KING AND KIN

Indiana Studies in Biblical Literature
Herbert Marks and Robert Polzin,
General Editors

Rembrandt, *The Sacrifice of Abraham* (reproduced by permission of Graphischen Sammlung Albertina, Vienna)

KING AND KIN

Political Allegory in the Hebrew Bible

JOEL ROSENBERG

INDIANA UNIVERSITY PRESS
BLOOMINGTON & INDIANAPOLIS

For Donald and Ellen
—friends and fellow readers

Manufactured in the United States of America

Library of Congress Cataloging-in-Publication Data

Rosenberg, Joel, 1943–
King and kin.

(Indiana studies in biblical literature)
Bibliography: p.
Includes index.
1. Politics in the Bible.   2. Symbolism in the Bible.
3. Eden.   4. Abraham (Biblical patriarch)   5. David,
King of Israel.   6. Bible. O.T.—Criticism, interpreta-
tion, etc.   I. Title.   II. Series.
BS1199.P6R67   1986   220.8'32   85-45160
ISBN 0-253-14624-0
ISBN 0-253-20396-1 (pbk.)
1   2   3   4   5   90   89   88   87   86

CONTENTS

PREFACE

Some years back, I became convinced of a simple and yet fundamental truth about the Hebrew Bible's continuous narrative: that, regardless of the alleged multiplicity of its sources, it formed a single, coherent, and integrated argument, of what I would call today "political" import. At the time, the larger contours of that argument were unclear to me, and at first I restricted my interest to what is commonly called the "Tetrateuch" (Genesis through Numbers). At the time, I also imagined I was dealing with a literary source in the conventional sense of the term: i.e., a document penned by a single author, bearing the hallmarks of a distinctive and idiosyncratic literary style—a terse, wryly ironic, and allusive style that required something of an esoteric, or, if you will, allegorical interpretation. Time and experience with biblical texts required me to modify my views somewhat, including both my sense of the text's message and my sense of its "authorship," but my basic conviction of its unity, style, and purposeful indirection has remained essentially unchanged. The present work seeks to demonstrate the shape, style, and argument of three narrative complexes taken from the larger continuous narrative of Genesis through II Kings—namely, the Garden story, the Abraham cycle, and the Davidic history—and to show their interrelation.

The first fruit of my researches was a doctoral dissertation in the History of Consciousness at the University of California at Santa Cruz, completed in 1978.[1] The present work began as a revision of that work, but, as such things often happen, the revision became a wholly new and unforeseen treatment of the subject. In the final paragraph of the dissertation, I suggested, perhaps somewhat tongue-in-cheek, that the Hebrew Bible was "the first work of rabbinic literature." By this I meant that it evinced an underlying critical intelligence that weighed, balanced, and contrasted traditionary[2] variants in a manner much analogous to that found in a page of Talmud. This critical intelligence, moreover, performed its work under cultural assumptions, and under historical and religious imperatives, also analogous to those of rabbinic literature; it affirmed similar values, and bespoke a comparable program of education for the people of its milieu and era. Although it would be tempting to try a rigorous and considered comparison of the two modes of discourse, biblical and rabbinic, it is neither feasible nor necessary to do so in the present work. It is sufficient to try to evaluate how biblical narrative talks and what it is saying.[3] The differences between the two modes, moreover, are as instructive as the similarities: the Talmud names its sources, the Bible does not; the Talmud is addressed to legal specialists, the Bible is not; the Talmud makes no attempt to maintain a continuous story, the Bible does. The end comment of my dissertation, however, is in some sense the point of departure for the innovations attempted here. I want to explore the Hebrew Bible's own internally exegetical dimension.

What, then, do I mean by "political import"? The makers of biblical literature were not solely concerned with advancing a particular view of God, or religious ritual, or moral law; on another plane, they were not solely concerned with telling a good story. Rather, they were deeply preoccupied with the nature of Israel's political community and were interested in the premises of political existence, addressing themselves to readers who thought about such things as leadership, authority, social cohesiveness, political order, rebellion, crime, justice, institutional evolution, and the relation of rich and poor. Any attempt to characterize biblical religion and culture that does not take into account the political dimension, that speaks in "eternal" verities and purely "spiritual" categories, will deeply misunderstand the subject. Similarly, any purely "literary" approach that sees in the biblical text a form of art and entertainment, or a purely psychologized kind of irony, or that tries to examine the narrative in isolation from its accompanying non-narrative materials, will likewise fall short of the mark. Biblical thought is rooted in its time and place, and, as such, is addressed to a particular kind of reader, one willing to undertake the deeply philosophical task of knowing "Israel" in all her dimensions. As such, this reader must be willing to ask what forces bind or divide the members of a political community—from the smallest scope of household and family, to the wider scope of village, tribe, and tribal confederation, to the widest scope of nation-state and kingdom.

For reasons obvious enough, the most sensitive period of Israel's development was her transition from confederation to kingdom, and it is no accident that the greatest narrative space is lavished on the figure who effected that change: King David. A study focusing on Moses—Israel's other formative leader—would have decidedly different contours from one focusing on David. If Moses and David are in some respects parallel figures, they are, in other respects, polar opposites: Moses was a reluctant leader, David an ambitious one; Moses was humble, David self-promoting; Moses clumsy of tongue, David a maker of songs and a genius of public relations; Moses a prophet who challenged a king, David a king who subverted the institutions of the prophets. Moses' grave-site is unknown, David's is Mt. Zion; Moses yielded to a successor from another tribe, David sired a dynasty; Moses wished for collective leadership (Num. 11:29), David centralized it; Moses administered before a traveling sanctuary, David planned a permanent one. The chief institutional polarities of ancient Israel's pre-exilic history are present in these two figures. Because King David stood at the threshold of Israel's written records—indeed, created the conditions for literacy as such—he is, properly speaking, the logical place to begin a study of Israel's institutional history. Moses, by contrast, remains shrouded in legend and oral history; his historical impact is best understood from the hindsight of Israel's monarchic era. I am at present undecided as to whether I shall attempt a Mosaic sequel to the present investigation, even if that is the logical destination of my studies. Meanwhile, I offer an examination of the Davidic complex, and of two legends closely related to it in typology and structure. To understand these materials is to advance a long way toward an understanding of biblical culture.

We do not, to be sure, know enough about ancient Israel to know how mainstream was "biblical culture" in the context of its time and place. The Hebrew Bible is a text and should not be confused with "ancient Israel," however much archaeology and historical science can tell us about the latter. An approach to biblical literature must tell us about its behavior as literature, and so must traffic in literary categories, to whatever extent our modern theories of literature (including those implicitly advanced by biblical form-criticism and biblical structuralism) are adequate for comprehending it. Yet it is not, strictly speaking, as literature that the Bible accomplishes its principal work, but as traditionary discourse. It is especially remarkable that the biblical story manages to unfold in a simple and natural way, yet cover all the bases, or "beats," dictated by an inherited lore, and to do so in a way that anatomizes the tradition and makes sense of otherwise often senseless or trivial traditionary data. The first two textual chapters of my study will seek to show how a biblical story's elements constitute carefully interlocking codes whose cumulative argument is more than the sum of its parts. My final chapter will seek a somewhat different entry into the components of a biblical story, one more centered in the literal meaning of the story itself, one less attuned to the allegorical and more to the mimetic, yet one no less alert to the story's symbolic and typological properties, and one that, whatever its rootedness in narrative realism, sustains my hypothesis of a biblical allegory—concerning which mode, more will be said shortly.

One could say that this study has two main phases, which I shall, by way of rough analogy, call a "semiotic" and a "deconstructionist" moment. The former seeks to show, as it were, the vertical system within which the story's various codes are deployed, and tries to comprehend the story as a static system. The latter, on the other hand, tries to

comprehend the text in terms of its intertextuality: its perennially centrifugal gestures toward other stories, other texts, other uses of a word,
its Heraclitean dynamism, its horizontal flux from one signifier to the
next, its hauntedness by the conflicting claims of texts, its key moments
and junctures, its silences and obscurities, its incommensurate themes
and preoccupations, its repetitions and obsessions. For reasons that will
become clearer as we proceed, the former mode is more appropriate to
the Bible's mythical and legendary material, the latter to its more mani-
festly historical and realistic material. The former looks at the completed array of biblical discourse, the latter at the unfolding moments of
a biblical story, or at the deeper dimensions of a word or theme. To be
sure, I could as well have switched the methods around, applying the
former to I and II Samuel and the latter to Genesis, but what is given
here is at least partly a record of discovery, in the manner and style in
which my unfolding research and deliberation developed. The radical
shift in method, at any rate, between chapters 2 and 3 does not quite
amount to a recantation.

Is my study a source-critical hypothesis? Emphatically not. There is a
logically prior task—to determine what the material is saying, and how.
This is, whether admitted or not, the hidden premise of all source
criticism. My own shifting judgments about source have taught me how
precarious are conjectures about the relative antiquity of a word, a form,
a pericope, a tradition, a story, or a corpus in the Hebrew Bible. All that
we can say is that what used to be called sources are more likely traditionary strands, that more attention must be accorded to the artistry of
editing, and that it is less productive to speak of four sources than of
many. This makes it all the more imperative to determine what the
material in concert is saying. While I shall, in deference to common
usage, occasionally refer to the assemblage, especially in my first two
textual chapters, as the work of a "redactor," this notion, too, is a relic of
source criticism's heyday that is perhaps better dispensed with in favor of
the more neutral and appropriate term "text."
   It should be noted that in demonstrating a certain unity to a skeletal
segment of Genesis–I Kings, I place myself at odds with one tenet of the
Bible's literary history that has enjoyed more or less of a consensus since
the publication of Noth's *Überlieferungsgeschichtliche Studien* (1943): the
notion of two independently evolving collections of biblical legend, a
"priestly" work, or "Tetrateuch," and a "Deuteronomistic" work comprising Deuteronomy–II Kings. This scholarly reconstruction contradicts the compelling affinities that exist between Genesis and I/II Samuel
(which an earlier generation of source critics, including Wellhausen
himself, was inclined to admit) and depicts the redactional process as a

listless and uninspired accumulation of available traditions, made for antiquarian and reverently *heilsgeschichtlich* purposes, rather than as an incisive and revolutionary critique of the national identity. The will to collect traditions does not arise from a leisurely, antiquarian curiosity, a self-effacing scribal transmission of whatever traditions arrived, by accidental accretion, at a state of collective venerability. Traditions are *selected;* their venerability is more often a *product* of their literary coherence in assemblage with other traditions than a *cause* of it.

Whatever the literary history involved, Genesis is, as I hope to show, nothing short of a companion work to II Samuel, a "midrash," if you will, upon the Davidic history, adumbrating the dichotomies articulated in the historical work by appeal to legend, myth, and primordial history. We must not assume, on the other hand, that the Davidic court history itself is, by virtue of its narrative realism, an "eyewitness" account, as is popularly maintained. "Realism" and "eyewitness account" are by no means synonymous; given the proper record, the court history of King David could have been composed in any era, including, for that matter, our own. The material could have served the interests of a readership concerned with issues we know little or nothing about. To confuse content with authorship is a fundamentalism of the very sort that scientific scholarship of the Bible has sought to leave behind.

In short, the biblical material we shall deal with appears to have formed a carefully premeditated program of personal and national education. In view of the patterns of leadership and education that emerged in Israel after the exile—a society under the guidance of literate elders, judging, teaching, transmitting, disputing, interpreting, and training in the art of interpretation; a society of the very sort that is portrayed *lacking* in the Davidic history and its related materials—it is not unreasonable to say that the biblical history is the first work of rabbinic literature. An analogous critique of centralized power was to be applied to the emperors of Rome, in the fullness of time.

ACKNOWLEDGMENTS

Ten scholars, biblical and literary, have knowingly or unknowingly played an important role in the unfolding of this book. These ten are James S. Ackerman, Robert Alter, Miri Amihai Collins, Michael Fishbane, Michael Fixler, Edward L. Greenstein, James L. Kugel, Alan L. Mintz, Robert M. Polzin, and George Savran. Their ready encouragement, feedback, or endorsement, and, in all cases, their example of creative accomplishment, have given life, in substance or in spirit, to the project enclosed within these pages.

A special measure of thanks is due, as well, to the persons at Indiana University Press entrusted with the acquisition and preparation of this work for publication. Their trustworthy vision and impeccable professionality have enabled me to feel proud and pleased about my association with this series.

A NOTE ON TRANSLITERATION OF HEBREW WORDS

The system of transliteration employed here is for the most part that employed in contemporary scientific scholarship on Bible and Semitics, with certain exceptions in the interests of simplicity, convenience, and aesthetics. I render aspirate "b" by "v," approximating more the contemporary Israeli pronunciation than the ancient bilabial "bh." Similarly, aspirate "p" is "f," not "ph." Aspirate "g," "d," and "t," are not rendered "gh," "dh," or "th," nor as underlined letters ("g," etc.), but simply as written. Aspirate "k," however, is rendered as "kh," and the letter *shin*, as "sh," rather than "š," except when rendering roots. The *ẓade* is rendered "ẓ," rather than the "ṣ" sometimes customary. All letters incorporating a *dagesh ḥazaq* are doubled in transliteration. Vowel quantities are not given. Personal and place names, when not quoted in Hebrew, are generally given in their familiar spellings in the Revised Standard Version. To summarize:

l	ל	ʾ	א
m	מ	b	ב
n	נ	v	ב
s	ס	g	ג
ʿ	ע	d	ד
p	פ	h	ה
f	פ	w	ו
ẓ	צ	z	ז
q	ק	ḥ	ח
r	ר	ṭ	ט
sh	שׁ	y	י
s	שׂ	k	כ
t	ת	kh	כ

·PRELIMINARIES·

THE QUESTION OF BIBLICAL ALLEGORY

FIVE WITS: Everyman, my leave now of thee I take;
  I will follow the other, for here I thee forsake.
EVERYMAN: Alas! then may I wail and weep,
  For I took you for my best friend.
                                        Everyman (c. 1485)

Or whatever it was they threed to make out he thried to two in the Fiendish park. He's an awful old reppe. Look at the shirt of him! Look at the dirt of it! He has my water black on me. And it steeping and stuping since this time last wik. How many goes is it I wonder I washed it? I know by heart the places he likes to saale, duddurty devil! Scorching my hand and starving my famine to make his private linen public.
                                        Finnegans Wake

And how was the Torah written? In black fire upon white fire.
                                        Midrash on Psalms

Is the Garden story myth or allegory? We know that it is figurative communication of *some* sort, and not mimesis, and it is likely that even ancient readers knew that. But what sort? What kind of figure does it articulate? What does it do for the kind of reader it addresses, and, indeed, what kind of reader does it address? Commentary on the story has tended to favor one or the other of the two options mentioned above, and critical commentary has not significantly departed from this tendency. Nowhere are the modern interpretive lines of conflict better apprehended than in the greatly contrasting commentaries of Hermann Gunkel and German-Jewish scholar Benno Jacob.[1] To enter the story through their eyes is to confront a dilemma posed by the story itself, one with consequences for our understanding of the Hebrew Bible's larger narrative. What, then, did they see, and in what sense do their responses to the text bespeak a strategy that originates within the text itself?

Gunkel: The Garden Story as "Myth"

Hermann Gunkel helped to open a fruitful new pathway in Old Testament studies by drawing a distinction between "history proper" (narrative produced by high court chroniclers aiming at a sober and realistic, if still tendentious, accounting of a nation's past—usually of its political history, especially of its wars) and "popular tradition" (poetic or bardic accounts of the legendary past, of the deeds of ancestors and prehistorical heroes, as well as folktales, etiologies, fables, and epigrams—all transmitted by oral means prior to the rise of kings and courts).[2] Outfitted with this distinction, he subjected the Hebrew Bible to an erudite and often incisive form criticism, supplying a refreshing change from the arid and sophistical pyrotechnics that biblical source criticism had fallen prey to since the generation of Wellhausen.[3] From Gunkel on, biblical criticism gradually transposed its interest from source questions (which were held to be more or less permanently settled) to the study of preliterary oral tradition, its forms and developments.[4]

It is worth noting, nonetheless, that Gunkel himself, in his commentary on Gen. 2–3, attempts to evaluate the character and outlook of the story considered as a literary composition (the "author" he has in mind is Wellhausen's "Yahwist," the allegedly earliest and most important literary strand of the Pentateuch). What stood out for Gunkel were the story's "mythic," "childlike," "earthy," and "naïve" characteristics:

2

The entire narrative, particularly in its archaic, earthy flavor, e.g., in its anthropomorphisms and vocabulary . . . , is significantly of a different character from P [i.e., the so-called Priestly narrator of Gen. 1]. . . . [Its] reflection on the human participation in God's creative work appears to us exceedingly naïve. . . . [Its penchant for folk-] etymology can only be the product of a peasant people. . . . [It] explains the riddle of human life in a childlike way: . . . so long as the human being has breath, he lives, but life forsakes the body with the breath. The myth explains now in its childlike way that God has breathed into the human being a portion of his own breath: this divine and wonder-working breath, however, would become—surely the narrator intends to say—an independent essence in the human body; . . . as naïvely told as this investiture might be, there lurks a notion more profound: the human being is akin to God, his breath of life a ray of God's effulgence. . . .

Why God forbids eating from [the] tree [of Knowledge] under penalty of punishment so terrible the narrator declines to say; . . . very often does this narrator omit communicating motives . . . and in any case, no reasons are here given to the human being; he must obey without reasons. Similar is Abraham in his migration and his offering-up of Isaac: childlike obedience. —That God's first commandment concerns eating is, likewise, childlike.

Aesthetically considered, the narrative, specifically in [chap.] 3, belongs to the most beautiful of Genesis . . . ; compare particularly the remarks of Herder, who articulated a truly poetic understanding of this narrative. The breath of the mythic has not yet evaporated from it, yet all foreign or barbaric touches have been driven out. Noteworthy is [chap.] 3's most complicated (for that time) depiction of the human personality . . . rendering the actions, through the beautiful appropriateness of sequences of situations and through a genius for arrangement; . . . to be noted also is the pristine delicacy in the handling of the sexual motif, as well as the immense earnestness with which the narrator speaks about God and sin. In short: (for that time) the most profound thoughts concerning man and God, and rendered in the most straightforward, vivid form; a wonderfully mythological content, distilled into a "nobler innocence." [It] is the pearl of Genesis.[5]

Starting from the premise that the early chapters of Genesis (from the second onward) had been put together by Wellhausen's "Yahwist," Gunkel viewed the Garden story as an artful, albeit naïve and childlike, expression of the early Israelite world-view, in which God is depicted unabashedly in anthropomorphic terms, the human being portrayed as a creature fashioned from the soil, and the origin of human suffering and of social customs explained through entertaining and enchanting etiologies, many of them stemming from a substratum of folklore, myth, and bardic art. Two key influences on Gunkel must here be kept in mind, one explicit, one implicit.

The explicit influence, whom he cites specifically, is Herder, who supplied the interest in "aesthetic" judgment, in the tale's "archaic,

earthy flavor," in its rustic *Sitz im Leben*, in the vision of an *Urzeit* within
which "the breath of the mythic has not yet evaporated," a time of "noble
innocence" in which ingenuousness and literary genius operate in harmony.[6] The echoes of Herder might also be detected in Gunkel's understanding of the text's narrative voice as "earnest" and "straightforward,"
two qualities of mind integral (to borrow the words of Hans W. Frei) to a
"natural and naive . . . expression of [a] way of life, [a] sensibility, [a]
natural and communal spirit."[7]

The implicit influence is that of Wellhausen himself, whose words are
neatly echoed in Gunkel's encomium for the "Yahwist's" art, and who so
persuasively had dated the four main alleged strata of the Pentateuch
(the so-called J, E, D, and P strata) roughly to the ninth, eighth, seventh,
and sixth centuries B.C.E., respectively—in other words, *not* to the era of
Moses. Attempting to present a coherent picture of the organic growth
of ancient Israel's religion, Wellhausen (many have said, upon Hegelian
paradigms, though it is surely a rather derivative Hegelianism)[8] had
sought to show how this religion evolved *toward* an ethical monotheism,
of a sort best exemplified in the teachings of the great literary prophets
from Amos (ninth century B.C.E.) to Deutero-Isaiah (fifth century
B.C.E.)—yet, in the process, to depict the full elaboration of Jewish law as
a comparatively late event in ancient Israel. Such a view suggests (in a
manner common to a long tradition of Christian scholarship on the
Hebrew Bible) that the "legalism" and "pedantry" of later Judaism had
originated mostly in the period of the Second Temple and after, leaving
the way clear for an understanding of primitive Christianity as a self-
conscious identification with the style and spirit of the Old Testament
prophets.[9]

We find in the perspectives held in common by Wellhausen and
Gunkel a strangely crossed set of models (a dialectical discontinuity
overlaid on a melioristic evolutionism),[10] and the peculiar double duty
of their criticism should be made clear: it tends simultaneously to extol
the vibrant, vivacious, and playful sensibility of the narrator (as forerunner to the parable-making kerygma of the Son of Man) and to pay
respects to the somber tones of that narrator's apparently pessimistic
theology (as forerunner to the doctrines of Paul, Augustine, and the
Protestant reformers of a later era). Thus, from the ninth to the fifth
century, according to this view of the Bible's literary history, Israel's
theological sophistication grew, while her art of narrative declined. As
Israel moved closer to a world-embracing ethical monotheism, manifested most inspiredly in the prophecies of Deutero-Isaiah, her legal and
ritual institutions proliferated out of hand and calcified, and so (these
critics maintain) her religious spirit fell prey to stultification and stagna-
tion in the ensuing centuries. What is important for our purposes is the

tendency of this type of literary history to exclude the possibility of any dynamic relationship among the alleged sources: each stage followed upon its predecessor as a separate sedimentation. The notion of a *usage* of parallel sources (or, speaking more flexibly, of parallel traditions) by an outside compiler was restricted to the dutiful "conflation" practiced by anonymous redactors, who were credited with little personality, intelligence, or originality in their own right (compared to "authors"), and who were often faulted for the clumsiness of a redactional surgery that left egregious contradictions in narrative detail and jarring transitions of style and focus. This particular view of the redactor depends on a model of literary history that stresses decline and decay. The latter generations ploddingly enshrine and polish the literary accomplishments of the former.

Gunkel shares with Wellhausen, then, a general indifference to the question of the interrelationship of sources, which both critics portray as one of steady accumulation or augmentation, or as the product of religious "polemics" that rode roughshod over literary coherence. When it comes to evaluating, then, the literary character of the "Yahwist's" product, Gunkel prefers to obscure the difference between a narrator and a compiler, and to treat the "Yahwist" as more or less identical with the totality of preliterary oral traditions, whose "charm" so engages his interest. He does this most of all, ironically, precisely where he tries to be the most explicit about their difference—as he points out, this is no individual, "spontaneous" creation, but a public art, ruled by a heritage of oral storytelling:

> The narrator must have been a particularly gifted master [*ein besonders begnädeter Meister*]; however, one would be in error to surmise that this story must be "a free creation of a storyteller." . . . In the book of Genesis, it is not a matter of an individual, poetic, but of a traditional creation, to which many generations have contributed their stamp, until at last the final master [Master?] could arrive. . . . [11]

Whether or not we have here a theological double entendre, we cannot help being struck by Gunkel's vacillation between a "Yahwist" who himself stood as a bard at cultic shrines, and one who mainly handed on the myths and tales of others.[12] In his capacity as a founder of Old Testament form criticism, Gunkel concentrates his interest, to be sure, on the oral prehistory of Genesis, and seems only secondarily interested in the final literary product, to which he devotes some hasty chapters at the end of his long introduction to Genesis.[13] Yet he was, in the end, still guided by the daimon of the older "literary" criticism, and so turns out to postulate, whenever he must be specific about a composite story's sutures and junctures, not a developed view of *oral* sources (i.e., of traditions),

but a modification and updating of Wellhausen: instead of "J," we have
"J¹" and "J²"—we have another *literary* theory, since the separate strands
of tradition that the one "J" made use of are themselves not merely
traditionary stocks but compositions.[14] Gunkel's successors, the tradition
historians, freeing themselves entirely from literary matters and devot-
ing attention more or less exclusively to the oral dimensions of the
legends, could much more easily postulate a "bardic" setting as the
original *Sitz im Leben* for many of Israel's traditions.[15] Gunkel, on the
other hand, seems caught between a bard and a compiler precisely where
he tries to reconstruct the fundamental formative influences in the
shaping of the biblical legends in our possession.

I belabor the foregoing matters not to stress the manner in which the
romantic and teleological biases of German historicism have shaped
Gunkel's perception of the literary character of Genesis, but to clarify his
use of the words "myth" and "mythic." Myth appears in Gunkel's Genesis
(here in terms harmonious with Herder, although Herder, for reasons
beyond our scope to discuss, carefully skirted the question of myth in his
treatment of the Bible)[16] as an expression of the solidarity of the social
unit—the clan, the tribe, the nation. It serves an affirmative, protective,
and sacral purpose, in which, above all, we find an identification of the
social group itself with the order of nature, verily an *assent* to nature—an
ascription of a lawfulness of natural causation to events that have been
shaped, at least in part, by caprices of human decision.[17] This is accomplished, paradoxically, by the story's weaving an aura of charisma, mystery, or holiness around the people and events the narrative describes.
Gunkel's narrator seeks to enforce authority—in the household, in the
tribe, in the tribal union—an authority consonant with the order of
nature itself:

> One can better understand [the mood of the Eden myth] if one calls
> to mind the relationship of the Israelite landlord to his tenant, a
> relationship which in ancient Israel was so often likened to the re-
> ligious. The overlord gives his tenant livelihood and protection; for
> this, in turn, the tenant must serve him. Between a good master and
> good servant is maintained a friendly intercourse; but there also stands
> between the two a difference, and this difference is in the order of
> things, and must so remain. The master, accordingly, does not think to
> elevate the servant to his own level, and to treat him as his equal; . . . if,
> however, such a servant might be pampered by the doting good-
> naturedness of his master, he may ultimately come to wish to be his
> master's peer. And this he must not do! For he must *fear* the master.
> —So the Hebrew viewed also his standing before God.[18]

It is by no means to be assumed that Gunkel himself regards this
feudal cameo as bearing in itself an enlightened theology, nor could he,

on the other hand, as a Protestant, have meant the image trivially. It is crucial for his reading, however, that he view the "Yahwist" as himself wholly at one with this view of divine-human etiquette. *"This difference is in the order of things and must so remain."* We have no better ground than this statement for a theory of the Garden story as myth—not in Grimm's sense of "a story of the gods" (a generic identification Gunkel handled with appropriate gingerliness around Scripture), but in the contemporary (and, perhaps, premodern) sense of a rhetorical strategy whose function is to delineate and guard a transcendent realm. Such a realm is constituted not by the presence of divine beings (as the taxonomy of Grimm would have it), but by the appropriate syntax: it is the *'al-ken* (therefore) of the naïve etiology in Genesis that serves as a mythic signature, the pseudo-learned justification of the present order of society and nature by appeal to fantasy, nostalgia, and the hallowed circle of ancestral deeds. Though it may raise more questions than it answers, this gesture must foreclose questioning. Faced with such a formula, we find no appeal to orders of reality outside the one presented in the narrative. The story is itself the last appeal; it refers only to itself, and elicits from its readers but one response: such is the way of things!

But is this, in fact, the main thrust of Israelite belief, which (however ironically we may, in the course of this study, come to read the pertinent texts) had emerged in its halcyon days as a *challenge* to the social and theological order of the late Bronze Age,[19] and, at least from the standpoint of biblical poetry, to the natural order as well? Or is Gunkel correct in observing mythological propensities at the beginning of a corpus so resolutely hostile, in the long run, to myth? This brings us around to the more specific question: is Gen. 2–3 a myth? This question will serve us as a useful point of entry into the commentary of Benno Jacob.

Jacob: The Garden Story's "Rationalism"

One can hardly say other than that Benno Jacob sought to *de*mythologize biblical legend. His efforts were aimed at correcting what he perceived as an overemphasis on the part of source and form critics of the generation that preceded his. His philological observations are closely related to his opinions on Wellhausen's hypothesis (and on those exegetical perspectives, such as Gunkel's, that had been constructed out of the matrix of documentary criticism), and in this regard Jacob resembles numerous other modern exegetes of Jewish origin who, while grounded in a scientific method and conversant with comparative ancient Near Eastern studies, sought to challenge, modify, or deemphasize the hegemony of source criticism, or (phrasing the matter to include Gunkel's form criticism) of *source-oriented* criticism.[20] Against the atomization of Scripture then prevalent, Jewish exegetes and translators such as Jacob, Buber, Rosenzweig, and later Cassuto, Segal, and others, stressed a *text-oriented* criticism, attuned to the synthetic crossweave of sources, motifs, and verbal figures of the *final* text—an entity to be dealt with in its own right and on its own terms, irrespective of its status as an individual or a composite product. It struck them as equally fallacious to ignore the larger unities of subject matter, style, rhetorical posture, narrative repetition and symmetrization, and verbal or motivic allusion in Scripture as to *establish* far-fetched correspondences unwarranted by the text itself or by whatever is known of its cultural and linguistic determinants.

Their plea was made not on grounds of religious orthodoxy (though, as we may see, it is incorrect to say that religious motivations did not lie at the heart of their arguments) but on grounds of philological and literary concern. This occasionally led them into some philologically questionable postures. Occupying themselves with the pedagogical aims of the received text, rather than with the purposes or historical contexts of the various voices that play off against each other in the text, these exegetes portrayed the received text as a "teacher" *par excellence*. This, for better or for worse, lent a fundamentalist tone to their arguments, which often rendered their specific judgments suspect in the eyes of scientific scholarship at large, all the more so given the apologetic context of their labors. I shall, further on, seek to substantiate that suspicion, but initially I must note that at least one implied consequence of their concern was about forty years ahead of its time: their insistence on a *contextual* understanding of divine names and other potential signs of multiple authorship in the Bible might have opened the way to a fuller discussion of the problems of intentionality and narrative voice in biblical literature, had not the problems of refuting or sidestepping Wellhausen loomed so large. Today, from the hindsight of Russian formalism, New Criticism, phenomenology, structuralism, deconstruction, and other epistemologically sophisticated disciplines in the study of culture, we possess more of the critical vocabulary and apparatus to make use of the Jewish exegetes' contextual reading.[21]

Awareness of the foregoing matters is necessary if we are to understand Jacob's exegetical standpoint toward Gen. 2–3. His opposition to source criticism, while not necessarily the central thrust of his scholarship, leads him to concentrate on two principal, and closely related, tasks: (1) to establish the narrative dependence of Gen. 2–3 on Gen. 1, and thereby to establish either the priority of the latter in time of composition or the continuity of the latter with the former as parts of the same composition; (2) to refute assertions as to the "primitive" or "naïve" character of Gen. 2–3, as inferred principally from the apparent anthropomorphisms in the story, over against the "later," more rarified monotheism and "priestly" concerns of Gen. 1. To cite some of his argument:

> ... Thus were heaven and earth, earth and heaven created hitherto [Gen. 1] and fashioned with regard to human history, which now henceforth will be narrated.... Chapters 1 and 2:4ff. are not just variant "creation stories" but relate to one another in the manner of a *kelal uferaṭ* [general-and-particular], for which purpose it readily could adopt as exemplary dictum the 13th of R. Jose haGlili's 32 hermeneutic rules: *kelal she'aḥaraw ma'aseh, 'eyno 'ela' feraṭo shel ri'shon* [A general statement followed by a detailed account: the latter is only an elaboration of the former]. ...
>
> [Concerning the Garden story's outlook:] Among all peoples do we find that human beings have had an aversion to work and fear of death. They would prefer that neither should exist. Their paradise, accordingly, is one of wishful dreams projected back upon an idealized antiquity. The biblical account, with a maturer wisdom, sets itself against such fantasizing, with so fine an irony that, even in our own day, grown-up children yet ignore. They think they should be told a wondrous story, a delightful fairytale, about how good humanity would have it were it not for the first Fall, through sin, of man and woman. No, the meaning here is something very different! Man was from the first created to earn bread by labor, woman to bear children in birthpangs, humanity to die. Adam here is man, not god, and his health consists in his obedience to God's command. To yearn for immortality on earth is presumptuous and vain, and man must find out for himself that Paradise is not cut out for him. All fantasy is hereby banished ..., and instead of myth we find religion, ethics, and psychology. ...
>
> [Concerning the story's style, compared to that of Gen. 1:] The enlightened and rationalistic cast of mind, shunning the fantastic and the mythological, displays itself in chaps. 2ff. as much as in chap. 1, as much in fundamental premises as in the details of the portrait of a paradise. Nowhere is it accurate to say that an alternative representation of God prevails. Even in chap. 1 does God directly speak to man, as later to Cain, Noah, and the Patriarchs. The alleged anthropomorphisms and childlike touches stem from errors of the exegetes. The customary view that sees in chaps. 2 and 3 an "idyll" lacks validity, for in such idylls a straightforward prohibition, transgression, and judgment would be out of place. Pastoral notions are forever inextricably bound up with childish fantasy, with superstition and with rustic poetry. But even if this were an idyll, we would still be wrong to think the author of chap. 1 incapable of such a task, or to assign the specialty of classic literary history to the *pre*history of Hebrew culture. It would be another matter if [chaps. 1 and 2ff.] were but the same story told twice in different ways. But this is not the case. ...
>
> How changeable aesthetic judgments are, at any rate, we can consider from the fact that in the time of J. G. Eichhorn the two "sources" were regarded exactly the other way around ...: then was chap. 1 seen as "high-poetic," the creation of the "fiery fantasy of a poetic

author," of an "ancient, prehistoric bard," a "national epic poem,"
whereas by contrast chaps. 2 and 3 bespoke "the learned acumen of
natural science, which assumes the medium of natural elements." It
was seen to be "a more historical representation of the earliest human
history, told only through sensory reflections suitable to mankind's
childhood." . . . In short: chap. 1 is poetry, chaps. 2 and 3 are prose, or
history, or philosophy. If these judgments seem but comic to contemporary pentateuchal criticism, which maintains exactly opposite conceptions, who can guarantee the latter against similar reversals of
opinion?[22]

Implied here is a certain circularity of method: Jacob would attempt to
prove the narrative dependence of the latter chapters on the first, and
therefore a conceptual unity; this paves the way to pointing up affinities
of *Zeitgeist* between both bodies of material, i.e., signs of an equivalence
in style, outlook, and sophistication that have largely been ignored by
modern commentators. Conversely, if he can demonstrate equivalences
of this sort, i.e., signs of a historical harmony between the alleged "late,
priestly" style of Gen. 1 and the alleged "early, bardic" style of Gen. 2–3,
then we have little need to view the chapters otherwise than as components of a single composition, which relate to each other as a *kelal uferaṭ*
(general-and-particular).

Numerous advantages accrue to the success of such an approach: the
text is carved up less; a continuity of style and content would pay more
respect to the great skill and subtlety that even Wellhausen and Gunkel
had conceded (albeit "for that time") to the Garden story. The story
would now gain scope, complexity, and new significance; the narrator
would now be seen as gifted with a keen ability to modulate his narrative
techniques to reflect changes in rhetorical intention; the design of *kelal
uferaṭ* removes the possibility of competition between the two accounts by
making each the function of respective purposes which stand in harmony together. Best of all is the intriguing proposition that the Garden
story is a comment on the *vanity* of paradisic fantasies, a notion that
suggests a certain *tension* between argument and nominal subject that
animates the strategy of narrative in ways familiar to us from the other
Western masters of the epic art, from Virgil to James Joyce (about
Homer, we cannot be so certain, though at least from the Hellenistic era
onward Homer was understood to speak allusively and esoterically). For
such rewarding gains, the sacrifice of documentary scholarship seems
such a small price.

But we soon find that the demand for consistency about the Garden
story's "rationalism" leads Jacob to some forced, perhaps even outland-
ish, refutations of the alleged magical character of events within the
story, especially that of the Tree of Knowledge and its forbidden fruit:

did the eating of it bring on changes in the laws of nature? Jacob wisely argues that the composition of the fruit is quite irrelevant to the problems of disobedience to God's command,[23] but instead of being freed by this point from a slavish obligation to the literal and physical dimensions of the story, he regards it necessary to refute even the slightest intimations of the uncanny: the "knowledge" that the couple gains is only the knowledge of their own transgression and its punishment;[24] the serpent crawled upon its belly all along, but then has this propensity *reformulated* as a "curse;"[25] Eve was destined from the start to bear children in pain, but has this fact "announced" to her—as to an adolescent daughter—and her "punishment" only consists of this new information;[26] and so forth.

There is a kind of flurried tailoring here, analogous to procedures we found at work in Gunkel, stemming from the commentator's position midway between a religious and a secular readership. Doctrinal ambiguities have to be ironed out, for the benefit of the person reading for a religious message, provided this does not compromise the interests of that readership concerned with philological and historical understanding. These limitations are more flexible than they may seem, insofar as they have given rise to radically opposed interpretations of Gen. 2–3—Gunkel was motivated to find mythopoesis lurking everywhere within the story, whereas Jacob was motivated to try to purge it—yet both commentators have, perforce, lapsed into a certain stiffness of canonical certainty in places where a blend of experimentation and tentativeness might have proven more useful.

In essence, Jacob's reflex devaluation of myth is as suspect as Gunkel's patronizing praise of it. His pat dismissal of the pastoral mode (what he here calls the "idyll") as the toy of children, peasants, shepherds, and the like ignores the use of the idyllic in the most sophisticated specimens of literary art (as, for example, works by Virgil, Spenser, Shakespeare, and Milton). His view of Gen. 2–3 as "banishing" all fantasy seems glib, as if such "banishment" did not comprise one of the central problems of a text whose literary subtlety has found, in Jacob himself, one of its most outspoken defenders. For precisely in the idyll is the problematic nature of idyllic thinking most self-consciously an issue.[27] Is it not, perhaps, quite possible to bring to Jacob's aid the very literary tendencies he here derides? For if, indeed, the declarations of "punishments" upon the primordial couple is a figurative way of expounding information that the couple would learn anyway, in the course of their normal lifetimes—if, indeed, beneath the supranormal wonders of "paradisic" life, there is something like a *normal*, biological life, then the depiction of a "garden" must emerge as a kind of code, or cipher—or perhaps allegory—of more familiar matters. As we shall see, Jacob's vision of the story as the product of a sophisticated and premeditating intelligence fits quite well with a conception of Gen. 2–3 as allegory, such that even Jacob himself is compelled to make use of the term. We shall return to Jacob's discussion in its proper place.

The Nature of Allegory

When we speak of literature as "allegorical," we generally have in mind any of several overlapping, but not synonymous, features.[28] We may think of allegory as a *genre*, by calling to mind various works that present personified abstractions, often with starkly emblematic names ("Hope," "Wisdom," "Sin"), and which trace not historical and factual events but the motions of thoughts, ideas, moral virtues, and other abstract qualities, and which do so with the self-conscious awareness of the conventions of allegory and with a clear sense of the shared assumptions between author and reader that make such a baldly allusive and abstract mode possible. Yet the very examples we could call to mind do not, in fact, reflect a single genre. Aesop's *Fables* are moral exempla; *Everyman* is a drama; Spenser's *The Faerie Queene* is verse romance; Bunyan's *The Pilgrim's Progress* is novelistic prose fiction. It is one of the curious paradoxes of allegory that while we can readily call to mind examples of it, we are hard-pressed to explain adequately what the examples have in common. The very general features suggested above do not in fact apply to all allegory but only to a special case of it. What, then, is allegory, if more than just genre?

Confusion about the nature of allegory stems from various factors. First, a distinction can be (but all too often is not) made between works that so thoroughly sustain an allegorical mode that they "are" allegories, and works, usually more complex and hybrid in nature, that *use* allegory, that bear allegorical features and resonances, or have among their many functions some limited allegorical purpose.[29] Such a distinction favors a view of allegory not as a genre but as (to use the words of Northrop Frye) "a structural principle in literature," or as a matter of rhetorical strategy, or, in the broadest sense, as a process of signification. With a work bearing only allegorical propensities, we are less able to speak of allegories *of* something (extratextual), but are required instead to focus on the ways we are led to perceive allegory *in* something (textual), on the ways an allegorical mode of meaning is making its presence felt in readers. To use the language of modern semiotics, we are drawn, in more complex and hybrid manifestations of allegory, more toward the signifier than toward the signified. We are led into ever more self-conscious awareness of how meaning is produced. As much as it may be "about" some extratextual referent, allegory must in some sense be about signification itself, and about the community of readers it presupposes.

A second source of confusion about allegory stems from the failure to distinguish between an allegorical *work* and an allegorizing *criticism*—the latter formally known as *allegoresis*.[30] Allegoresis may be applied to a work that is not, in itself, an allegory but that, for one reason or another, either encourages or demands a figurative interpretation—which interpretation, in its turn, may or may not see the work in question as intrinsically allegorical, but only as consonant with an allegorical meaning. The Hellenistic allegorizing of Homer, which began in the embarrassment of the academies over the anthropomorphisms and unseemly conduct ascribed by Homer to the divine world,[31] was compelled, in order to "save" Homer for a certain respectable readership, to attribute an allegorical intention to Homer himself.[32] Yet medieval allegorization of the Bible, which started from analogous premises (the need to justify anthropomorphisms or other apparent crudities in the description of divinity), nevertheless preferred to keep allegorical interpretation as an *option*, one among several interlocking and possibly complementary modes of interpretation that presuppose at least the formal priority, if not the primacy, of the literal or historical mode of meaning.[33]

Whence the notion of interpretive *layers*, which found expression, in Jewish and Christian exegesis alike, as a "fourfold" system.[34] Jewish exegetes spoke of "PaRDeS"—the late Hebrew word means "orchard," "garden," or "paradise"[35]—whose consonants were the acronym of *peshaṭ* (simple, literal, or historical sense), *remez* (allusive, conceptual, or allegorical sense), *derash* (homiletic, exemplary, or moral sense), and *sod* (esoteric, mystical, or eschatological sense).[36] In the fourteenth century, Nicholas of Lyra epitomized a similar garland of interpretive options with the following doubly symmetrical epigram:

> Litera gesta docet; quid credas allegoria.
> Moralis quid agas; quo tendas anagogia.

> The *literal* betokens actions [gests];
> what you should believe, the *allegory*.
> The *moral*, what you should do;
> where you are heading, the *anagogy*.

One should not assume that these interpretive modes were, in practice, employed in the neatly complementary way this finely crafted dictum implies—efforts such as the thirteenth-century Jewish exegete Bahya ben Asher's "fourfold" Pentateuchal commentary notwithstanding.[37] The three nonmimetic modes of biblical interpretation, in fact, continually overlap in nature and function: drawing a moral is a type of allegorizing, for example, as is drawing theosophic or eschatological conclusions, since the text is shown in each case to speak in a roundabout and cryptic manner. All three figurative modes, moreover, in order to exist at all, have to take root in the soil of the literal meaning. The rabbinic dictum "A biblical verse [*miqra'*] does not depart from its plain meaning" (Shab. 63a) held sway in medieval Jewish commentary, even where allegorizing was sanctioned. Patristic commentary, similarly shunning gnostic and sectarian excesses, early on held to a similar exegetical hierarchy, despite its preoccupation with moral and philosophical meanings, its opposition to "Jewish" literalism, and its orientation to typological parallels between the testaments. Even so great a friend of allegory and typology as Augustine saw fit to valorize the literal meaning of Scripture: "Brethren, I warn you in the name of God to believe before all things when you hear the Scriptures read that the events really took place. . . . Do not destroy the historic foundation of Scripture, for without it you will build in the air."[38] Augustine's sense of the allegorical dimension of the Garden story was firmly anchored in a historical understanding of the text. In the *Civitas Dei*, he holds allegory optional and secondary:

> . . . some allegorize all that concerns Paradise itself, where the first men, the parents of the human race, are, according to the truth of holy Scripture, recorded to have been; and they understand all its trees and fruit-bearing plants as virtues and habits of life, as if they had no existence in the external world, but were only so spoken of or related for the sake of spiritual meanings. As if there could not be a real terrestrial Paradise! As if there never existed these two women, Sarah and Hagar, nor the two sons who were born to Abraham, the one of the bond woman, the other of the free, because the apostle says that in them the two covenants were prefigured; or as if water never flowed from the rock when Moses struck it, because therein Christ can be seen in a figure. . . . No one, then, denies that Paradise may signify the life of the blessed; its four rivers, the four virtues, prudence, fortitude, temperance, and justice; its trees all useful knowledge; its fruits, the customs of the godly; its tree of life, wisdom herself, the mother of all good; and the tree of the knowledge of good and evil, the experience of a broken commandment. The punishment which God appointed was in itself a just, and therefore a good thing; but man's experience of it is not good.
> . . . These and similar allegorical interpretations may be suitably put upon Paradise without giving offense to any one, while yet we believe the strict truth of the history, confirmed by its circumstantial narrative of facts.[39]

It is easy to understand the reasons for this hegemony of literal interpretation: the historical communities constituted by biblical revelation had to understand their respective scriptures as speaking historically. Even the paradigmatic and sapiential elements of the Bible were historicized quite early in the history of biblical interpretation (if not in the evolution of the canons themselves): the Psalms were attributed to David's authorship, Proverbs to Solomon's, and Job to Moses';[40] and the Garden of Eden, Mt. Ararat, Babel, Sodom, and Mt. Moriah were understood as historical locales, even where their specific locations were disputed. Figurative and typological exegesis had to begin on the premise of the biblical text's historicity, and was seen to proceed from the initiative of the interpreter, rather than from cues intrinsic to the text—except where such cues (as, for example, evidence of Christ's "fulfillment" of Hebrew prophecy; or, in rabbinic exegesis, textual peculiarities summoning adumbrations of the "Oral Law") were themselves held (like the "Oral Law" itself) to be part of the text's historical substance.

A third source of confusion about allegory stems from the presence in classical rhetoric of apparently competing figurative modes, which, despite their remaining ill defined in their interrelation, are weighted with the aesthetic value judgments of particular cultures and eras. So, roughly from the late eighteenth to the late twentieth century, "allegory" had generally come to be seen as something "bad," by virtue of its mechanical nature, its artificiality, its extraneousness to its referent, and the like, and "symbolism" as something "good," by virtue of its organic concreteness, its naturalness, its fusion of sign and meaning, and the like.[41] Myth, metaphor, metonym, synecdoche, trope, topos, etc., have fallen into one or another position along the spectrum of this polarity, but the modern critic's sense of the overall interrelationship of classical figurative modes has tended to remain vague and ad hoc.

The decline of allegory, of course, must be seen as a significant trend in Western literary history, and can be correlated with such interdependent developments as the decline of the Bible's authority, the growing obsolescence of epic and didactic poetry, the corresponding growth of realistic prose fiction, the rise of secular cultures founded on scientific monosemy and historical self-consciousness, and the development of highly technical abstract languages predisposing (in a manner that *competes* with allegory) to the demystification of natural language and of literary expression. Whether allegory has rebounded in the form of modernism—in the surrealism, polysemy, and self-reflexiveness of such writers as Kafka, Joyce, Nabokov, Pynchon, and Borges—remains to be determined in the light of future literary history. Our present uncertainty on the matter must remain in effect whether we adhere more to the opinion of Maureen Quilligan, who, in the voice of a renascent Christian humanism (and of an informed and empathetic reader) hails the resurgence of allegory in modernism:

> . . . we seem in the last quarter of the twentieth century to have reentered an allegorical age.

... allegory reflects not so much the dominant assumptions about value prevailing in any cultural epoch, but rather the culture's assumptions about the ability of language to state or reveal value; that is, value conceived in an extramundane way, not mere marketplace value, or the goings on in the *agora*, but something *allos*. To define the generic focus of allegory as language is to remove it from the stifling confines of service to a dogma (any dogma) which thereby emphasizes a narrative's essentially static superstructure. It frees us to see allegory's characteristic concern for process, for the complicated exfoliation of interdependent psychic, intellectual, and cultural revelations, which can all be spoken of only in terms of the force that shapes them all: language.

... so that we can judge just how well its reading serves our humanity. Once we get past the necessary complexities of the text and have a measure of control over our response to it, we will be able to see that the proper reader of allegory has never been [Northrop] Frye's impatient literary critic, but someone who is willing to entertain the possibility of making a religious response to the ineffability invoked by its polysemous language.[42]

or whether we hold closer to the views of Hungarian philosopher Georg Lukács, who, in the voice of a maverick Marxism, sees allegory as an expression of literary decay:

Allegory is that aesthetic genre which lends itself par excellence to a description of man's alienation from objective reality. Allegory is a problematic genre because it rejects that assumption of an immanent meaning to human existence. . . . transcendence, which is the essence of allegory, cannot but destroy aesthetics itself.[43]

Lukács draws in this instance on the philosophical aesthetics of Walter Benjamin in *The Origin of German Tragic Drama*:

In Allegory, the *facies hippocratica* of history looks to the observer like a petrified primeval landscape. History, all the suffering and failure it contains, finds expression in the human face—or, rather, in the human skull. No sense of freedom, no classical proportion, no human emotion lives in its features—not only human existence in general, but the fate of every individual human being is symbolized in this most palpable token of mortality. This is the core of the allegorical vision, of the Baroque idea of history as the passion of the world; History is significant only in the stations of its corruption. Significance is a function of mortality—because it is death that marks the passage from corruptibility to meaningfulness.[44]

Curiously, this starkly negative sense of allegory, stressing its preoccupation with mortality and decay, approaches, in certain respects, at least the negative component in the biblical view of history to be expounded in the present study. The apparent dualism of allegory seems to place it in the service of an intelligence committed to anatomizing and debunking.[45] Allegory has often been associated with irony and satire, domains in which the moralist and the immoralist in the writer often merge, but in which moral or social *critique* of some sort remains central to the text's concerns. If, in the manner of Benjamin's "passion of the world," remedy and renewal seem no longer retrievable, it is possible to imagine a sort of allegory whose preoccupation with decline leads to a certain mordant clarity of moral vision, attuned to paradox and dialectical contradiction, which exercises its claim in the midst of the tragedy and disorder it recounts. We must envisage here a kind of discourse subversive to the sense of time and historical change expected by the reader of mimetic narrative—here I borrow the words of Paul de Man:

> Allegory is sequential and narrative, yet the topic of its narration is not necessarily temporal at all, thus raising the question of the referential status of a text whose semantic function, though strongly in evidence, is not primarily determined by mimetic moments; more than ordinary modes of fiction, allegory is at the furthest possible remove from historiography. The "realism" that appeals to us in the details of medieval art is a calligraphy rather than a mimesis, a technical device to insure that the emblems will be correctly identified and decoded, not an appeal to the pagan pleasures of imitation. For it is a part of allegory that, despite its obliqueness and innate obscurity, the resistance to understanding emanates from the difficulty of censorship inherent in the statement and not from the devices of enunciation: Hegel rightly distinguishes between allegory and enigma in terms of allegory's "aim for the most complete clarity, so that the external means it uses must be as transparent as possible with regard to the meaning it is to make apparent." The difficulty of allegory is rather that this emphatic clarity of representation does not stand in the service of something that can be represented.[46]

In his essay "The Rhetoric of Temporality," de Man elaborates on the pseudotemporal and countermimetic properties of allegory, which is here placed into a functional complementarity to irony:

> The fundamental structure of [an] allegory [appears] in the tendency of the language toward narrative, the spreading out along the axis of an imaginary time in order to give duration to what is, in fact, simultaneous within the subject.
> The structure of irony, however, is the reversed mirror image of this form. . . . irony appears as an instantaneous process that takes place rapidly, suddenly, in one single moment. . . . In this respect, irony comes closer to the pattern of factual experience and recaptures some of the factitiousness of human existence as a succession of isolated moments lived by a divided self. Essentially the mode of the present, it knows neither memory nor prefigurative duration, whereas allegory exists entirely within an ideal time that is never here and now but

always a past or an endless future. Irony is a synchronic structure, while allegory appears as a successive mode capable of engendering duration as the illusion of a continuity that it knows to be illusionary. Yet the two modes, for all their profound distinctions in mood and structure, are the two faces of the same fundamental experience of time.[47]

It can be seen that the most sympathetic explainers of allegory share an assumption of a text whose unfolding moments are as essential to the reader's consciousness as the instantaneous structures of irony it comes *in toto* to lay bare. The narrative's illusion of continuity, its evasion of synchrony, its pointed presumption of its own "historicity," are far more dominant ingredients in the workings of allegory than the "message" in whose service the text signifies. The veritgo of the text's irony must be prepared by an imagined stability of temporal succession. Yet the allegorical text must somehow, by the details and contradictions of its own unfolding, invert or destabilize that succession, providing the clues to the sense of disjunction and otherness that eventually awakens in the mind of the reader. Such clues can often be quite faint and obscure—a word, a turn of phrase, an invasive discourse, any small linchpin of temporal structure whose enunciation loosens and collapses the temporality into the ruin (one could say, rune) of allegorical insight. One can see that this process involves a crossing of semantic frames, a juxtaposition of literary or cultural codes, a revisionary upheaval of the meaning of words used earlier in the text. One can also see that the "horizontal" progression of signifiers is a far more important determinant of the character of allegory than the "vertical" relation to a signified. The latter relation is more the preoccupation of allegoresis than of allegory, as Quilligan points out:

> The inappropriate terminology of *allegoresis* (verticalness, levels, hidden meaning, the hieratic difficulty of interpretation) continues to contaminate the reader's appreciation of the peculiar process and values of narrative allegory. Hunting for one-to-one correspondences between insignificant narrative particulars and hidden thematic generalizations, he is frustrated when he cannot find them and generally bored when he can. This state of affairs leads logically to Coleridge's strictures against an inorganic, mechanical, and thoroughly unappealing kind of literature.[48]

Quilligan counterposes to this "imposed" allegory and its tyranny of the vertical, an understanding of allegorical narrative as a necessarily linear, and thus "horizontal," progression:

> . . . this vertical conceptualization of allegory and its emphasis upon disjunct "levels" is absolutely wrong as a matter of practical fact. All reading proceeds linearly, in a word-by-word fashion, but allegory

often institutionalizes this fact by the journey or quest form of the plot, journeys which are, futhermore, extremely episodic in nature. It would be more precise to say therefore that allegory works horizontally, rather than vertically so that meaning accretes serially, interconnecting and criss-crossing the verbal surface long before one can accurately speak of moving to another level "beyond" the literal. And that "level" is not above the literal one in a vertically organized fictional space, but is located in the self-consciousness of the reader, who gradually becomes aware, as he reads, of the way he creates the meaning of the text.[49]

One can, to be sure, carry this insight too far, for, indeed, there is *order* in allegory—even the ecstatic verbal soup of *Finnegans Wake* has both rhyme and reason—and if that order is not hierarchical, it still may be described in synchronic terms that approach in abstractness and exteriority the hieratic style of interpretive priesthoods nurtured on allegoresis. Modern literary theory is at present uncertainly poised between two great moments—some would say conflicting moments, some complementary: a "semiotics" that reaches into texts with the confidence that they can be known in terms of the *langue*, the system of abstract codes that makes them possible; and a "deconstruction," a playful poststructuralist skepticism, rooted in the aphoristic tradition of Kierkegaard, Nietzsche, and the later Wittgenstein, that seeks to make of the unraveling of texts only further texts: to compound the enigma and persistence of the signifier, to uphold the anteriority of writing, and to match rune with rune. If the structuralists and semioticians are the priesthood of allegoresis, the deconstructionists—the otherwise unlikely camaraderie of Derrida, de Man, Lacan, and Bloom, among others—are, in their subversiveness, jocularity, and preference for oracles, the shamans or court fools in the commonwealth of reading, and the true allegorists, whose "allegories of reading" are, for their recipients, as unsettling as premodern allegory was to its readership. Jonathan Culler calls this dichotomy one between "canny" and "uncanny" critics, but also warns us that one can underestimate the extent to which a structuralist continues to inhabit a deconstructionist.[50]

In any case, the temporalizing enchantments of allegorical narrative rarely yield, as de Man almost suggests, a smooth and hermetically sealed surface, or as Quilligan sometimes hints of, a Heraclitean swirl of names and codes, but something in between: a rational text riddled with explicable gaps, discontinuities, and irresolution, whose uncertainties are part of the reading adventure it poses. Such a text has both structure and a certain portentous despair of structure, a tendency to gesture deferentially toward silence, while gnomishly enticing its readers (if I may here wax allegorical) across the precarious floes of fractured language, atop a sea of polysemy, toward wisdom. If the situation of modern literary theory is easily made into an analogy for a problematic that, in different ways, inhabits biblical narrative, the history of biblical interpretation, and modern critical study of the Bible, it is because today's readers share certain fundamental assumptions with the makers of that book, with its interpretive tradition, and with the historical sciences born out of it. The conflict of a hieratic priesthood with a subversive, ecstatic, and shamanistic prophethood seems very ancient and very persistent in Western cultural history.

Allegorical Readings and Biblical Readers

The scholarly investigator of biblical narrative[51] will readily agree that the problem of the figural status of the Bible's narrative is a worthwhile one to ponder, and will willingly concede that the problem has something to do, among other things, with the representation of time, with the role of wordplay and polysemy, with the status of ironizing, with the structures of quotation, with intertextual relations, with structural analogues, and with the manipulation of folk stereotypes. What this scholar may not always readily concede is that the Bible is wholly a *literary* entity, that it is fiction, that its discourse is not wholly earnest, that its largest units, indeed, are a "text" altogether, in anything other than the most formal and canonical sense. Such a scholar is understandably wary of any critical language that can be applied with equal facility to the Bible, to Rabelais, to Goethe's *Faust*, to *Ulysses*, and to *Pale Fire*. He or she may likely not always concede the notions of discursive space taken for granted by the literary theorist of either the semiotic or the deconstructionist persuasion. And where the biblical scholar may concede that determining the oral or written character of a biblical narrative is a worthy task, the same person will stress the contradictory and inconclusive nature of the data, will usually resist speculation on the nature of the written sign or of signification, and will probably oppose efforts to weave from the biblical text metascientific sophistries and gnomic counter-texts.[52]

Most suspicious of all to the biblical scholar is a notion of biblical allegory. It smacks of medieval allegoresis and seems to promise only the tautology of a translated code—in which ideology and dogma control the movements of the text—while at the same time seeming to express only the private meanings of the allegorizing interpreter. This distrust of allegory is probably rooted in a more general belief in the "heavy-handedness" of allegorical interpretation, especially one alleging political allegory, since the allusions must be either so precise that they are unrecoverable or so general that they are uninteresting. The allegorical correspondences are generally understood as a one-for-one homology—rather than as a dynamic system of syllogistic and dialectical transformations, in which words and figures change meaning across time. To pick up on a motif of Quilligan's quoted earlier, opponents of allegory judge it by the standards of allegoresis, and this results in a curiously circular dilemma: expecting too little of allegory, they fault it for providing too little.

In one respect, this valuation is correct, or, to be more precise, half-correct: readings of an allegoretic type (and this includes much that structuralism has done for the Bible's narrative) are dissatisfying. Biblical allegory, if it exists, must do more than provide a set of static contemplative patterns of mechanistic transformations. It must hit its readers where they think, but must do so in a way that involves their life postures, their passions, their prejudices, their hopes and fears—in short, all of the faculties to which they believe themselves "organically" connected—testing, in the process, their understanding of the social and cultural realities that make literature possible or necessary in the first place.

Which brings us to consider more carefully the notion of "political" allegory. Theorists of allegory have tended to speak of two great strands of allegory in Western literary tradition: one variously construed as moral, psychological, or religious, dealing, one should say, with matters pertaining to the mind and spirit; and a political strand, dealing with the social and relational aspects of human existence.[53] Biblical literature, on the other hand, does not recognize this neat distinction. If it is the aim of allegory to sketch out the lineaments of a cultural self, biblical allegory sees that self as both individual and collective. The civil society of a given era may try to split the functions of knowledge—relegating knowledge of the human body, the daily and seasonal cycle, the perception of time, and the domain of moral choice to the consciousness of the individual; and knowledge of the body politic, of ethics, authority, the state, and the wielding of power to a public consciousness. The Hebrew Bible resists that split, not as a form of resistance to civil society, but as a form of critique from within it. Between the individual and the tribe, it poses the indissoluble mediation of the houshold; between the individual and the state, it poses the indissoluble mediation of the tribe. And it uses the conflicts of the household, the tribe, and the intertribal order as means of anatomizing the strengths and weaknesses of state and empire.

A biblical political allegory, therefore, would not admit of a simple, one-for-one correspondence between a story and the political events it "refers" to. Its correspondences, if they are directly translatable, are multiple and embrace a variety of cultural codes. Its exact historical context is beyond our power to determine fully, precisely because its montage of traditionary discourse has succeeded in standing, to use de Man's words, in the service of something that cannot be represented. The reader's experience of such a text (and we must assume that this text is indeed addressing *readers*) is gradual and cumulative, and it is the unique crossweave not just of traditions and of narrative moments but also of propositions and syllogisms that comprises the essence of allegorical communication. A story proceeding, as it were, enthymemically (concealing unstated premises) gradually cultivates its proper readership and establishes the need for multiple readings. The esoterism of the allegory emanates, to borrow again de Man's words, "from the difficulty of censorship inherent in the statement and not from the devices of enunciation." This censorship is not always that of a political despotism; it can arise in constraints of propriety, of expedience, of sensibility—constraints that the allegorist may often recognize as legitimate. When Leo Strauss, in *Persecution and the Art of Writing*, stated the conditions of indirection in serious writing, he overstated, perhaps intentionally, the "totalitarian" context of esoteric discourse:

> . . . We can easily imagine that a historian living in a totalitarian country, a generally respected and unsuspected member of the only party in existence, might be led by his investigations to doubt the soundness of the government-sponsored interpretation of the history of religion. Nobody would prevent him from publishing a passionate attack of what he would call the liberal view. He would of course have to state the liberal view before attacking it; he would make that statement in the quiet, unspectacular and somewhat boring manner which would seem to be but natural; he would use many technical terms, give many quotations and attach undue importance to insignificant details; he would seem to forget the holy war of mankind in the petty squabbles of pedants. Only when he reached the core of the argument would he write three or four sentences in that terse and lively style which is apt to arrest the attention of young men who love to think. That central passage would state the case of the adversaries more clearly, compellingly and mercilessly than it had ever been stated in the heyday of liberalism, for he would silently drop all the foolish excrescences of the liberal creed which were allowed to grow up during the time when liberalism had succeeded and therefore was approaching dormancy. His reasonable young reader would for the first time catch a glimpse of the forbidden fruit. . . . Reading the book for the second and third time, he would detect in the very arrangement of the quotations from the authoritative books significant additions to those few terse statements which occur in the center of the rather short first part.[54]

Such a method of artful quotation is indeed at home in any situation where a writer (or "quoter") wishes to cultivate "contemporaries" in future eras. This may express a kind of alienation, but one must remember that the alienation is twofold in nature: the esoterist wants neither a mass readership nor a narrow coterie. His literary indirection, to use Strauss's words, creates a work "addressed, not to all readers, but to trustworthy and intelligent readers only. It has the advantage of private communication without having its greatest disadvantage—that it reaches only the writer's acquaintances."[55] The work creates its own readership, for it contains within itself the necessary tools of interpretation, which are discovered by the serious reader over the course of multiple readings, and are discovered chiefly from the text. It presupposes a milieu extending over several generations, and in its main thrust is a justification of that milieu. Yet it makes its peace with the "priestly" concerns of its own era, choosing instead a quiet and understated form of subversion. It makes its peace with its own "literal" (and illiberal) meaning. Strauss's self-censored writer here expresses the conditions of literacy itself.

With Leo Strauss, we come one step closer to a more native theory of biblical allegory, since the three subjects dealt with in *Persecution and the Art of Writing* are three serious and important readers of Scripture—Maimonides, Judah Halevi, and Spinoza, whose treatises are something other than mere allegoresis. It could be argued, and Strauss approaches such a notion, that these three, who stood upon the threshold where philosophy and religion meet, were "contemporaries" of the Scripture they interpreted. They understood the divided nature of their own discourse, and they took their cues on such matters from Scripture itself, and from the politics of biblical interpretation in postbiblical times. The realm they embraced spoke to the competition of the rival faiths, and to that of interpretive rivalries within the respective faiths. They were keenly aware, with varying degrees of sympathy or antipathy, of the intervening claims of the Oral Law and the Christian New Testament, and of the patristic and rabbinic interpretation these texts generated, if not also of the Qur'an and the Hadith, and certainly of the Graeco-Latin philosophic tradition. And they were, in varying ways, ideal respondents to the allegorical dimension of Scripture, rather than practitioners of allegoresis, for they spun from their readings allegories of their own.

Philo: Biblical Allegoresis

In this one important respect—in the making of allegory from allegory—Strauss's three biblical readers differ markedly from the presumed father of biblical allegoresis, Philo of Alexandria, who has never appeared hesitant to declare openly to his readers the esoteric meaning of biblical narrative. What is striking about Philo's exegetical method is how much it often resembles the interpretive techniques of rabbinic discourse: quotation and intrabiblical allusion, etymological and nu-

merological argument, tendency to see in the biblical character a hero
of virtue, recourse to parables, willingness to abstract.[56] Where Philo
stops short of rabbinical method is in his discursive format, his concealment of his sources, and his single-minded commitment to one openly
understood interpretive position, which is, nevertheless, not always generalized as plainly as one might expect: "The migrations [of Abraham] as
set forth in the literal text of the scriptures are made by a man of wisdom,
but according to the laws of allegory by a virtue-loving soul in its search
for the true God."[57] Philo omits to explain what are the "laws of allegory," and in this respect he is far less explicit than his rabbinic counterparts, who have supplied very detailed hermeneutic rules for determining figurative meanings in Scripture. Here and there, he will reveal the
apologetic and rationalizing context of his labors, as, for example, in his
contention that the plain sense of the biblical text, when presenting
events contrary to the laws of nature, is myth (and therefore abhorrent to
the sophisticated reader).[58] Yet his generalizations about the intentions
of Scripture itself seem curiously disjointed and noncommittal, as, for
example, the opening of the treatise from which the above quotation is
drawn, the *De Abrahamo*:

> The first of the five books in which the holy laws are written bears the
> name and inscription of Genesis, from the genesis or creation of the
> world, an account of which it contains at its beginning. It has received
> this title in spite of its embracing numberless other matters; for it tells
> of peace and war, of fruitfulness and barrenness, of dearth and plenty;
> how fire and water wrought great destruction of what is on earth; how
> on the other hand plants and animals were born and throve through
> kindly tempering of the air and the yearly seasons, and so to men,
> some of whom lived a life of virtue, others of vice. But since some of
> these things are parts of the world, and others events which befall it,
> and the world is the complete consummation of them all, [Moses]
> dedicated the whole book to it.[59]

   Philo hints of, but does not develop, connections between the theme of
"peace and war" and those of "fruitfulness and barrenness," "dearth and
plenty," etc., though, to be sure, the mastery of the passions he is to find
everywhere in Scripture is seen as conducive to both peace and fruitfulness, to the flowering of nature, to the staving off of fire and flood, to the
tempering of the air, and to the life of virtue.[60] The harmony of Mosaic
and natural law is a frequent theme in his writings:

> Moses extolled [the righteous] for two reasons. First, he wished to
> show that the enacted ordinances are not inconsistent with nature; and
> secondly that those who wish to live in accordance with the laws as they
> stand have no difficult task, seeing that the first generations before any
> at all of the particular statutes was set in writing followed the unwritten

law with perfect ease, so that one might properly say that the enacted laws are nothing else than memorials [*hypomnēmata*] of the life of the ancients, preserving to a later generation their actual words and deeds.[61]

One must not assume from these words that Philo is advocating a reverence for the past as such, or a mystical communion with the life of the ancients for its own sake. Still, a linkage of historical generations by the mediation of recorded "deeds and words" is by no means an obvious boon, given Philo's belief in the universal and timeless accessibility of philosophical wisdom. Why write history? Why record for posterity? Why not learn all from oracle, maxim, and treatise? Why the descent, if you will, into *res gestae* and personification? Why does a latter-day generation need *story* as a means of inculcating wisdom, and why, in particular, stories of life in former eras? As cut-and-dried as Philo sounds in asserting a pedagogical linkage between an ancient generation and his own, he here reveals certain a priori assumptions, perhaps biblical and Jewish in origin, concerning the role of memory and story in the formation of character. The Greek term *hypomnēma* (memorial, mention, monument, symbol), while not identical in semantic field, bears useful comparison to the Hebrew *zikkaron* and *zekher*,[62] which, in the Sabbath wine benediction, cast the ritual into a radically bold intrabiblical typology: ". . . a remembrance [*zikkaron*] of the work of Creation . . . a reminder [*zekher*] of the going-out of Egypt. . . ."

If for Philo memory only serves the greater glory of the timeless "unwritten law," its presence in his argument is significant nonetheless. Philo seems to accept as a given that an account of the lives of the ancients would reach his era, but he leaves unspecified the factors motivating and enabling the intervening generations to preserve a record of the past in the first place. While one finds in Philo's psychomachian landscape a relentlessly one-way allegorizing, and while in the statement quoted above Philo seems strangely to ignore the element of *struggle* in the life of virtue (which, to be sure, does surface in his actual exegeses), nevertheless one almost finds in Philo's words an accurate assessment of biblical tradition's pedagogical task: the cultivation of virtue and memory as mutually reinforcing structures. We cannot say for sure, however, whether Philo saw this as anything other than a one-way process: memory serving virtue (and conformance to the "laws of nature"), but not the reverse. His textual interpretations are certainly more than "mere" allegoresis, but they fall short of responding fully to the real allegory Philo may have seen in Scripture. The allegorical trope of the soul's confrontation with the sensible world (which would become, in Christianity, Gnosticism, and in medieval Kabbalism, a myth of incarnation and

descent) is, indeed, cognate to certain motions in the Garden story and
the Abraham cycle, but Philo's explanatory posture is not that of the fully
engaged reader of biblical allegory. His explanations are too fluent, too
discursive, too informative. Philo forgoes the condensed silences of biblical language that rabbinic Oral Law (in the form of Judah ha-Nasi's
otherwise by no means lexically deficient Mishnaic Hebrew) managed to
reproduce. So while Scripture itself very likely registered in Philo's mind
as allegory, the commentary he wrote is essentially allegoresis—an imposed meaning, narrower in scope than allegory, and lacking the constraint of silence and indirection that allegory typically imposes on its
readers.

Maimonides: A Polis of Readers

Let us return to the matter of "political" allegory. Philo (*De opif.* I, 3)
speaks of the adherent to the (pentateuchal) Law as a "world citizen"
(*kosmopolitēs*), as though the cosmos itself were a polity, but on the whole
he prefers something of a reverse emphasis: the natural, political, and
historical realms are a sign of the soul, its virtues and vices. These realms,
including the narrated world of biblical history, signify an inner, intrapsychic reality, more than the reverse. For Moses Maimonides, some
1100 years later, the signification process was decidedly two-way and
complementary: the political and spiritual functions of Scripture are
interdependent, a matter Maimonides states with the utmost clarity:

> The Law as a whole aims at two things: the welfare of the soul and
> the welfare of the body. As for the welfare of the soul, it consists in the
> multitude's acquiring correct opinions corresponding to their respec-
> tive capacity. Therefore some of them [namely, the opinions—tr.] are
> set forth explicitly and some of them are set forth in parables. For it is
> not within the nature of the common multitude that its capacity should
> suffice for apprehending that subject matter as it is. As for the welfare
> of the body, it comes about by the improvement of their ways of living
> one with another. This is achieved through two things. One of them is
> the abolition of their wronging each other. This is tantamount to every
> individual among the people not being permitted to act according to
> his will and up to the limits of his power but being forced to do that
> which is useful to the whole. The second thing consists in the acquisi-
> tion by every human individual of moral qualities that are useful for
> life in society so that the affairs of the city may be ordered. Know that
> as between these two aims, one is indubitably greater in nobility,
> namely, the welfare of the soul—I mean the procuring of correct
> opinions—while the second aim—I mean the welfare of the body—is
> prior in nature and time. The latter aim consists in the governance of
> the city and the well-being of the states of all its people according to

their capacity. This second aim is the more certain one, and it is the one regarding which every effort has been made precisely to expound it and all its particulars. For the first aim can only be achieved after achieving this second one.[63]

While postulating the formal interdependence of the Law's two functions, Maimonides seems to recognize the priority "in nature and time" of the political function. Without political stability and "the abolition of reciprocal wrongdoing" (ibid. 60a), the quest for intellectual and spiritual perfection is impossible. This is true on both an individual and a communal level: adherence to the Law is prerequisite to the personal endeavor of philosophical study, and a community's adherence to the Law's moral and political norms sets the social climate within which intellectual perfection is possible. The human being's bodily well-being requires such basic amenities as food, shelter, and hygiene, and since these are not things that can be dependably secured by individuals alone, political association (*'al-'ijtama'u-'l-madaniyu*) is necessary. Such association, by definition, thrusts together people widely differing in capacities and temperaments, who must achieve, however tenuously, a consensus on their shared symbols, words, and moral imperatives. The Bible's miracle tales, cultivating in naïve readers the faith and motivation necessary to participate in Law and tradition, likewise provide them, albeit in a much disguised form, with the rough outline of the "correct opinions" on whose possession their immortality hinges. These stories are thus parables, were understood as parables by their rabbinic interpreters, and were explicated *by* parables in the Talmud and Midrash, and a large part of the task of the *Guide* is the training of a parabolic reader.[64] Whence the *Guide*'s own elliptical and spare design, its esoteric caveats, and its preoccupation with language and signification. If the uneven capacities of the Law's adherents require that they each read the biblical text in different ways, this uncertain meshing of sensibilities itself comprises a political problem *par excellence*. The gulf between the elite and the naïve reader nevertheless conceals a deep symbiosis and cooperation, the reasons for this cooperation evident to each individual in a manner suited to his or her unique capacities. Exploring the homonymic properties of biblical words is a necessary first step toward a higher wisdom, but a part of that wisdom is the willingness to leave the homonymy, and the confusion it generates, in place.

The "political" dimension of esoteric communication, according to the paradigms offered by Leo Strauss, rests in the writer's awareness of a conflict of sensibilities between a mass and an elite (or persecuted) readership. It comprises a political problem because careful and careless readers share, sometimes physically, sometimes culturally, the same "polis." The careful writer has just as much interest in preservation of the whole commonwealth of literacy (including its careless readers) as he has in preservation of his careful readership. Knowledge of political evolution is thus important to the writer and is a necessary component of his program for readers. If the careful reader's gradual transcendence of Scripture's literal and mythic meanings is a kind of private purgation, a purifying of the intellect, it nevertheless must culminate in public restraint and circumspection, in a willingness to allow other readers whatever understanding their motivations and capacities dictate, within the bounds of the exoteric Law. The tendency of allegory to beget allegory is rooted in this transferability of silence and indirection from text to commentary.

At the end of his introduction to the *Guide*, Maimonides cites seven causes for the presence of contradictory statements in a text.[65] The first—collection of the views of several authors—he attributes to Mishnah. The second—preservation of an author's original and changed opinion—he attributes (together with the first) to Talmud. The fifth, sixth, and seventh—pedagogical simplification, unintentional loss of consistency through multiple premises, and partial concealment of the subject—he attributes to aggadic, midrashic, and philosophical texts. The third and fourth causes, which he attributes to Scripture, should be quoted here in full:

> The third cause. Not all statements in question are to be taken in their external sense; some are to be taken in their external sense, while some others are parables and hence have an inner content. Alternatively, two apparently contradictory propositions may both be parables and when taken in their external sense may contradict, or be contrary to, one another.
> The fourth cause. There is a proviso that, because of a certain necessity, has not been explicitly stated in its proper place; or the two subjects may differ, but one of them has not been explained in its proper place, so that a contradiction appears to have been said, whereas there is no contradiction.

The two conditions described here—parables and apparent non sequiturs—are stated without much elaboration, so it is difficult to see the role they play in relation to each other, or within the total picture Maimonides will present of biblical discourse, but it is important to understand that these modes of indirection are not merely casual or decorative in function. They are integral to a unified subject and consistent strategy that we can perhaps designate by the single term "argument." That the Bible has an argument means both that it is more than an encyclopedic hodge-podge and that its line of argument is not plainly expounded. It must be discovered by the reader slowly and laboriously—

much like the argument of the treatise Maimonides himself writes. Elucidating the parables alone—the domain of Maimonides' "third cause"—would leave us with little more than allegoresis. Understanding the *progression* of the text—which Maimonides' "fourth cause" would seem to necessitate—that is, apprehending the shifts in semantic field and cultural code that the biblical text, moment by moment, conditions us to expect, is to approach a more intrinsically allegorical reading.

Allegory as Parable

We have so far touched upon numerous, possibly conflicting, theories concerning allegory, which bear, in differing degrees, on an approach to the Bible as allegory: that allegory is a genre or convention; that it is a pictorial and narrative means of representing abstractions; that it is a rhetorical strategy or structural principle within works that include non-allegorical functions; that it is often indistinguishably intertwined with other figurative modes; that it is associated with irony and satire; that it is a false temporalization of something simultaneous within the subject; that it is a gesture "otherwards" from its nominal subject; that it is an internal and verbal landscape; that it is an art of polysemy; that it is an art of quotation; that it is a correlation of political and psychological realities; that it is a form of esoterism; and that it is a form of syllogistic argumentation, both systematic and indirect in its exposition. Concern for method and pedagogical clarity would seem to dictate that we simplify our canvas somewhat, or at least that we draw the existing definitions into some sort of functional relation.

The ensuing chapters will, I hope, accomplish the latter task, through the interpretation of specific texts. Meanwhile, without renouncing the complexity of allegory's multiple capabilities, let us seek a simpler paradigm for understanding concrete manifestations of allegory. Picking up on Maimonides' repeated emphasis on parable, I would like to focus upon allegory's behavior as parable. It is appropriate here to return to Benno Jacob's commentary on the Garden story, specifically to his remarks on the function of the serpent in the tale:

> . . . The serpent cannot here personify a superhuman principle of evil, either a devil or some disguised form thereof, as in the ancient Persian serpent-myths, in which Dahaka, first created being, enables Ahriman, who takes on serpent-form, to work corruption in the earlier-created world of Ormuzd. Here, in contrast, is the serpent expressly a creature of God [see Gen. 3:1], and even later [i.e., after the "curse" of 3:14–15] this *naḥash* still does not embody the personified power of evil, who, out of hatred of God and His kingdom, must act destruc-

tively. The dogmatic Christian explanations are as unacceptable as
mythological conceptions that would retrieve from the serpent-figure,
in however pale a form, a primal demon, bringing in for proof thereof
all sorts of parallels, as in the *märchen* types supplied by Gunkel ("Peasant myths"). Equally invalid are the over-rationalized platitudes of
pure historicism, as we find even in Köhler. . . . Most admissible, in
harmony with the enlightened outlook and the ethically inclined perspective of the Torah, is a moral allegory where the serpent represents
no cosmic, antigodly power but an inner tendency in man himself in
his capacity as *nefesh ḥayyah* [=animal; cf. Gen. 2:7, 19], which incites to
disobedience of the divine injunction. . . . For such purpose is no animal more suitable than a simple garden snake, which insinuates itself,
twisting and slithering, unnoticed. . . . the embodiment of cunning and
seduction.[66]

"*. . . a moral allegory, where the serpent represents no cosmic, antigodly power,
but an inner tendency in man himself.*" Several important ideas about allegory are condensed in this phrase: that it is concerned with moral choice;
that its proper focus is the individual, intrapsychic sphere; that its *apparent* focus is cosmic and mythic history, the clash of good and evil, of godly
and antigodly, on a scale larger than life.[67] The apparent confusion
between personal and suprapersonal domains, which Jacob sees in the
history of Garden-story exegesis, and which he attributes to a mistake on
the part of readers, may be more integral to the textual dynamics of
allegory than Jacob was inclined to admit. For Jacob, as for Philo, the
reading process seems to involve a simple and one-way decoding that
ends with the internalization of the insight and the discarding of the
mythological husk. In this manner, an analogy is made whose outer
appearances are merely provisional, approximate, and inferior to the
insight ultimately conveyed. This purely functional import of the story's
imagery, by making proper interpretation depend on the good offices of
a reliable interpreter, suits a conception of allegory that is closer to the
notion of allegoresis outlined earlier.

Maimonides, we should note, similarly denigrates the intrinsic importance of a parable's imagery, and seems initially to suggest that the
intervention of a qualified interpreter is necessary to the reader's proper
apprehension of the text. Yet he repeatedly belies this apparent stance
by the opacity and indirection of his own discussion, and by his obvious
assumption that a reader's own initiative and choices are essential to the
interpretive venture. Having the textual image's "translation" alone is
insufficient. The reader must not only know what the image means, he
must know what orders of meaning are being invoked. He must know
how much of the image means what it means, and how much of it is
ballast, accoutrement, or decoy. He must know when he is being addressed parabolically, and must be able to gauge the extent of the text's

concealment or incongruity. Such matters are dependent not on an interpreter's intervention but on the reader's own instinct, preparation, and effort. Maimonides employs as his rabbinic precedent for this notion the statement in Mishnah *Ḥagigah* 2:1 that certain esoteric mysteries of Scripture are not to be expounded by a teacher unless the pupil "is a sage who understands of his own accord" (*ḥakham hammevin midda'ato*). What one communicates in that circumstance are "chapter headings," which the listener must fill in on his own initiative and out of the resources of his own training and intellect. The recipient's own active involvement in the interpretive process is necessary to fuse the disparate hints into a meaningful pattern.

Elsewhere in the same discussion, Maimonides cites another rabbinic statement on the nature of *mashal* (parable). His quotation of it is imprecise, and we should here juxtapose his rendition of it with the original:

> Our rabbis say: A man who loses a sela or a pearl in his house can find the pearl by lighting a taper worth an issar. In the same way this parable in itself is worth nothing, but by means of it you can understand the words of Torah. (*Guide*, I, Intro., 6b—translator's italics)

> Our rabbis say: Don't let this parable be trivial in your estimation, for by means of parable, a man can understand the words of Torah. It is like a king who lost a gold piece from his house or a fine pearl: Is it not by means of a candlewick worth an *issar* that he finds it? Thus, let not this parable be trivial in your estimation, for by means of parable a man can understand the words of Torah. (Midrash on Song of Songs, I, i, 8)

Maimonides' version of the statement seems, indeed, diametrically opposed in meaning to that of the original: the original warns us not to underestimate the figures of a parable; Maimonides' version warns us not to overestimate them.[68] The two statements taken together neatly epitomize the polarity of the conscientious reader's dilemma: when to read meaning into a figure, and when to cease doing so. Restraint of one's interpretive faculties is as important as the spurring of them. This insight would be less apparent had Maimonides quoted the statement correctly, and his apparently purposeful deviation from it creates a conflicting claim of texts that cannot be solved or mediated simply by saying that one text is correctly rendered, the other not; or by weighing, at this early stage of the *Guide*'s unfolding, how much accident or design underlies the swerve.[69] Perhaps only the full unfolding of the *Guide*'s argument can make evident the relative weight of the respective claims (and then again, perhaps not), and the reader must not only hold in suspension the solution, if one exists, to the discrepancy, but must remain, at least for the nonce, admonished in equal measure by both the "correct" and the "incorrect" version. The decoding of parables thus involves much more than a simple replacement of opacity with clarity, or a simple one-for-one decoding of a cryptic message: it requires a trained and subtle awareness of the context, timing, intertextual discrepancy, and cumulative argument that in concert determine the figurative weight to be given to a scene or image. The reader's active and informed participation in this process is essential.

The "correct" version of the rabbinic dictum is, for its part, a characteristically self-reflexive manifesto on the nature of *mashal*: it talks about parable by means of parable, and it, too, like Maimonides' misquotation, makes an unacknowledged intertextual swerve of its own. The "king" who has lost a "pearl" has precedents in Hellenistic myth and gnosis,[70] and, whether or not the synagogue recipient of the rabbinic homily was aware of these resonances, the homilist was certainly aware of the tug on his listener's fancy exerted by the trope. Mythological enchantment—the seduction of the recipient's imagination, the appeal to his nostalgia and sentimentality—is essential to the "disenchantment" of which allegorical insights are made. It plays a role in stimulating the reader to make analogical associations on several levels at once—for the sense of mystery and enigma it evokes is an encouragement to reflection and sustained attention, to the extended (perhaps lifetime) gaze by which alone higher understanding is possible. Not all overinterpretation is dysfunctional.

Restricting ourselves to the purely analogical function of the *mashal*, we still find that its manifestation is anything other than static or one-dimensional. In the *mashal*, a scriptural verse or situation is rendered clearer by reformulation into certain key stock figures and locales: king, princess, merchant, student, wise man, old wife, young wife; palace, marketplace, boat, law court, foreign country, etc.—which, simple in themselves, are juggled into endlessly ingenious new combinations. Here, mimesis is decidedly not the purpose; to all appearances, it is the *logic* of a textual moment that the *mashal* aims at illuminating. The imagery is at all times bound up with a particular verbal and syntactical musculature, which, far more than imagery per se, is what is remembered about a *mashal*: a tone of voice, an inflection; a turn of surprise, perplexity, or sarcasm; an exclamation of discovery, wonderment, or triumph. Always there is comparison, but the similarity resides in the coincidence of naming and utterance between the scriptural verse and its commonplace analogue, and in some conceptual kinship between the two, not in the imagery. Since the varieties of remembered human utterance are far more numerous and expressive than those of remembered visual information, the suppleness of the *mashal* medium is virtually limitless. We could call these phenomena "habits of mind," but they are always verbal, and always specific. A *mashal* elicits not just a "message" (a *nimshal*, a thing analogized) but a broader and more nuanced set of implications, connotations, socially responsible conclusions, and encouragements to further private speculation—all through the medium of words and verbal figures.

It is the *kakh* (the "thus" or "so it is") of the *mashal* that triggers this complex response in readers, and it is precisely here that we are poles apart from the *'al-ken* ("therefore") of naïve mythology, which subdues and reassures and forecloses further speculation—assuming, that is, that we can take the latter formula at face value, as the form critic would often have us do with its occurrences in Genesis. Suffice it to say that the affinities between *mashal* and allegory are self-evident. The weight of cognitive activity falls on the hither side of the word "thus," i.e., outside the text, within the reader and the reader's world, after the imagery of the *mashal* has dissolved, to reconstruct itself thereby as proverb, maxim, insight. It is significant that Hebrew knows no lexical distinction between parable and proverb: both are rendered by the single word *mashal*—they are two halves of the same operation: one might think of proverb as a sort of collapsed parable, and parable, conversely, as an expanded, pseudochronic, narrated exposition of the insight of a proverb.[71]

Parable in the Hebrew Bible

The *mashal* did not originate with rabbinic literature; it has had a long history in Hebrew literature, and, for that matter, in literature of the ancient world as a whole. The biblical examples—by which I mean those texts that self-consciously present themselves to the reader as parables in some formal sense[72]—seem largely to have a political context: they are typically addressed to a secular sovereign, to city elders, or to the political community as a whole:

> Joseph said to Pharaoh: "Pharaoh's dreams are one dream. What God is to do He has told Pharaoh. The seven good cows are seven years, and the seven good ears of corn are seven years. It is one dream. And the seven lean and deficient cows which came up after them are seven years; the seven empty and wind-battered ears of corn will be seven years of famine. That is the matter I have spoken unto Pharaoh: that which God is to do He has shown to Pharaoh. [Etc.]" (Gen. 41:25–28ff.)

> Israel took all of these cities. Israel dwelt in all the cities of the Amorite in Heshbon and in all its dependent regions. For Heshbon was the city of Sihon. (King of the Amorite he was: He fought with the first king of Moab, and took all his land from his hand up to Arnon. Therefore do parablers [*moshlim*] say:

"Come, Heshbon, be built; be established, city of
    Sihon,
for a fire has gone out from Heshbon; a flame from
    the district of Sihon,
it has devoured the cities of Moab; the *ba'alim* of
    the high places of Arnon,
Woe to thee, Moab; thou art lost, o people of Chemosh!
He has made his sons refugees; and his daughters cap-
    tives—to the Amorite king Sihon,
We have shot it to death—Heshbon as far as Dibon,
we have laid it waste unto Nophah—as far as Medeba."
                                                    (Num. 21:25–30)

YHWH placed an oracle in the mouth of Balaam. He said, "Return
to Balak, and say thus . . ."
    He returned to him, and behold, he was standing by his sacrificial
offering, he and all the princes of Moab.
    He took up his parable and said:
            "From Aram Balak has led me, king of Moab from the
                hills of the East,
            [saying:] 'Come, curse Jacob for me; come, fulminate
                against Israel. . . .'
            How can I curse what God has not cursed? How should
                I fume against whom God has not fumed?
            For from the clifftops I can see him; from the hills
                I mark him out,
            yes, he dwells as a people apart; among the nations
                he is not counted.
            Who has counted the dust of Jacob? Who has numbered
                even a fourth of Israel?
            May my soul die an honorable death; may my fate re-
                semble his!"
                                            (Ibid., 23:5–10; cf. ibid.,
                                                18–24; 24:3–9, 15–25)

All the lords of Shechem and all the house of Millo gathered together. They went and crowned Abimelech as king, by the terebinth of
the pillar, which is in Shechem.
    They told Jotham, and he went and stood at the top of Mt. Gerizzim.
He raised his voice and said to them:
            "Listen to me, lords of Shechem, and God will
                listen to you:
            The trees up and went to anoint themselves a
                king over themselves.
            They said to the olive: 'Rule over us!'
            And the olive said to them: 'Should I leave
                behind my fatness, whereby God and men
                have honored me,
            and should I go to swagger o'er the trees?'
            The trees said to the fig: 'Come thou, rule over us!'
            And the fig said to them: 'Should I leave behind my
                sweetness and my good produce,

and should I go to swagger o'er the trees?'
The trees said to the vine: 'Come thou, rule over us!'
And the vine said to them: 'Should I leave behind my
    choicest wine, that gives joy to gods and men,
and should I go to swagger o'er the trees?'
And all the trees said to the bramble: 'Come thou,
    rule over us!'
And the bramble said to the trees: 'If, in truth,
    you are anointing me as king over you,
come, take refuge in my shade! If not, let fire
    come forth from the bramble,
and let it devour the cedars of Lebanon!'"

                        (Judg. 9:6–15)

". . . Take up this parable against the king of Babylon, and say:
    'How has the oppressor ceased, she who extorts
        gold, how she has ceased!
    YHWH has broken the rod of evildoers, staff of
        governors,
    which struck in wrath the peoples, with unceas-
        ing stroke,
    ruled in anger nations, with a persecution unre-
        strained. . . .'"

                        (Isa. 14:4–6ff.)

The word of YHWH came to me as follows: "O human being, read out a riddle, and parabolize a parable unto the house of Israel. And say: 'Thus says my master YHWH:
    "The great eagle, great of wing, long-limbed,
    replete with feathers, with a dappling of colors,
        comes toward the Lebanon,
    he takes the choicest of the cedars, crops the
        heads of saplings,
    and he brings them to the land of Canaan, sets
        them in a town of traffickers.
    He takes some of the region's seeds, and plants
        them in a seeding-field,
    he takes them to the edge of plenteous waters;
        plants them as a willow,
    and it sprouts, becomes a vine: spreading, and
        low of stature,
    turning its tendrils toward him, the roots of
        it are under him.
    It has become a vine: it brings forth branches,
        and it shoots forth sprigs.

    "There was a single great eagle, great
        of wing, and plenteous of feathers,
    and behold, this vine has bent its roots toward
        him,
    its tendrils it extends to him, to water it, from
        the furrows of its planting,

on a good field, next to plenteous waters, it is
   planted,
making branches, bearing fruit, becoming a majestic vine."'

   "Declare:
        'Thus says my master YHWH: "Shall it prosper?
        Shall he not cut off its roots? its fruit, so
          that it withers?
        It dries, in all its sprouting leaves it dries, etc." '"
                      (Ezek. 17:1–9ff.)

   "Then from before Him was sent the palm of a hand, and this
writing was inscribed, and this is the writing that was inscribed:
          MENE MENE TEKEL UPHARSIN
   "This is the interpretation of the words; MENE, God has numbered
[*mena'*] your kingdom and brought it to an end; TEKEL, you have
been weighed [*teqiltah*] in the scales, and have been found wanting;
PERES, your kingdom has been divided up [*perisat*] and given to
Medea and Persia." (Dan. 5:24–28)

   What do these examples have in common? They are by no means all
akin in a form-critical sense. The first and last are of a type commonly
called the "wise courtier,"[73] more properly a story of a wise *outsider*,
whose intervention at court is understood as an exceptional event (for
the customary courtiers are typically perplexed where he is not). Yet
these episodes of a wise intercessor present a type of oblique discourse
(the dream; the writing of a heavenly hand) worth comparing to the
mashal proper. Jotham's fable likewise lacks the designation *mashal*, but it
presents a similarly oblique communication whose figural status resembles that of a *mashal*, and this fable has, in any case, often been termed a
"parable" by modern investigators. All of the examples, then, are similar
in presenting a message, specifically a warning, signaling the onset of a
major historical and political crisis. The message usually arises as an
interruption of the milieu's usual discourse, and as a surprise to its
habitual community of speakers, causing (or expecting to cause) consternation and perplexity among them. The recipient of the oblique communication is always a person or group whose fortunes are directly
affected by its message. And the warning is always, at least initially,
opaque and stylized—couched in dream language, poetic or oracular
utterance, or exotic apparition.
   Here we can again benefit from the distinction between allegory and
allegoresis. If the first and last examples resemble allegoresis more than
allegory, it is because of the presence of a demystifying interpreter, who
provides the "correct" interpretation in the name of a higher power. The
other examples are presented without an interpreter, as if their inter-

pretation were obvious to those privy to the parable's code, though not *yet* obvious to the immediate recipients. These uninterpreted parables—mystifying, but spoken from a vantage point that is demystified—momentarily bring the reader into the circle of perplexity depicted of the court milieu. The reader's (at least, the postbiblical reader's) perplexity is, in any case, short-lived, for this reader normally possesses a hindsight on the event foretold, such that the parable's meaning is usually apparent before the figure completes itself. Indeed, in the Sihon oracle, the events of the Israelite invasion of Heshbon and environs are presented in the framework of an *etiology*, culminating in the quotation of anonymous "parablers," whose words are *recalled* from the vantage point of a latter-day narrator and reader.[74] Since biblical prophecies of imminent events are sometimes spoken in a "prophetic perfect" (Gesenius-Kautzsch §106n), the oracle recalled, itself recalling, could be viewing future events, future even to the latter-day readers, such that its exact temporal applicability is left tantalizingly uncertain. This promiscuous confusion of time-frames, and partial concealment of tradent and secondary recipient, are devices rooted in principles of allegory we have considered earlier in this discussion. We see again that quotational structures, homonymy, alliteration, artfully naïve fabulation, and a general contagiousness of polysemy, all at play in varying degrees in the examples quoted, are essential ingredients of biblical allegory.

The confusion of time-frames likewise occurs in another usage of the word *mashal* in the Hebrew Bible: quite frequently, the word is employed for situations that, like the above examples, represent the fulfillment of a reciprocal justice, but seen from the perspective of its victim or of persons and nations looking on from without. Here, the word is best translated as "proverb": ". . . and you shall become a source of astonishment, a proverb, and a byword among the nations . . ." (Deut. 28:37); ". . . to be a reproach, a proverb, a taunt, and a curse . . ." (Jer. 24:9); "I will set My face against that man, I'll make him into a sign and a proverb . . ." (Ezek. 14:8); ". . . and I became a proverb of theirs" (Ps. 69:2); ". . . He has made me a proverb among the nations" (Job 17:6). In these examples, one's fate is a lesson, a text. We should savor here the matter-of-fact way that the fate of persons or nations could be taken as a *sign* in the discourse of future generations. The cultural linkage of generations is presupposed. Again, there is a curious mingling and convolution of time-frames, as if every deed or event, whether promised or remembered, has a simultaneous textual life—a fate in the retelling and in reading, to be sure, but one that is already read and retold in the utterance of its first declarer, already an item of tradition and lore.

In fact, we are dealing in all cases with a distinctive symphonics of narrative and non-narrative discourse that is common to biblical literature as a whole. For most of its continuous narrative (Genesis through II Kings), the Bible speaks in a manner ever midway between story and traditionary discourse. This dichotomy more or less exactly mirrors the sociocultural duality that inhabits the people whose story is told: as story, the text projects successive chapters of a national mythology for the precarious entity known as "Israel"; as traditionary discourse, it displays the centrifugal momentum and fragmentary character of tribal or regional utterance. As story, it appeals to the reader's sense of universality and comon history; as traditionary discourse, it bespeaks parochiality and dialectical conflict, subverting the artificial harmonies and fluencies of story, riddling it with quotation and digression, complicating the historical tableau with a multiplicity of voices and tradents. If modern source critics see themselves as demystifying the biblical text, that demystification was already anticipated in the text itself, and was not only dependent for its effect on the mystifying properties of story and myth, but itself resulted in new enigmas for one trying to make sense of the multidimensional whole. The reader's discovery that a scene is "only" this or "actually" that (but always something *else*) is only the beginning of a deeper, more far-reaching exploration of the story's meaning. With this often vertiginously dawning realization, the reader gains a wider sense of what vistas of meaning are possible, and thus of what interpretive faculties must be mobilized over time. A first corollary of this process is the obligation to *reread* the text, to reconsider what has already been digested in the light of the new parameters of interpretation.

This gradually self-compounding text presents story as the reality of a *polis*—a political community, whether city- or territorial state—and traditionary discourse as the prepolitical and postpolitical constant against which the world of the story, of the *polis*'s history, takes shape. Behind and beneath all history is a kind of chatter or gossip—we could call it traditionary gossip, for it is traded across generational lines—but one should not take the term "gossip" as implying a triviality of import or function. Gossip presupposes memory and renown, takes for granted a prior historical *impact* that has reverberated in the preoccupations and hushed whispers of the gossipers. Yet the idioms of gossip transcend time and history, serving as the foil of the story and its heroes. It is the hidden community of rehashers and evaluators ("washers" in the Joycean conceit quoted in the headnote of this chapter) that supplies biblical narrative with its unique textures. The *meshal 'ammim* (popular proverb) that registers the latter-day knowledge of former deeds functions, in a sense, in a kind of eternal present. Yet without it, we would not have history at all, for the historical record itself is constructed out of such mosaic tiles, out of the very same "documentary" shards with which the modern historian reconstructs the past.

Nathan's Parable: Two Men in One City

The brief story recounted by the prophet Nathan to King David in II Sam. 12:1ff. is a *mashal* in all but name only. Its fabular language is rhythmic and stylized, its figures sketched in the most minimal manner. The reader knows from the last half of the last verse of the preceding chapter (11:27: ". . . and the thing which David did [to Uriah the Hittite] was evil in the eyes of YHWH") that Nathan comes as YHWH's emissary, and in specific response to the crimes committed by David in the episodes that preceded. For the reader, though not for the unwary king, the *nimshal* is clear: the simple, bold strokes of the parable are an analogue for the situation of David and Bathsheba and her murdered husband, Uriah. The king, however, remains unaware not only of the parable's referent, but of the fact that it *is* a parable. For him, it could be a case to adjudicate—until its proper interpretation is read out to him:

> And YHWH sent Nathan to David, and he came and said to him: "Two men were in one city, one a rich man and the other poor. The rich man had a lot of sheep and cattle, but the poor man hadn't any, but for one small ewe which he had bought with hard-earned money, and he nurtured it so that it grew and lived together with him and his sons, and from his bread it ate, and from his cup it drank, and under his protection slept, and became like his daughter. And there came a wayfarer unto the rich man, but the latter was too sparing [*wayyahamol*] to take of his sheep and of his cattle, to prepare for the guest who had come to him, so he took the poor man's ewe and prepared it for the guest who had arrived."
>
> David's anger flamed against the rich man, and he said to Nathan: "By the life of YHWH, the man who did this truly deserves to die! He should repay the ewe's cost four times over for this thing he did, for he has acted without pity [*we'al 'asher lo' hamal*]!"
>
> And Nathan said to David: "You're the man. YHWH God of Israel has said thus: 'I have anointed you as king of Israel, and have saved from the hand of Saul, and given to you, into your very bosom, the house of your lords and women of your lords. I've given to you Israel and Judah, and if that were not enough, I'd add on for you this way and that. Why have you acted contemptuously against the word of YHWH, doing what is evil in His eyes? Uriah the Hittite you have struck by the sword: his wife you have taken for yourself, and him you have killed by the swords of the sons of Ammon. So now I say, the sword will never let up from your house, because you have despised Me, and have taken Uriah the Hittite's woman for your own!'
>
> "So says YHWH: 'Behold, I am bringing upon you evil from within your household. I will take your women before your eyes and give them to your neighbor [MT: neighbors] and he will lie with your wives in the glare of this sunlight—for you have acted in secret, but I shall enact this thing before all Israel and in broad daylight.'" (II Sam. 12:1–12)

As noted earlier, the biblical parable almost invariably arises in a political context, in that it is most frequently aimed at figures in the ruling circles of the nation, or at the nation as a whole. As also noted, the distinction between moral-psychological and political allegory breaks down before biblical examples. In Nathan's parable and its dramatic setting, no priority of one concern over the other can be deduced: the psychological disorientation and moral misbehavior of the king is made synonymous with a misuse of public power, but in another sense, the strength wielded by one man over the other, rooted in factors the parabler leaves unstated, already predisposes to abuse and immorality. The very courtly structure that permits a king to stay at home while generals and their hapless underlings engage in war has generated a climate of moral laxity and wanton irresponsibility that reaches even unto Israel's greatest soldier.

The crime itself, in a manner typical of biblical narrative, had been presented as an item of discourse. The account of its execution, which takes up the latter half of II Sam. 11, is given over almost completely to surveying the progress of a message from one social stratum to another: David's surreptitious order to eliminate Uriah in the thick of battle— conveyed back to camp by the hapless victim himself (11:14)—must travel several stages before it translates into action, and news of the order's completion must similarly pass by stages back to the king (25).[75] More than a narration of a private intrigue, this account surveys the total social structure of the nation that permitted such an action to take place. We learn of the implication of David's general Joab in the affair; we are left to speculate on his exact motives and the exact tenor of his participation. We learn of the cost in soldiers' lives required to expose Uriah to the Ammonite sword. We perceive something of an acerbic tone to Joab's instructions to the return messenger, noting his apparent preoccupation with the timing and sequence of his dispatched reportage. We witness the garbling of this timing and sequence by the anonymous messenger himself, and are left to speculate whether this is a stylistically motivated condensation of the narrator's or a meaningful lapse in understanding on the messenger's part. As J. P. Fokkelman has observed, the total configuration of the palace-to-battlefield-to-palace sequence is symmetrical.[76] It thus forms a complete cameo, whose import, one must say, is collective: it is the people Israel (including Uriah) who slay Uriah. It is the people Israel who slay the people Israel.

What is arresting about the conspiracy's aftermath in Nathan's parable is the manner by which the relation of a *mashal* to its *nimshal* is conveyed: the bridge is Nathan's well-aimed "You're the man." By this means are the moral-psychological and political domains of allegory merged. What had been thought of as exterior ("the man") is made interior ("you").

Only at that moment, conversely, do the details, contours, and logical force of the external representation (the parable of the ewe) fully come into their own, at least for the king.

We have no assurance that such a confrontation between king and prophet "really" happened: it could have been an actual court practice for a prophet to address his sovereign in the mode of parable; or it could as well have been projected *ex post facto* by a writer with a larger scope of pedagogical design in mind. If the latter, then the parable is aimed at least partly at the ordinary Israelite, and King David's misbehavior is at least partly that of the nation as a whole—or, at least, of those who failed to heed the warning from the prophet Samuel (I Sam. 8:10ff.) as to what the choice of monarchy would bring as consequences. Nathan's startling and satisfyingly resonant announcement ("You're the man": a classic moment of allegorical rhetoric—one may compare the *kakh*, "thus . . . ," of the rabbinic *mashal*) is ultimately capable of being turned against the reader, who has thus far been habituated to imagine villainy primarily in the third person, just as has the king himself. The sting of this parable gathers force precisely from the satisfaction we derive as readers at the springing of this trap upon a character in the story. Only as an after-thought (or perhaps not even until the impending civil war is recounted in II Sam. 15–19) does the multivalence of the prophet's stratagem occur to us. The "you're the man" of allegorical discourse is distressingly contagious, but it likewise can appear to quarantine and reassure ("Yes, *he's* the one, all right!"). It much depends on the type of reader facing this material.

Actually, this transfer mechanism (more correctly, a detransference mechanism) often may be absent from an allegory or a parable. In the example cited, we possess a much clearer model of the typical form of parabolic discourse than can be obtained from most examples. We have here a three-stage transaction: (1) presentation of a story or announce-ment to the king; (2) the king's emotional reaction to the story while he yet believes it to have happened to some other people; (3) application of the story to the king himself. This pattern, while not identical in form, bears useful comparison to that of the rabbinic *mashal* quoted earlier, which essentially sandwiches the story (stage 1, above) between two statements of its application (stage 3), leaving the recipient's reaction (stage 2) to the reader. In the Nathan episode, it is important that neither the king nor the reader has any clear signals initially as to the nature of Nathan's communication. As it happens, this device is tried out on the king no less than three times in four chapters (II Sam. 11:8ff., 12:1ff., and 14:ff.). The narrative seems preoccupied with the dynamics of oblique discourse necessary in a royal court. This pattern seems partly rooted in the office of sedentary king: the king as a symbol of consensus does not guide but ratifies; he is a channel or focus of information and policy, a court of appeal and guarantor of justice, but not himself (qua king, that is) an engaged political actor. This is true irrespective of any good or bad deed David the person commits, of the personal responsibility he bears for his action, and even of the *political* deeds that David, though he be king, may continue to perform. David, to be sure, remains a political actor to the end of his days, but where he serves the role of council king, and serves it well, he must place his own personal and political actions under public scrutiny, and abide by the "objective" justice he represents. For this reason, it is possible, as for the Tekoite woman in II Sam. 14, to maneuver the king into passing judgment on his own actions: "But why," she exclaims, "have you considered such a thing against a people of God?—for the king speaks this matter as one guilty of not returning his own estranged one home!" (14:13). This, of course, was the core of her mission, and the reason for the concocted story, placed into her mouth by Joab, of her son's exile by blood avengers. The story itself, like Nathan's, begins under disguise of a matter for adjudication, and is seen, in hindsight, to be a parable. The resemblance of parable to casuistic law is striking.

One should not construe the idea of a "triggering device" too literally, since the exact moment of recognition, whether for the king or for the reader, is anything but mechanically predictable. The last half of 12:6 (literally: ". . . *and* because he did not pity . . .") has the character of an interrupted sentence. Does David perhaps halt in the middle of a sentence because he already perceives the prophet's drift? It is as if by repeating the verb *ḥamol* (be sparing/have pity) in such a radically different sense from Nathan's, he is brought fact-to-face with the true character of events and is stopped in his tracks even before Nathan's "You're the man." The prophet's delicately sarcastic use of *wayyaḥamol* (was sparing) both contrasts sharply with David's fuming earnestness, and contributes, from its demystified standpoint, a conceptually precise insight about the nature of covetousness: that it is not merely greed for another man's lot but a doubting of the sufficiency of one's own. The rich man "was sparing" in the wrong direction: toward his own wealth. The first thing stated in Nathan's open declaration of YHWH's wrath (vv. 7ff.) is a catalogue of YHWH's long history of beneficences toward David, which, not coincidentally, is a remarkably accurate and dispassionate account of the usurpations and dispossessions that brought David to power. "And if that were insufficient," roars the prophet's deity, "I would add on this way and that [*kahennah wekhahennah*]! Why have you despised the word of YHWH. . . ?!" (8). Here, we find a much larger *nimshal* than even the crime against Uriah: David has acted contemptuously toward YHWH Himself, holding as trivial the stewardship of His people's destiny that had been given to him in trust. It is such contempt for the historical mission of his own kingship that led David to covet Uriah's wife in the first place, and it is contempt for his own people that he expresses when he rationalizes the deaths of Uriah and compatriots at the wall of Rabbat Ammon by saying: "Thus say to Joab: 'Let not this matter be evil in your eyes, for this way and that [*kazoh wekhazeh*] consumes the sword. Strengthen your war, etc.'" (11:25).

Within and Without the Garden

The David/Nathan episode is a key text for understanding the nature of allegorizing in the Bible, for it allows us to see one character allegorizing for another. It is thus a kind of allegory of allegory, for the whole transaction ultimately serves another oblique purpose, whose target is the reader. This is true howevermuch we might debate the "oral" or "written" character of the Bible. The semantic operations that we witness between one character and another are transacted again between the text and us. We have seen the way that key words, motivically orchestrated, bind the various frames of meaning to one another. We have seen the tendency of story to embed itself amid ever-widening circles of discourse. The *mashal* is a kind of Chinese box: the structures that surround it are not extraneous to it, howevermuch its paint or inscribed designs may differ. "It," therefore, is not the innermost box alone, but the totality of boxes. And just as we reach the innermost with a sense that only the imperfect technology of miniaturization stands in the way of further reductions, so are we left in doubt as to the outermost. If the traditional form of the Talmud page (text flanked by commentary flanked by reference apparatus flanked by readers) epitomizes this sense of elaborately interlocking scales, it has been conditioned for such by the text that forms its centertext's center: the Hebrew Bible itself.

The question "Is the Garden story myth or allegory?" is, then, not a question of genre or of referent but one of signification in the broadest sense. We are dealing here not simply with a text whose "story" wrought enchantment upon later generations, but with one whose *use* of story drew subsequent generations of readers into a cooperative and interpretive relation, to the text and to one another. We are dealing with a complex system of discourse of which the printed text itself is only a partial and visible register. To state, as Jacob and Cassuto have, that the serpent is an allegorical representative of the tendencies operating in the minds of the first human pair presupposes a species of human talk in which such representation is possible—and once such a mode is possible, it is difficult to contain. This does not mean, of course, that anything can be made to mean everything. We do well to take seriously Maimonides' cautions: there are parables in which every element is meaningful, and there are parables in which only some of the elements are meaningful. There is a time to interpret and a time to leave off interpreting. Wisdom in such matters is cumulative without being architectonic: the deepening of one's textual acquaintance does not lead to a dogmatic edifice (Maimonides' notion of "correct opinions" notwithstanding), but to new textual indirection. Correct opinion spawns further correct opinion; it does not spawn incorrect opinion. That, in a sense, is the test of its correctness. The contagion of meaning does not rest in the full picture's being deciphered, as in Augustine's parody of biblical allegoresis, where each element of the Garden—rivers, gemstones, trees, animals, and the like—is assigned an emblematic meaning. It rests in the text's preparing the reader to pursue its related texts, and to stand in a community of related interpreters.

I envisage in the ensuing chapters three explorations of biblical texts, one a story, one a story cycle, and one a history combining several cycles. None of these explorations will supply "commentary" in either the premodern or modern sense of the term. The episodic structure that a commentary must adopt serves in the end to render all of its exegetic conclusions merely episodic in their force. Any commentary, moreover, that is structured on a verse-by-verse format lends to the text a canonicity at odds with its contemporary impact (taking "contemporary" in the double sense suggested in the present essay: the text's first readers, and the text's "contemporaries" beyond the generation of its emergence). To recover such an impact requires a more synchronic orientation, at least to begin with. Precisely where we deal with allegorical dimensions of the text must we put forth a kind of questioning that cuts through the line of narrative and causes us to rearrange its elements in other ways that best explain the underlying principles of subject and narrative design.

A procedure of this nature is at odds with any mythologically oriented reading that might seek to place a barrier of mystified nostalgia between us and the material of the story, unless it is carefully explained what role that nostalgia plays in our reading process. Such a reading is in danger of appealing only to that part of us that would wish to share a fancied solidarity with a bygone world, while we temporarily abandon a more complicated world that is, alas, too much with us. Any reading that encourages a hypnotic fixation on the narrative trajectory does essentially *half* the job of allegory (or of criticism that reveals an allegorical process at work). This is true whether such a reading occupies itself with a mimetic or a mythic mode of narrative—both types of exegesis, mimetic and mythological, assume accounting of "what happened" as the critic's major task; both modes make the story's (and its author's) world something quite "other" than the reader or his world.

To read biblical narrative, on the contrary, in ways that will do justice to its more enduring subtlety requires that we see ourselves as its contemporaries in a painful, demanding sense of the term: namely, that we remain rooted in our own world and understand the story to be addressing itself to us where we stand. I do not wish to encourage here a "kerygmatic" conception of the biblical story: the text does not—at least, not through the inquiry we shall make—mobilize our existential engagement or the affirmation of a particular religious confession. Rather, it will draw us into its cognitive operations, by means of our awareness of our own. We must attempt to understand the concrete work the biblical story poses as its task; to see the story aimed in part toward a restricted readership (whatever other public functions this material may have served, or come to serve), a readership concerned with Israel's politics and history, and one ready to submit itself to a rigorous training in the art of reading.

It need no longer cause surprise among biblical scholars if one proposes a study in which source-critical considerations are set aside. It may cause surprise if one asks that they be both bracketed and kept in view. Even if it is not relevant any longer to say, for example, that Gen. 2–3 was written by the ninth-century "Yahwist" and Gen. 1 by the fifth-century "Priestly" writer, it *is* relevant to postulate great differences in subject matter, rhetorical structure, and literary style between the two accounts, and it *is* relevant to inquire about the structure and progression of the whole sequence of Gen. 1–3 (though that will not be attempted in the present study), and about whether the relation between the two (or more) texts is one of "general-and-particular." There is little need to posit any radically broad *temporal* gap between the alleged "Yahwist" and the alleged "Priestly" writer. The text may be representing a *social* gap, explainable in terms of the conflicts that rent Solomon's kingdom apart in the era after Solomon's reign (by "era" I mean the whole span between the schism of Jeroboam I and the Babylonian exile). Any more precise "dating" of source is unavailable to us until we determine precisely what the text is saying. I shall, as it turns out, suggest a relation between the three texts studied here that is not fully explained by the presently regnant source hypotheses. But the thrust of the argument advanced here is not toward any solution of source questions.

It is, indeed, significant that modern commentators (here excluding the defenders of a literary unity between Gen. 1 and Gen. 2–3) have sought to deflect the force of contrast in the material in question by attempts at a historical breakdown of sources, offering as arguments thereto the very reader's responses the text had carefully anticipated. The defenders of a literary unity have, for their part, likewise deflected any force of contrast by seeking a picture of the text as something seamless and organic, without contradictions or discrepancies that, indeed, as the source critics would argue, *are* a matter of provenance. The pertinent question is whether the *text* reflects an awareness of its multiple origins, and whether the very obvious stylistic and rhetorical differences are used as part of a larger statement—in which case, we have little choice but to regard the text itself, for all practical purposes, as the "author," quite without need of a term like "redactor."

On the other hand, there is every reason to avoid dispensing with the mythological "charm" of the narrative. We must travel its trajectory before we try to offer any exegesis. We must understand the tug on our attention exercised by myth and fancy, then politely disengage ourselves from it, and reconstruct the concrete, if textually absent, social setting to which the story "refers," and in the presence of which it dissembles.

·I·

THE GARDEN STORY
FORWARD AND BACKWARD:
THE NON-NARRATIVE DIMENSION
OF GEN. 2–3

> Turn it around and around,
> for everything is there.
> —Ben Bag-Bag, *Avot* 5:27
>
> Madam, I'm Adam.
> —Popular palindrome

No story seems more unidirectional than the Garden story (Gen. 2–3). Tracing, among other things, the origin of death, of procreation, of cultivation, of social discord, of human knowledge, of guilt, punishment, and suffering, it portrays these changes as something unprecedented and irreversible. If any tale could symbolize the flow of time, or, indeed, could epitomize that distinctly temporal art, the art of narrative, it would seem to be this one. Yet the very telescoping of the Garden story's manifold cultural concerns into so compact a form suggests a subtler and more complex discourse, less temporal and less narrative in character, for which the purported time-scheme of the story serves as a kind of armature. Perhaps the encapsulation of these "non-narrative" concerns into a simple fable, convenient for repetition and folk transmission, is itself a more remarkable labor than its reverse, the unfolding of the non-narrative discourse through exegesis and analysis, but it is possible to show that such discourse is already in the text, and not merely a construction of postbiblical commentary.

Premodern biblical exegesis more or less took for granted a non-narrative dimension, as the "fourfold" medieval systems of biblical interpretation would imply.[1] Exegetical lore of a rabbinic type, among others, by virtue of its preoccupation with wordplay, by its feel for parenthesis and quotation, has much to teach us about biblical narrative. Moreover, its patterns of accretion and transmission are often analogous to those of Scripture, and of similar antiquity.[2] The evolution of Israelite traditionary lore was a continuous and multilayered process, in which the isolation and declaration of a "Scripture" was only a comparatively late event,[3] and even at the earliest known stages of canonization, interlinear extratextual elaboration in public recitation may have been common,[4] suggesting that interpretation has, in a sense, always been a part of the text, as the Jewish notion of an archaic "Oral Torah" implies.[5] The boundary between Scripture and interpretation is fluid, and it is possible to show that Scripture itself may represent a commentary on a prior tradition or scripture, its traditionary elements arranged in a manner that suggests an exegetical rather than a narrative voice.

Modern exegesis of the Garden story, as of Scripture in general, focuses on reconstruction of its alleged sources, whether literary (the domain of "documentary" criticism)[6] or preliterary (the domain of form criticism and tradition history).[7] The union of sources, in the light of this criticism, would seem to represent a more or less accidental accretion of elements, cleverly woven, if not always consistently or unobtrusively so, into a continuously "temporal" pattern of narrative exposition. The segments of the story occupied with the creation of man from dust, the creation of woman from man's rib, the location of Paradise at the fount of "four rivers," the temptation and disobedience of the human couple, their judgment and punishment, the "Tree of Life," the "Tree of Knowledge," the expulsion from Paradise and installation of an angelic guard, all have been proposed as the nuclei of originally independent stories or traditionary complexes.[8] Each of these analyses has its advantages, but none satisfactorily accounts for the literary structure of the final product,[9] or for the non-narrative discourse that results from the synthesized text. This chapter attempts to supply a model of such a structure—one far more interesting conceptually than that afforded by a merely accidental accretion of elements, and one whose elements have been combined in a precisely crafted manner into a whole that expresses a complex and consequential thought.

The Nature of Authorship in Gen. 2–3

Insofar as source analysis of the Garden story has yielded conjectures about both preliterary and prior literary elements in the story, part of our task is to obtain a clearer picture of the nature of "authorship" in the Garden story. Biblical higher criticism has changed considerably since the days of Wellhausen in its concepts of biblical authorship. The notion of a biblical story as an invention *de novo* from the mind of a literary artist has come under increasing attack as more has been learned about the processes of oral transmission and traditionary evolution.[10] Certain schools of biblical form criticism have gone so far as to abolish "authorship" altogether as a meaningful category of explanation in biblical studies.[11] On the other hand, as scholarly interest becomes progressively diverted from "documentary" sources onto preliterary or prior literary units, or as attempts to clarify the viewpoints of the "Yahwist," "Elohist," "Deuteronomist" and "Priestly" source become progressively more arid and hair-splitting, we find that "authorship" in something resembling its familiar modern sense returns through the back door, as well it should wherever we are concerned with understanding the mediating intelligence (whatever its period of principal emergence) that gives shape and meaning to a biblical story or story cycle. Thus, the comparatively new discipline of "redactional" criticism[12] has come to concern itself with the very "authorly" tasks and processes that were once attributed to the four major "documentary" sources identified by Wellhausen.[13] In recent times, for example, Michael Fishbane has advanced a persuasive reading of the Jacob cycle as forming a chiastic or concentric pattern of motifs that centers on Gen. 30.[14] In establishing such a pattern, Fishbane

effectively demonstrates the existence of principles of redactional art
that are as subtle as those of composition at the level of "authorship"—
principles that indeed raise the question of whether such redactional art
should not, for all practical purposes, be understood as the main "authorship," and the preliterary and prior literary elements as matters of
the stories' respective prehistories.

Such an understanding demands that we comprehend a biblical story
as an integral part of a story cycle, and the internal movements of a story
as serving the thematic developments of the larger sequence of which it
forms a part. It is possible, nevertheless, to reverse this stipulation and to
posit the existence of a story that itself serves to define the movements of
a story cycle, or even of whole biblical books or collections of books. This
seems most likely the case for the opening chapters of Genesis (1–3),
which have long been understood to form a kind of overture to the
Primeval, Patriarchal, and Mosaic histories that constitute the remainder
of the Pentateuch.[15] I do not mean to suggest that the latter cycles and
books were necessarily written or compiled to conform to the lineaments
of a previously written Creation or Garden story—on the contrary, the
prefatory stories more likely presuppose the thematic interests of the
materials they introduce—but rather, that a sharper understanding of
the literary structure of Gen. 1 and 2–3, respectively (our concern here is
solely with the latter), might enable us to form better judgments about
the nature of the subsequent biblical material.[16] I stress here, as well, that
I intend no literary-historical hypotheses as such. For present purposes,
"received text," "composition," and "redaction" are all more or less
synonymous. I retain the last term primarily as a way of indicating that
the author of the story's finished structure was, after all, a traditionary
collector, limited by the obligation to preserve the character and unique-
ness (if not the actual verbatim formulation) of each inherited element
while simultaneously seeking an arrangement of elements that would
make a statement of its own. This is a type of "authorship" obviously
quite different from that in the modern sense of the term, although it
does resemble, in certain respects, the techniques of a documentary
movie.[17]

One way or another, the existing hypotheses outlined earlier regarding the preliterary and possible prior literary elements of the story are
not wholly irrelevant to our investigation. One can grant a provisional
reality to the divisions of elements made by modern commentators and
investigators (Westermann's, being the most atomistic and bibliographi-
cally the best annotated, are perhaps the most useful), for the sake of
determining which of such divisions might play a role in the story's
structure. Since it is here a matter of the relations between possible
traditionary elements or compounds thereof *within* a story, rather than
between stories, it might seem appropriate to call any resultant pattern

(for want of a better term) a "microredactional" structure, i.e., an arrangement of elements that are not large enough or detailed enough to form independent stories, but which, nevertheless, because they each express a complete and nontrivial thought, could have circulated independently at an oral or prior literary level.[18]

Some confusion is likely to arise, however, from the fact that modern commentators have apportioned their commentaries to units varying greatly in size, alleged literary type, and semantic weight. For purposes of structural analysis, great disparities in size between comparable elements should at least be accounted for, and a mixture of generic with semantic levels should, as much as possible, be avoided.[19] One should, accordingly, establish an appropriate priority of analytic stages, remaining careful, if possible, not to mix generic with semantic levels within each stage, unless it is to establish the congruence of the total structure under consideration with those established by preceding stages of analysis. It is perhaps better, then, to reserve the term "microredactional" structure for that comprising the broadest type of *formal* distinctions, and to progress from there to a more detailed "motivic" structure, comprising the story's specific units of *content*. In this manner, one avoids a mixture of generic with semantic levels within a given proposed structure, while still showing the interrelation of elements across several levels. Ideally, such a reading should pay equal respect to matters of generic and traditionary origin (as much as these are given to be known) and to matters of textual design and meaning in what is currently fashionable to call the "synchronic" sense.[20] In practice, most readings are provisional, tentative, and intuitional, and an adequate accounting of both generic-traditionary and literary-textual factors may well be impossible, though an attempt is surely worthwhile, and is my task here.

The Microredactional Structure of Gen. 2–3

Let us begin by noting that certain elements of the Garden story present themselves more immediately and explicitly to the reader's attention as non-narrative elements: pauses in the story's action for the sake of thematic enhancement or amplification. Namings and etiological statements are the most obvious of such pauses, although in some sense it is possible to say that *all* elements of the story have a non-narrative dimension, as we shall see more fully later on, and in any case, quite a number of alleged traditionary elements of the story have been adjudged "extraneous" or "supplementary" by commentators (cf. above). I shall try to restrict myself here to those elements that appear distinct *formally*, rather than merely by virtue of motivic content.

I shall provisionally distinguish three main types of departure from

narrative action. The first is best represented by the parenthetic description in 2:10–14 of the "four rivers" that emerge from the Garden to
water the four major regions of the world. This idiosyncratic item of
geographical lore can be regarded as a more or less autonomous motif
within the story, in the sense that no other aspects of the story (other
than the overall implicit equation of the Garden with a cosmological
"center")[21] are hinged upon its information, and we may, for present
purposes at least (without discounting the importance of the cosmological theme to the story's meaning), regard 2:10–14 as part of the main
stock of narrative, and its role in the unfolding of the story's microredactional structure as subordinate to that of the narrative segment in which
it occurs.[22] (One should, as well, regard the etiologically weighted divine
pronouncements in 3:14–19a as a departure of this type: important to
the unfolding of the story's symbolism from the standpoint of motivic
content, but structurally subordinate to the narrative segment in which it
occurs, although later it will be necessary to specify the function of this
departure more explicitly.)

The second and third types of digression, on the other hand, namings
(2:23, 3:20) and explicit (not implicit) etiological statements (2:24, 3:19b)
are significant structuring elements, first, by virtue of their occurrence as
doublets, and second, because of their placement.[23] The ancestor of
humanity is portrayed naming his female companion twice, first *'ishshah*
("woman"), secondly *ḥawwah* ("Eve," or possibly "Life-giver"), with the
story's main action intervening between the two namings. The etiological
statements likewise occur twice, once just after the first naming, once just
before the second.[24]

The resultant microredactional picture of Gen. 2–3 (implicit etiologies
are spelled out as such) is as follows:

> Narrative (2:4–22): Creation of man, garden, beasts, woman (2:5 and
> 18–22 are laden with implicit etiologies: origin of rain and tilling;
> origin of animal names, of woman from man's rib, of human so-
> ciety).
>
> Naming (2:23): Man calls his companion "woman" (*'ishshah*) and him-
> self "man" (*'ish*).
>
> Etiology (2:24): "Therefore does a man leave his father and his mother,
> and cling together with his woman, and the two of them become one
> flesh."
>
> Narrative (2:25–3:19a): The temptation, transgression, and punish-
> ment (14–19a laden with implicit etiologies: origin of snake's pos-
> ture, of enmity between snake and man; of woman's pain in child-
> bearing, of her passion for and dependence on her male companion;
> of hard labor, tilling, breadmaking and, above all, of death and
> burial).

Etiology (3:19b): "For dust thou art, and to dust thou shalt return."

Naming (3:20): Man (*'adham*) calls his companion "Eve" (*ḥawwah*).

Narrative (3:21–24): God clothes human pair, expels them from garden (3:21 is an implicit etiology: origin of hide-clothes—cf. 3:7b: origin of plant fiber clothes). Birth of a child (4:1) completes one generation.

This scheme the reader will readily recognize to be palistrophic:[25]

> Narrative
> Naming
> Etiology
> Narrative
> Etiology
> Naming
> Narrative

The story's broadest formal subdivisions thus manifest a quite orderly symmetrical arrangement. Moreover, in its palistrophic formation, the resultant structure bears strong resemblance to the redactional arrangement Fishbane showed operating between stories in the Jacob cycle, thus further justifying our characterization of it as microredactional. We should be aware, as well, that this analysis does not interfere with any of the hypotheses proposed regarding prior literary and/or additional preliterary sources: the segments here designated "narrative" could still reflect composite segments of narrative or traditionary units, such as those suggested at the beginning of this essay. The division of elements I have proposed, however, makes clearer that at least some of the inherited elements of the story are intended to exhibit parallel relationships—something we would not see as clearly if we treated all of these elements as equivalent in weight or function. The author's task seems not merely to have been to weave a connected narrative from available traditions, but to combine traditions into a conceptual framework.

Comparison of the Narrative Segments

Before we examine the parallel relationships of the conspicuously non-narrative material, some remarks are in order regarding the interrelationship and progression of narrative segments. As noted above, it is possible that independent traditionary pericopae underlie these segments. But their fusion into a continuous story is not only smooth and (almost) seamless, but appears, as well, to explore consistently a single problem: the relation of man, woman, and beast. Each narrative segment advances a particular permutation of that relation (what follows is not intended to serve as a detailed critical analysis of the narrative, but merely to highlight the changes in the relation of the three principals of the story):

(1) In 2:18–23, man is shown asserting his independence from and mastery over the animal kingdom by his preference for one of his own kind as sexual and social companion. The motif "man's preference of woman over beasts" is a key theme of at least one major ancient Near Eastern parallel to the Garden story, the epic *Gilgamesh*, where Enkidu's sexual initiation by a prostitute is followed by the shamed revulsion of the members of the animal kingdom, who had hitherto been his beloved consorts.[26] This event portrays the first step in the humanization, socialization, and urbanization of the wild Enkidu. Preference for the social and sexual companionship of one's own species is here the symbol of species awareness—a prerequisite to the development of culture and the mastery of nature.

(2) Understanding Gen. 2 this way helps clarify the serpent's role in Gen. 3. We can see him as the instrument of a revenge by the animal kingdom against its defecting kin, man, as, in a roundabout way, the water serpent in *Gilgamesh* effectively avenges the theft of the animal kingdom's former guardian and companion Enkidu by robbing Gilgamesh of his hard-won plant of eternal life.[27] 3:1 explicitly identifies the serpent as a "beast of the field which the LORD God had made," thus tying him thematically to the events of chapter 2. Whether he is a representative of the animal kingdom per se, or whether he is to be seen as an embodiment of the animal principle *in man* is a matter of debate,[28] but either way he helps articulate a problematic in the unfolding identity of humanity: the extent to which man, kindred both to immortal divinity and to perishable animal life, can assert his independence from and rulership over the rest of the natural world. The story's preoccupation with this problem is further underscored in the palistrophic cameo of 3:11–19, by which the respective guilt and punishments of God's creatures for their rebellions are assigned (judicial inquiry proceeds from man to beast; God's curses, in the reverse direction),[29] and man is made aware for the first time of his own perishable nature and so (at least with respect to mortality) his animal identity. At the same time, the respective buck-passings of the participants (the serpent's implicit in his "dumb brute" silence, which contradicts his eloquence in 3:1–5) form, together with the divine curses that cancel their pretensions, a symbolic tableau of a new, postlapsarian order: beast subordinated to humankind, woman to man, man to the ground from which he sprang.

(3) In the third narrative segment (3:21–24), the human pair is de-

scribed as receiving "skin clothes" from God, a detail that, if interpreted as meaning "clothes made of skin,"[30] suggests a new, deadly stance of opposition between man and beast, as promised in 3:15. Simultaneously, the introduction of mythologically weighted material in verses 22–24 (divine jealousy, intimation of a celestial hierarchy, installation of cherubim and a "revolving flaming sword," second and final mention of a "Tree of Life") suggests that God's earthly creatures must now take their places within a wider hierarchy of which they occupy the bottom rungs.

The above will suffice to show that each narrative segment, despite its probably separate (and even internally composite) traditionary origin, advances a single consistent theme: the development of human identity against the backdrop of nonhuman factors: earth, vegetation, animal life, the celestial and divine world. Man is first shown rejecting the kinship and companionship of the animal world, and thus denying his own earthly nature; he is then shown tempted by an animal to strive beyond his human status toward divinity, thereupon finding himself censured and punished by God, though apparently also given (3:16) the capacity to subdue woman (or fellow human being) and (3:15) to destroy animals; he is last shown with his destructive power over animals an apparent *fait accompli,* and his own mortality sealed. He is also shown in a newly hostile relationship to earth (3:17), now required to perform the harder labor of tilling, milling, and baking instead of the token labor of pruning a bounteous orchard; now dependent on capricious seasonal rainfall instead of on the uninterrupted flow of underground springs (cf. 2:5b, 6).[31] In this progression of events, we witness, of course, the gradual coalescence of the world as we know it.

Understanding the progression of the story's narrative segments alone, however, leaves unanswered the more fundamental question of the rhetorical purpose underlying this progression: what is to be gained by portraying familiar life in relation to a favored garden or "paradise"? The answer, I shall argue, lies in the shaping or structuring effected by the conspicuously non-narrative materials that supply the story with a symmetrical design, namely, Gen. 2:23–24 and 3:19b–20. The parallel relationship that they form enables us to understand the story's scope and meaning, its topic and argument.

Comparison of the Etiological Statements

Considered together, the two etiological summaries (2:24 and 3:19b) dovetail in interesting ways. One stresses "leaving," the other "returning." The first can best be understood in the context of the "rejection of beasts" theme I discussed earlier: the first human being, in rejecting the companionship of beasts—his siblings, as it were, co-born of the soil (2:19)—accomplishes an exodus repeated typically in every human lifetime, namely, the leaving behind of one's original household to create a new household with a conjugal partner. The second etiological summary is best understood in relation to the first: at some point in his lifetime, the human being is made to understand that he must return to the place whence he was taken, the earth. As such, he is, to some extent, held in thrall to his original household. We perceive here two parallel moments in the human life-cycle.[32]

It is important to note that both etiological summaries represent breaks in the story's temporal framework. Strictly speaking, 2:24, in its present form as a subordinate clause introduced by *'al-ken* (Therefore . . .), requires the information of verses 18–23, or something comparable, to make sense; yet in the context of the story, it seems to depart from the events narrated to refer to a custom presumably prevailing in the narrator's "present" time—matrilocal marriage. Quite apart from the content of the etiological ascription, this temporal break is significant, in its suggestion of a narrative voice ensconced in a later epoch from that of the story's events and intrusive into the action where an "editorializing" function is called for. Such an impression should not rule out the possibility that the juxtaposition of 18–23 with 24 (or, perhaps more plausibly: 23 + 18 → 22 + 24, in that order of accretion) is a traditionary sedimentation that was already completed at the preliterary level. One way or the other, we do well to keep in mind that verse 24 is both distinct from what precedes it and a commentary on it. It is not a merely incidental "aside" that enriches the story with ethnographic coloring.

Similarly, we must recognize 3:19b ("For dust thou art, . . .") as both traditiohistorically distinct from the main body of narrative,[33] and bound up with it as commentary. Minus the word *ki*, 19b very likely had a preliterary career as independent as its postbiblical one. Its appearance in the Garden story serves to invest the repeated motif of "dust" (2:7, 19, 3:14; cf. 19aβ) with a wider philosophical significance by identifying it with a well-known proverbial truism. This perhaps vertiginous leap from divine pronouncement to aphoristic homily is in character with the other major leap in narrative voice or perspective established previously in the story (2:23–24). Its conceptual progression is something like the following: "'. . . until you return to the earth, for from there you were taken,' for [as we say unto this day]: 'Dust thou art, and to dust thou shalt return.'"

We can see, then, that both etiological ascriptions occupy roughly the same function in the narrative: both shift the narrative perspective to a later "present" time, and both generalize the narrative by appeal to widespread human custom or proverbial insight. I again must stress what I stated initially, something the commentaries of my acquaintance have generally ignored: the passages' parallel relationship. Both statements stand for comparable moments in the human life cycle: the point at which one's natural origins are set aside or forgotten (the moment of betrothal or marriage, the moment of leaving one's parents' house and establishing a conjugal household) and the point at which they are recalled (the moment when one becomes concretely aware of the fact of death; a moment not synonymous with the moment of death itself, but rather with the *awareness* of one's perishability that normally accompanies the onset of middle age).

It serves for the present simply to note the distinct relationship of the two ascriptions as two parallel moments of the human life-span (the cessation of adolescence; the onset of senescence), and the fact that they enclose the central narrative segment, the story of the temptation, transgression, and punishment of the first human pair. It follows from this that the narrative core is best construed as something transpiring neither in adolescence nor in senescence, but at maturity's apex, the era perhaps most occupied with sexual and social relations, the era of full and vigorous adulthood, the human being's most "political" era. It is in the light of this pattern that we must understand those elements of the story which, in their turn, bracket the central elements, i.e., the namings, to which we must now turn our attention.

Comparison of the Namings

We must now ask whether and how the parallel namings support thematically the "life-cycle" pattern established, as outlined above, by the parallel etiological statements. I prefer not to discuss in isolation from the story the meanings of the names given by the first man to his partner, *'ishshah* (woman) and *ḥawwah* (Eve), but rather to concentrate on the manner in which these namings, and the narrative events they enclose, affect the terminology for man himself—for it will be seen that the first naming, at least, entails something of a de facto change in the term for "man." I noted briefly in the preceding section that the narrative events leading up to the naming in 2:23 (verses 18–22) seem to be traditiohistorically posterior to the naming itself. The latter, by reason of its thrice-stated verbal leitmotif *zo't* (this one) and its archaic grammar,[34] seems to suggest an ancient, independently circulating, poetic gnomon.[35] The narrative material seems to have been chosen specifically to illustrate the reason for the

similarity of names for man and woman (*'ish/'ishshah*). This montage could
have been, as suggested earlier, a natural traditionary accretion of a
preliterary nature, or it could indicate a distinctly literary manipulation, of
a type common in midrash collections of later eras: a narrative situation is
constructed to culminate in the quotation of a proverbial truism familiar
to all readers or listeners, which may, nevertheless, become revalued in
meaning by being placed into a narrative context.[36]

The species of wit involved in this particular example is clearer in the
Hebrew, where paired names for male and female members of the same
species, e.g., *par/parah* (cattle), *kelev/kalbah* (dogs) or *sus/susah* (horses),
are more common than in English, though it is somewhat obscured by
the omission of specific names from the story. Nevertheless, the implication is clear enough: in 18–20, man is described as trying to find a female
partner in the animal kingdom similar enough to him in physical appearance and behavior to merit being called by a name similar to his. It is
this situation that has led at least one commentator to shun the commonly proposed emendation of *ule'adam* in 20b to *wela'adam* (and for the
man),[37] and to translate, according to the Masoretic vocalization, "and
for 'Human,' he [sc. the man] did not find a partner corresponding to
him."[38] This accentuation of the verbal nature of the problem established by 2:18–20 renders the resolution in 2:23 all the more satisfying
and delightful: the man surprises the reader by changing his own designation from *'adam* ("human," i.e., according to the implicit folk etymology of 2:7, "humus-born") to *'ish* ("man" as partner to "woman," *'ishshah*).

The narrator, in other words, begins with two facts that are purely
linguistic, and from them weaves a narrative segment conforming to the
larger themes and issues in the Garden story. These linguistic facts are
the following: (1) that there are two chief names for "man" in Hebrew;
(2) that only one of them can be used as a companion term to "woman."
To this set we might add a third linguistic fact established by the folk
etymology of 2:7: (3) that the rejected term strongly resembles the word
for "earth." Thus, in choosing the newfound feminine companion as his
mate, the man must pick a twinlike name that expresses his affinity for
and kinship with the woman, and renounce the name that signified his
kinship with, and possibly his affinity for, his place of origin, the earth.
This procedure of "betrothal" is, as we noted earlier, summarized by the
etiological statement of 2:24. As with the etiology, the renaming makes
the most sense when placed into the context of the human life-cycle: the
age of courtship and marriage is the time when the human being seems
most alive, most mobile, most independent from parental bonds, most
inclined to seek out partners and associates (not just spouses) from

among his own generation, and perhaps also (assuming that sexual equality might have been as much an issue for our ancient author as for us today, as 3:16 suggests) the most equivalent in stature to a sexual counterpart. It is, in other words, the time of a human being's greatest independence from the earth, which otherwise (3:17–19) collects the remains of all completed lives and imposes economic hardships that necessitate the division of labor and the establishment (3:16) of social caste lines and sexual inequalities. Free of such pressures, the time of betrothal is, in short, a time of "paradise."

Turning to consider the relative distribution in the story of the words *'adam* and *'ish*,[39] we find a pattern supportive of the thematic progression I have outlined thus far. We must note, first of all, that the narrator, with one notable exception, never uses the term *'ish* to refer to the particular man who is the story's protagonist; *'adam* remains the preferred term for "man" (i.e., as *ha'adam*, *"the* man") throughout. There are, in all (counting the exception just mentioned), only four uses of the term *'ish* in the entire story: (1) the naming in 2:23, (2) the etiology in 2:24, (3) the story's central event in 3:6: ". . . and she gave [the fruit] also to her man with her [*gam le'ishah 'immah*], and he ate," (4) God's curse of the woman in 3:16: ". . . and toward your man [*we'el 'ishekh*] shall be your longing, and he shall govern you." Of these only the third can be regarded as a mention by the narrator of the protagonist; the others all represent proverbial or archetypic ascriptions with applications beyond the individual character, and are either spoken by the characters or are quotations from the "tradition," or both. All represent "man" only in relation to "woman." All fall either in the central narrative segment or in the non-narrative materials introducing it, strengthening the impression that *'ish* is an interlude in the life-history of *'adam,* and that the central narrative segment is somehow testing the conception of human nature introduced in 2:23–24—namely, that man is closer to his adopted relations than to his place of origin, or (phrasing the matter in the context of the human life-cycle), that the marital bond is stronger than the filial, the conjugal household stronger than the parental.

The test yields a negative answer. The bond between *'ish* and *'ishshah,* like the conspiratorial or competitive relation between *'ish* and *'ish* in subsequent biblical stories, proves volatile and fragile. The human pair's association becomes progressively discredited. Again, it is a verbal subtlety that drives home the point. The clause "to her man with her" (3:6) could have made equally good sense in omitting the prepositional qualifier *'immah* (with her). The word, moreover, introduces to the plot an ambiguity whose solution presumably is crucial to our understanding of the action: *where* was the man during the woman's dialogue with the serpent, and can he be said to have undergone the temptation "with her"? As if to harp on this unexplained detail, the man's words in 3:12 prove equally disturbing. Faced with God's anger over the transgression, he states, confusedly, "the woman whom you gave [to be] with me [*'immadi*] she gave to me from the tree and I ate." The preposition *li* (to me) presumably would have made more sense than *'immadi* (with me), but here the man, precisely at the moment he hopes to disclaim responsibility for his actions, is unable to erase the intimacy of his association with the woman.

By this time, the reader is perhaps conditioned to anticipate the verbal dyad *'ish(shah)/'im* ([wo]man/with) where the two characters are mentioned together, but in 3:16, we are presented with a surprising resolution to the progression: God says, ". . . and toward your man shall be your longing." The word "with" is pointedly withdrawn where it might have been appropriate, whereas previously it had been present where it was inappropriate. Henceforth, man and woman are to occupy separate domains of daily life and separate frames of discourse. Henceforth, the relation of the sexes will be a matter of contact across barriers. It is the dawning reality of death that makes it so. The change in man's relation to woman coincides with the change in his understanding of his own existence: woman must cease to be close cohort and companion and must now become primarily a bearer of children, because the human being's earthly lot is now seen to be limited in time. The mutual personal fulfillment afforded by an indefinite extension of man's and woman's "twinlike" association must now be subordinated to considerations affecting survival of the human species, and the man's and woman's equivalence of social function must now yield to a division of labor appropriate to their newly stressed biological differences and fostering their mutual isolation. Neither partner has cause to rejoice.

It is a moot point whether, prior to mankind's fall, the biological differences between man and woman existed, as numerous commentators have debated;[40] the story traces not the origin of the differences per se, but that of the *awareness* of differences—which, once we again translate the story into the context of the human life-cycle, is shown to be most pronounced not at the time of pubescence but at the time of childbearing. (At pubescence, to be sure, the sexual equipment of man and woman begins to function, but the structure of social and economic organization that supports the production of children in the conjugal family is yet dormant.) The fact that it is a mental rather than a physical transition that forms the subject of the Garden story raises certain questions about the story's mode of allegorical signification, which I shall deal with in the last sections of this chapter.

It is in the light of the above considerations, at any rate, that we must understand the otherwise senseless nonsequitur of 3:20: "And the human being called his wife's name 'Eve' [*Ḥawwah*], for she was mother of all living." The name "Ḥawwah," which resembles the *pa''āl* noun-pattern denoting the practitioner of a craft, skill, or habit, may be translated as "Life-bearer."[41] It is significant that this naming occurs precisely at the moment that the man has been made aware (3:19) of his own mortality. Recorded here with considerable irony is the male spouse's sense, perhaps universal to the whole animal kingdom, that the production of offspring is the beginning of the end of his own flourishing vitality. The woman is "life-bearer" to the future generations, but she is "life-taker" to her mate. Indeed, insofar as his exertions of physical strength become redirected to the welfare of his wife and children (as well as livestock), the man is literally sacrificing his own vitality (quite apart from whatever mystical significance was invested by ancient society in the transmission of seed). It is for these reasons, and not because of any innate "perversity" of woman, that Eve is blamed for the "fall." That the name "Ḥawwah" also resembles the terms for "beast of the field" (*ḥayyat hassadeh*), "animal" (*nefesh ḥayyah*), and, marginally, "serpent" (Aramaic *ḥiwya'*)[42] lends additional depth and wit to the story: the man's second naming expresses his profound sense of isolation not just from his conjugal partner but from the whole of animal life, which is now seen to have a dimension that is temporal—the man is initiated involuntarily into a new body politic with which he must cooperate to sustain life on earth, which includes the lives of those yet unborn.

The foregoing discussion is, I hope, sufficient to make clear the foundation of the Garden story in the human life-cycle, and its very precise use of the conspicuously non-narrative elements: namings and etiologies. I must now offer some concluding interpretive remarks, followed by some observations on the type of literary art represented by the Garden story.

The Motivic Structure

Earlier in this chapter, I outlined what I called the "microredactional" structure of the story. There, we saw how drawing a provisional distinction between narrative and conspicuously non-narrative elements yielded a symmetrical design. Subsequent discussion sought to show how the parallel relations thus established between like elements were clear and logical. Thus far, I have made no attempt to differentiate elements or motifs *within* the narrative segments, although I offered a brief summary of the manner in which the narrative segments represented evolving permutations of the triad man/woman/beast. I now wish to translate the microredactional structure into a more detailed motivic structure, which would look something like fig. 1.

FIG. 1

a   Headnote: "These are the generations . . ." (2:4)
  b   No field economy: ". . . no man to till the soil" (2:5–6)
    c   Man given life, installed in Garden (2:7–17)
      d   Man prefers woman over beasts (2:18ff.)
        e   Names (*'ish/'ishshah*) express equality (2:23)
          f   Etiological summary: "Therefore, etc." (2:24)
            g   Human couple "naked and unashamed" (2:25)
              h   Serpent promises "eyes will be opened" (3:1–5)
                i   Transgression (3:6)
              h'   The couple's "eyes are opened" (3:7a)
            g'   They experience shame (3:7b–10)

Postmortem on the event—a sub-palistrophe:

    x   God questions man; man points to woman (3:11–12)
      y   God questions woman; she points to serpent (3:13)
        z   [Serpent is silent]
        z'   God passes judgment on serpent (3:14–15)
      y'   God passes judgment on woman (3:16)
    x'   God passes judgment on man (3:17–19a)

---

          f'   Etiological summary: "For dust thou art . . ." (3:19b)
        e'   Names (*'adam/ḥawwah*) express inequality (3:20)
      d'   Man and woman wear skins of beasts (3:21)
    c'   Man expelled from Garden, denied immortal life (3:22–24)
  b'   Field economy begins (implied; cf. sub-palistrophe and 23b)
a'   Birth of a child completes one generation (4:1)

Two irregularities in this pattern should be noted. First, it is not a simple palistrophic pattern but a compound one: while the "postmortem" sequence is critically important to the unfolding of the main structure, it does not participate in it. Second, the completion of the parallel b/b' is only implied, although the nearest equivalent of b' (2:23b: ". . . to work the ground from which he was taken . . .") stands in close proximity to it, imbedded in c', and the sub-palistrophe itself is closely related to it in theme.[43] Here, the merging of different traditionary complexes may be in evidence. Strictly speaking, God's "judgment" of the couple is already contained in 3:22–24, verse 22 forming a continuity with verse

10. The more expanded "judgment" sequence (the sub-palistrophe) provides a more adequate transition to the second etiological summary ("For dust thou art . . . ," 19b), where, in the context of the life-cycle, it is *knowledge* of impending toil and death, not the woes themselves, that is at issue.[44] All material from c to c', exclusive of the sub-palistrophe, fits within a complex of traditionary themes we might call "the Garden of Immortality." The sub-palistrophe and b/[b'] form a complex of traditionary themes we may then call "the plights and responsibilities of post-Garden life."

The two bodies of traditionary themes establish a contrast between "Garden" and "Field" fundamental to the story.[45] The former deals with the human individual in his precultural innocence, the latter with the hard facts and necessities burdening human culture. Only in the layer labeled d/d'—man's rejection/exploitation of the beasts, i.e., his choice of human partner and, later, the couple's wearing of animal skins for clothes—does the theme of "culture" invade the "Garden" material, and, in so doing, it establishes the ground for the story's central action: man's victimization by beast, as in *Gilgamesh.*

If we thus abandon our habit of reading the Garden story as a connected narrative describing a "historical" event unfolding in a unilinear time, and view it instead as an artful symmetrical arrangement of traditionary motifs revealing certain logical or causal relations, we gain a better picture of the type of insight the story embodies. This becomes clearer if we examine (a/a'), the outer perimeter of the story. Gen. 2:4 begins the story under the rubric (frequently assigned to a "later" author than that of the Garden story): "These are the generations of heaven and earth. . . ."[46] But the first human couple is not said to conceive a child until 4:1: "And the human being 'knew' Eve his wife, and she conceived and bore Cain." One might well construe the entire Garden story as a midrashic elaboration upon the sequence formed by the two verses 2:4 and 4:1, thus tracing the origin of the world's first "generation," and as such preoccupied with the pattern of human perceptions attendant upon the task of procreating.[47]

In this light, the story's ground-plan of the human life-cycle becomes clear. That no explicit act of sexual relations is mentioned (though "desire" is mentioned in 3:16) is inconsequential to the story's unfolding. It is the noetic structure of the human life-span that is shown here, i.e., the changing configuration of personal space and interpersonal relations through a lifetime. Commentators who have seen in the couple's partaking of "the fruit of the Tree of Knowledge" a sexual awakening are perhaps right for the wrong reasons.[48] They are reasoning backwards from the very symbolic resonances the story itself helped to create. There is nothing intrinsically "sexual" about the events recounted, unless the evasive or suggestive power of metaphor ("phallic" serpent; "womb-like" fruit; "oral" gratification; "parental" prohibition, etc.) is taken as hinting of sexual activity. But the changes in mutual perception and interaction that accompany the event do suggest the evolution of a conjugal bond, including the disillusionments that, alas, all too often assail such bonds. If anything, we have a story of a *post*-sexual awakening: the dawning of biological and cultural imperatives affecting the illusory autonomy of the conjugal family even as it breaks free from the sway of the patriarchal family.

The Meaning of the "Two Trees"

It is useful at this point to examine a motif about which, because of its importance, I have postponed discussion thus far: namely, the "two trees" (Tree of Life; Tree of the Knowledge of Good and Evil) that are central to the story's action and thematic development—and here we may find some "diachronic" considerations useful to this discussion.[49] It is clear that the "two trees" fit most appropriately within the "Garden" traditionary complex, and that they are tied integrally to the disobedience and transgression that are acted out in the story's core (h–h'). It is by no means agreed by commentators, however, that the respective *proper* names of the trees ("Tree of Life," 2:9b; 3:22b, 24b; "Tree of the Knowledge of Good and Evil," 2:9b, 17a; cf. 3:5b, 22a) are part of the original traditionary core of the story, which in its main contours seems to speak mainly of a "forbidden" tree (so the sense of 3:3b, 11b, 17aβ) or of a "tree which is in the midst of the garden" (3:3a). The proper names occur only in the comparatively outer layer c/c', a matter that bears out the traditiohistorical picture advanced by Westermann: that the "Tree of Life" motif was a secondary accretion, and "Tree of the Knowledge of Good and Evil" a tertiary accretion that evolved by analogy (out of 3:5b and 22a) to the proper name "Tree of Life."

Westermann's proposal, however, is deficient in one respect: it over-looks the antiquity and persistence of the mythological dichotomy "Knowledge vs. Life" that forms the subject of the Garden story's nearest analogues, especially the myths of *Gilgamesh* and *Adapa*.[50] The fragmentary *Adapa* describes a kind of "Catch-22" situation, in which the hero Adapa (name cognate to "Adam"?) must refuse a food allegedly conferring immortality, which he knows is poison to mortals.[51] An epigram (or epitaph) in the opening lines of Tablet A sums up the situation in its most fundamental contours: *'ana šu'atu nēmeqa 'iddinšu, napištam dā'irtam 'ul 'iddinšu* (To him [the god Ea] gave wisdom, [but] eternal life he did not give him).[52] Indeed, Adapa's survival in the short run depends on his knowledge of his death in the long run, i.e., on his knowing the ineluctable difference between mortals and immortals. In *Gilgamesh*, similarly, the hero's "acculturation" (prefigured in his companion Enkidu's loss of innocence) rests in his change of aspiration from the immortality of deeds that confer lasting fame to the qualified immortality of deeds that benefit a community. Only the certain knowledge of his own mortality can bring about such a change.[53]

Westermann's notion of a secondary addition of a "Tree of Life," and a tertiary renaming of the "forbidden" tree to a "Tree of the Knowledge etc." is plausible enough from a traditiohistorical standpoint, but it is important to stress that from a compositional standpoint the modifications were most likely conceived as a unity—i.e., that a typological dyad "Tree of Knowledge"/"Tree of Life," or, more simply, "Knowledge"/ "Life," was superimposed upon the primitive narrative stock that originally comprised only the motifs "garden"/"forbidden tree"/"disobedience." Indeed, the Garden story's nearest intrabiblical analogue, Ezekiel's oracular lamentation over the King of Tyre, who is said to have dwelt "in Eden, the garden of God" (Ezek. 28:12ff.), merely concerns itself with "garden" and "disobedience" motifs, omitting the "forbidden tree" theme altogether, thus further isolating for us its metaphorical elaborations "Tree of Knowledge"/"Tree of Life."

Why, then, the addition of a "Knowledge"/"Life" dichotomy? The answer remains obscured as long as we cling to the story's mythological causality: that because man sought knowledge, he was denied immortal life, or, in other words (reading with the kind of antitechnological bias characteristic of religious fundamentalism), that man's quest for knowledge begot death. If we adopt the reading I have proposed in the present study, namely, that the Garden story is modeled on the human life-cycle, the reverse causality is more plausible: that death begot knowledge, or, more precisely, that the dawning awareness, in any one generation, of human perishability characteristically gives rise to efforts to transmit knowledge to a successor generation, and to develop institutional structures designed to facilitate that transmission. The Garden story, seen in this light, accomplishes a remarkable triple function: (1) to make clear the genesis of the motivation in the *individual* to cooperate with his successor generations; (2) to account for the *cultural* origins of generational continuity, which, in tandem with the evolution of such cooperative ventures as language, education, politics, technology, and law, represents a major leap forward in human evolution; and (3) to justify the particular *religious* preoccupation of Israelite society with the formation of a *tradition*, seen as a chain of "generations" acting in cooperation to ensure the transmission of the values, laws and insights (believed to be God-given) that enable life to survive on earth.

This reading helps us to understand better the larger redactional design of Genesis, and, indeed, of the whole narrative corpus of Genesis–Kings—which remains relentlessly, at times slavishly, "chronological," even where discrepancies of narrative consistency result, and even where the analogical force binding some of the narrative sequences is sacrificed. The principal thematic issues in biblical narrative are those that touch upon generational continuity, a delicate condition requiring both harmony between parents and children and harmony between siblings, but which is seriously menaced in every generation. This problem is clear enough in Genesis, where family relations occupy center stage; it is possible to demonstrate its presence in the books Exodus–Judges, where tribal and national history are more the focus. In the books of Samuel, the family returns to center stage, especially in the court history of King David (the longest and most detailed narrative cycle in the Bible), where a father-son conflict is held accountable for the lives of 20,000 people in Israel's bloodiest and most tragic civil war. The opposition of David and Absalom can be translated into the language of the Garden story: the son is *'ish,* but the father is *'adam.* The loyalties formed by adoptive association are different from, and at war with, the loyalties of bloodline, of kinship. Both sets of loyalties being volatile and fragile, the formation of "tradition" is at all times an uphill battle. The account of the forces imperiling tradition is the closest Genesis gets to a concept of "Original Sin." God's "curse" is the insufficiency of the individual. Man as an individual is barred from access to a "Tree of Life," yet the human family branches out in Genesis and beyond quite literally as a "Tree of Life." Immortality becomes the qualified immortality of generational succession, a cooperative venture, and access to the "Tree of Life" is made equivalent to the collective (and, as such, accursedly difficult and hazardous) self-realization of humanity through time.

The Garden Story as Literary Art

Some brief conclusions are in order regarding the type of literary art we have been examining:

(1) *It is an art of quotation.* The legendary material and much historical material of the Bible rely on an oral tradition, and possibly on earlier written collections. It is quite possible that only a small portion thereof is represented in the Bible, and that the Bible is, as it were, only the tip of an iceberg—though it is still apparent that the extant form of the tradition seems to have a comprehensiveness and authority sufficient to have made the collection a "holy Scripture," a "Bible," with canonical status. This canonicity should not obscure the fact that the biblical

traditions in our possession have been *selected* from a larger stock whose form and order are by no means identical with the present canonical form and order, and which are, in any case, partly unrecoverable. Only one thing is certain from the analysis I have offered: the selection is artful, precise, and intricate, and constitutes a deeper level of textual meaning, which is sometimes at odds with the story's plain or apparent meaning. I have tried to show that the logical analogies established in the story arise from relations of its traditionary units, and that any "structural" analysis of the story should not deal in mental categories (such as some of the anthropological, economic, or psychoanalytic abstractions currently fashionable in structuralism) that are unduly remote from the pattern of differences established by the text itself. That I have called this material's art an art of quotation suggests its formative relation to later traditionary collections in Judaism, Christianity, and Islam. Although I have suggested, in passing, its analogies to the midrashic method, one major difference should be kept in mind: in midrash, traditionary sources are attributed to named individuals; in the Bible, they are left anonymous.

(2) *It is an art of verbal irony.* We have seen the manner in which the presence or absence of a single word can shape the story's meaning. Indeed, more: we have seen how the story is itself built around key words.[54] That acts of naming form part of the plot does not, should not, obscure their genesis as plot elements, i.e., as reasoned backwards, so I maintain, from key words. Such a model is best understood as an art of traditionary quotation, analogous to (though not identical with) the rabbinic art of midrash. Both Bible and midrash select from, and/or comment upon, an inherited scripture or tradition; both seem polemically committed to a justification of the inherited tradition, of the need for tradition as such, and of the need for a well-diffused educated class capable of shaping and transmitting the tradition. Because both biblical and rabbinic literature are founded at least in part in a kind of plea for traditionary literacy, it is no accident that the reader's *verbal* literacy is exercised and trained, as well—by which I mean the reader's ability to distinguish subtle differences between key words and their puns, assonances, repetitions, and even anagrams, as guides to narrative meaning. I have called the literary art at issue here an "art of irony" because quotation of either a word or a traditionary unit (epigram, etymon, song, etc.) aims to subvert, by complicating, the quoted material's conventional meaning, and to supplant it with deeper levels of meaning. I have called it an "art of *verbal* irony" to distinguish it from the ironies of plot and character long noticed by more mimetically oriented biblical criticism.

(3) *It is an allegorical art.* Because the Garden story is symmetrical and largely concentric (the one major deviation itself a symmetry), it neces-

sarily establishes parallel relations among its elements, and, as such, analogies. At the same time, for these relations or analogies to be perceived requires that the story be apprehended as a unity, and only as *completed*. All elements of the story, regardless of the fictitious "time" progression they purport to advance, must in the end be perceived instantaneously and paradigmatically. This atemporal type of counter-meaning, subversive to the story's ostensible chronology, is, as Paul de Man argues in his essay on allegorical temporality, a device that lies at the heart of allegorical discourse.[55] The chief preoccupation of such discourse is not the affective domain we associate with the story's familiar mimetic dimension, which, to be sure, it certainly exploits (such matters as dramatic irony, "pity and fear," plot and character development, or even the "mythic," "symbolic," and "psychoanalytic" factors),[56] but rather a conceptual and logical domain more akin to the instantaneous insight of proverb, maxim, and parable. Such understanding of a biblical story accords with Maimonides' reading of Scripture (*Guide of the Perplexed* I, Intro., 3a/ff.) not as narrative but as a systematic map of "equivocal," "derivative," and "amphibolous" words—concerning which, we must, with him, concede an often perplexing difficulty of access: "And even this small light that shines over us is not always there, but flashes and is hidden again, as if it were [Gen. 3:24] the *flaming sword which turned every way*."

·II·

IS THERE A STORY OF ABRAHAM?

הלוא זה אוּד מֻצל מאש
Zech. 3:2

Is there a story of Abraham? To ask this question is to inquire after the literary coherence of Gen. 12–25; to determine its unities of space, time, plot, and character; and to show a more or less continuous trajectory of action and causality, an orderly relation of plot to subplot, and a continuity of thematic concern. To accomplish these tasks is a process that, while riskily based on subjective responses of a reader, nevertheless has a rich critical language to draw upon, both premodern and modern, and by now there is ample precedent within modern biblical studies for a "synchronic" mode of analysis, whose general premises no longer need be justified at length.[1] Use of this method does not, however, absolve the analyst from stating clearly to what extent, and in what ways, the text studied is a work of *literature,* whose modes of composition, performance, and dissemination have at least some formal comparability to literature in the modern sense.[2] It has justly been argued that literary study of the Bible can never afford to disregard the biblical reader's literary competence.[3] With Gen. 12–25, that requirement poses a serious problem, for biblical form criticism, our best arbiter of the biblical reader's literary competence, has made quite clear that the text does not comprise material entirely written in origin, nor material entirely oriented toward reading pleasure per se, and that, to the extent that it can be called "literature," Gen. 12–25 is not one but *many* kinds of literature.[4] By this reckoning, there is not a single Abraham *story,* but an *anthology* of Abraham stories, redactionally doctored with great ingenuity to form a roughly continuous chronology, but bearing little true continuity, and presuming no unified performance context.[5]

Is there, then, an Abraham *cycle?*[6] To put the question this way is to inquire after the patterns of order in the redaction of Gen. 12–25, adopting, where necessary, source-critical, form-critical, and traditiohistorical judgments, and to view the text's principles of order on a different plane from that of the story's plain sense and temporal plot-line. Here, it is often a matter of establishing motivic and thematic *parallels* within the cycle, and, quite often, *symmetries* of compositional sequence. Symmetry in the Bible has, by now, been both extensively argued[7] and articulately challenged,[8] but it appears, at present, to be less a question of *whether* there is symmetry, and more one of *why,* and what functions it serves.[9] For this reason, it is not sufficient to identify symmetry in a biblical story or cycle, and to leave the matter at a purely formalist solution. One must specify, as well, the semantic nature of the points of articulation between alleged terms, and thereby specify a *functional* relation between them. To do so is to revive the question: Is there a story of Abraham? For the traditionary montage of Gen. 12–25 can be shown to comprise articulations that are fundamentally etiological in nature, and that form a single argument presupposing a unified story at the plain sense of the text.[10] ("A biblical text never departs from its plain sense" [Shab. 63a] is a sound rabbinic dictum, whose application to the present inquiry must be remembered throughout—even where an allegorical or homiletic dimension can be shown to exist.) Ask any child in a yeshiva, and he will tell you that there is a story of Abraham—though his rationale for this belief transcends story: quite simply, there was an Abraham.[11] Since even the child will agree that Abraham did not write his own story, he likewise means that there was an Abraham *tradition* by which the events of Gen. 12–25 progressed from historical fact to written text.[12]

So it has further been asked: Was there an Abraham tradition? Was there an Abraham? At this point, the field of research on Abraham polarizes into competing professional bailiwicks, each insisting on a different locus of meaning for the material of Gen. 12–25. Those following the lead of archaeologists and biblical historians such as Albright, Bright, and de Vaux find the text pulsing with the life of the Middle Bronze age, representing authentic historical memories of Amorite and *'apiru* population movements; legal and social customs of Mari, Nuzi, and pre-Amarna Canaan; and divine and theophoric names suggestive of pre-Israelite thought patterns and cultic deities.[13] (Those arguing for the "historicity" of the patriarchal narratives, it should be noted, do not try to say that there was an Abraham, Isaac, or Jacob, as such—only that there is a strong resemblance between the milieu of the patriarchs and that portrayed by archaeologists of the Bronze Age.) Others, such as Thompson and Van Seters,[14] disparage the usefulness of archaeology for an interpretation of Gen. 12–25, and challenge the historicity of Abraham, arguing instead that the stories reflect the concerns and idioms of the monarchic and exilic eras—thus directly or indirectly vindicating that regnant voice in biblical studies prior to the rise of biblical archaeology, Julius Wellhausen.[15] Those of the anti-"historicity" persuasion presumably see Gen. 12–25 as *literature,* but their methods are not always those of literary study.[16] They have, in any case, introduced a misleading either/or conception of "historicity" into the discussion, which has made it seem as if Gen. 12–25, if "true" in some historical sense, cannot also be story, and, if "story," cannot also have at its core an authentic historical memory.[17]

Meanwhile, tradition historians such as Clements and Westermann have taken a middle ground in the debate, insisting on the need for bridging the some 800-year period between the era of Abraham and the earliest written accounts of his life, with a history of an Abraham tradition, and an accounting of the diverse oral and written forms comprising it, each with its original life-setting, its performance context, and its unique role in the gradual crystallization of the whole.[18] Clements has supplied a very worthwhile traditiohistorical study of Gen. 15, tracing the Abrahamic covenant/promise described there from its origins among Calebite settlers of Hebron; through its political use by David, first in the Judahite league based in Hebron, and later, in a pan-Israelite context, in Jerusalem; to its neglect in the era of the prophets and the Deuteronomic reforms; and finally, to its revival in late monarchic and early exilic times, as a message of hope to a badly demoralized community of Israel.[19] Westermann, for his part, applying his characteristic bibliographic thoroughness and comprehensive overview, has supplied a useful accounting of the redactional junctures binding the diverse elements of the Abraham cycle, and has supplied a simple and plausible symmetrical model of its elements, somewhat akin to a model proposed in the present study.[20] On the face of it, tradition history would seem to have the most balanced perspective, neither purely archaeological nor purely literary. But its methods still withdraw us from the reading experience into a highly conjectural pretextual realm, and share with source analysis the fallacy of parlaying up a developmental pattern out of the two-dimensionality of the text. Where Gen. 12–25 is concerned, tradition historians are on especially weak ground, because of the paucity of references to Abraham outside of Genesis.[21] We may prefer to affirm, with tradition historian Martin Noth, the fundamentally literary nature of the Abraham "tradition,"[22] and to confine our interest in traditiohistorical factors to the question of the cycle's role as *evaluator* of traditions whose preliterary history must remain largely a matter of conjecture. We thus return again to a chiefly literary conception of Gen. 12–25, though we need not thereby confine our interest to narrative alone, nor need we categorically deny the material's "historicity" or traditionary antiquity.

The present study seeks to show the coherence of Gen. 12–25 both as *story* and as *cycle*. We cannot easily separate the two functions, of course, and I therefore propose a reading that is neither purely literary nor purely traditiohistorical, but adapted to a text that is midway between narrative and traditionary discourse. We will attempt, in particular, to understand the cycle's unique manner of *balancing* traditions while *advancing* a plot. I will show that it does this by presenting like traditions in a sequence of increasing elaboration or development, while maintaining a roughly symmetrical array of parallels, each layer bearing a particular functional relationship to the whole—the center term serving as the prototype of the two episodes that stand most conspicuously apart from the cycle's symmetrical component. Stated so abstractly, the pattern does not do justice to the lively *internal exegesis* I will attempt to show at work: between the parallels, among the layers of parallels, and between the plot and the oracles that punctuate it. The cycle, in other words, expresses both a developmental configuration and a conceptual framework that together suggest deep reflection on the available traditions about Abraham, a reflection closely bound up with individual details of the narration at almost every point.

An Inventory of Repetitions in Gen. 12–25

Abraham, one easily notices, does certain things more than once. Twice he migrates on divine command. Several times he builds an altar. Twice he represents his wife to foreigners as a sister. Twice he has a hand, direct or indirect, in the expulsion of his servant Hagar. Other episodes that may or may not include Abraham likewise happen more than once: of hospitality to strangers; of disaster at Sodom; of a parent driven into the wilderness with a seemingly doomed child; and so forth. Certain of the cycle's repetitions have provided source critics with a notion of "parallel accounts," namely, of the Yahwist ("J") and the Elohist ("E").[23] But, in fact, the pattern of repetition extends across the familiar lines of source division—occurring *within* an alleged source (episodes of hospitality to strangers occur only in "J"), or between sources not viewed as parallel (twice, for example, Abraham asserts himself on behalf of Sodom: once in "J" material, 18:24ff., and once in the anomalous and apparently unclassifiable material of Gen. 14).[24] If we thus broaden our conception of what constitutes a repetition, and compile a simple inventory of every repeated action or motif in the cycle, we emerge with a useful starting point for determining the cycle's unifying principles:

Unhesitating response to a divine command to migrate: 12:1ff., 22:1ff.

Building of altars: 12:4–9, 13:18, 22:6; cf. 15:9–11, and (the planting of an *'eshel* to mark a human covenant) 21:33.

Divine promises to Abraham: *without dialogue*—12:2–3, 7, 13:14–17; 21:12 (preceding verse implies dialogue, but does not represent it), 22:15–19; *with dialogue*—15:1ff., 17:1ff., 18:1–15 (18:16–33 an independent pericope dealing with the fate of Sodom, but predicated on divine promise to Abraham; see vv. 17–18). Chapters 15 and 17 are also generally understood as "covenant" pericopes.

Divine promises to Hagar: 16:10–12, 21:17–18 (both without dialogue).

Sodom motif: 13:10–13, 14:1–24, 19:1–38 (cf. 18:17–33).

Hospitality extended to strangers: 18:1–8, 19:1–14. Cf. 24:25ff.

"Wife-sister" episode: 12:10–20, 20:1–18. Cf. 26:1–16.

Border covenant settling servants' quarrel: 13:5–11, 21:25–34.

Exchange of goods or money as covenant: 14:21–24, 21:27–30, 23:1–20.

Parent driven into wilderness with child (or conceived seed): 16:4–14, 21:8–21, 22:1–18.

Genealogy of Abra(ha)m and Nahor: 11:27–32, 22:20–24. 24:1–67, in entirety, resolves a genealogical issue. Cf. 10:1ff., 11:10–26, 25:1–11, 12–20.

The following will be less central to our discussion, but should be kept in mind, as well:

Naming of a child: 16:11, 15 (cf. 17:20), 17:17–19 (cf. 18:11–15), 19:37–38, 21:3, 6–7.

Place-naming at site of theophany or settlement: 16:14, 19:23, 21:31, 22:14. Cf. 14:3, 13, 24–implied etiology of the name "Hebron."

Change of ancestor's name: 17:5, 15.

Episode or pericope introduced by "After these things . . ." 15:1ff., 22:1ff., 22:20ff.

Episode introduced by ". . . there appeared . . .": 17:1ff., 18:1ff.

I will attempt to show that, although exceptions to the pattern exist, most of the categories in the first list reveal a pattern of increasing elaboration, and manifest features of an increasingly "literary" nature: dialogue, suspense, irony, dramatic development, and psychological emphasis.[25]

Command to migrate. Investigators have noted the striking similarity of phraseology and analogy of theme between Gen. 12:1ff. and 22:1ff. (a correspondence embarrassing, perhaps, to source critics, who would assign the episodes to "J" and "E" respectively).[26] Equally important are the differences. Abra(ha)m's obedience to God's command in 12:1–3 is told in only a few sentences (12:4–9), whereas in 22 it occupies most of the chapter. Whereas in 12 no access to Abraham's psychological state is permitted, in 22, the information established throughout the cycle, the painstaking detail lavished on Abraham's obedient response, and the short dialogue with Isaac (the only place in the cycle that Abraham converses with one of his children), all create a wealth of psychological depth (while still not entering explicitly into Abraham's thoughts) that makes the events of 22 seem light-years removed from 12. In both cases, the command involves repudiation of kin—in 12, the parents' household; in 22, Abraham's own offspring Isaac. The blessing of fertility in 12:1–3 resembles those in 15:5, 17:2, 5ff., 17:20, 21:18b, and 22:17. Because of the purposeful ambiguity of 12:1b, no land is promised until the command is fulfilled, in 12:7.

Altars. Abraham's building of altars is first recorded perfunctorily in 12:4–9 and 13:19. In chapter 15, while the *building* of an altar and *locale* of the altar are not specified, we are given a detailed account of the activity at an Abrahamic altar, here the sacrifices that elicit the famous "covenant between the parts."[27] In 22, the building of an altar is again, as in the first examples, stated explicitly, but this time as the crux of a narrative episode (22:9), and here—by virtue again of the child-sacrifice theme, and of the full trajectory of Abraham's experience preceding the story—the moral and psychological dimensions of 22 far exceed the simple lineaments of Abraham's altar building in chapters 12 and 13.

Promise. At a first perusal, it would seem that the promises to Abraham are most elaborated at the center of the cycle, and least elaborated at the periphery—for it is only in the central chapters (15, 17, 18) that Abraham engages in dialogue with God over one or another aspect of the promises he receives. This constitutes the one major exception to the pattern of increasing elaboration among the narrative units, and, as we shall eventually see, it is an important guide to the cycle's overall structure. But it should be noted that up through chapter 18, the pattern of increasing elaboration still holds: the promises increase in length, and the narratives in which they are set grow in complexity and dramatic subtlety. Chapters 15 and 17 have been seen by investigators both as "promise" narratives and as "covenant" narratives,[28] and, as we shall see, they form a parallel set in the cycle's overall structure. Some investigators, however, have questioned the narrative nature of these chapters, and have seen in them "artificial narratives" specially constructed to frame promises to Abraham of land and progeny that originally had independent histories as oracles.[29] Chapter 18, by contrast, has been seen as a true narrative, in which the promise of a child is not merely a disembodied oracle inserted into an ad hoc framework of dialogue, but rather is integral to the unfolding story—a story of a type with parallels in Ugaritic literature from the patriarchal era itself.[30] All three chapters, in any case, bear, in their present form, certain features more reminiscent of the "prophetic call" type-scene, which I will discuss in more detail further on in this study.[31] The form and content of the promises to Abraham have been much debated by investigators, but since the now-classic study by Albrecht Alt, the two most basic elements have generally been understood as promises of land and progeny.[32] The promises of progeny, it should be noted, increase in specificity.[33] The promises to Hagar, and the placement of the Hagar episodes in relation to the Abraham promise narratives, will occupy us further on in this study. The culminating promise to Abraham of land and progeny in 22:15–19 introduces a new theme (war of conquest) whose specific weight and meaning in context will likewise occupy us further on.

Sodom and Gomorrah. The three places in the cycle where Sodom and

Gomorrah are a theme likewise reveal increasing elaboration. The first mention of the locale is brief, but rich in associations that reach out through the cycle and beyond, both backward (to the Garden story, the Flood, and Babel) and forward (to other episodes of disasters among foreign peoples, such as Gen. 34, Ex. 4–15, and Josh. 6): "And Lot lifted up his eyes and saw the whole Jordan plain, that all of it was well watered, like a garden of YHWH, like the land of Egypt, all the way to Zoar—before YHWH's destruction of Sodom and Gomorrah" (13:10).

Later, after Abraham turns to settle in Canaan, the following is said: "And the people of Sodom were exceedingly wicked, and sinful to YHWH . . ." (ibid., 13).

Sodom returns as the major theme of the next chapter (14), this time amid a wealth of geographical, apocryphal, and historical detail (especially vv. 1–9). Life in Sodom, however, is still not shown. Only in 19 is there elaboration on the city and its people. (Sodom is allowed to return one final time as a fully *internalized* reality, when Abraham, twice an intervener on behalf of Sodom, is led to commence an abomination similar in gravity to, or even exceeding, those of the Sodomites, in Gen. 22.)[34]

Promises of land and progeny correspond roughly to the foreign and domestic domains of the cycle, respectively. The Sodom and Gomorrah episodes contain both sets of elements, but feature a land theme, namely "the iniquity of the Amorite," stated most explicitly in 15:16. Here, the implication is clear; the destruction of the lower Dead Sea region, still proverbially evident in the bituminous wastes even today visible to the traveler, is taken as the first installment of the divine promise to replace the Canaanite (or Amorite) peoples with Israel. It is important to keep in mind here that title to the land is established not by historical precedence or by divine election in any absolute sense, but by continued maintenance of behavior pleasing to God. Not that Israel will settle the destroyed region (though today, of course, she mines it for valuable ores)—rather, the cycle holds the destruction up as an omen of the future destiny of the Canaanite peoples, who otherwise are portrayed in the cycle as living side-by-side in comparative peace with Abraham and his household.

The progression 13–14, 18–19 clarifies the gradual separation (and mutation into a neighboring people) of Lot and his household from the household of Abraham; and Abraham's fruitfulness (and so, his inheriting progeny) is finally guaranteed, in the annunciation of the birth of Isaac (a tradition, one can say, of separate origin,[35] but here woven integrally into the Sodom narrative through the linkage of 18:16–19). This pattern, whereby the ascendance of one clan is matched by the decline, migration, or estrangement of another (and the latter's redefinition as a border people), is repeated in the material about Ishmael, and, in the Jacob cycle, in the material about Laban (31:43–32:1) and Esau (33:1ff., 36:1ff.). The irony and dramatic justice are especially ripe in the Lot material, since it was Lot who had chosen the richer of the two lands.[36] Not only does he disinherit himself from western Canaan, but the land he chooses is withdrawn from him, as well. There is also special poignance in the fact that Abraham, though his favored posterity will be the principal beneficiaries of a divine dispossession of the Canaanite peoples, is consistently represented as a *defender* of Sodom, in 14:14ff. and 18:23ff.

Hospitality. Closely bound up with the Sodom and Gomorrah stories are the narrative sequences illustrating the hospitality of a Terahide ancestor (Abraham or Lot) toward three "strangers" who turn out to be angelic emissaries on a divine mission. The essential detachability of the Abraham "hospitality" episode from the Sodom story (the first mention of Sodom is only at the departure of the angels, 18:16), contrasting with the integrality of Lot's hospitality to the Sodom story (it is as Lot's guests that the angels first meet the Sodomites and strike the first blow against them, 19:4ff.), makes it clear that a distinctly literary manipulation of separate traditions (annunciation of Isaac;[37] destruction of Sodom) has taken place. It is not our task here to evaluate which of these traditions is "older," or which episode is modeled on the other. It is only clear that, in the light of the cycle's thematic concerns, the two episodes stand as inverse parallels to one another, and that the latter episode emerges, in effect, as a satire on the former. Lot's hospitality, while certainly as generous in main outline as Abraham's (and in one respect, 19:8, more so), is a poor copy of his kinsman's.[38] His willingness to sacrifice his daughters (and thus his posterity) to the whim of the Sodomites stands in bold contrast to the importance of a posterity to Abraham. And whereas the Abraham episode treats with delicate humor the question of Abraham's sexual role in the conception of Isaac (18:11–15), the Sodom episode and its aftermath in Zoar make Lot the progenitor of his posterity by the very daughters he was willing to cast into the lustful mob. Again, it is fair to say that of the two "hospitality" episodes, the latter is the more elaborate.

"Wife-sister." The "wife-sister" motif, considered as an item of history and tradition, is an obscure and suggestive theme whose full meaning will probably continue to elude us.[39] Its role in the cycle, however, is reasonably clear and does not require extratextual evidence to yield meaning. Its importance to the unfolding of the cycle is twofold. First, it is one of several kinds of episodes illustrating Abraham's contact with foreigners, and one in which the question of foreignness, as such, is most at issue. A situation evolves whereby Abraham, to the extent that he

acknowledges Sarah as kin, must repudiate her as spouse, a matter eventually resolved into harmony, and into a qualified rule: spouse = kin; foreigner = non-spouse. By virtue of these elements, the "wife-sister" material thus meshes in a quite logical manner with the Lot-Sodom material: Abraham's balanced endogamy contrasts with both the unbridled exogamy of the Egyptians/"Philistines" and the unbridled endogamy of Lot.[40] Second, because the "wife-sister" episodes describe a moment in which the survival of Abraham's conjugal household is most endangered, it touches on the issue of Abraham's promised progeny through Sarah, namely Isaac and the entire succession from Isaac that results in the people Israel. That the yet-unconceived Isaac is the hidden focus of both stories is suggested to us again in an unusual way in Gen. 26, where the third "wife-sister" episode in the patriarchal narratives turns out to have as its hero Isaac himself.[41]

The second of Abraham's "wife-sister" episodes is, in any case, the more elaborated of the two accounts: God communicates to Abimelech in a dream; to Pharaoh by a plague. Abimelech consults with his courtiers, then summons Abraham; Pharaoh simply summons Abraham. Abimelech asks: "How have I wronged you that you could do a great wrong to me and my kingdom? . . . What were you intending?" Pharaoh simply asks: "Why didn't you tell me?" Abraham replies in detail to Abimelech, not at all to Pharaoh. And his untruth to Abimelech turns out to be qualifiedly true: she *is* a kin. In the Egyptian version, we are left thinking that Abraham has told an untruth.

Border and resident covenants. Two other types of narrative motif not yet mentioned concern Abraham's relations with strangers (or estranged). These are: (a) border agreements settling servants' quarrels (13:7ff., 21:22ff.),[42] and (b) exchanges of goods in the form of tithe (14:21ff.), oath (21:28ff.), or purchase (23:11ff.), to clarify an issue connected with residence. These episodes belong together as a group and express a progression from informal to formal idioms of agreement. Abraham and Lot simply turn in opposite directions (13:11; cf. v. 9). Abraham the resident, however, insists to the Hittites of Kiriath-Arba (Hebron) that his acceptance of burial land for his family be a real-estate transaction "at the full price" (23:9), and the entire episode is occupied with the elaborate transaction. The progression reflected here again brings to bear the problem of consanguinity/non-consanguinity: in the course of ten chapters, Abraham has gradually become a stranger to his kinsman Lot and, by adoptive rite and exchange of goods, a friend and neighbor of foreigners (here, the Hittite Hebronites). The act of estrangement from kin acted out *in extremis* in 12:1ff. and 22:1ff., and mirrored in the dissembling near-estrangement of the "wife-sister" episodes, is told more or less non-catastrophically and realistically in the border and resident covenant episodes.[43] Abraham's key allegiances, prior to the courtship of Rebecca, are adoptive relations. The sole "blood" relation to whom he maintains a continuous loyalty throughout his active career is his own spouse. It is as if this very contraction of kin allegiances to the conjugal family in the very narrowest sense (but including the offspring of that relation) allows Abraham the geographical mobility and contractual freedom he needs to enter into such fruitful and peace-promoting relations with strangers. This, in fact, is what enables him to cease being a stranger in his final environment (Hebron), and to become a resident—one could say, a citizen—while at the same time maintaining the integrity of his chief kin allegiances and ethnic identity. This pattern of development, by diminishing the importance of Abraham's horizontal kin allegiances, increases the importance of the vertical nexus: namely, the succession through Isaac—a matter which, by the end of chapter 23, is all but completely settled. There remains the acquisition of a wife for Isaac—paradoxically, from among the very kin Abraham left behind in chapter 12, in his first historical act.

Together with the building of altars, Abraham's human covenants help establish the initial steps in the fulfillment of the "land" aspect of the divine promises, and, indeed, the total pattern of points crossed in these episodes gives us a full outline of Abraham's Canaanite itinerary. I will have more to say further on in this chapter about the geographical trajectory recorded in the cycle, and its importance for our understanding of the material.

Household narratives.[44] If Abraham's success in dealing with strangers (and so, in establishing a foothold in the land) is partly dependent on his simplification of horizontal kin allegiances, his success in establishing a line of succession (and so, of establishing a foothold in time) is partly dependent on the clarification of his vertical kin allegiances. This matter is developed chiefly in the narratives of the intra-household competition of Sarah and Hagar. Whereas Abraham's household is shown very little in the early chapters (up through 15), it gradually grows to occupy almost all of the latter chapters. Strictly speaking, the "wife-sister" episodes and the "Lot/Sodom" episodes pose for Abraham a household and succession problem as much as a diplomatic and land-settlement problem—but they do not, at any point, state the succession issue as their explicit subject, and, but for a brief glimpse in 18:1–8 of activities in and around Abraham's tent, do not reveal the interaction of Abraham's conjugal family. That interaction is reserved almost exclusively for the narratives dealing with the temporary exile of a parent and offspring, and the near-fatal menacing of the offspring.

The Hagar narratives both consist of two segments: events leading up to the exile (in which the principal actors are Abraham, Sarah, and

Hagar), and events following the exile (in which the principal actors are Hagar and God/angel of God). I will have more to say later about the narrative syntax of the Hagar episodes, but here it suffices to point out that the flow of events in the second segment of both narratives is strikingly similar in configuration to the story of the sacrifice of Isaac. Both involve a parent driven into the wilderness with a child (or conceived seed). The latter Hagar episode, like the Akedah story, involves a mortal danger to the child, and in both, the child is rescued at the last moment by divine intervention. (Rabbinic exegesis, we should note, is sufficiently attuned to the close relationship between the Hagar episodes and Gen. 22 as to make the latter likewise flow from the rivalry of Sarah and Hagar).[45] Other correspondences will be dealt with later.

With this similarity in mind, we can see more clearly that the progression between 16:1–16, 21:1–21, and 22:1–19 is one of steady elaboration and deepening of the succession problem. As in other narrative motifs we have surveyed, the Akedah story serves as both a dramatic culmination and a paradoxical twist of the motif. After Abraham, for a second time, drives out Hagar, he then in a very fundamental sense *becomes* Hagar—recapitulating her major movements, her dread, forlornness, and uncertainty, and arriving at a similar vindication. The differences, of course, in both context and tone of the migration, are equally fundamental, and here we must take into account the one other place in the cycle where Abraham is set into a "type-scene" parallel to a subplot figure, namely, in the "hospitality" episodes: there, he served as the *pattern of a parody;* in chapter 22, while enacting high tragedy, he serves as the *parody of a pattern* already doubly established by Hagar. The parallel is especially important because it constitutes part of the trial of faith Abraham undergoes: having not long before enacted the role of one abruptly dismissing a servant, he is left to wonder if a similar fall from favor is what motivates the inexplicable command to sacrifice Isaac. The reader, of course, is alerted (22:1) that this is a "test" of Abraham, and a test, as suggested by the Prologue of Job, is predicated precisely on divine *favor.* Since Abraham's passage of the test hinges on his maintenance of the faith conspicuously lauded in 15:6 ("and he believed in the LORD, and He accounted it for him as righteousness"), it is therefore in his interests to *know* that this is a test. It is not Abraham's willingness per se to give up his son that is at issue (as a cruder, more "Canaanite" interpretation of the gesture might dictate, and as apparent divine approval to this effect in verse 12 might lead readers to assume);[46] rather, it is his belief in the promise of a posterity. As such, only one option is open to him: to proceed to sacrifice his son while knowing that the gesture *must* have another outcome—the "Hagarite" outcome, in fact, namely, the last-minute divine intervention her story has conditioned us to expect. But in place of her wailing despair, we are shown quiet certitude and veiled words. Erich Auerbach's by now classic observation that Gen. 22 exemplifies the tendency of biblical narrative to conceal its characters' psychological states[47] can only be fully understood in the light of the intra-exegetical function of the cycle. It is not simply that the story's actions, to use Auerbach's words, "call for interpretation"—rather, they call upon the reader to make explicit the interpretation they already are.

Genealogy. Finally, the cycle records a gradual separation and re-merging of the genealogies of Abraham and Nahor. In the preceding chapter, I have shown how a genealogical nexus is, in a sense, the primary pretext for narrative elaboration, forming, as it does, the outermost parenthesis of the story, and making the story itself an episode of *toladot* (literally, "begettings"; metaphorically and intrinsically: "history"). A genealogical nexus likewise frames the Abraham cycle.[48] The information in 11:27ff. is perfunctory—our knowledge of Abraham at that point is minimal, and our knowledge of the eventual child of Nahor's line, Rebecca, who will be a mate to Isaac, and thus a crucial link in the lineage of Abraham and Israel, is altogether nonexistent.[49] When the genealogy of Nahor returns in 22:20ff., it is still with minimal reference to what is to come; only a gloss makes the link: "After these things, Abraham was told: 'Milcah, too, has borne children to Nahor your brother . . . [including] Bethuel.'— Bethuel is the father of Rebecca" (22:20–23). Yet the placement of this genealogical note immediately following the events of the Akedah (22:1–19) can only have the most studiedly paradoxical effect: the very next tangible sign in the fulfillment of God's promise to Abraham of "innumerable" descendants (22:17) is not a new descendant of his own, but one to his nearest living relative who stayed in the Syrian homeland— Nahor. It is not until the elaborately developed story of the proxy courtship of Rebecca in chapter 24—outside of the Joseph story, the most detailed and finely drawn narrative in Genesis—that the otherwise obscure genealogical note finally acquires meaning and depth.[50] If the genealogical information of chapter 22 is seen in relation to the more extensive genealogical material of chapter 25, then the materials they bracket—chapters 23 and 24—serve as a double thematic coda to the whole cycle, exhibiting the cycle's most decisive realization of the double promise made in 12:2–7: land and progeny.[51] Again, what this amounts to is a pattern of increasing elaboration: the first genealogy is uncomplicated by the weight of narrative factors; the latter complex of narrative and genealogy (22:20–25:18) is a self-contained composition in its own right, and dependent for its meaning on narrative information established throughout the cycle.

To sum up our inquiry thus far: We can see, first of all, that all of the major thematic units of the cycle follow a carefully modulated overlapping progression from simple to complex, from oral and archival fragments to realistic stories, from external to domestic relations, from neu-

tral to emotionally charged (if still laconic) reportage, from ingenuous to
ironic tone. The traditional synagogue lectionary division of the cycle
(through chapter 22) into two *parshiyyot* (12–17: *"Lekh Lekha"*; 18–22:
"Vayyera'") gives us a reasonably exact picture of where the cycle begins,
as it were, to shift gears. All of the basic thematic elements of the second
parashah are contained in the first, but the first has far less of the
narrative power and dramatic subtlety of the second. This theme-and-
variations progression is more or less the reverse of a pattern I have
shown operating in the Garden story:[52] there, we find a relatively heavy
concentration of narrative elaboration into the first half of the story's
palistrophic structure, the second half reserved for more distinctly non-
narrative and etiological fragments; in the Abraham cycle, by contrast,
the second half of the cycle[53] expands, deepens, and sometimes twists or
overturns the meaning of thematic elements set forth in the first. What
source critics have seen as an "Elohistic" appendix (specifically, 20:1–18;
21:6–32, 34; 22:1–19),[54] may, in fact, be part of a larger redactional
pattern of narrative elaboration on preliterary units, which themselves,
in the first half of the cycle, are arranged in a pattern of increasing
elaboration. What is especially remarkable about this pattern is that it
remains more or less in harmony with the story's temporal progression:
the thematic elements of the first half depict Abraham's world before the
conception of Isaac, the destruction of Sodom, and the purchase of land.
Those of the second half represent both traditionary *variations* and
narrative *developments* of their predecessors in the first. Even where
narrative credibility is strained by the repetition of a theme (did Abraham not learn the dangers of representing his wife as a sister? Is not the
second expulsion of Hagar presented as if it were a new idea?), we find
the narrative details maintaining consistency of a sort: no motive clause
introduces the second "wife-sister" episode, as in the first, and where
Abraham's motives are allowed to surface (in 20:11–13), we find that his
deception was not an untruth after all, but a partial withholding of the
truth, thus revealing Abraham as one who, for pressing reasons, under-
took a calculated risk twice, from fear of a greater risk. Similarly, in the
second expulsion of Hagar, it is not Hagar's behavior per se that is the
issue, but inheritance, an issue now made more real by the presence of
Isaac.[55] And whereas the first time Abraham's response was immediately
to support Sarah, the second time he is displeased (a displeasure made
more real by the presence of Ishmael!) and must consult God for guidance.

   Second, we can see that the thematic development of the cycle throws
into relief two principal themes—land and progeny—corresponding to
the two chief elements of the divine promises given initially, in 12:2–3, 7,
and that the principal episodes of the cycle focus on one or the other of
the two issues, with the promise dialogues mediating between the two.[56]

Finally, we can see the special role that Gen. 22 plays in the cycle, the several ways it supplies a resolution to thematic tensions established throughout the preceding chapters. It contains the last of God's commands to Abraham, which, like the first, is obeyed instantaneously (thus boldly contrasting to the places where Abraham enters into disputation with God). It contains the last altar he builds, which, unlike the first (where no victims are mentioned), bears a named and speaking victim. Its locale, as I will try to show more fully later, is at the center of Abraham's geographic itinerary (on both a N/S and E/W axis) and is to become the center and capital of the land Abraham's descendants will inherit. The story's action, involving no dialogue between Abraham and God, has as its central action a divine voice restraining a human hand. In a cycle rich in allusions to Abraham's vast retinue and to crowded foreign courts, the story portrays the moment in Abraham's life when he is most alone. (His leaving his servants behind in 22:5 is thus a highly weighted and conspicuous moment.) As a parody of the Hagar narratives, the Akedah story supplies both a traditionary variant (on the theme: Abraham imperiling the life of his own child) and a literary culmination of the cycle's household focus. And since the succession through Isaac can be shown to be the underlying issue even of narratives where Isaac is not explicitly mentioned (e.g., the "wife-sister" episodes and the Lot/Sodom material), the Akedah story supplies a chilling reversal of expectations generated throughout virtually the whole cycle. To view the story in this manner—as a composition functional to the *cycle*—does not rule out the possibility of its independent composition (by the hypothetical "Elohist," for example), but its force in context derives from the structure of the whole. What is especially striking is the manner in which Gen. 22 sweeps up into its vortex virtually every major theme and motif set forth in the preceding ten chapters. During the few, swift strokes of its progression, it momentarily *represents* the cycle, refracting it in an enigmatic and nightmarish inversion. The fuller import of this stratagem can only be seen when we explore the cycle's relation to the rest of Genesis, and to related texts outside of Genesis.

Having surveyed the internal progression of each category of duplicated theme or motif in Gen. 12–25, and having made some preliminary observations on their external interrelationships, we are now ready to observe more carefully the structure of their layout as a cycle.

The (Nearly) Symmetrical Component of the Cycle

Provided that one's observations are accurate and one's terms properly defined, it is no less useful to identify a *near*-symmetry in a story cycle than to identify a perfect one.[57] If, out of an approximate total of eighteen thematic elements, only four, let us say, were to converge in a symmetry, while the remainder lay outside the symmetry, we would find a symmetrical model quite suspect. But if *twelve* elements converged, and the remainder could be accounted for without postulating them as extraneous to the composition, we would have strong evidence for at least a symmetrical *component* in the composition. It is better in such circumstances to argue a symmetrical paradigm and account for divergences than to start with *no* paradigm and articulate a more idiosyncratic model. In fig. 2, at any rate, the symmetrical component of the Abraham cycle is indicated (square brackets denote material violating symmetry *within* the schema; material excluded from the schema is accounted for separately).

FIG. 2

a   Genealogical framework (11:10–25, 26–32)
  b   Migration from Haran; separation from Nahor (12:4–5)
    c   Building of altars; land promised (12:4–9; [13:14–18])
      d   "Wife-sister" episode (12:10–20)
        e   Border agreement with Lot (13:1–13)
          f   Sodom episode and rescue of Lot (14:1–24)
            g   Covenant of sacrifice (15:1–20)
              X   Expulsion and rescue of Hagar (16:1–16)
            g′   Covenant of circumcision (17:1–27)
          f′   Sodom episode and rescue of Lot (18:1–19:38)
      [e′   Border agreement with Abimelech (21:22–34)]
      d′   "Wife-sister" episode (20:1–18)
    c′   Building of altar (22:6); land promised (17b); acquired (23:1–20)
  b′   Migration to Haran; reunification with Nahor (24:1–67)
a′   Genealogical framework ([22:20–24;] 25:1–18)

To account first for the divergent material within the schema: (1) The latter half of the "c" element (13:14–18) belongs conceptually to "c," even though out of sequence, because it completes the set of *peripheral* altars along a N/S axis of the future Israel's chief sanctuaries. Its appearance at the end of chapter 13 thus has the effect of a "footnote" to the earlier episode, its location at this spot according more plausibly with Abraham's settlement in Hebron following Lot's departure. (2) The border agreement with Abimelech is, from a form-critical standpoint, ideally matched to the quite similar episode with Lot in chapter 13,[58] but occupies a different position in the actual text apparently to improve the chronological plausibility of the well dispute with Abimelech—for the episode presupposes that Abraham is already known to Abimelech, whereas the "wife-sister" episode of Gen. 20 requires that he *not* be known to him.[59] (3) Finally, the genealogical information in 22:20–24, while belonging to the genealogical framework of the cycle (a/a'), occurs in the actual text as a "footnote" to the Akedah story; it must occur *before* chapter 24 in order to serve the thematic demands of 24, and it cannot *immediately* precede 24 because of the considerable chronological gap between the birth of Bethuel and his activity as a grown man in 24. (I have already noted the coda function of 23–24.)

Properly speaking, the first fifteen verses of the second "Sodom" episode are, as already noted, a traditionary unit (annunciation of the birth of Isaac) of separate origin, but its function in the "Sodom" episode is clear from its role as the paradigm of the "hospitality" parody in 19:1ff., as already noted.

This leaves only the second Hagar episode (21:1–21) and the bulk of the "Akedah" story as standing outside the pattern. The similarity of both Hagar episodes to the "Akedah" story has already been noted, and it seems no accident that the *central* term in the symmetrical schema presented above should be the pattern for its most conspicuous divergences. The narrative syntax of these examples should be compared in more detail (fig. 3).[60]

FIG. 3

a Rivalry of Sarah and Hagar embroils Abraham (16:1–5)
  b Sarah requests that "the LORD decide" on her favored status (v. 5)
    c Exile of pregnant Hagar (6)
X: Hagar I   d Encounter with angel of YHWH (7–8)
      e Angel proclaims reversal of situation (9–12)
        f Naming of well at site of theophany (13–16)

a Rivalry of Sarah and Hagar embroils Abraham (21:1–11)
  b God reminds Abraham that child of Sarah is favored (vv. 12–13)
    c Exile of Hagar; endangering of her child (14–16)
Y: Hagar II   d Encounter with angel of God (17a)
      e Angel proclaims reversal of situation (17b–18)
        f Appearance of well at site of theophany (19)

a God, "testing" Abraham, commands sacrifice of Isaac (22:1–2)
  b God reminds Abraham that child of Sarah is favored (v. 2)
    c "Exile" of Abraham, endangering of his child (3–10)
Z: Akedah   d Encounter with angel of YHWH (11)
      e Angel proclaims reversal of situation (12; 15–19)
        f Appearance of ram, and naming of site of theophany (13–14)

Term "a" of the third episode is more homologous to its counterparts than it seems, for it is the rivalry of Sarah and Hagar, as noted earlier, that underlies the test of Abraham and supplies its principal ironies. We have already seen that the succession question is a theme that builds, explicitly and implicitly, throughout the cycle, and thus the departure of this most volatile of issues from the symmetrical framework may be quite integral to the composition: as progressively greater order is manifested in Abraham's extradomestic life, the glaring disorder of his household relations remains to be resolved, and the idiosyncratic nature of the resolution is heightened by its extraneousness to the symmetry. Here it is not a matter, as in the other divergences from symmetry, of adjustment for plausibility of plot, but rather one of thematic culmination. For such a function, any rigid conformance to the cycle's symmetries is no special virtue.

The subtle interplay of symmetrical and asymmetrical elements in the cycle must, in any case, be understood as distinctive features of a kind of textual *bricolage:* fusion of inherited materials whose combined narrative and transnarrative functions could be stretched only so far. What is especially remarkable is how much symmetrical regularity there is for a cycle whose *narrative* progression (and thus its thematic "irreversibility") is otherwise so decisive, and whose traditionary units manifest increasing elaboration.

The symmetry's parallel elements are not always evenly matched in size and genre (when considered according to their separate functions), but as a motivic structure, the scheme in entirety works quite well, and each parallel from "b" to "e" expresses a geographical polarity or term of one: b/b' implicitly establishes Israel's northeastern border (Syria), d/d', the southwestern (Egypt/Philistia); c, the peripheral altars (Shechem/ Bethel-Ai/Hebron), and c', the central altar (Mt. Moriah is sometimes identified with Jerusalem);[61] e, the eastern extremity (the Jordan), and e', the western (the Shephelah). Whereas c begins with the northernmost settlement of Abraham (Shechem), c' ends with the southernmost (Beer-sheba). Sodom (f/f') stands apart from what surrounds it in representing an "Amorite" community destroyed by God for its sinfulness, and the two episodes, in turn, sandwich a promise in which God alludes to "the wickedness of the Amorite" as the circumstance that will permit Israel to occupy the land which otherwise (c–e/e'–c') Israel's progenitor Abraham is shown acquiring by purchase, treaty, and altar building. The segment f/f' thus expresses a moral and retributive aspect to Israel's conquest of the land, less akin to the pacific and legally or cultically based acquisitions of the patriarchs, one more akin to the retributive motifs of the primordial history (Gen. 1–11) and the Exodus (Ex. 1–24, 32–34). In this manner, the Abraham cycle's framework establishes links with the story cycles preceding and following, and articulates a dichotomy that underlies much of the narrative history from Genesis to Kings, one noted by numerous observers:[62]

Israel's acquisition of the land is *permanent,* rooted in ancestral purchases, treaties, and cults, and in unsolicited divine promise.

Israel's acquisition of the land is *contingent* upon Israel's fluctuating worthiness (like all other nations of Canaan) before God.

We should note, in this regard, the special position occupied by Gen. 22. While the altar building described there (c'; 22:6) stands parallel to the distinctly non-warlike altar building of c (12:4–9), the promise it eventually elicits is partly warlike and retributive in nature: ". . . and your offspring shall inherit the gates of their [lit. 'his'] enemies . . ." (22:17).

The oracle seems to tap a body of tradition preoccupied with a type of historical rupture in Israel's earliest life—one in which, perhaps, parents and children were set at odds, in which divinely mandated action yielded up morally questionable acts, and in which the pacific bonds of historical "promise" and human covenants, in the highly balkanized region that was Canaan, were temporarily overturned in favor of a more retributive covenant, a more partisan conflict, a more warlike destiny.[63] It is not especially surprising that the bellicose oracle of 22:17 (the first such oracle that directly implicates Abraham's descendants through Isaac)[64] should surface in the Akedah story. There is no more apt metaphor for the ravages of war than a parent's sacrifice of a child. Here we may take into account an important pretextual factor. From the standpoint of traditionary discourse, the future nation (or nations) prophesied throughout the cycle loses its oracular innocence, so to speak, only here, at the moment that Abraham has lost his biographical innocence. The coincidence seems more than fortuitous. It shows the manner in which traditionary voices are carefully orchestrated within the text. It matters not whether the oracle alludes to conflicts in the eras of the Exodus, the conquest, or the monarchy—though the second seems the likeliest; the adjoining eras are not far out of view. More important is the function of the oracle in the cycle. Picking up resonances from the center of the palistrophe, fgXg'f' (the only other place in the symmetrical structure where the upheaval of nations is suggested), the oracle in 22:17 makes explicit what had hitherto been only implicit: that the future Israel will itself help the hand of destiny through its wars of conquest—which, remembering "the iniquity of the Amorite," we must understand at least partly as partisan and religious conflict. To understand this pattern better, we will examine in more detail the core gXg'.

The Two Covenants, and the Paradox of Hagar

If the cycle is perceived by its reader as symmetrical, that perception would begin, however faintly, with the first major narrative repetition, namely g′, the second "covenant" episode. The two covenant episodes (chapters 15 and 17) arguably resemble prophetic "call" narratives, along lines analyzed for other texts by Habel, Richter, Zimmerli, and, most recently in *Prooftexts*, Uriel Simon,[65] who have identified such features of the genre as introductory word, commissioning, hesitation or objection, reassurance, and sign—all of which, with some variation, apply to Abraham's interactions with God in these chapters.[66] There are actually three such narratives, if we count the angelic theophany at Mamre in chapter 18—a highly original variant that still preserves classic "call" features—but only the first two contain the terminology and rituals of covenant. In the actual sequence f→f′, the reader's sense of symmetry is artfully delayed by a succession of thematic echoes incidental to the cycle's symmetry: 18:1–15 and 16–33 share elements of the "call" genre; chapter 19 echoes the hospitality motif of chapter 18, while continuing the Sodom theme begun in 18:16ff. (19:29 explicitly alludes to the debate on Sodom begun in 18:16ff.: "God was mindful of Abraham, and removed Lot from the midst of the upheaval"); and Lot's dispossession from the land he chose, and the desperate and demoralized aftermath in Zoar (19:30–38), echo the fate of Hagar and Ishmael: less favored kin and household are consigned to live as a border people, where their behavior descends to a norm repugnant to Israelite sensibilities (cf. 16:12: "[Ishmael] will be a wild ass of a man; his hand against everyone, and everyone's hand against him"). It is only by hindsight that the reader can see the totality of 18:1–19:38 as a single episode, matching the earlier Sodom episode of chapter 14. This delay in the cycle's closure, or masking of it, is especially important to our understanding of symmetry in a biblical narrative cycle: symmetry is not a straitjacket, not a blindly pursued aesthetic norm, and rarely an exclusive formal element in the composition. Like a musical *ostinato*, it creates a kind of trelliswork, into which is woven a more dynamic progression of narrative events.

The two covenants, at any rate, seem clearly parallel. Biblical source criticism has understood these episodes to represent the JE and the P versions, respectively, of the Abrahamic covenant.[67] But the oracles themselves suggest a different dichotomy: in 15:13ff., the Exodus is foreseen, and the conquest in the days of Joshua; retributive justice and a cycle of iniquity seem to supply the motive force of divine action; in 17:1ff., the cultic rite of circumcision is the focus, and it is closely linked with motifs of fertility (2, 4, 5, 6, 16, 20), royalty (6, 15–16, 20), an "everlasting" covenant (7, 9, 12, 13, 19), and Israel's "everlasting" possession of the land (8). These oracles imply a time of wealth and even slave owning in Israel (13). Their cosmopolitan vision stresses consanguinity in Abraham of a multitude of peoples (5, 6, 16); a spirit of generosity toward Ishmael; and memory of his inclusion in the covenant of circumcision; and, in general, a sense of Israel as a people blossoming in unbroken prosperity and tranquility in a region bountiful enough to sustain all, under the divine protection presumably guaranteed by cultic propriety. To be sure, fertility and cultic rite are present in the first covenant (15:5, 9–12, 17), and displacement of Canaan is suggested in the second (17:8), but the overall difference in emphasis is undeniable and quite striking.[68] We have essentially the same contrast outlined earlier: between a conditional and an unconditional sense of Israel's tenure—and here one might add: between a confederate and a royal polity.

Between the covenants is suspended—indeed, enigmatically—the expulsion of Hagar. On the face of it, Hagar seems a potential embarrassment to both covenants. The unspecific promise of seed, in 15:5, certainly includes Ishmael, and the promised heir in 15:4 *could* be Ishmael. Similarly, chapter 17, while granting Isaac the more favored status (implicit in the form of prophetic dialogue in verses 15–22, where Isaac is mentioned on God's initiative, Ishmael on Abraham's), speaks about Ishmael quite benignly, clearly viewing him as a sharer in the covenant of circumcision, and bearer of a kindred duodecimal tribal structure, and thus as kin to Abraham in a deep sense. If this reflects well on his bearer, then Hagar is, by one way of reckoning, seen favorably, even in the context of her officially subordinate status to Sarah. But it is precisely there that the problem represented by Hagar acquires a new dimension.

For Hagar is an Egyptian. Abraham's contact with Egypt in the first "wife-sister" episode (12:10–20) made clear the vulnerability of Abraham's domestic and familial structure to Pharaoh's manipulations, and yet in chapter 16, the situation is reversed: an Egyptian is subordinate to an ancestor of Israel. Were it not for her rebellion against the plan, her child would have been hers to present to her *mistress* for adoption as her own (16:2: "so that I might be built up [or 'enchilded'] through her"). This ravaging of Hagar's own kinship rights is pointedly analogous to the narrowly averted exploitation of Abraham's family by Pharaoh in chapter 12. Indeed, in the light of 15:13 ("Know indeed [*yadoaʿ tedaʿ*] that your seed will be a sojourner in an alien land whom they will serve; [their oppressors] will afflict them 400 years . . ."), the situation of Hagar in chapter 16 is clearly part of a delicately balanced causal scheme reaching back to the first Egyptian sojourn and forward to the second. Hagar's position at the end of 16 must be seen as a qualified but hard-won victory: Sarah's symbolic motherhood of Ishmael is *not* recognized, even as Hagar's servitude to Sarah is affirmed. Ishmael will become a people apart, volatile and treacherous to all, yet used by all, maintaining marital and trade ties with Egypt and sufficient commercial contact with Canaan to traffic in the captive Joseph (37:28)—and so, indirectly, agent in the future Israel's descent to Egypt.[69] In turn, implicit punishment is visited on Abraham's descendents (a punishment "to the fourth generation" stated in principle in Ex. 20:5 and 34:8) for the callousness toward Hagar and her offspring manifested in complicity by Abraham and Sarah in chapters 16 and 21, albeit with apparent divine validation (16:9 and 21:12). If God is later to harden Pharaoh's heart (Ex. 10:1), he has first hardened the hearts of Abraham and Sarah—who, as servant masters in their own right, try to borrow the baby of an Egyptian subordinate, as Pharaoh's daughter in Ex. 2:9ff. is to borrow that of an Israelite subordinate. This complicated web of moral compromise and reciprocal political vicissitude[70] makes clear the relation of Gen. 16 both to the Egyptian episode in chapter 12 and to the Egyptian sojourn oracle in chapter 15. The placement of the Hagar episode between the two Abrahamic covenants, and at the center of the Abrahamic palistrophe, is thus less enigmatic than it initially seemed, even if its historiosophic symmetries are a bit convoluted.

It is ironic that the episode in which Ishmael's kinship to Abraham (and Israel) and independent greatness as a people is most affirmed, chapter 17, is one whose oracles most self-consciously portray a royalized Israel, a stratified and slave-owning society, prefigured in the wealth and entourage of Abraham. Ishmael, with his Egyptian affinities, would understandably be seen in a more favorable light in the more "Egyptianized" social context of early monarchic Israel (the source of chapter 17's *traditions* about Abraham and Ishmael, whatever its literary history).[71] But in the larger setting of 12–25, this Egyptianization of Abraham is deeply rooted in his close affinity to Sarah first defined in chapter 12—in the very tale that most clearly articulated the ancestral couple's *separateness* from Egypt, and their at least metaphorically endogamous bond. There, the Egyptian urban environment was seen as an erosive force on the cultural and tribal solidarity of foreign residents, as, indeed, it is quite forcefully portrayed in Ex. 1–2.[72] The survival of Abraham's nuclear household in Gen. 12 carries with it a chain of consequences that reveal the steady contraction of Abraham's chief loyalties to his kinspouse Sarah alone—the culminating matter being his actual expulsion, abrupt and ungenerous at that, of Hagar and Ishmael, in chapter 21. Abraham's choice for kin against Egyptian servant is likewise a *class* loyalty, and so, in a sense, "Egyptian," though without the courtliness of Pharaoh in 12:20. Chapter 22 carries the theme a step further by showing the simultaneous "Hagarizing" and "Canaanizing" of Abraham—his exile with a seemingly doomed child, and his offering of the child on an Amorite mountain. Yet, however inverted or grotesque these cultural paradoxes become, they are consistently shown to stem from a miraculous and otherwise favorably viewed process in Abraham's household: the birth of a son by a kindred wife—a child of old age, announced by divine prophecy, and surviving past weaning (21:8). The cumulative argument in this array of traditions and literary elaborations affirms, it seems, the divine and historical necessity of Isaac's election and Ishmael's expulsion; but it is a clouded destiny, one that has the outer contours for Abraham of a fall from idyll. The dark "knowledge" vouchsafed to Abraham at the end of chapter 15 is echoed in his own life in two ways: (a) by the strife within his inner household; (b) by his offering of the favored son, with bellicose associations evoked in oracle. In this manner, a considerable range of Israel's later history is embraced, in which the human costs, for better or for worse, of Isaac's election are to become evident. For all of his idyllic dealings in Canaan, Abraham does not emerge unscathed, either personally or eponymously.

Looked at in the context of the primeval history (Gen. 1–11), and especially of the Garden story (2–3), this is a quite ordinary human fortune, one rooted in the life-cycle itself, both of an individual and of a people. It is perhaps a pessimistic view of human nature, but one coupled with a recognition of God's rule, and with an impartial affirmation of the distinction between good and evil. And since it is firmly grounded in an awareness of human mortality, and sees in generational continuity alone a kind of qualified immortality, it shows how each generation must live with a merely partial view of its own history—all else is a matter of faith, but a faith tested even as to its own moral purpose. One implication of the foregoing analysis, at any rate, is clear: the Abraham cycle cannot be seen in isolation from what comes before it and after it, nor is the Abrahamic covenant one different in nature from that formed in the book of Exodus—however different a tradition history the two bodies of material may have had.[73] The trials of Israel's confederate history, and the cycles of retributive justice that underlie it, are as present in the Abraham cycle as the glories of her monarchic history—indeed, the corruptions of monarchic society are there, as well, along with their consequences. This darker vision of Abraham's destiny is not merely effected by the affixing of an "Elohistic" appendix, with its allegedly "northern" and "confederate" perspective. On the contrary, the pattern can be seen to be inherent in the structure of the cycle as a whole, which, with its Egyptian and Sodom sequences, I have here shown to contain all of the relevant moral and theological polarities of Israel's later history, and of the world's earlier history. Abraham and his child through Sarah are granted no blessings or preeminence that are not paid for by the blood, sweat, and tears—and corruption—of their later descendants, for all of which there is significant foreshadowing in even the first ancestors' generation: a descent to Egypt; pressures toward familial attrition; a military clash with Assyria; adoption of the Egyptian practice of slavery and oppression; exile of a household member and kin; prophecies of royal rule; fraternal strife; dynastic struggle, waged by rival wives; acquisition of wealth and worldly power; famine and disease; economic competition; divine destruction of sinful communities. If a kind of "eminent domain" is asserted for Abraham and Isaac (and so, for Israel), it carries full "knowledge of good and evil," and from the Nile to the Euphrates (Gen. 15:18), there is plenty of both.

The Etiological Argument and the Core Problem

In most discussion of symmetry in biblical narrative, it is not sufficiently appreciated that a symmetrical framework is also a parenthetic one— built from the periphery inward, and expressing a series of interlocking etiological explanations, whereby each successive layer answers a question or problem established by the one surrounding it:

a/a' shows the genealogical continuity of the line of Nahor that will lead eventually to the people Israel.

b/b' explains how this continuity was maintained despite the migration of Abraham: when the time was ripe, a bride was secured from among the kin left behind in the Syrian homeland.

c/c' shows where the migration led, how altars were built as destined sites in the promised land, and how the land was decisively promised at those sites, and its first parcels acquired, along with promises of an inheriting progeny who would occupy the land.

d/d' clarifies the relation of the ancestral father to the ancestral mother, and recounts their miraculous rescue from situations that almost prevented the destined progeny from emerging.

e/e' shows Abraham severing from a "horizontal" kin allegiance (Lot) that would endanger both his hold on the land and the clarity of a line of succession, and, conversely, establishing allegiances with non-kin that will further secure his hold on the land. This step, however, throws into relief the absence of a *specific* heir in the vertical line.

f/f' traces the fate of the kin who departed, and introduces another aspect to Abraham's occupation of the land: that, in addition to human agreements necessary for the acquisition, there is a moral factor—those unworthy are displaced by the hand of God.

g/g′   clarifies, through the "promise" dialogues, the specific intentions of God, regarding Abraham's heir and the exact pattern of
the future progeny's acquisition of the land: they will not fully
occupy it until "the iniquity of the Amorite . . . is complete," and
they will, in the interim, sojourn "in a land not their own."
Ironically, because of Abraham's wealth and retinue, his household already resembles (in g′) the stratified and slave-owning
societies his heirs will displace.

While "development" of a sort can be said to occur between the first
and the second member of each layer, and certainly between the outermost and the innermost layer, the pattern as a whole seems static and
tautological. Its function is to frame and focus the core problem, namely,
the question of Abraham's inheriting progeny, comprising the thematic
complex I have labeled X, Y, and Z. Only this latter complex concerns
itself exclusively with Abraham's domestic life, and it is here that a
different kind of development asserts itself, both structurally and thematically—though it is one carefully prepared by the surrounding
framework, and standing over against it in a delicate orchestral balance.
Originating at the core of the symmetry (X), the domestic complex soon
proceeds somewhat at odds with it (Y interrupts it; Z partly overlaps it),
unfolding the succession conflict at the heart of Abraham's household,
and introducing a moral failing in Abraham that clouds the destiny of his
heirs, and clarifies why the Egyptian sojourn to come would be necessary.

This analysis sheds light on the question raised at the beginning of this
chapter: Is Gen. 12–25 primarily *story* or *cycle?* It is clear from the
foregoing discussion that it is both: that the symmetrical array of traditions forms, quite literally, a "cycle," against the background of which
arises a gracefully asymmetrical thematic signature that carries the principal weight of the "story," namely, the story of Abraham's volatile
household as it is affected by Abraham's unfolding destiny in the promised land. It is clear that the deep interdependence of "story" and "cycle"
makes it impossible to speak of the one concept in isolation from the
other, except insofar as each serves a distinct function within the text as a
whole. All elements, both of story and of cycle, combine to mediate the
paradox of an inheritance that is simultaneously a dispossession—a
matter on which I will address some concluding remarks.

Abraham in Genesis; Genesis in Abraham

The foregoing study has, I hope, made clear that the arrangement and
interplay of stories in the Abraham cycle are wrought with great preci-

sion, literary subtlety, and exegetical consequence. The cycle's flexible symmetry allows an elaborate, polyparenthetic discourse, busily etiological on one plane, and single-mindedly narrative on another. This is a type of communication midway between storytelling and traditionary gnosis. The cycle's progression from simple to complex suggests an effort to represent the history of discourse about Abraham, from oral to written, from archival to novelistic. Abraham is presented in a curiously double subjective function: as one who *learns* of his descendants' future, and as one who *portrays* it.[74] Each new oracle is progressively more weighted with the burdens of historical existence, and as Abraham is made privy to them, his familial and personal fortunes begin to take on shadows. The cycle's innermost term, like that of Gen. 2–3, has the character of a transgression. As in the Garden story, the process is initiated by a woman. The language of the two passages is strikingly similar (". . . took . . . and gave to . . . her husband . . . and he . . ."):

> wattiqqaḥ Sarai 'eshet 'Avram 'et Hagar hammiẓrit shifḥatah mikeẓ 'eser shanim leshevet 'Avram be 'ereẓ Cana'an wattitten 'otah le'Avram 'ishah, lo le 'ishah, wayyavo' 'el-Hagar . . .

> Sarah, Abram's wife took Hagar the Egyptian, her servant woman, at the end of ten years of Abram's dwelling in the land of Canaan, and gave her to Abram her husband, his as a wife, and he cohabited with Hagar . . . (Gen. 16:3–4)

> wattiqqaḥ mippiryo watto'khal, wattitten gam le'ishah wayyo'khal.

> She took from its fruit and she ate, and she gave also to her husband, and he ate. (Gen. 3:6)

Other reverberations suggest themselves, as well: "Abram listened to Sarai's voice . . ." (16:2); "Listen to her voice . . ." (21:12); "Because you listened to your wife's voice . . ." (3:17). But what, in the Abraham cycle, is the action at issue? Indeed, what is it in the Garden story? Disobedience of a divine command? Inauguration of a chain of events leading to offspring? Or aspiration to a higher rank? The multiple etiological function of the story allows it to be all three. In the Abraham cycle, we may state the dimensions of the problem confronting Sarah and Abraham in less abstract terms, and here we must try to enter into the motivation of Sarah at the moment of her decision to mother a baby by proxy. It is "at the end of ten years of Abram's dwelling in the land of Canaan." Sarah, from the perspective of her social world, has reasons to be anxious at this natural time of taking stock, for she has not given birth. She is no doubt privy to the information revealed to Abraham, namely that one of his own loins will succeed him, but the identity of the mother has not been specified. Her age is well past childbearing, by any normal reckoning, so her subterfuge is perhaps an honest bid for a qualified motherhood, courageous in its swallowing of pride, yet prideful in its legal and class hubris. For it is a highly problematic action she proposes, a questionable and exploitative legal fiction, predicated on the availability of a servant whose own parental rights will be severely circumscribed.

Almost from the start, the plan goes wrong. The servant—serving a household perhaps unused to postures of mastery—easily rebels, and Sarah is driven to acts of oppression that complicate her error still further. Not only are Hagar's mother-rights affirmed, but she remains in the household as a long-term thorn in Sarah's side, and a threat to Sarah's preeminence. Abraham, meanwhile, is haunted by the presence of Ishmael, and twice he pleads on his behalf. As the proposed expedient union is, from the start, a compromise for both Sarah and Hagar, it is one for Abraham, as well. He will eventually make clear (24:3–5) the importance of a kindred wife, such as Sarah is to him (20:12), but he will stress, even so, the importance of Isaac's dwelling away from the ancestral homeland (24:8). Sarah's choice to affect the legal fictions of a slave society is based on an unwarranted, if seemingly necessary, despair in her own capacity for natural motherhood, and is a "descent to Egypt" every bit as analogous as Abraham's actual descent there by constraint of famine. But Abraham's complicity in this second descent is a descent for himself as well, and his primary loyalty to Sarah, both in accepting Hagar and in repudiating her, leads him to complicate his error by giving a free hand to Sarah to oppress Hagar.

At that moment, perhaps, Abraham makes a critical decision, for which no divine voice has yet prepared him: to forgo his one tangible chance at parenthood on the expectation of a child through Sarah. While it is an act of faith quite characteristic of Abraham, and a repudiation of an Egyptian near-spouse in harmony with the ending of chapter 12, its effect is to inflict hardships on a servant. If a later Israel will be admonished to remember that they were slaves in the land of Egypt,[75] Abraham's actions reflect a forgetting that they *will* be there. For this carelessness, a child will be born whose descendants will, as it were, serve the extradition papers.

Like the Garden story, the Abraham cycle must be seen in its genealogical context. The former story traced the evolution of the first human generation, suspended, as it were, between Creation and procreation. The story itself could be thought of as a genealogical digression, tracing the shifts in domestic protocol surrounding the production of the offspring that would soon become a genealogical statistic. As such, the story is quite naturally preoccupied with the turning of the phases of the life-cycle, the evolution of the primordial pair from parental to conjugal to parental household. Abraham and Sarah follow the same path. I have shown in chapter 1 that in the Garden story, the main boundaries of the primordial couple's "paradisic" life are marked out by the use of the word *'ish* ("man") for the story's male protagonist, and that this usage coincides with that period of the human life-cycle when one is neither child nor parent, neither part of one's parental household nor yet the founder of one's own. With such founding come the first intimations of mortality. *'Ish* becomes *'adam.*

Abraham, significantly, only becomes an active character at the moment of the command to leave his father's house in 12:1ff., and ceases to be one only after founding a lineage and securing burial land. (Just as return to the ground is a key motif in the Garden story, so it is in Gen. 23). The large age leap in 24:1ff. and Abraham's drastic withdrawal from the narrative limelight must be seen in this context. Abraham's prosperity, good fortune, and, miraculously, fertility do not wane (25:1ff.), but clearly his most active years were prior to the birth of Isaac, and he recedes from the eye of history, back into genealogy, once Isaac's survival is assured. *'Ish* becomes *'adam.*

Other parallels with the Garden story are at the level of motivic echo: Sarah, like the first woman, is a "sister" wife. The two covenants, one with its motif of "knowledge" of future evils, the other with its motifs of everlasting life in the promised land, bear an uncanny relation to the two trees of the Garden story—Tree of Knowledge of Good and Evil, and Tree of Life. Abraham, like the first human being, begins his active career repudiating the kin of his place of origin (Gen. 2:18–24||12:1ff.), and ends it by resuming his tie with his ancestral lineage (3:19–21||24:1ff.). If we extend the borders of the Garden story into Gen. 4, we find that each patriarch in Genesis recapitulates the major lines of the primordial story: experiences radical severance from kin; experiences collaboration and scandal with a closely kindred wife; acquiesces in the advancement of one child over another; witnesses the exile of a child; experiences a first taste of mortality through the presumed death of a child.[76]

Throughout the Abraham cycle, Abraham is shown severing from kin and household in more than one way: leaving his father's house, temporarily losing his kindred wife to a foreign king, expelling Hagar and Ishmael, offering up Isaac, burying Sarah. Erosion of the family seems a constant process and constant threat. All of this occurs before there is even a family lineage to speak of at all. Abraham, after all, is not the parent of Israel per se, but the grandparent of the eponymous ancestor, and the great-grandparent of the tribes. Jacob's fecundity, and that of his descendants, is not shared by Abraham or Isaac. That "innumerable" descendants should spring from but a single child whose survival and succession remain in doubt throughout the cycle is sufficient to make the later Israel aware of their extreme contingency as a people. This brings the "progeny" theme of the cycle into close harmony with the "land" theme: Israel's title to existence and her title to the land are contingent upon one and the same factor: continued worthiness (like all other nations) in the sight of God. "Is this not a brand plucked from fire?" (Zech. 3:2).

Meanwhile, *each* generation, in the light of its handicaps and hazards, is made to seem a miracle. There is, one might say, a "vertical" and a "horizontal" dimension to procreation. In the "vertical" dimension, parents pass on their substance to the next generation and are assured the continuity and survival of the lineage; in the "horizontal" dimension, parents must witness or mediate, often haphazardly, the struggles and unequal distribution of virtues among the children, turbulence that embroils the parents themselves, and may, at times, even set a parent into mortal conflict with a child. With the exception of the time of Egyptian slavery, when Israel's procreative power seems to have been at a peak, the very begetting of children either presupposes or signals significant changes in the class and material status of the parents that constitute, at some level, a moral compromise. That this compromise is often unforeseeable or unavoidable makes of procreation a kind of originary sin, though not "Original Sin," in any metaphysical sense. The Hebrew Bible's means of retaining a critical perspective on human morality while championing and celebrating the survival of the people Israel is to keep strict accounting of the failings of Israel's progenitors, while silently maintaining an elaborate system of *quid pro quo* justice, in which the sins of the parents are visited on the children "to the third and fourth generation"[77]—a karmic arithmetic whose main practical effect is to cloud *every* generation's life and chance at life, but whose terms do not, in themselves, amount to certain or immediate extinction as a people. Indeed, its workings more often resemble ordinary life.

In this manner, the Abraham cycle allows personal and national destiny to mirror each other. But between them operates a third type of destiny, political in nature. Abraham's political destiny resembles that of the "new man," a type ubiquitous to world history from ancient times to the present, best known to Western culture from certain key junctures in that history: Alexander's Orient, late republican Rome, Jacobean England, prerevolutionary France, America, and Russia. Writing of the eve of the English revolution, Michael Walzer shows "a movement away from . . . familial ties and from the forms of authority that it imposed . . . [and] from the patriarchal to the conjugal family. This transformation in the nature of family connections parallels and supports the rise of secular political sovereignty."[78] The Bible, on the other hand, carries the process further:

for it is the destiny of the "new man" to become old. The advent of both personal and political senescence is a phenomenon on which the biblical narrative lavishes the bulk of its attention. Abraham's political senescence is surprisingly benign, as, indeed, is the case throughout Gen. 12–50, which, curiously, is an idyll only at the political level. The gracious foreigners of Genesis behave with uncommonly fair and courteous demeanor toward the ancestors of Israel, as the latter settle among them and entwine their lives with their lands, and even estranged kin sportingly find their niches in the social ecology of greater Canaan. These bonds of interdependence go sour beyond the third generation, and even the third (Jacob's) has ills not previously experienced.

This is not "salvation history" (*Heilsgeschichte*), in the sense envisaged by much contemporary biblical scholarship, but simply history. Given the certain link between the fault within and the enemy without, each generation's life is a delicate balancing act. "Not because you are the most numerous of all peoples has the LORD your God desired you and chosen you, for you are the merest of all peoples" (Deut. 7:7). All the more remarkable, then, is the establishment of a *culture* with generational continuity. For only in continuity can there be survival, and thus only in continuity can there be "innumerability" (Gen. 15:5). In a responsum on the apparent paradox of a decimated people that is also innumerable, Saadya Gaon[79] makes clear this temporal extensibility of the Israelite commonwealth:

ולא יכחישו זה את זה שני הכתובים.
כי בניו המעט בעיני נפשם ומספרם ככוכבים,
ואם כמה פעמים היו קצותם נחשבים.
אבל כלם לא נספרו משלם ולא נכתבים.

These two verses [Gen. 15:5 and Deut. 7:7] should not contradict, for [Abraham's] children, seeing themselves as few, yet number as the stars. And if, at times, their census has been reckoned [lit. "their extremities considered"], yet the whole of them were never numbered totally, nor written down.

·III·

DAVID WITHOUT DIAGRAMS: BEYOND STRUCTURE IN THE DAVIDIC HISTORY

LEAR: Meantime, we shall express our darker purpose. . . .
King Lear I, i, 37

Of all the literary estimations by historians of the court history of King David, Julius Wellhausen's is one of the briefest and most engaging. He speaks, in his famous *Prolegomena,* of a narrative in which events are "faithfully reported, and the palace intrigue which placed Solomon upon the throne is narrated with a naiveté which is almost malicious."[1] Historical verisimilitude and literary artfulness are by no means synonymous or even complementary capabilities, but their marriage has been a more or less consistent theme in modern characterizations of the story, in investigations of a historical or source-historical type:[2]

> ... the creation of a genuine historian, who conceals rather than reveals his historical purpose, especially by his expert handling of a narrative style based on that of the saga in the arrangement of the individual scenes. ... In this literary account there is reflected a tremendous heightening of the historical conscience of the Israelites. (Alt)

> ... a masterpiece, unsurpassed in historicity, psychological insight, literary style, and dramatic power ... [its] vivid descriptions and characterizations and ... lively dialogues have seldom if ever been surpassed in the literature of mankind. (Pfeiffer)

> ... historical writing ... mature and artistically fully developed to an extent which makes it impossible to envisage further development in this direction. (von Rad)

> ... a composition presented and embellished with great narrative skill, a composition which has in it something of a *good* historical novel. (Eissfeldt)

> For the last years of David we have in the [sc. literarily] matchless "History of the Throne Succession" ... a document with an eyewitness flavor. ... (Bright)

> The presentation of the Court History of David, which is a historical source equal in importance to the narrative of David's rise, has rightly been rated an unequaled masterpiece of ancient Near Eastern historiography. Besides the realistic and true-to-life portrayal of people and events, the artful and dramatic structure of the narrative contributes much to its success. The author was undoubtedly an eyewitness to the events and a member of the royal court. (Sellin/Fohrer)

Wellhausen's bon mot is the freest from superlatives and stereotyped formulations, but perhaps also one in which the contradictory impulses of faith in reportage and deviousness in art seem the uneasiest and most polarized of bedfellows. The remaining expressions, stated with greater or lesser degrees of restraint, blur this polarity by making access to the events and artistry of the representation seem like inevitable partners. The relation, of course, is not as equal as it may seem. The skill in telling, in the long run (once the historians get down to the business of perform-ing *their* craft), is always the adjunct member of the partnership. It is a bonus in the historian's quest, but not an essential component of what he is seeking. It is not credited with any true role in the historical subject's *being* history, only with the power of making this history come alive for posterity, of making it *seem* factual. The relation works precisely because it is *not* seen as essential. The craft of the literary artist is the humble servant of events, not the agent by whose mediation the events were constituted as "events" in the first place.

Yet one senses that the blur already begins with the *Prolegomena* themselves: for there, too, the court history is seen to have "an essentially historical character," one that "affords us a glance into the very heart of the events, showing us the natural occasions and human motives which gave rise to different actions"—such that the artistry of malicious naïveté consists chiefly of the story's presence to the events, its transparence in rendering the occasions and motives of which history (considered as an array of "actions") is made. It is taken for granted that all powers of artistry would be bent toward showing, through a diligently mustered "circumstantiality," what the teller saw, or otherwise *knew,* as one situated close to the "heart" of events.

Various theories have of course multiplied about the identity of the court-history author—as if it were possible to determine the identity of any biblical author, and as if knowing such a fact explained anything more than the text itself explains. The candidates are most often chosen from among named personages in the narrative, or are linked as "par-tisans" to one or another of such figures. Theories such as these can get quite ramified and embracing, as in the work of Hannelis Schulte, for example, where four distinct sources are perceived in I Sam. 9–I Kings 2, the last two of which—the second half of the "Saul-David history" (I Sam. 21–23, 27, 29–30, II Sam. 1–2:8, 5) and the "Davidic history" (II Sam. 2–4, 6, 21, 24, 9–20, I Kings 1–2) are attributed respectively to Abiathar and Jonathan ben Abiathar, members of the ill-starred priestly family of the line of Eli, banned to Anathoth after Solomon's succession.[3] Schulte's study is in other respects a sophisticated and suggestive work, and one cannot say for certain that her hypothesis is *not* correct, any more than one can say that it is. What is not unique about her argument is the assumption she shares with her predecessors that circumstantial detail and "eyewitness flavor" somehow add up to an eyewitness ac-count.[4]

We should note that such studies often rely heavily on linguistic and lexical criteria. Yet to affirm the linguistic datability of sources may create more problems than it solves. Linguistic history itself, for better or for worse, is partly based on accepted views of literary history and is sharply circumscribed by the sparseness of the texts themselves. We simply know too little about biblical Hebrew to use linguistic criteria with any confidence. Linguistic antiquity, in any case, does not in itself establish "eyewitness" origin.[5]

Something in us rebels, to be sure, at the notion that the materials of II Samuel are *not* history. The material seems too specific in factors of personality and locale, too idiosyncratic in its partisan loyalties, not to emanate from circles closely involved with the events. One feels too strongly the obvious impact that David's revolution wrought upon the consciousness of the narration to deny that the Davidic court history has its origin, one way or another, in Davidic court history. Certainly, the Hebrew Bible—by its concern for chronology; its interest in political and military events, in origins and long-range causality, in the growth and elaboration of Israel's national sovereignty, in the wielding of power and the conditions of justice; by its explicit and implicit claim (especially in Deuteronomistic passages) to historical witness; by the realism and sobriety of its narrative style; and above all by its preoccupation with continuity—takes its reported events seriously as history. Between cycles, the Bible moves to ever less symbolic, ever more elaborated modes of representation. We are too indebted to the generosity of the court history's author for the wealth of place-names, personages, and factions the story affords us—amid a Middle Eastern literary and historiographic milieu otherwise dominated by mythical, official, and stereotyped modes of representation—to dismiss lightly the text's "historicity."[6] And certainly, for reasons other than the story's alleged "eyewitness" perspective, as we shall see, it must be understood as a historical *interpretation* of first magnitude.

But the impossibility of establishing the "eyewitness" status of the account remains curiously untroubling to historians, the very persons charged with upholding firm criteria of historical attribution.[7] This is not to say that historians do not take judicious account of the obvious fact that events such as David's adultery with Bathsheba, Amnon's crime against Tamar, or David's testament to Solomon, were not likely to have been "witnessed" events, let alone all witnessed by the writer, let alone by the *same* writer. (Certainly, Thucydides and other historiographic realists in the ancient Mediterranean world were not above inserting type-scenes into their accounts when it suited their purposes. That, in itself, does not compromise their reputations as historians, though we do well to bear in mind an instructive difference between the biblical author and Thucydides: the latter makes sure to proclaim at the outset the nature of his access to the events he will describe; the former apparently senses no such need, but assumes the same neutral, omniscient voice that prevails throughout the Bible.) What remains unexamined, however, is the notion that it is the presence or access of the writer to the events that constitutes what is most significant, interesting, or usable—in short, most "reliable"—about the Davidic court history as a source for modern historiography.

The assumption is, of course, belied by the modern historians themselves when they actually get down to using the source for their discussions: for they do not talk, when at their best, about the influence of the court scandals, of David's tragic chastening, of the play of domestic feuds and intrigues, and the like, upon Israel's early monarchic history. They talk, rather, about institutional relations; about military, diplomatic, and geographical factors; about socioeconomic and class conflict; about structural and political contradictions in tenth-century Israel; about the struggle between confederate and royal ideologies; about the complex and constantly shifting balance of power in the rise of Israel as a state. These are matters about which the biblical account speaks only elliptically and obliquely—if tellingly, nevertheless. To that extent, even the historians view this most historical of biblical narratives to be a sort of allegory—in the sense that it must be decoded for its otherwise very substantial content. In the long run, it seems as if the story's "actions" are the least substantial of its riches, if still invaluable as the point of departure for the rest.

Once one severs the "eyewitness" connection, once one recognizes that it was not necessary to *be* present at the events reported in order to understand and report them, there is theoretically no firm basis for placing the work's time of composition in any one era over another in the next four centuries or so after the events it records.[8] Thomas Mann, after all, did not need to live in ancient Canaan or Egypt in order to retell, in "eyewitness" detail, the story of Joseph and his brothers. And once one severs the "eyewitness" connection, one is talking about a way of representing events (even contemporary events) that is very different from what historians customarily assume when they talk about the court history as a historical account.

Yet it is their view of the material as *literature* that seems most puzzling. After some initial genuflections in homage to the work's literary greatness ("masterwork," "masterpiece," "excellent," "unsurpassed," "unequalled," etc., almost begin to sound like jacket copy), investigators often happily move on to its *historical* substance, without a word about the problems of literary representation that are at stake in any historical interpretation. And the "history" thus mined extends little or no explicit recognition to the text that frames what they see—or *is* what they see. The text has disappeared, or diaphanized, and what stand revealed are "events" (or "actions"). At this level, a certain act of faith is required, not so much faith that the events really happened, but faith that the telling of the events can make them comprehensible, can make them "history." Whether the events are accepted as factual or are taken as a cipher of historical phenomena that are reconstructed according to the hermeneutics of the historian, what usually is not examined is the relationship between the institutional categories wielded by the historian, on the one hand, and the family jealousies and intrigues, the seductions, betrayals, homages, allegiances, personal terrors, omissions, and excesses that make up the conceptual province of the storyteller, on the other. But the failure to raise the question of this relationship is not that of historians alone. The full dimensions of the problem become clearer when one turns from historians' evaluation of the Davidic court history as literature to the evaluation of (or, more often, the refusal to evaluate) the King David narratives as history by literary critics.[9]

Literary study of the Bible these days is all too often identified with "synchronic" approaches, which have all too often been defined by what they are not: source criticism (what *used to* be called "literary criticism"), which is taken as the core concern of a "diachronic" approach. One easily forgets that non-source-critical literary study has its own diachrony: the temporal unfolding of the story, whose configuration of action must be *played* to be fully perceived. This is where so-called literary and synchronic analyses are the most disappointing. They have come to be trapped by their own tools. The charts, statistics, and catalogues that are supposed to provide a way into the story violate its spirit and lead to inconsequential and formalist generalizations, clouding whatever good insights the studies advance (and they do advance them) with a thicket of technical language, textbookish reifications, and numbing efforts at hard science.

This is not to suggest that studies of this sort have no value. On the contrary, such works on the Davidic court history as Charles Conroy's *Absalom, Absalom!—Narrative and Language in 2 Sam. 13–20* and J. P. Fokkelman's *Narrative Art and Poetry in the Books of Samuel* (Volume I),[10] boggish as they sometimes are to read, supply very useful physiognomies of the text. Their authors would seemingly be the first to admit that their discussions could never substitute for a reader's firsthand confrontation with the narrative. They would perhaps like to think of their critical paraphernalia as transparent guidelines to what is, once played out in the reading experience, a set of essentially qualitative contours. But these studies leave us, in the long run, with little more than a set of tautologies. The translation of the story's motions into the vocabulary of a modern technical discipline is a useful exercise, perhaps, for the practitioners of that discipline, but it does little to explain or interpret the story. It simply introduces new complications and superfluities, of a sort for which the biblical text itself is an appropriate Occam's razor. So, when Fokkelman

tells us that this or that occurrence of an event in threes is a manifestation of "the ternary principle" (namely, of the tendency to happen in
threes), one wonders what has been gained for interpretation. Or when
Conroy, speaking of the story's "microcontextual narrative patterns"
(which is to say, things that happen in the story) lists with great sobriety
"the 'command/execution' pattern," "the 'request/granting' pattern,"
"the 'news or message' pattern," and "the 'accusing question/excusing
answer' pattern," together with their various subtypes, useful as these
abstractions sometimes are, one wonders what they can do for our
understanding of the story, when so neatly divorced from character and
context, disassembled, labeled, and shelved. The investigator moves
through the material with the calm certainty of the taxonomist, surrounding everything with the comfortable buzz of a domesticating discourse, but leaving the story essentially untouched.

Now, it is too easy—to borrow a familiar motif from Wordsworth—to
complain that critics "murder to dissect." A frequent corollary of this
complaint is the problematic insistence that criticism be an art rather
than a science, a matter that can never serve as a critical manifesto, since
the status as art usually depends on the specific wielder of the art, and
criticism can, in any case, both *be* an art and, in having (literary) art as its
subject, be something quite other than "Art." No, what is especially
troublesome about studies of the structuralist and "synchronic" persuasion is not their scientism per se, but the ahistorical, apolitical, and
contemplative stance they encourage toward the material. Conroy informs us that the court history is in Northrop Frye's "autumn mode,"
and notes further on that "the pervasive presence of contrast and reversal gives something of [!] a tragic tone to the story"—as if tragedy were
possible in such fractional and half-hearted measure, and as if tragedy
could set down roots in anything other than the most specifically en-
dured political and cultural contradictions, common to the biblical author and at least his initial audience. Fokkelman, who is certainly bolder
than Conroy in his willingness to interpret, still ends up with strikingly
tepid, banal, and overpsychologized conclusions. "Have vengeance and
the callousness that war brings upset David's balance?" he asks, concerning David's crimes against Uriah—to which one might answer: How can
we know? The insight explains nothing of the specifically political and
institutional vertigo that afflicts the king and underlies his action toward
Uriah. Fokkelman largely contents himself with the explanatory categories of Gestalt psychology and various "New Age" disciplines, investing
the story with meanings distinctly foreign to it: "energy," "chakra," "peak
experience," "growth process," and the like. (His use of the term "kar-
ma," on the other hand, may have some merit, provided we remember
that there is no biblical Hebrew equivalent of the word.)

To the credit of both authors, one should say that a bracketing of

historical questioning such as theirs is in itself a commendable procedure. In some sense, it represents a worthwhile and refreshing change
of emphasis. It had, after all, long been respectable in biblical criticism to
see in almost every biblical text the propagandistic angling of one or
another party, sect, or class, or the self-congratulatory contortions of
blind ideologies able only to speak in reflexes. Wouldn't it clear the air to
divest oneself wholly from historical interpretation and simply concentrate on the text as a story—or, without apologizing for the abstraction,
as a "narrative"? The text can't, after all, *avoid* being literature.

But can the synchronic critic avoid the text's being itself an interpretation of some sort of history? Can one do without the political vocabulary
that is the stock-in-trade (but not the monopoly) of the historian? Isn't
the text's meaning *as literature* dependent on the weight and moment of
its deliberations as history? On the bite of a historically informed wit,
whose pungent orchestration of Israel's institutional contradictions is, in
some sense, the core experience for the reader—for elucidation of which
the renunciations, usurpations, resumptions, transfers, and misuses of
power and authority in and around the Davidic court are the key gestures?

Reflection on this matter should help us understand why synchronic
studies of the type discussed here are so profoundly dissatisfying as
literary interpretation, and why the most suggestive and interesting
interpretations of I/II Samuel and I Kings 1–2 (assuming one is not here
comparing apples to oranges) continue to be, not the literary studies, but
rather those of a more explicitly diachronic bent, such as Wellhausen's
inquiries, Alt's "The Origin of the Israelite State," Bright's and Noth's
chapters on the Saul and David eras in their respective histories of
ancient Israel, Cross's chapter on royal ideology in *Canaanite Myth and
Hebrew Epic,* and various other studies of comparable importance. One
feels enriched by these examinations in a way one does not by excessive
diagrams, inventories, and colometry, and one appreciates that these
investigators generally muster the full dignity and proportionality of
essay form in service of their tasks. Somehow, our understanding of the
text as a *story* improves with immersion in its dimensions as *history,*
though, obviously enough, the historians just mentioned were not attempting literary study, in the contemporary sense of the term, and, as
we have seen, their own spotty attention to the connection between story
and history, and between the domestic and public domains of the story,
remains problematic.

Somewhat closer to the mark, perhaps, is David M. Gunn's *The Story of
King David: Genre and Interpretation.*[11] Gunn steers a middle course between a synchronic and a diachronic approach, faulting the historians
for their overemphasis of propagandistic and ideological factors, chal-

lenging the widespread assumption of the story's tenth-century origin, and that of its written origins, stressing instead the presence of folk motifs and oral storytelling patterns (thus, in contrast to the synchronic efforts, remaining involved with factors of the story's origin and transmission, as his chapter on the story's borders especially demonstrates), and, in offering his own interpretation, drawing useful models (though not very useful diagrams) of the interplay of personal and political factors in the story. Gunn, moreover, argues his case with a certain "biblical" economy and sense of proportion. Yet Gunn, too, remains overly aestheticized and contemplative toward his subject. While his chapter on "prevailing views" is a compendium of good sense about the shortcomings of his predecessors (his generally close involvement with the critical literature throughout his work is quite impressive), he seems somewhat less convincing when advancing his own alternative:

> My own suggestion . . . is hardly radical. It simply takes seriously as a major clue to the basic genre of the narrative the one aspect of the work that has commanded the most widespread agreement, namely its quality as a work of art and entertainment. The argument of the previous chapter showed the problems inherent in current classifications of the narrative as history writing, political propaganda or didactic literature. The case for viewing the narrative as a story in the manner of a modern novel or short story (*novella*) remains persuasive. My proposal is that the primary generic classification of the narrative should be as a story in the sense of a work of art and entertainment.[12]

Now, we have already seen what a flimsy edifice the story's literary reputation is (quite aside from its actual literary merits), since the "widespread agreement" about "its quality as a work of art and entertainment" is largely linked to efforts to outsmart or defeat its literary function, in order to arrive at the historical "kernel." But, far from providing a conclusive answer to the question of the story's generic identity, this thesis only raises new questions. It presumes that "art and entertainment" can be neatly divorced from the social, cultural, political, and religious matrix in which they flourish. It tends to sidestep the fact that people learn from their art and entertainment, and the possibility that for an adult, pre-exilic Israelite, this may have been a chief de facto arena of instruction. Those stories memorable enough to sit among the culture's chief classics and sacred texts are not there simply because of their beauty or their power to divert. To put it another way, their beauty and power to divert may stem, in part, from the elegance and force of their power to explain, and from the need of the culture for particular kinds of explanation. This is perhaps recognized by Gunn himself in his earlier discussion of the question of *Tendenz* in the David story:

> To deny that the narrative is a document of political propaganda is not
> to deny any political interest within the narrative. To do so would be
> absurd. . . . Shakespeare's "historical" plays are clearly "political" in
> terms of subject-matter and themes explored, and few in an Eliz-
> abethan audience could have failed to appreciate the undercurrent of
> comment on contemporary political life and institutions; yet they are
> above all *plays*, works of art for the purpose of serious entertainment,
> and least of all are they "propaganda."[13]

Yet even here, in the midst of his well-taken analogy between the biblical
author and Shakespeare, Gunn clings to a belief in the autonomy of art.
It is "the undercurrent of comment on contemporary political life and
institutions" that sends some Shakespearean scholars, quite justifiably, to
the English constitutional histories of Maitland and Elton, as a way into
Henry IV, or *Richard III*, or even *Coriolanus* and *Julius Caesar*. This is not
to suggest that a Tudor or Stuart audience needed to read such histories
in order to understand their poet, only that some members of those
audiences possessed the political and institutional sophistication required to make full sense of Shakespeare's political themes, and that
such understanding was a principal ingredient of the literary delight
they certainly experienced. Gunn makes the political dimensions of the
King David story an incidental bonus in its unfolding as art, just as the
historical investigators of the story made its artistic brilliance an incidental bonus in its unfolding as history. This persistent blind spot shared by
the two disciplines—the absence of a sense of necessary connection
between the story's historical knowledge and its literary modes—is curious and interesting. The connection between the family intrigues of
Israel's leaders—the specific gestures traded between kin—and the
larger history of Israel's moral and political institutions has been, as yet,
insufficiently explored.

As for source criticism, there is a persistent and curious contradiction
that prevails in the critical discourse about the Davidic court history. On
the one hand, there is widespread agreement that a tenth-century source
underlies at least some of the history.[14] On the other hand, there is
widespread disagreement about the borders of that source, and, as such,
little unanimity about its exact form and message.[15] Even Leonhard
Rost, whose study gave authoritative expression to the notion of a "Succession Document," had found the need to see the alleged document as
something other than a continuous account. Though the document
extended into I Kings 1–2, it did not include II Sam. 21–24, but must
surely have included the story of Michal's childlessness in II Sam. 6, since
this crisis of the inability of the houses of David and Saul to merge was
for Rost the conceptual underpinning and point of departure for the

whole "Succession" theme.[16] Rost's study did not provide a comprehensive study of the sources of I/II Samuel, but instead focused only on the traditionary complexes dealing with the Ark, the Ammonite war, and the Davidic monarchy and its succession. The story of the house of Eli, the account of the founding of the monarchy, the story of the house of Saul, and that of the rise of David are not examined, which may weaken a bit Rost's argument, since the "Succession" history, which seems so distinctive next to the folkloristic "Ark" narratives, seems far less so next to the omitted materials. Still, Rost's analysis is substantial enough to imply a complicated pattern of traditionary accretion and infixing, at least some of which, in Rost's view, may have been undertaken by the "Succession" author himself. This entails (though neither Rost nor his successors have made this explicit) a pattern of internal exegesis, whereby texts that on stylistic or other grounds are wholly unrelated are made to stand in a certain affinity, such that their juxtaposition rereads (or, to use the revisionary language of Harold Bloom, "misreads") one or another of the texts so assembled, so as to supply some new angle to the larger story being related.

This is a reasonable enough principle by which to understand the interrelation of the Bible's heterogeneous sources, since it is unlikely that the sources would have come together in the first place if there were not some basis, narrative or otherwise, for relating them. Indeed, the persistent intercutting of narrative with genealogical, archival, cultic, legal, etiological, proverbial, poetic, and prophetic data—always in ways that underscore the development of the narrative themes—is a hallmark of biblical style, and there is no reason why we should expect I/II Samuel to behave any differently from the norm. The problems arise when a critic attempts to determine which texts are the "leaders" in the process, and which are the "followers." Is a folkloric or archival fragment infixed to a narrative cycle by the narrative author, or is it an addendum by a later editor or redactor, humbly annotating what is, by then, an ancient and venerable story with a long history of transmission? Here, we find ourselves in an area of decision where caprice and fashion tend to rule, and where, given the text's two-dimensionality, firm conclusions—that is, conclusions able to survive the erosions of further critical fashions—are unlikely. Much depends on what we decide is the principal thrust or meaning of the narrative cycle we examine. Whereas for Rost, it was the question: "Who shall sit on the throne of David?" for some of his successors, it could be alternatively defined, such that the "Succession" narrative, in recent years, has tended to go by more neutral aliases. We may speak of the monarchic history (I Sam. 8–II Kings 25), the Saul cycle (I Sam. 9–14 et al.), the history of David's rise (ibid., 16–26 et al.), the Davidic history (ibid., 16–I Kings 2), the court history (II Sam. 2–I

Kings 2), and of course "I/II Samuel." If a certain consensus prevails on where the court history ends (I Kings 2:46: " . . . and the kingdom was secured in the hand of Solomon"), the story's beginning has been allowed to slide back and forth (Conroy places it at II Sam. 13, Fokkelman at II Sam. 9, Rost at II Sam. 6, Schulte and Gunn at II Sam. 2–4).

Paradoxically, the synchronic studies have tended to get drawn back into diachronic concerns precisely where they search for the entity that is to be considered as a synchronic whole. Every selection of material entails a rejection of other material, and the rejection all too often implies a judgment as to the extraneousness of what is excluded. Such judgment has one of four possible foundations: either it rests on some previously established diachronic criticism; or it rests on a diachronic hypothesis newly advanced by the synchronic critic; or the excluded material's relation to the whole is simply not understood (a fact seldom admitted); or the excluded material is deemed *possibly* relevant to an understanding of the whole, but, for reasons of the space and format of the study itself, must be excluded from view. Now, every analyst is vulnerable to being superseded on the grounds that the material he or she selects is incomplete. Obviously, different readings of the King David story are possible, depending on whether we read it by itself (or through some smaller component of it), or as part of the book of II Samuel, the complex of I/II Samuel, the Septuagint's "Book of Kingdoms" (comprising our I/II Samuel, I/II Kings), the Masoretic text's "Former Prophets" (Joshua–Kings), the alleged Deuteronomistic history (Deuteronomy–Kings), the whole continuous narrative corpus Genesis–Kings, the canonical Hebrew Bible, or the canonical Christian Bible. We should accept this as a fact of life, and recognize that the large corpora seem deliberately structured on a principle of open-ended textual interface: each seemingly self-contained intermediate member has both a prefatory and culminatory function. Despite the occasional abruptness of transitions, and despite the post-biblical division into books and lections, the progression of time is essentially continuous. Yet the changes in narrative scope and focus create a relentlessly self-transcending structure, built partly out of materials that themselves encouraged a pattern of transcending misreadings. In such a way, each major unit is both an addition to the whole and a microcosm of it.

The fact that different totalizations of biblical material are possible should discourage efforts, such as Fokkelman's, to disavow source criticism and simultaneously to claim one is offering "a full interpretation" of material that is treated, for all practical purposes, like a source within a wider collection of sources—any *"full* interpretation," after all, would have to account for its larger meaning in whatever redactional or canonical structure the analyst happens to recognize as lying beyond its borders. But even assuming that, once one faces up to the partialness of one's scope, a certain measure of completeness is possible with the restricted material chosen for interpretation, one still faces curiously diminishing returns upon the expanding space of one's interpretation. Fokkelman, for one, seems to confuse "a full interpretation" with belabored colon-by-colon and scene-by-scene analysis. It is not the totality of one's interpretation that matters, but the consequentiality. One can perhaps accomplish more with selective sallies into isolated moments and junctures in the text, or by a reading that deliberately distributes its attention across seemingly noncomparable domains of textual lattice, including intrabiblical networks of symbolism and typology, and postbiblical networks of commentary and exegesis, both predmodern and modern.

The Present Approach

At this point, it is necessary to explain the plan of exposition undertaken in the following pages. The task here will be to explore the King David story (and the closely associated complexes of Davidic tradition) without the aid of lists and diagrams, without any learned shifters of academic prose that might supply illusory notions about the unity or totality of the subject, and without any structural or interpretive generalizations that cannot be stated mostly in plain English and in essay cadences. Without necessarily imitating the biblical text, we should try to discuss it in ways that do not stand in the way of the literary experiences it embodies. Accordingly, I propose a series of short, interlocking essays, each seeking to pinpoint some moment in the institutional history of ancient Israel brought to bear in the narrative action or dialogue. We will in particular try to see how the contrast between a confederate and a monarchic standard is evident in the interaction of the story's characters, or how, in the clash and interplay of the two standards, certain institutional contradictions reveal themselves. In pursuing this plan of discussion, I will try to show how the categories wielded by our contemporary historians are, in some sense, shaped by the literary devices of the text itself—how, for example, the very contrast between "confederation" and "kingdom" is a problem for the *storyteller,* and not simply for modern historical exegetes seeking to outsmart the text.

The plan of discussion may initially seem aimless and meandering. It will not examine the court history in chronological sequence but will intercut an unfolding sequence of scenes with examination of scenes from David's earlier career, or with a survey of one or another key word, or with discussion of an individual character, or with exploration of more conceptual issues, or with a look at Psalms or other related materials. In this manner, I will try to show the text in its *plurality* (a notion I borrow from Barthes),[17] that is, in the complex intertwining of a variety of literary and cultural codes, whose modest and experimental unraveling here will, I hope, enable them to show themselves more fully for what they are once *reread* in their proper sequence.

The reader must not expect a complete exposition of every text or topic dealt with in the ensuing pages, nor will we be able to survey in the present study every topic relevant to an understanding of the Davidic history. Though we shall occasionally view the events shown by the text as if they had the solidity of real history, it is not real history that we shall be uncovering here but historical interpretation. One must not, however, expect any generalizations about the structure of the Davidic history analogous to those attempted in the preceding chapters. This is not to imply that such generalizations cannot be made or that structural parallels to the Garden story and the Abraham cycle do not exist (cf. my Epilogue)—rather, that in the light of the excessive and often confusing adumbrations of structure adduced by Fokkelman and others, another type of discussion is in order, in which structure is experienced from *within* the unfolding moments of the text, experienced as reading pressure, as echo, as momentary cadence, as delayed resolution, as contradiction and paradox. For such observations, we do not need charts or statistics, but only the tools of memory, common sense, and, wherever possible, plain speech—the same apparatus that the anonymous ancient author/tradent demanded of his readership, and that remain, whatever the technical advances of scientific scholarship, the most reliable tools of biblical study.

FROM HOUSE TO HOUSE

You turned my lament into dancing,
  You undid my sackcloth and girded me with joy,
  that [my] whole being might sing hymns to You endlessly . . .
                       Ps. 30:12–13 (NJPS)

The duplicity, the manifoldness of "house" begins at least with the expression "indoors/homeward" (*habbaytah*) in the instructions of Philistine diviners to their people in the so-called Ark account (Rost's *Ladeerzählung*) in I Samuel (6:20): the people are to transport the captured Israelite Ark of the Covenant back to the Israelites in a cart drawn by two cows, whose calves are returned "indoors/homeward." The Ark is to be sent, together with certain fetishistic tokens of Philistine appeasement, without a driver, and if the cows' random wandering goes up to Beth-Shemesh (lit. "House of the Sun"), the Philistines will know that the hand of YHWH is behind their misfortunes. And so it occurs: moving "neither to the right nor to the left," their calves having been returned houseward, the cows went, lowing as they walked (or, by another reading of *wyšrnh:* "walking straight"), accompanied by the lords of the Philistines as far as the borders of the House of the Sun. The inhabitants of Beth-Shemesh, receiving the wandering Ark in festal rejoicing, offered the cows as a burnt offering, along with other sacrifices, and the Philistine lords, having viewed the scene from a distance, returned to Ekron. YHWH later struck the people of Beth-Shemesh for having "looked into" the sacred Ark. Whether the offense was one of looking, touching, approaching, challenging, or otherwise unwarrantedly possessing, the Ark had consistently brought disaster to its violators. As a precaution, the Ark was moved again, now to Kiriath-Yearim.

The word "house" (*bayit, bet-*) first appears in the books of Samuel in the expression, in I Sam. 1:17: " . . . whenever she [Hannah] went up to the house of YHWH [at Shilo]. . . ." This usage is repeated at the end of the chapter: " . . . [Hannah] brought him [the young Samuel] to the house of YHWH"—leaving us with a sense of thematic completion: the spot that had been the scene of Hannah's torment at the hands of her rival Peninah now becomes the site of her victorious dedication of her newly weaned son Samuel to the service of YHWH. As Samuel had been foretold at the house of YHWH, so he is inaugurated there in the priestly vocation.

But in what sense can YHWH be said to have a "house"? Does not the song of Hannah that ensues celebrate a deity so ubiquitously mischievous, so unbounded in the scale of his historical interventions, that the conception "YHWH's house" must appear, as it were, as a kind of blasphemy? Truly, "the pillars of the earth are YHWH's"—how, then, a *"house* of YHWH"!

Yet, apparently, "houses of YHWH" are said to have existed in the days before kingship, and the detail is presented in I Sam. 1:7 in a manner and context suggesting that the locale at Shilo had all the marks of stability and venerability that the people of the time would associate with a sacred "house": a sacrificial altar; a perpetual, and apparently hereditary, priestly service; an annual pilgrimage of the populace; and fixed seasons of pilgrim-offering. It is only in the ensuing chapters that qualifications of this picture begin to appear: the priestly family that ministers at the "house of YHWH" is by no means permanently hereditary, and YHWH is not bound to one site. When the sons of Eli sell their beneficences, unjustly exploiting the people and committing other immoralities, YHWH withdraws his favor, leaving this family but a "house" in a narrower sense: a father's-house, a household or kin-grouping that enjoyed purely historical (and so temporary) prominence in YHWH's plan. "Behold, I showed myself to your father's house, when they were in Egypt subject to the house of Pharaoh" (2:27). In the politics of generational succession, the paternal household is but a party, a faction, a sect—whose strength lies partly in the vulnerability and vicissitudes of other houses, and whose fate is eventually many vulnerabilities of its own.

So the "house of YHWH" at Shilo cannot mean, in any strict sense, a shelter *for* YHWH, for those who administer it operate in the shelter *of* YHWH, and the term "house" in this context must be but a convenience for "seat of reign," "place of YHWH's manifestation," "site of pilgrim offerings," or the like—one place among many possible ones, in one era among many. Even when, in 3:3, that site's physical structure is called by the cultic term *hekhal* ("palace, temple," from the Sumerian *e-gal*, "great house"), the unfolding context requires that we understand it as bearing only provisional and relative sacredness in the economy of Israel's worship.

YHWH's words to Eli in 2:30 reveal a divinely centered perspective on the role of the familial "houses" of human beings in YHWH's plan, which we may take as fundamental to the unfolding story of the books of Samuel and Kings: "Truly, I had said, 'Your house and your father's house will walk before me forever,' but now, says YHWH, 'far be it from me! rather, I shall honor those who honor me, and they who scorn me shall be dishonored!'" (cf. Gen. 12:3, Ex. 33:19). Every presiding house begins with the *divine* (!) hope of perpetual divine favor, yet it is the behavior of that house's members that ultimately determines *how* perpetual its preeminence will be—at least, in the theodicy of 2:30.

I Samuel 3 introduces a new angle to our conception of Shilo as a sacred site: the era is one of failing prophecy, and, despite their possession of the ephod of divination (2:28), the household of Eli is not generally privy to the word of YHWH, which "was rare in those days; no vision broke through/appeared aplenty" (3:1). The manifestation of this word to the non-Elide boy Samuel is thus not a product of normal cultic functions but an extraordinary occurrence, and, not surprisingly, it turns out to bear the message of the fall of Eli's house: " . . . I will fulfill against Eli all that I spoke concerning his house . . . the iniquity of the house of Eli shall not be expiated by sacrifice." Given that Eli himself had opposed his sons' iniquities (2:22–25), we see from YHWH's oracle to Samuel that a "house," when it means household or family lineage, includes forces beyond the control of its nominal head—it is a cauldron of potential anarchy, of decay, of conflicting wills and cross-purposes that undo even those with the best intentions. That which lives in the shelter of YHWH is not sheltered from itself.

The actual fall of Eli's house in I Samuel 4 is interwoven with another set of traditions—those of the Ark—which introduces yet another perspective on our understanding both of the "house of YHWH" and of the "house of Eli." It is only here that we learn, though we had known it in other contexts at least as far back as Num. 10:33–36, that the Ark may be moved from place to place, and, in particular, may be moved from its resting place at a cultic shrine to the battlefield, where, in the hour of need, it is expected to strike terror into the hearts of Israel's enemies. Indeed, in the present instance, it works so well that the enemy, in the intensity of its fear, rallies to defeat Israel. Is the text playing a joke? The story that follows keeps its comical edge, but the serious component of the story's theme has already been driven home by the mere moving of the Ark: lifting it from its ground at Shilo changes the definition of Shilo and its Elide guardians. They are now relativized, their fortunes cast in with the success of the battle to which they lend their precious relics, and, despite the jocularity of the Ark's capture and Philistine sojourn, a low point is reached both in Israel's fortunes and in those of the house of Eli. With the battlefield death of Eli's dissolute sons Hophni and Phineas, the "house" of Eli more or less fatally collapses, as does Eli himself upon learning of the capture of the Ark. One feels a certain sympathy for this aged, crustacean figure, undeluded about the virtues of his sons, unmoved by report of their deaths, eager only for news of the Ark, and struck down finally by recognition of the decisive breaching of a "house of YHWH." Phineas's surviving newborn son is named by his dying mother "Ichabod" (lit. "Inglory!"), and both the Elide dynastic house and the Shilo "house of YHWH" are in decisive eclipse. The Ark does not return to Shilo. The remaining priests of Shilo move to Nob.

At this point, as noted, the story turns comic. At this most despairing moment of defeat for Israel, the story laughs. What is funny about this? The joke, it seems, is on the conquerors. The Ark is easier to capture than it is to contain. Waylaid to a "house of Dagon," the Ark begins, like the trickster-deity of Hannah's song, to play games with its captors. A statue of Dagon falls on its face. A second fall breaks its limbs. A plague strikes the inhabitants of Philistia, first in Ashdod, then in Gath, then in Ekron, afflicting the people with . . . hemorrhoids!—frequently fatal, to be sure, but a particularly ignoble and humiliating affliction, appropriate to satire written by the victims' enemies. It now seems, in any case, that the Ark can take care of itself.

It is this apparent divine self-sufficiency, and the finely emblematic scene, in the chapter that follows, of the driverless cows bearing the triumphant Ark back to Israelite territory that enable us to understand the otherwise obscure incident that marks the eventual return of the Ark to a shrine of prominence in II Samuel 6. The two episodes (I Sam. 6 and II Sam. 6) are similar enough to suggest the lineaments of a type-scene: in both, there is a triumphal procession; in both, there is great rejoicing and the offering of thanksgiving sacrifices; in both, there is a wagon and oxen; in both there is retribution for unwarranted proximity to the Ark; and in both, the itinerant Ark proves its sufficiency against its enemies and against the hazards of travel. Only in the second episode is YHWH's vengeance against the one who touches the Ark sketched as a dramatic episode, with a named victim: it is Uzza—son of Abinadab, the Ark's erstwhile host in Kiriath-Yearim—who ventures forth his hand almost involuntarily to steady the teetering Ark when one of the animals stumbles, and for this indiscretion he is struck dead. The medieval Jewish commentator Kimhi, among others, stressed the deficiency of *faith* that underlies Uzza's fateful action—for, presumably, he should have known that the Ark of YHWH would not stumble! Uzza, to be sure, is unimportant: his role in the story, like that of Aaron's ill-fated sons Nadab and Abihu in Lev. 10:1–3 and of the rebelling party of Korah in Num. 16:1–35, is simply to throw into relief the power and transcendence of YHWH. Their deaths are even made to seem a consecration (cf. Lev. 10:3; Num. 17:1–3). There is perhaps no better divine gesture to underscore the presumption of David in ordering the Ark removed from Kiriath-Yearim (or Baalim), presumably to a more "secure" house. If Abinadab and his sons were dubious guardians of the Ark, its new chief protector, David, is made to understand how pretentious is the bid to "protect" the Ark. David is perturbed enough to halt the Ark's progression, and he diverts the Ark to the house of Obed-Edom the Gittite. Throughout the chapter, we find the repeated word "house"—first in the sense of provisional shelter for the Ark (6:3–4); then in the unusual expression "house of Israel" (cf. 7:2–3) in the verse that follows: "David and the house of Israel danced before YHWH . . . ," thus here in the sense of "community," "polity"; then again, as a second provisional shelter, "the house of Obed-Edom," but also calling forth mention of Obed-Edom's "household," and here YHWH's behavior is unexpectedly benign: "The Ark of YHWH remained in the house of Obed-Edom the Gittite, and YHWH blessed Obed-Edom and his whole household" (6:11).

David, though chastened by the death of Uzza (see v. 8), takes the good fortune of Obed-Edom as a sign that the victory processional of the Ark may continue. One must note here that the intended destination of the Ark has not yet been mentioned. Finally, verse 13 reports that, as the Ark enters "the city of David," David, wearing a linen ephod, whirls and dances like a dervish, apparently offending Saul's daughter Michal, who glimpses the event from a distant vantage point. Michal, a onetime beloved and ally of David's, is here shown registering the understandable dismay of the surviving members of the house of Saul, to see the seat of YHWH's rule moved southward to the makeshift capital of Saul's chief rival. Later confronting David directly, she attributes her disaffection to David's "exposing himself in the sight of slave girls, as the riffraff do," but it is unlikely that the antipathy was new, or that the jibe was any more than an attempt to trivialize what David had made a cause of great significance. Once a protector of David against the wrath of her father, Michal had been absorbed back into the concerns of her father's house, and, though betrothed to David, was married by Saul to another man. Later taken back by David, on grounds of Saul's prior obligation, Michal left her husband's house apparently with reluctance and bitterness. The rehousing of the Ark is thus intertwined with another "house" problem, one of household, which David states with uncharacteristic meanness and frankness in his reply to Michal's insult: "[I dance] before YHWH, who chose me over your father and all his household, and appointed me prince [*nagid*] over YHWH's people Israel! I will dance before YHWH!" (6:21).

David's dance, as noted, is not simply offensive to Michal because of the sexual impropriety she finds in it, but because of her antipathy to

David, and perhaps from her misgivings about the cultic innovation that is occurring. The linen ephod, the ecstatic dancing, and the apparent ritual nakedness of the king are motifs of ancient Near Eastern mythology and priestly liturgies. David's role here is institutional, and bespeaks changes in Israel—a return, perhaps, to the sense of king and temple that prevailed in the heyday of pagan culture in the land. The king's house, already constructed before the Ark was removed from Kiriath-Yearim (see 5:11), is to be the sanctuary of divine law—seat and tabernacle of the earthly indwelling of YHWH. The king, conforming to his mythological archetype, is chief steward, the "gardener" of the divine world and feeder of mankind. He dispenses nourishment to the populace (6:19) and sends them "each man to his house" (*'ish leveyto*). Yet his own household, as the confrontation with Michal shows, remains in a precarious state. David's ungracious sentiments toward the house of Saul, spoken to Michal with a bald clarity, state the fundamental fact of his reign: that it is born out of warring houses, and that victory is YHWH's alone.

Had David and Michal produced an offspring, the question of monarchic succession would perhaps have been closed. Israel's and Judah's kingly houses would have become one, and political turmoil would presumably be averted. Reality, however (6:23), is not so simple. David, despite his sanguine demeanor, begins his Jerusalem-based pan-Israelite reign in uncertainty. Michal, who sees the king in his moment of greatest triumph, sees him, as it happens, through a window from the inside of a house (v. 16). The ecstatic king is framed as in a picture, or viewed as text by a commentator: the house of David as seen from the house of Saul. The king's presumably exposed genitals house the "house" that is to replace Michal's, yet momentarily she is housed, and the king (and his privates) unhoused. Past and future mingle uncomfortably. Michal has *seen* David—and the symbols and instruments of dynasty—in an archetypally improper way reminiscent of the espying of the drunken, unclad Noah by his elder son Ham (Gen. 9:22), and, traditiohistorically speaking, the incident has much the same effect: an estrangement, a malediction, a subordination of the one who espies. Though the indiscretion was first that of the dynastic father, it is the intruder who pays the penalty. Yet the etiological summary is here neutral and unspecific—as if the estrangement were mutual; less of a dispossession than a deadlock, a collapse of dialogue: "And Michal, daughter of Saul, had no child, unto her dying day" (6:23). Despite their uncomfortable interdependence, house has parted ways with house.

It is at this moment, and against such a background, that the famous episode of dynastic covenant is introduced, and with a thematically resonant transitional verse: "It happened, *when the king sat in his house,* and YHWH had given him rest [*heniaḥ lo*] from all his enemies, that the king spoke to Nathan the prophet . . ." (7:1).

We are again inside a "house" that seems like shelter, but that shelters only by the shelter of YHWH. At this moment of idyllic good fortune (the verb *heniaḥ lo* is distantly cognate to *wayyanniḥehu*, "He set him down," in the Garden story, Gen. 2:15), the king is moved to ponder the apparent irony that he lives "in a house of cedar, whereas the Ark of God dwells within a tent-curtain" (v. 2). There is a ritual and rhetorical quality to this question, as if the answer were already long-known—and, traditiohistorically speaking, it was. It is, indeed, the etiological founding moment of Solomon's Temple, and at first it seems as if this moment is to enjoy a certain ideological tranquility: "Nathan said to the king: 'All that is in your heart, go and do. Truly, YHWH is with you'" (7:3).

But other claims assert themselves. What source historians find as sure signs of "composite" authorship in the account—as if authorship were any other than composing!—is a dialogue of traditions. The king's ritual astonishment is matched by a divine ritual astonishment:

> It happened that night that YHWH's word came to Nathan, thus: "Go, and say to my servant David, 'Thus says YHWH: Shall you indeed build me a house to sit in? Truly, I have not sat in a house, since the day I brought up the children of Israel from Egypt unto this very day! I went about in a tent and in a tabernacle. Wherever I have gone about, with any of the children of Israel, have I so much as spoken a single word to any of Israel's tribal chieftains whom I commanded to pasture my people Israel, to say "Why haven't you built me a house of cedars?"'" (7:4–7)

At first, the rejoinder appears to direct itself at the presumption of the king's intention to shelter the Ark in a more secure house. As the etiological fables of I Sam. 6 and II Sam. 6 have shown, the Ark knows its own way home. YHWH's question carries the echo of an undoubtedly widespread parochial skepticism and resistance to David's brand of sacral kingship, quite understandable for the time and place. But it soon turns into what we might call the Deuteronomic boast—that is, the familiar *magnificat* of covenant formulary, the formal recitation of a patron king's beneficent acts to his vassal, as a preface to the latter's covenant obligations. This formula is rooted in ancient Near Eastern, not specifically Israelite, idioms—praising the divine covenanting king for daring to do the cosmically unprecedented with his protégé:

> "Thus say to my servant, to David: . . . I took you from behind the sheepfolds to be a prince [*nagid*] over Israel. I was with you wherever you went, cutting off all your enemies before you, and I shall make for you a great name, like the name of the great ones who were in the land,

and I shall appoint a place for my people, for Israel, so that they dwell
[securely], and tremble no more. No evildoers shall continue to oppress them any longer, as in former times, ever since I appointed
chieftains over my people Israel. I shall give you rest [*wahanihoti lekha*]
from all your enemies. . . ." (7:8–11a)

Thus far we find the covenant form quite classical—just as YHWH
had demanded to Israel, at the end of her wilderness sojourns (Deut.
4:32–34):

> Truly, ask now of the former days that were before you, from the time
> God created a human being (*'adam*) upon the earth, from one end of
> the heavens to the other: Has such a great thing come about, has its
> like been heard? Has a people heard the voice of a deity speaking from
> the fire, as you have heard, and yet lived? Or has a deity attempted to
> come take a people for himself from amid a nation, with trials, signs,
> wonders, and wars, and with a strong hand and an outstretched arm,
> and with great terrors . . . ?

All of this conforms to a rhetoric of hyperbole more or less traditional in
covenant formulary. Yet the text, however precedented its form, typically claims the unprecedentedly new. And what, indeed, is without
precedent in Israel prior to this historical moment? This text points to it
(v. 10) by the double declaration of what shall be done "no longer"
(*lo' . . . 'od, welo' yosifu . . .*): no longer a trembling Israel; no further
oppression from without. Has anyone in Israel, even Saul, been able to
promise more than *temporary* rest from Israel's enemies? Indeed, it was
judged (then, as now) a viable peace if "the land had rest from its
enemies forty years"—how, then, *perpetual* peace! But henceforth would
come to be, if not perpetual peace then at least a perpetual *peacekeeping:*
namely, a permanent structure responsible for the civil tranquility, a
nation-state of Israel, and a transtribal sacral/temporal power permanently charged to impose order in the land and among the people. This
structure, symbolically tied in perpetuity to the house of David, would
remain in Israel even after the house of David itself relinquished active
sovereignty.

The manifold sense of "house" is nowhere better concentrated than in
the verses that ensue:

> And YHWH declares to you that He, YHWH, *shall make for you a house.*
> When your days have been fulfilled, you shall lie down with your
> fathers, and I shall raise up your seed after you, who shall go forth
> from your loins, and I shall establish his kingdom. *He will build for me a
> house,* and I'll make firm [*wekhonanti*] the seat of his kingdom unto
> eternity. I shall be a father to him, and he a son to me: if he deal
> perversely, I'll chasten him with the rod of men and by human afflic-

tions. But my love shall not depart from him, as I had withdrawn [it] from Saul, whom I made to fall away before you. *Your house and your kingdom are true [ne'eman]* unto eternity [text adds, uncertainly: ahead of you]; your seat will be secure [*nakhon*] unto eternity. (Ibid., 11b–16)

House as physical shelter of the Ark; house as ruling family; house as patrimony, posterity, and dynasty; house as temple and sanctuary; house as seat of YHWH's reign—these senses of "house" have mingled at least as far back as the opening of I Samuel, and here they are allowed a brief semantic harmony in the utopian typology of Davidic Yahwism. Yet the oracle does not place the house of David, so to speak, "beyond good and evil." It operates in YHWH's shelter: "Unless YHWH builds the house, in vain do its builders toil over it" (Ps. 127:1). It is a haunted house— visited by the memory of houses that have fallen, warned by proverbial examples of unfulfilled housedom. But its role, both in Yahweh's plan and in the economy of Israel's culture and religion, is permanent. Its rulers are to be held accountable, in ways they have yet to know, both for their own moral behavior and for the moral health of the realm. But their permanence, their indispensability, and, in some sense, their internal necessity, are acknowledged by YHWH, and so the ruling house will not perish, but will be chastised "by the rod of men, and by human afflictions" (*beshevet 'anashim uvenig'ey bene 'adam*—a plural version of the often-attested poetic dichotomy *'adam/'ish*). This house's turns of destiny will themselves be the emblem of the fate of the people—the "house of Israel"—as a whole. It is the unique combination of Israel's internal evolution with Israel's external pressures (the Philistines) that created the royal house. The harmonious mutuality of divine sheltering and human tabernacling that this creation seems to embody is the product of a unique and unprecedented rapprochement between the house of David, the house of Israel, and the "house" of YHWH. It is that rapprochement alone which guarantees Israel's continued existence, and, as it turns out, despite the permanence of David's rule in Israel's historical memory, the Davidic house is no more secure than the house of Israel as a whole. If David's house will suffer "the rod of men, etc.," surely the house of Israel will not escape the same—as the covenant curses of Deut. 27–28 make clear. The Deuteronomist's parallel history of the house of David and the house of Israel (I Kings 12–II Kings 25) will also make clear that the troubled symbiosis between the two houses will lead to a dubious kind of exemplary mortality for the house of Israel and a dubious kind of symbolic immortality for the house of David—"dubious," because the one never fully dies and the other never fully lives. The "house of YHWH," born out of divine as well as human compromise, suffers analogous vicissitudes. "Who am I, Lord YHWH," asks David in ritual astonishment, in his reply to his patron king, "and who is my house that you have brought me to this point? . . . Is this the manner/law of a human being [*wezo't torat ha'adam*]?" Not exactly. Only the full Davidic history is *torat ha'adam*.

But the motivic use of "house" has a wider scope. The sons of Zeruiah, for example, hear David curse their house (II Sam. 2:28ff.). Ishbosheth is killed within the false security of his house: "[The assassins] killed [him] in his house, upon his bed" (II Sam. 4:11; cf. 4:6–7). So, too, David would ask after the ramshackle remnant of the house (dynasty) of Saul, "Is there yet any who is left of the house of Saul, to whom I may show love on Jonathan's account?" (9:1; cf. 9:3). As the Ark and its relics had been moved to the city of David, so the lame son of Jonathan, Mephibosheth, is moved to the shelter (and supervision) of David's table (9:4–7). Bathsheba is espied from "the king's house," but after her eventual dalliance with the king, returns "to her house." When Uriah is later told "Go down to your house" (12:8), the text wavers between the sense of physical house and that of conjugal household, for it is conjugal relations David hopes to precipitate. The double meaning is preserved in the verse that follows, as is the contrast between king's house and Uriah's house: "Uriah lay down at the entrance of the king's house . . . but to his house (and household) he did not go down" (cf. vv. 10–11, 13). After Uriah's death, the distinction between Bathsheba's (Uriah's) house and David's is obliterated: " . . . and he gathered her unto his house" (11:27)—an act that, as for the house of Judean Nabal (I Sam. 25:42) and for that of Benjaminite Saul and Mephiboshet (II Sam. 9), was intended to be construed as an act of sheltering, patronage, leviratelike responsibility. But YHWH leaves no illusions about *whose* gift this was: "I [YHWH] gave you the house[s] of your lords, and the wives of your lords into your intimate control. I gave you the house of Israel and Judah, and if that weren't enough . . ." (12:8).

And so, this new manner of chastising the ruler (and, indirectly, his people) "by the rod of men, etc." will take the very permanence of the ruling house into its dynamics: it will be evil *from amid* that house that will undo the realm. "Behold," says Nathan's deity, "I bring upon you evil from your house. . . ." And so it happens: "David sent for Tamar [to come] to the [king's] house, saying, 'Go to the house of Amnon . . .'" (13:7–8); "The king said: 'Let [Absalom] be returned to his (familial) house . . .'" (14:24); "Joab rose and went to Absalom, to [his] house . . ." (ibid., 31); "The king left ten concubine women to tend the house" (15:17); "And Ahitophel said to Absalom: 'Go into the concubines of your father whom he left to tend the house, and all you have will be secured'" (16:21). And so on. The motif continues well into the next books, but one must note the special sense of closure that is accorded to the "Ark/house of YHWH" theme in the final chapter of II Samuel.

Where, as in the earlier stations of the Ark, there is a context of plague or random destruction, the aid of certain solid, otherwise obscure, citizens (here Araunah) is enlisted, and a makeshift dwelling place is secured for an altar of YHWH. Perhaps the name "Araunah" contains a conscious play on *'aron* ("Ark"), but the latter word does not otherwise appear in the story, nor does the word "house" in the sense of physical shelter. We read here only of a "threshing floor" (*goren*), a place, to be sure, for theophany and oracle (Judg. 6:37, I Sam. 14:2, 18–19; cf. II Sam. 6:5), but probably not a walled site—nor, despite its presence in Jebusite Jerusalem, and its precedent as a pre-Solomonic Davidic altar, can it be firmly identified with any known locale. This houseless house of YHWH was associated only by a later religious imagination with Abraham's Mt. Moriah and Solomon's Temple Mount.

GOING INDOORS

Ask for the peace of Jerusalem,
May those who love you be at peace.
Ps. 122:6

The transformation in narrative topography that begins with the Davidic court history is seemingly unheralded and minimally noticeable, but it is decisive for our understanding of the continuous narrative history that runs from Genesis through II Kings. Prior to this juncture, Israelite history had been either eponymous or collective—that is, it was essentially a corporate history, whether of ancestors or tribes, and when leaders arose in the narrative, the pattern or timing of their leadership was made to reflect in some way the religious and moral condition of the community as a whole. It was, moreover, largely an *outdoor* history—a chronicle of tent and field, of wilderness and mountain, of oasis and vineyard, of riverbed and cairn, of terebinth and palm, of city rampart and village gate. Henceforth, it will be largely a chronicle of palace life, of the dynasty and its counterdynasties, of throne and bed. A history of ancestors and tribes will become a history of kings and their prophetic adversaries, of the dynastic chains and dynastic begettings, of decisions made within that enclosed space *par excellence:* the royal house.

We behold in this transition, properly speaking, not a shift from a public to a private domain, but one from body politic to body paradigmatic. The rich lore of kingship that extends indefinitely into the archaic past, and forward into postbiblical religion and culture, is muted in the prose tradition of the Bible (though untrammeled in Psalms and the poetic tradition), but it is never far out of reach. Its assumptions are fundamental to a reading of II Samuel. Most of the motifs of enthronement psalms and divine-warrior poetry are present in some form in the prose tradition:[18] the massing of hostile troops; the clamor of the people or the council for a ruler; the designation, secret and public anointing, and divine adoption of the king; the king's protests of youth, innocence, and inexperience, and the divine reassurance of support and guidance; the symbolic ride of the king upon an ass amid the populace; the

124

emergence of the king in his chariotry and battle gear; the routing of the enemy, with hornblasts and cries; the processional return with the Ark of the Covenant; the ecstatic dancing, the ritual nakedness of the king, the clash of bells and timbrels; ululating throngs and women's choruses of tribute; the king's deposit of the Ark and tablets of the law inside a sanctuary; purifying of the sanctuary, and the foundation of a temple; enthronement of the king, and royal marriage; identification of the king's order with the creation of the universe from out of chaos; New Year festival, atonement, reading of the law.

Were we to possess only the poetic tradition alone, we would simply say that ancient Israel partook of a common complex of myth and symbolism familiar to her from the Canaanite milieu and general Near Eastern usage. The elaborately polytheistic trappings of the pagan lore of kingship translated with surprising ease into the psalmodic conventions of YHWH and his council of (lesser) divine beings, and the microcosmic parallel of earthly king to heavenly remains more or less intact. If we turn from psalms to the prose tradition, however, we find these motifs severely qualified by narrative context.

The pivotal figure in the biblical lore of kingship is of course King David, to whom more narrative space is accorded than any other biblical character, including even Moses. Though he is not Israel's first king (and, given the typology of rulership in the era of "judges," perhaps not even the *second* king), he is the first successfully *dynastic* king, and, as such, the character through whom the presuppositions of dynastic institutions are anatomized. In Israel of the eleventh and tenth centuries B.C.E., as our text unfolds its history, the merits of dynastic leadership seem by no means self-evident or widely appreciated. The organs of institutional continuity were sustained by a fragile tribal consensus,[19] which initially accorded monarchs only the most tentative and conditional exercise of power, and which threatened to come apart numerous times during David's reign itself, and did so decisively, if still only partially, after the reign of his first dynastic heir. In that I Sam. 8—the story of Israel's demand for a king in the days of Samuel—makes kingdom a project of the king's subjects, reflection on the fate of kingship in Israel must be seen as the vehicle of a reflection on Israelite society as a whole.

If David is the pivotal figure in that reflection, the David-Bathsheba episode in II Sam. 11 is pivotal to our understanding of his reign—not simply because Bathsheba is the dynastic mother, a status that (like that of Sarah's as ancestral mother) will be clarified only at the end of a long narrative cycle, but because the melodrama of David's illicit affair is the occasion of a whole complex of routine gestures and messages, of terrain traversed and terrain avoided, of verbal choices and verbal slips, that do more to explain Israel's institutional changes than even the sober and discursive pen of the historian.[20]

The story opens with a curious textual ambiguity, seemingly only a problem for so-called lower criticism (namely, of textual editing, vocalization, and emendation), but one that, intentionally or otherwise, conveys a perplexity crucial to the story's unfolding: "It happened at the turning of the year, the time when kings/agents go forth [to battle] . . ." (II Sam. 11:1).

The consonantal text reads "agents" (*mal'akhim*), but the Masoretic vocalization reads "kings" (*melakhim*), the latter being the most widely accepted reading.[21] While it seems unwise to accord conflicting versions of a biblical word *equal* weight (the two words, after all, are unrelated and spelled differently, and only one of the two can occupy the textual space accorded it), the fact that the ambiguity exists at all suggests that conflicting interpretive pressures (what Barthes in another context called *pressions de lisibilité*)[22] may themselves have helped shape the history of the text. This is, after all, the first place in the Bible that a leader of Israel stays off the battlefield in time of war,[23] and the question of the role of agents in the conduct of kingly business returns again and again throughout the story (and, indeed, throughout the court history). Since a king, as defined in I Sam. 8, is *himself* an agent of the people, and his exit to battle a constitutive moment of his authority,[24] we find ourselves with an oddly convoluted inversion of kingly function in the king's preference of agents to represent him. In this transition to a sedentary monarchy, the agent within the king and the king within the agent seem at war with each other, a struggle indeed analogous to the opposition of consonantal and spoken text, the *ketiv* and *qeri*. (Similarly, if Joab's literal taking of Rabbat-Ammon in 12:26 is thought of as a *ketiv*, the king's symbolic possession of the city in 27–31 constitutes something of a *qeri*.) The contradiction, at any rate, is borne out further by the details that immediately follow: " . . . that David sent Joab, and his servants with him, and all Israel, and they laid waste to the Ammonites, and laid siege upon Rabbah. David stayed in Jerusalem" (ibid.).

The inversion is made clear by the apparent hierarchy: Joab, second (or first) in command; his servants, i.e., the professional elite guard and largely foreign mercenary troops that had constituted David's extra-Israelite power base since his exile from Saul's court;[25] only last is "all Israel," namely, the tribal muster that comprised the oldest institution of warfare in ancient Israel, and that made the battle a specifically Israelite battle in the first place. It is unclear here who is hiring whom to do what. The pointed reference to David's remaining in Jerusalem, in any case, makes clear to us that war is being conducted in a very different way from that of the archaic tribal muster, whose dynamics (and defects) we are familiar with from the Song of Deborah (Judg. 5). The rational and bureaucratic mode of statecraft that is David's specific innovation has better uses for the king than the charismatic and warlord functions that elevate a man to kingship in the first place. The advantages of a sedentary monarch are both practical and symbolic: as strategist, the king can move troops and materiel with greater freedom and suppleness than his location amid the heat of battle would permit; and, as symbol of the unity and continuity of the territorial state, the king's immobility creates a semantic and mythological bulwark of immense psychological value against any enemy—especially against one, like King Hanun ben Nahash of Ammon, whose challenge had specifically represented an attack on the legitimacy of the cisjordanian ruler (II Sam. 10:1–5).[26]

David's genius as a monarch is here shown resting in his overcoming a certain literalism of kingly function that had plagued both the reign and the mental tranquility of Saul. Saul, to be sure, is shown anticipating the kingly style of David in certain important ways—by his movement within a cloud of agents, henchmen, and informers; by his responsibility for orchestrating the instrument of war; and by his establishment of the rudiments of a court and dynasty.[27] But Saul's power rested—as the beginning of his reign suggests (I Sam. 11:5–13; cf. 10:9–13)—in his personal military prowess and in the vagaries of prophetic inspiration. Both his reputation and his mind begin to come apart with the inevitable rise of younger rivals (like David, and, indeed, his own son Jonathan) from within the ranks. Saul remains a kind of prisoner to the typology of judgeship. "Is Saul also among the prophets?"—the obscure gnomon that appears in an etiological context in I Sam. 10:9–13 and 19:18–24— hauntingly expresses Saul's inability to control the conditions of his own inspiration and ecstasy, and serves as a kind of emblem for the curiously hybrid and unrealized nature of his kingship. David's public career remains largely untroubled by such imperatives. Strategy, deceit, and a certain aloofness from the sweat of battle characterize his reign. Whereas Saul has staked his legitimacy in a kind of frenzied effort to reduplicate his early successes on front after front, David discovers that a king's success can be predicated on the deeds of others. If the king does not have to be everywhere, he does not have to be anywhere but his home base.[28]

Thus far, at any rate, II Sam. 11 proceeds on the level of institutional history: it is the office of king and the conduct of war that form the principal subject of the opening verses. Yet the outcome of the battle against the Ammonites (along with David's symbolic assumption of the mantle of military success) is not recounted until 12:26–31. If the pattern of parenthetic interpolation, which we know to be common to biblical narrative in general, holds true here, the tale of personal intrigue

that is now to be related will comment in some way on the institutional
and military history that forms the framework. This is borne out by the
words that follow:

> And it happened one evening that David arose from his couch and
> went for a walk atop the roof of the King's house, and he saw from the
> rooftop a woman bathing. The woman was very beautiful. David
> inquired about the woman, and was told "Why, that's Bathsheba,
> daughter of Eliam, wife of Uriah the Hittite." So David sent agents,
> and summoned her, and she came to him and lay with him—she had
> just formally ended her monthly impurity—and she returned home.
> (II Sam. 11:2–4)

A fairly ramified web of assumptions underlies these spare, rapid, almost
calligraphic details. The otiose king is portrayed neither in ceremonies of
state (as in numerous psalms) nor at work with his palace councils (as in
the mythological examples found amid certain other psalms), but rather
in distinctly private, and perhaps pointedly unflattering forms of leisure:
napping, strolling, running after his eyes.[29] We note that he is not called
"the king," nor "King David," but simply "David"—yet the rooftop he
treads rests on "the king's house" (*bet hammelekh*), a tension in terminology that hints of one between man and role. "He saw from/atop (*me'al*)
the rooftop . . ." presents a syntactic ambiguity that prompted the Stuttgart editors, at least, to cite textual variants at this point: is the word
referring to the king's rooftop or Bathsheba's?[30] One way or another, the
visual trajectories formed by the precipitous inclines of the City of David
make such an accident of espying something quite ordinary. Whether
the woman was *placing* herself in the path of the king's gaze (she does,
after all, create a bit of a stir here and in the ensuing verses) can neither
be concluded from the text nor excluded from its interpretation. We are
not explicitly apprised, at this point, of David's thoughts about what he
sees, but the narrative caesura effected by "the woman was very beautiful" (*weha'ishshah ṭovat-mar'eh me'od*)[31] creates a voice that is neither
purely narratorial nor purely words of David's thoughts. Momentarily,
all attention is focused exclusively on the spell exerted by the bathing
woman.

"David sent and inquired . . ." can, at least on initial appearance, admit
of two interpretations: either he summoned someone to the rooftop to
gaze at the woman with him and to tell him who she was; or he sent a
messenger to the woman's house to ask for her name. Either way, the
ease with which aides are ever present to the king's (and, for that matter,
to David's) bidding is masked only by the minimal way in which this court
background is represented: informers, spies, and gossipers abound in
the palace milieu, but their faces and names are obliterated—their dis-

course a ubiquitous murmur cradling the action of the story's named persons, threatening their privacy and reverberating their deeds. Yet it is the very milieu on which the king's political and military success is founded. When the Aramaeans under Hadadezer, for example, massed troops at Helam (II Sam. 10:15–16), "David was informed of it" (*wayyug-gad le-Dawid*, ibid., 17).[32] Israel's dependence on informers at and around the Syrophoenician borders is a security policy not unique to the twentieth century.[33] Indeed, the Ammonite king Hanun, the man who had begun the conflict between Israel and an Ammonite-Aramaean league, may have had good reason to fear David's legates as spies, or known of his reputation for mobilizing intelligence operatives. The answer David seeks now, at any rate, is clear in its essentials: "Why, that's (*halo' zo't*) . . . !"—a style of exclamation suggesting the former of the two alternatives mentioned above, namely, that someone is guessing the woman's identity from the king's vantage point—followed by her patronymic and her marriage bond. While the information is presumably helpful, it is a double-edged sword: the king himself is a prisoner of his own network of gossip, as the unfolding of the story will make clear.

The information itself is revealing in other ways. Setting aside the question of the identity of Eliam (or of his anagram Ammiel in I Chron. 3:5), we note that "Uriah the Hittite" seems a curious way of designating one with a clearly Yahwist name—unless, to be sure, it is a Hebraization of a Hittite name (such as the more identifiably Hittite name "Araunah"—Hit. *a-ra-u-wa-ni*, "freeman, aristocrat"—in II Sam. 24:18ff.).[34] Yet a Hittite presence in David's Jerusalem is, if uncertain, within the realm of possibility,[35] and it has been suggested that Uriah, as a member of the entrenched aristocracy that antedated David's conquest of the city would, in good Canaanite fashion, have sought the protection and patronage of the new strongman of the region, much as the Hittites (*beney Ḥet*) of Hebron had paid homage to David's literal and typological ancestor Abraham in his day, and intertwined their interests with his.[36] The "Yahwism" of Uriah's name is thus an appropriately patriotic concession to the winds of change. Uriah's position as one of David's *gibborim* ("strongmen"—see II Sam. 23:8ff., I Chron. 11:10ff.) should cause us to modify somewhat our conventional picture of Uriah as a humble foot soldier, a conception that certain other details of the story and its framework encourage.[37] One whose dwelling is located so near "the king's house" is very likely an honored member of royal-military circles, one well enough known to the king's courtiers, if not to the king himself, that his naked wife seen from an adjacent rooftop would trigger astonishment of a rather precise nature.

David now sends "agents"—again, a conspicuous choice of words that perhaps suggests a cloak of secrecy (the legates that had been sent on

David's *public* mission to Ammon in 10:2 were called *'avadaw,* "his ser-vants," not his "agents").[38] The agents fetch Bathsheba—by what means we are not told, nor do we learn of the woman's reactions, nor of the nature of the blandishments, threats, or other inducements that motivate her to lie with David. The simplicity and rapidity of the action at this point suggest that her resistance, if any, was minimal, or perhaps (within the scope of this chapter, at least) irrelevant. The general appearance of the woman as passive and acquiescent at this stage of the court history stands in sharp contrast to her boldness at the end of the history, when her decisive intervention will throw the dynastic succession to her son Solomon (I Kings 1)—only by hindsight, blurred by the passing, within the text, of nearly twenty turbulent years, do we recall the Bathsheba of II Sam. 11, and only then, much belatedly, do we wonder about her possible hidden assertiveness in the first encounter. By then, of course, her boldness may owe itself to other factors—her years of (unreported) experiences of court life, the clear favor that Solomon occupies in David's eyes, or the enfeeblement of the aged king—so again there is no clear clue as to her behavior in the adultery episode. In any case, the dispatching of "agents" is a detail conforming to the larger pattern of the king's reliance on agents for the conduct of state business—the adultery with Bathsheba thus shown as a by-product of more or less the same apparatus that enabled David to know in advance of Aramaean troop movements, and matters of similar strategic import.

The seemingly parenthetic annotation "—she had just formally ended her monthly impurity—" (*wehi' mitqaddeshet mittum'atah*), as commenta-tors have observed, sets the framework for the action that is to follow: if Uriah had left for battle prior to or during Bathsheba's isolation from conjugal relations, her later pregnancy (11:5) cannot be attributed to him—unless he can be brought home and somehow induced to cohabit with her.[39] David now embarks on such a plan. His first interchange with Uriah takes only two verses, but again a number of institutionally weight-ed factors are brought to bear in these compressed sentences:

> Uriah came to him. David asked about the welfare of Joab, the welfare of the people, and the welfare of the war. David said to Uriah: "Go down to your house, and wash your feet." Uriah went out from the king's house, and the king's provisions went out after him. (Ibid., 7–8)

The priorities of protocol in David's amenities are similar to the palace-downward hierarchy presented in the story's opening verses—with the notable absence of Joab's "servants," the elite military body to which Uriah belongs, and with the notable addition of "the war," as if political disorder itself were somehow part of the ranks. No specific conversation is recorded at this point, though we must assume that more detailed words would have been exchanged, and that the three subjects mentioned delineate the main parameters of their discussion, in the order of their importance to David. Because, with one exception, the thoughts and words of Uriah are nowhere recorded in the story (and David's thoughts, while deducible from his words, are not stated by the narrator), we have no idea of the specific tone, tenor, or tensions of their conversation. We have no idea of whether Uriah was used to serving this function as bearer of battlefield tidings, whether David routinely asked the questions he asks here, or whether both men were struggling through an uncomfortable encounter. Yet we do know, without being informed directly, something of David's preoccupations at this point. Our awareness of context supplies a new meaning to David's words that may or may not be perceived by Uriah.[40] It is worthwhile here, however, to concentrate not so much on speculation about Uriah's thoughts, but on the relation between what David's words mean and what they purport to mean. We see here that the split between "David" and "the king" can again be observed, even if David is, in a sense, hiding behind "the king" (as in: "the king's provisions"). David relies at this moment on a certain kind of kingly chatter, which *sounds* like a gracious king bestowing rest on his hard-working and loyal messenger. It is of course in David's interest that these words not be perceived by Uriah as too obtrusive or jarring— one can well imagine a thoroughly neutral and uneventful official conversation preceding this invitation, a conversation from which David hoped to glide imperceptibly into the hidden agenda. Yet, the words jar, if only for being the first direct discourse of the exchange, and because they cannot avoid intruding one half-clause too far ("and wash your feet") into the delicate intangibles of Uriah's domestic life, in order to press upon Uriah a trajectory of action that David hopes will lead further. In a sense, it may not even matter to David whether the action proceeds further—Uriah's return to his house is all that matters, and the appearance that he has come home to resume all normal domestic activities: for this is sufficient to sow the appropriately neutralizing rumor on the winds of gossip.

At this point, however, David makes a fateful miscalculation, for which his command of protocol and his assumptions about Uriah have not prepared him. In a story where such a clear division was made from the start between the elite guard and the Israelite muster, David would have no particular reason to believe that members of the respective bodies would observe the same religious code in respect to war duties and grounds for relief thereof. He, more than any, knows what a mixed multitude he had created through his years of isolation from Israelite institutions, and through his gradual incorporation of Philistine, Canaanite, and Hittite elements into his ranks. While David was particularly sensitive to the semantic nature of his actions and restraints with regard to Israel's religious sensibilities, we may assume that he would have displayed a certain liberal courtliness (out of the same instincts for tact and expedience) toward his marginal Israelites and adopted Yahwists. We have other examples of David's worldly pragmatism and his accordingly cavalier attitude toward religious ritual.[41] So it makes perfectly good sense at this point that David should extend furlough from all battle duties, and that he assume it within the prerogatives of the monarch to grant such dispensations, even where they might contradict the practices and institutions of Israelite holy war. For this reason, David is caught by surprise in what follows:

> Uriah lay down at the gate of the king's house, with all his master's servants. He did not go down to his house. They reported to David: "Uriah did not go down to his house." David said to Uriah: "Haven't you come from a journey? Why didn't you go down to your house?"
>
> Uriah said to David: "The Ark and Israel and Judah are dwelling in makeshift dwellings (or: in Succoth), and my master Joab and the servants of milord are camping on the face of the field—and I should go to my house to eat and drink, and lie with my wife?! On your life, as your soul lives, I shall not do this thing!" (Ibid., 9–11)

There is no clearer expression of the clash between cultural codes. The king's appeal to the commonsense propriety of resting from a journey in wartime presupposes an essentially secular use of the instrument of war, whereas Uriah's reply presupposes the confederate standard of the holy war: the highest symbol of authority is the Ark; the tribal muster is mentioned next, conspicuously ordered by region ("Israel and Judah"); they dwell in booths (or, recalling the typology of Exodus and wilderness, "in Succoth"); only last is "my master Joab and milord's servants," the ambiguity of the "milord" (Joab or David?) suggesting to us both the king's remoteness from the core and Uriah's sincere grounds for doubt about David's involvement in the events at all. Uriah's name turns out to be Yahwist, after all. In the heart of the imperial phalanges we find an orthodox Israelite, quietly observing the wartime soldier's ban against conjugal relations (cf. I Sam. 21:4–7). The significance is double: it compounds the enormity of David's crime (a violation of a marriage is bad enough; a violation of a marriage under sacred conjugal suspension is a particularly cruel and nasty offense); and it attests to the vitality of the confederate faith that it could take root amid the ranks of those structurally the most independent from the confederate polity.

YHWH'S ANOINTED

. . . difficulties in walking straight and standing upright. —Lévi-Strauss

"This day I have begotten thee . . ."

Ps. 2:7

I Samuel 24 and 26 are traditionary doublets on the order of, say, the "wife-sister" episodes of Genesis or the dual "covenant" narratives of Gen. 15 and 17, except that the I Samuel materials are much more precise in their historical scope, slower in their temporal unfolding, and more detailed in their narrative verisimilitude, if not necessarily more "factual." The points shared in common by the stories have been adequately summarized by Culley, among others, and there is no need to recapitulate these matters here.[42] For present purposes, it suffices to note that several distinct items of tradition are comprised in each version: Saul is shown seeking David's life between battles with the Philistines; David is shown advised by impulsive aides whose recommendations must be sometimes resisted and always suspected; he is shown refusing to harm the person of "YHWH's anointed" (*meshiaḥ YHWH*); he is shown choosing a token form of attack (cutting a piece of garment; stealing a spear and water cruse) as a means of signaling to Saul both that the young fugitive refuses to harm him and that he possesses the capability to do so.

In certain respects, the episodes differ: in the former, David criticizes Saul directly and outspokenly, whereas in the latter, he goes out of his way to spare Saul from blame.[43] In the latter, likewise, he is shown criticizing Saul's aides, both for their slander of David and for their failure to protect the person of Saul. And while, in both episodes, Saul is shown conceding to David the justice of the latter's criticism, only in the former does he acknowledge the inevitability of David's eventual rule, and extract a vow from David not to wipe out the Saulide line. It is also worth noting that only in the second episode are David's aides mentioned by name: he is accompanied by Ahimelech the Hittite and by Joab's brother Abishai, son of Zeruiah, and it is Abishai who makes the offensive suggestion.

133

Across both episodes, David's words are addressed in altogether three directions: to his aides, to the aides of Saul, and to Saul. At points, these words become quite finely nuanced and expressive; at other points, they are hackneyed and formulaic—almost heraldic. Let us look first at David's words to his own aides:

> David's men said to him: "Here is the day YHWH had told you about: 'Behold, I am giving your enemies [Masoretic vocalization: enemy] into your hands—do to him whatever is good in your eyes.'"
> David arose and cut the corner of Saul's robe, stealthily. But afterward, David was struck by remorse that he had cut the corner of Saul's robe.
> He said to his men: "Horrors to me from YHWH if I should do this thing to my master, YHWH's anointed, to put forth my hand against him—for he is YHWH's anointed!"
> David restrained [lit. excoriated] his men with words, and did not permit them to rise up against Saul. (24:5–8)

> Abishai said to David: "God has today sealed up your enemy into your hand! So now, please let me strike him with a spear into the ground—one time, I won't deal him a second!"
> David said to Abishai: "Do not harm him! Truly, who would put forth his hand against YHWH's anointed and be found innocent?" David [further] said: "As YHWH lives, truly YHWH will afflict him, or his day will come that he dies—or loses in war and is finished off. Horrors to me from YHWH for putting forth my hand against YHWH's anointed! So now, please take the spear that's at his head, and the water cruse, and let's go."
> David took the spear and the water cruse at Saul's head, and they went away. No one saw or knew, and no one woke up, because all of them were sleeping, for a deep slumber of YHWH had fallen upon them. (26:8–12)

and then at David's words to Saul's aides (latter episode only):

> David said to Abner: "Aren't you a man [*'ish*]? Who is like you in Israel? But why haven't you kept watch over your master the king? For truly, one of the people came to harm the king your lord. This thing is not good that you have done; as YHWH lives, you deserve to die, for you did not keep watch over your lord, over YHWH's anointed! So now, look: where is the king's spear and the water cruse that were at his head?" (26:15–16)

and finally at David's words to Saul:

> David said to Saul: "Why do you listen to the words of a mortal [*'adam*]: 'See, David only seeks your misfortune!'? Behold, this very day my eyes have seen how YHWH has given you into my hand, in the cave, and said to kill you! Yet my eye was sparing of you, and I said: I

will not put forth my hand against my master, for he is YHWH's anointed!

"My father! See, yes, see the corner of your robe in my hand: yes, I clipped off the corner of your robe, yet didn't kill you! I haven't sinned against you—yet you are hunting me for my life!

"May YHWH judge between me and you, and may YHWH exact for me justice from you. But *my* hand will not be upon you!"

"As the ancient saying goes: 'From evildoers will come forth only evil.' But my hand will not be upon you. After whom has the king of Israel gone forth [to battle]? After whom are you pursuing? After a dead dog! After a single flea! YHWH will be a judge, and he will render judgment between me and you. He will look, and will plead my case, and get justice for me from your hand."

When David finished speaking these things to Saul, Saul said: "Is this the voice of David, my son?" And Saul raised his voice and wept. He said to David: "You are more in the right than I, for you have bestowed upon me good, and I have bestowed upon you evil. For you, you have told me today that you have done good with me, in that YHWH had sealed me up into your hand, and yet you did not kill me. And, indeed, does a person ['ish] find his enemy and put him forth onto a good road? May YHWH pay you good in exchange for what you have done for me today!

"So now, behold, I know that you shall surely reign, and the kingdom of Israel will rise up into your hand. So now, swear to me by YHWH lest you cut off my seed after me, and lest you destroy my name from my father's house." (24:10–22)

Saul recognized the voice of David, and he said: "Is this the voice of David, my son?" David said: "It is, my lord king." He said [further]: "Why is this that my master pursues after his servant? Truly, what have I done, what evil is on my hand? So now, let my master the king listen to the words of his servant: if YHWH has incited you against me, let Him receive an offering. But if it is human beings [*beney ha'adam*], cursed be they before YHWH, for they have driven me out today from adhering to the inheritance of YHWH, saying: 'Go, serve other gods.' So now, let not my blood fall to the ground away from the presence of YHWH, for the king of Israel has gone out [to battle] against a single flea, as one hunting partridge in the hills."

And Saul said: "I have sinned again, David, my son! Truly, I will not do evil to you again, in exchange for my soul having been precious in your eyes this day. Behold, I have been foolish, and I have erred quite greatly."

David answered and said: "Here is the spear of the king. Let one of the servant boys come and get it. And may YHWH return to the man [*la'ish*] his justice and faith, in that YHWH has given you today into my hand, but I did not desire to put forth my hand against YHWH's anointed. And behold, as your life was held important this day in my eyes, so may my life be held important in the eyes of YHWH, and may He save me from every trouble!"

Saul said to David: "Blessed are you, my son David, you will both truly achieve and truly prevail!" David went his way, and Saul returned to his place. (26:17–25)

There are essentially two chief themes, both political themes, at focus in the episodes, both of which pertain to the person and office of the king. The first is David's emphatic declaration of the sacredness of the king's person as "YHWH's anointed."[44] David here stresses a concept of royal ideology that may not have been very central to the original confederate investiture of the king, but that would have been familiar from the Canaanite, Philistine, and Egyptian milieus.[45] In certain respects, it runs counter to the prophetic doctrine of charisma by which the judges and Saul were elevated to leadership—for their charisma was seen as temporary, and dependent on the approval of the prophetic or priestly leadership, whereas David's respect for the king's person is extended even to one who has acted in a patently illegal and irrational manner, and who represents a direct and immediate threat to David himself.

The second theme, a corollary to the first, is a doctrine of the relation of the king to his aides.[46] Their job, as David conceives it, is unstinting protection of their monarch, not only of his physical person, but also of the political neutrality of his office. Aides who counsel precipitous and shortsighted acts of retaliation or who mislead their leader, or enlist him in a private vendetta (a problem for David the nonmonarch as much as for Saul the monarch), represent as much a breach of the integrity of the office they are protecting as do lapses in security around the king's physical person.

It is especially important at this stage that David represent himself as a *nonmonarch*, even though he was previously anointed for at least the prophetic (i.e., minimal) style of kingly office. In a sense, he presents himself here as a kind of ideal *subject*—adhering in loyalty to his monarch even though, on grounds of self-defense, he had cause to harm him. He is teaching the king's subjects the art of obeisance. Three times in chapter 24, twice in identical words, David affirms that his hand will not be upon Saul (11, 13, 14). He refers to himself as "a dead dog, a single flea" (cf. 26:20), and the vindication he anticipates is not that of the rightful ruler, but that of the powerless and oppressed: "YHWH will exact justice for me from you, but *my* hand will not be upon you!"—more or less the prose equivalents of the psalmist's cry of distress, an appeal to the invisible order of divine recompense, the justice of the underclass and servant.[47] David, to be sure, does not spare the king the full brunt of accusation, or underestimate the king's wickedness, but he emphasizes that under no circumstances will he personally be the agent of the justice he invokes. There is a curious kind of congruence here between the powerlessness of the victim, who anticipates help from without, and the unassertiveness of "YHWH's anointed" (Davidic version), who delegates both offense and defense to trusted (and, at times, distrusted) aides. His victimship is thus embryonically a study in kingship. The vulnerable and contradictory nature of Davidic kingship is nowhere better epitomized than in his recognition that the treachery of aides, his own and Saul's, is responsible for both his own and Saul's troubles, and that king and victim alike must perennially steer cautiously through the perilous shoals of their counsel. So, while he teaches servants the art of obeisance, he teaches kings the art of rule.

What is essential to note here is that David is represented constructing, as it were, out of whole cloth a fully imperial conception of kingship at the moment of his greatest and most ideal victimship—psalmodically speaking, at the moment of slander, dishonor, persecution, flight, and exile; that condition which the psalmist metaphorizes as the "depths," the "straits," the "seaswells," and the "murmurers." At this moment of greatest personal jeopardy (prior to kingship, that is), David is shown as a kind of ombudsman of royal custom, laying the foundations for the throne he will eventually occupy, yet without showing himself as a *seeker* of rulership, or as anything other than a humble and devoted servant of the reigning monarch.

It is all too easy to view these speeches as constituting royal propaganda or policy from after the fact—of this, there is little need for dispute (though it is still uncertain whether it is royal propaganda or someone's view of it). This notion, however, slights the subtlety with which David is drawn in both episodes, and fails to appreciate the more or less consistent line of theme and problematic with that of II Samuel. While the premonarchic David is drawn in a radically different manner from the later King David, the continuity of policy makes up for the seeming discontinuity of character. The young David is articulate, outspoken, sharp-minded, legalistic (the rabbinic portrait of David as a Talmudic scholar could be partly rooted in this evident skill with which David sketches the legal and typological lineaments of kingly office).[48] The older David will seem, by comparison, tired, vague, jaded, long used to (and dependent on) the ten thousand small acts of evasion and self-forgiveness, the royal loopholes and exculpations, that the king, as arbiter of the sacred and the profane, is empowered to wield. Yet the same institutional tenets represented in I Sam. 24 and 26—the inviolability of the King's person, the neutrality of his office, the condemnation of blood vengeance, the affirmation of YHWH's help to the oppressed, and the insistence on meticulous royal security—are more or less the doctrines put to the test in II Samuel and I Kings 1–2. Moreover, the same key words abound: "lie down," "this thing," "man" ['*ish*], "human being" ['*adam*], "good and evil," and the like.

I Sam. 26 adds an additional Psalm motif (one also akin to Jonah's poetic cry of distress in Jon. 2), that of exile from "YHWH's inheritance" (*naḥalat YHWH*), namely a sanctuary or tabernacle where the divine presence dwells.[49] David here dips deep into common ancient Near Eastern usage, echoing alike the lore of kingship and soteriology, and the myths of sacred enclaves and royal gardens that abound in Ugaritic and Akkadian texts. The exact referent of David's coinage is perhaps more modest: the migrating Ark of the Covenant, whose earlier vicissitudes had formed part of the opening of I Samuel (chaps. 4–7), and to whose protection David was a sworn servant. But the reader's hindsight on David's eventual career makes the reference a synonym or synecdoche for "Jerusalem." David here seems to protest Saul's enmity as a type of *religious* persecution: " . . . for they have driven me out today from adhering to the inheritance of YHWH, saying: 'Go, serve other gods'" (26:19). (The episode in fact prefaces David's entry into the service of the Philistine king Achish of Gath, if not thereby into service of the *gods* of Gath.) All of this before there is a Yahwistic Jerusalem to speak of, or a permanent abode for the Ark. Again, since the taking, losing, and retaking of Jerusalem will be a chief theme of II Samuel (and finally, in the book's last episode, the divinely mandated ground for a temple is secured), we again find the "legalistic" David establishing the issues of the book to come, and affirming the very norms of cultic and legal propriety before which he himself will fall as personally culpable in II Sam. 11–12. The later repeated strategy by which David's underlings allow the king to trap himself by his own words, is applied proleptically by the narrator as early as I Sam. 24 and 26.

Apart from the presumably more cultic emphasis of 26, one other major difference between chapters 24 and 26 must, as noted earlier, be that in the latter episode David is far more sympathetic to Saul: he castigates Saul's protectors and he curses Saul's advisors as the possible inciters of the king's malice, emphasizing his own loyalty to and esteem of the king (26:24). So the two "protection" themes mesh quite intricately in this episode: David as (wronged, exiled) protector/protégé of "YHWH's inheritance" (land, Ark, tabernacle), accuses the protectors of "YHWH's anointed" (Saul, and, proleptically, David himself). Their slander of him and their neglect of Saul are presented to Saul as two sides of the same coin.

Though David seems to mean Saul when he speaks of "YHWH's anointed," the reader is aware that *David* knows (insofar as he can, in a composite text, *know*) that he himself has been anointed (by Samuel in I Sam. 16). With all of the obeisance David pays to Saul throughout the latter half of I Samuel, the reader can never escape the knowledge that David is defining his own kingship. Saul's suspicions of David seem in fact quite well-founded. If the institution of kingship seems to congeal around the younger man independently of the intentions of either, it is because of his superior mastery of the symbolism and protocol of kingship. Here, as throughout the Davidic history, it is the semantics of sovereignty that comprises the true arena of political struggle. It is all the more infuriating to the overwrought Saul that his young rival has no openly stated designs on the throne. It is sufficient for David to design the *constitution* of the throne to which he pays obeisance.

Saul, meanwhile, is represented in the unflatteringly prosaic postures reserved for kings in decline: urinating, napping, dropping his guard. It will be yet some space of text before the younger master will be depicted (II Sam. 11, 13, 14) in a similarly unvigilant state. Paradoxically, the very conception of king that David champions here reduces kingly activity to the most immobile of executive functions: the king is a pure conduit of information, a kind of *corpus angelicum*,[50] making strategic decisions for the realm on the basis of data brought to him by others, and carrying the long hand of royal justice to the realm by verbal fiat alone, enacted by the hands of others. This immobility, however integral to the king's role as gatherer of intelligence and orchestrator of troops, closes him in, pressing him into an ever more cloistered and dependent state, ever more conducive to the kind of luxuriating and personal sloth that the biblical narrator typically, as for Canaanite kings, epitomizes by the most private and compromised of daily actions.

AMNON AND TAMAR

"And he will take your daughters to be grinders, cooks, and
bakers . . ."

I Sam. 8:13

My sister, my bride . . .

Song of Songs 4:9 et al.

David's firstborn son, Amnon, is initially shocked at the idea of violating
his half-sister Tamar (II Sam. 13:2b), although the key verb's literal sense
and its supporting syntax permit a double entendre: "And it was awe-
some in the eyes of Amnon to do something to her." Biblical usage
militates against translating this verse as does, say, the Revised Standard
Version, "and it seemed impossible to Amnon to do anything to her."[51]
It may, indeed, have seemed quite possible to Amnon—and, in any case,
"wonderful," at least at the level of echo, subliminal suggestion, and
affinities in the biblical concordance.

This ambivalence in Amnon's mind is partly illuminated by the story's
setting and context. This is the first full glimpse of the domestic life of
David's children, or indeed, of his household altogether. As is well
known, it is also the first in a chain of events that will constitute the
punishment and chastening of David foretold in Nathan's prophecy in
the first part of chapter twelve.[52] In the Amnon episode, David's related-
ness to the personages who appear is stressed three times in the opening
verses of the chapter: "Absalom, David's son . . . ," "Amnon, David's
son . . . ," and "Jonadab, son of Shimeah, David's brother." Yet David is
conspicuously absent from these verses, and does not enter into the story
until Jonadab has provided Amnon a scheme for approaching Tamar.
What is important here is the transition wrought in Amnon, which
depends precisely on a double sense to the word *wayyippale'* (was wonder-
ful/was unthinkable). Prior to Jonadab's intervention, we are tempted to
read the verse in the RSV's sense, though even in that case, it is made
clear that the thought of doing something to Tamar is a fixation or
fascination in Amnon's mind. After Jonadab's intervention, the thought
becomes, as if automatically, a *permitted* rather than a forbidden thing, a

plan rather than a dispiriting unattainability, and we are required to rethink the word *wayyippale'*.

Who is Jonadab, and what is his motivation here? We note that he is a nephew of David's (13:3), and that he conspicuously addresses Amnon as *ben hammelekh* ("king's son," with perhaps the weight of "crown prince"). Born of a brother of David named Shimeah, who had been bypassed for the crown of Saul along with six other sons of Jesse (I Sam. 16:9, where, however, he is called "Shammah,"), Jonadab could have any of a variety of motives for his exertions in this story. Is he maneuvering himself up the ladder of succession? Or is he a partisan of someone else?—Absalom, for example, as his role in II Sam. 12:32–33 suggests. Or is he simply a sort of busybody? A gossip? A sycophant? A jester? It seems important here that the reader be kept in the dark about the exact nature of Jonadab's agency, both to deepen the sinister aura about the court and to emphasize the manner in which the most intimate domains of the king's household are continually vulnerable to manipulation by the very sedentary milieu that the king himself has worked to create. The court is still faceless, even if the conspicuous precision of identification by which Jonadab is introduced (" . . . Amnon had a companion whose name was Jonadab ben Shimeah, brother of David . . .") brings the court into a decisive intersection with the familial and biographical data on David introduced elsewhere in the cycle. Court and household, two promiscuously mingled senses of the word *bayit* ("house"), are here represented in a particularly volatile overlap. It is intersections such as these, one should note, that have provided historians with their understanding of the royal court as a place of idle courtiers, Machiavellian schemers, royal pretenders, and "new men," or, to use Max Weber's felicitous term, "Catiline conspirators."[53] It is this sudden shift of the action to David's offspring that lends credence to the well-known view of this and the ensuing chapters as recounting a "succession" battle,[54] even though the weighty question "Who shall sit on the throne of David?" will not be asked until the opening scenes of I Kings, and even though succession itself is nowhere raised as an issue until the rebellion of Absalom at the beginning of II Sam. 15. We sense the seemingly *crowded* nature of the royal house, its casual mingling of public and private life, the steady access of court and household to one another: this uniquely textured hybrid society seems purposefully chosen as a means of epitomizing a moment of crisis in Israel's institutional history. Yet the narrator makes no explicit reference to political or institutional factors per se: it is timing, montage, placement, and identification of character that convey the impression.

As an analogous verse from the Garden story (Gen. 3:1: "And the serpent was subtler than every beast of the field which the LORD God had made") might serve in its context, a reference to Jonadab's cleverness ("Jonadab was a very smart man [*hakham*]") invites the reader to assume that the ensuing verses will exemplify, in some way, this courtier's slyness. The echo here of the rhythms of morality fable is one of numerous ways that "wisdom" idioms, frequently alleged to be prominent in the court history, assert themselves.[55] (We will have occasion elsewhere to touch on the question of the role of "wisdom" in the court history, along with the related, though not identical, question of the role of the "wise courtier.") We cannot avoid this analogy to the serpent, even if a full-fledged typological correspondence is neither possible nor necessary—if Jonadab's motives are allowed to lie shrouded in innuendo, so are his intertextual affinities. But, as in other scenes of the court history, the problem of agency is particularly prominent, and a kind of triad of man/woman/agent particularly essential to the plot's unfolding. The resonance with the Garden story seems thus more than casual, and it is further borne out in Jonadab's actual proposal:

> He said to him: "Why are you so glum morning by morning? A king's son! Won't you tell me?" Amnon said: "Tamar, the sister of Absalom my brother, I love."
> Jonadab said to him: "Lie on your bed and pretend to be sick. When your father comes to see you, say to him, 'Please let Tamar come feed me a meal [lit. bread]. Let her prepare the food in my presence so that I might see and eat from her hand.'" (13:4–5)

The motivically repeated words evoke the classic temptation motifs of "seeing" and "eating," and specifically eating out of the hand of a sibling and would-be sexual companion. Perhaps the connotation of the name "Tamar" as a type of tree adds to the reverberation, as does the reference to "bread" (cf. Gen. 3:17–19). But another set of associations is perhaps more pertinent, namely to the story that has just preceded: Jonadab's name evokes echoes of the name "Joab"; we must ask if Joab's role as an agent in sexual intrigue is parallel in some way to Jonadab's. In certain respects it is not: Joab is not represented in the David and Bathsheba story as a tempter, and his agency, as such, is far more encompassing than Jonadab's—for he is both intermediary in the fatal dispatching of Uriah and general representative of David in the conduct of the war against Amnon. Jonadab, moreover, does not act *for* Amnon, but provides him with a plan whereby he may act directly. Yet, as Joab's orientation and motivation in the Bathsheba episode are unclear, Jonadab's are similarly unclear. In both cases, the possibility is left open that the agent's role as facilitator of a crime is serving some unspecified conspiratorial purpose for which the episode's tempted party (David and Amnon, respectively) is made himself an "agent." As the latter episode proceeds, however, it becomes clear that the true tempted party in the transaction is not Amnon but David himself, who enters the action only belatedly, and under conditions that make him, in a sense, the main issue in the story.[56]

We are already indirectly prepared to focus on David by Amnon's curiously worded reply to Jonadab (the Hebrew word order is here left intact in the translation: "Tamar, sister of Absalom, my brother, I love"). Again, as in the introduction of Jonadab, kinship factors are made conspicuous, and here allude to a structural peculiarity of David's monarchy important to the court history's development, even as it pinpoints an understandable evasion on Amnon's part. For Amnon does not refer to Tamar as his sister but as "the sister of Absalom, my brother." David's freewheeling political and military dealings have helped create a large number of marriages (see II Sam. 3:2–5, 5:13–16), and a similarly large number of offspring who stand in a half-sibling relation to one another. Absalom is in fact also a half-sibling to Amnon, but Amnon prefers to see Tamar in this instance as the more distant of the two relatives. That she is child of the same father but not of the same mother bears a significance that is, like so much else in this history, of simultaneously political, psychological, and typological weight.

First, if Amnon is indeed crown prince (a fact by no means assured), a *permanent* union with a half-sister—disregarding for the moment the vexed question of the permissibility of half-sibling marriages, and disregarding the matter of Amnon's true intentions—would by no means be altogether disadvantageous to the royal house. It would further cement the union and interdependence of families that David's acquisition of the respective mothers as wives had inaugurated, and would create a vast extended family with the king, the dynastic father, as its focal point. A house so structured by the father's almost promiscuous accumulation of wives and children, a house with the structural contradictions born of this hoarding of alliances, such a house has the oddity of being both the monument to a policy of the father and a consequence of the policy. It is both a trophy of David's wars and a time-bomb in the midst of the supposedly peaceable kingdom he labors to create. The bellicose David is set at odds with the sedentary king. What is so peculiar is that at no point prior to, during, or long following this scene is David's specific attitude about succession made known—quite apart from the more oblique rubric stated at the birth of Solomon in 12:24–25: "David consoled Bathsheba his wife. He came to her and lay down with her, and she bore a son and called his name 'Solomon.' YHWH loved him. David sent by the hand of Nathan the prophet, and called his name 'Yedidiah,' in deference to YHWH." The reader's knowledge that Solomon was the successor creates the necessary link between this brief genealogical notation and the actual succession in I Kings 1–2. But Solomon himself plays no role at all in the chapters that lie in between. From Solomon's birth to Solomon's succession, there is no Solomon in the narrative. The vastly complex civil education of Solomon presupposed in his legendary "wisdom" (a curriculum that surely would have begun prior to his father's death) is nowhere mentioned in II Sam. 13–24, as if these chapters were some sort of parenthetic departure within an otherwise largely archival history of reigns. The pattern of mixing narrative and non-narrative data is familiar to us from Genesis through II Samuel, so its manifestation here should not be particularly startling. The king's succession by the king is laid out as a historical moment with its own counterhistory— in which the play of charismatic fantasy and political folly threatened its very birth. These twelve chapters entertain a time when the eventual succession was troubled, and the survival of the Davidic line itself a contingent matter. But it is Davidic *policy* that is most on trial.

And so, to return to Amnon's words, we see that his roundabout way of describing his relation to Tamar thus covertly alludes to a family structure that is part of a larger military and political program of the king, designed to render the key families of Judah and Israel personally dependent on the king by making the king kin to all. (One thinks of the Anglo-Saxon *cyning* [king], the "kin-ing"). "Behold, we are your bone and flesh," say the tribes to David (II Sam. 5:1). "I have given you the houses of your masters, and the wives of your masters into your very bosom; I gave you the houses of Israel and Judah, and if that is too little, I would add on this way and that," says Nathan's oracle of YHWH to David (12:8). Clearly, a certain kind of genealogical gerrymandering lies at the heart of David's philosophy of state. By its own internal dynamics, such a policy must inevitably generate incestuous bonding. It is perhaps for this reason that traditions associated with David's lineage (as far back as Moab and Lot, in Gen. 19, and Abram and Sarai in Gen. 12:10–20) seem unusually preoccupied with incest, endogamy, and (Gen. 38; Ruth) the in-law endogamy known as levirate marriage.

Second, this unwieldy structure is portrayed on the verge of certain major changes (if, perhaps, temporary ones) in the consciousness of kinship, which take root first and foremost in the royal household itself, amid the generation of those raised at the royal court, at the moment of their sexual ripening. These are the first Israelite brood among whom the more complex and sophisticated aristocratic marriage patterns in Egypt and Mesopotamia are capable of being taken seriously. Amnon, of course, may not be taking anything seriously but his own lust, but the delicacy in his mention of Tamar suggests that even he is sensitive to matters of kinship. Yet it is not Amnon, after all, who seeks a rationalization, but (for very different and thoroughly legitimate reasons) Tamar:

"No, my brother, don't force me, for such a thing isn't done in Israel! Don't do this horrid thing. And I, where would I carry my disgrace? And you would be one of the most despised in Israel. So now, please speak to the king, for he won't keep me from you." (13:3) If Tamar, who is the unwilling victim of Amnon, entertains the possibility of royal half-sibling marriage in Israel (or concocts it, to buy time against Amnon's advances), then it is not necessary to wonder if Amnon does. Her pleas take root in a context seemingly well used to such ingrown alliances. As commentators justly note, Tamar is protesting the rape, not the incest.[57] Indeed, in such a moment of desperation, it is worth paying close attention to the supposedly responsible doctrines she clutches for. She seems to speak with emphatic certainty that the king would *welcome* the alliance, and perhaps speaks in the belief that such an outcome is well known to Amnon as well. Again, our attention is indirectly brought to focus on the king and his policy.

As for Amnon, there is very little explicitly said about his character. The typological concurrences with Genesis and with II Sam. 11 (via the *Leitwörter* "see," "eat," "lie with," etc. that occur throughout II Sam. 13) make clear that he is seen as a yielder to temptation and a sinner. Jonadab's epithet *ben hammelekh* places him as the recipient of a certain forktongued flattery: Amnon's blue blood is both a mark of distinction and a sign of unearned preeminence. Amnon is thus shown as a type of *pawn* in both the king's marriage schemes and the courtiers' possible succession schemes. The very fact that the king's policy on succession is deliberately withheld in II Samuel suggests that his offspring are pointedly kept in the dark about his intentions, until his understanding of his options be fully ripened. Meanwhile, they are vulnerable to each other, and to their own passions and fancies.

Whatever the shortage of narrational explanation of Amnon's character, we see that he is quick to adopt Jonadab's plan without protest, ruthless in his ravishing of Tamar, and unable to tolerate her presence after the act. There is a curious syntactical echo between the words that describe his postcoital revulsion (" . . . for greater was the hate with which he hated her than the love with which he had loved her . . ." [ibid., 15]), those that describe Tamar's reaction to it ("She said to him: No! Not this evil which is greater than the other that you have done to me! Don't send me away!' " [ibid., 16]), and those of an earlier comparative statement:

> I am bitter, my brother Jonathan,
> pleasant to me thou wert exceedingly,
> more wonderful [*nifla'thah*] to me your love
> than love of women!
>
> (II Sam. 1:26)

where, not coincidentally, the verbal root *pl'* is a key word. Again, as in
the David/Bathsheba episode, two cultural codes are juxtaposed: the
ascetic (and vaguely homophilic) camaraderie of arms and the lustful
and incestuous passions of the idle and cloistered royal child. Amnon is
significant only insofar as he is seen as the fruit of David's special brand
of matrimonial statecraft. If we read the story at the level of morality
fable alone, whereby David's previous transgressions are punished by a
gruesome but typical and appropriate kind of reciprocal justice, we miss
the specifically institutional dimension of the story. There is not merely a
moral *quid pro quo* in the chastening of the king (though certainly that,
too), but a unique flourishing of political consequences to a long-prac-
ticed political strategy, now called to account by a portrait of its moral
and psychological effects on the king's own household.

All vectors in the story thus point to David: Amnon orients himself by
David's multiple marriages; Jonadab hatches a plot to make David unwit-
ting accessory to Amnon's designs on Tamar; and Tamar appeals to
David's presumed readiness to tolerate half-sibling marriage within his
household. David's threefold appearance in the story, ostensibly as a
peripheral character, in fact reveals him as the focus of concern. He is
the source of the ideological threads from which the story's ruses and
rationalizations are spun. Yet his behavior is curiously minimal and
retiring in all three instances. When Amnon feigns illness, David accedes
to his demand for Tamar's care, with a perfunctory and seemingly
absentminded recapitulation to Tamar of his son's request. As in previous staged confrontations (11:18–25, 12:1–14), he is represented as
unaware of the full import of the news presented; he is set up in a snare,
whereby his own words are made to betray him. The very network of
gossipers and observers that David had established for his political business is a milieu that turns out to have its own particular uses of *him*. The
omnipotence with which David seemed to act in the beginning of the
David/Bathsheba episode is also a vulnerability to many. The royal order
is a kind of plastic medium in the hands of at least some of the royal
subjects.

Similarly, when David learns of the rape, the text merely says: "And
King [!] David heard all these things, and was very angry" (13:21). The
Septuagint text adds the following words: " . . . but he did not rebuke his
son Amnon, for he favored him since he was his firstborn."[58] This
ambiguity in the textual history seems to reflect conflicting impressions
of the degree to which the king would favor a firstborn son—a natural
point of contention, given the ambiguously hybrid state of David's kingship. The ambiguity is already contained in the designation "King David." What is clear is that no rebuke *or punishment* is recorded. What,
then, is he angry at, and qua whom, "King" or "David"? What sort of

anger leads to both private and official silence? Is it not clear to the king that with the destruction of the reputations of both Amnon and Tamar, two of "King David's" key assets in the politics of *cyning* are irretrievably lost—*unless* a policy of coverup can be invoked, as David had attempted in the case of Uriah? Yet it is still possible (or *also* possible) that David's softness or immobility in the matter is the result of a purely private doting—one may compare his treatment of Adonijah in I Kings 1:6. Or it is a function of his preoccupation, or advancing age, or a certain *avoidance* of love (and preference for stereotyped and stilted forms of behavior) likely to take root in the household interaction of those who have too long lived at an official level—concerning which more will be said in its place.

This failure of will—rooted in habit, impasse, and shame—is most evident of all in David's third appearance in the story:

> It happened two years later that Absalom had [a] sheepshearers' [festival] in Baal Hazor, which is in Ephraim. Absalom invited all the king's sons. Absalom came to the king [*sic*] and said: "Please see, your servant has sheepshearing. Please let the king and his servants go with your servant. And the king said: "No, my son, let's not all go, that we may not be a burden upon you." But he prevailed upon him, and yet he did not wish to go and gave his blessings.
>
> Absalom said to him: "If not, please let Amnon, my brother, go." The king said to him: "Why should he go with you?" But Absalom prevailed upon him, and he sent with him Amnon and all the sons of the king. (13:23–27)

Here, the name "David" has retreated from the text altogether. Absalom addresses the king in the groveling tones seemingly demanded by protocol—or flatteringly adopts them beyond the measure required. He calls him "the king." He refers to himself as "your servant." He alludes to the king's sons (cf. verse 27) as "his servants." And he makes free use of the hortatory particle *na'* ("please"). The king's answer, *'al beni, 'al-na' nelekh kullanu, welo' nikhbad 'alekha* ("No, my son, please let's not all go, etc."), which envisages his own participation in chiefly official and ceremonial terms (the royal *retinue* would be a burden), is curiously reminiscent in syntax to Tamar's pleas to her brother: *' al 'aḥi, 'al te'anneni* ("No, my brother, do not force me . . .")—and again a motif from David's wartime lament for Saul and Jonathan is brought to mind: *'al taggidu be-Gath, 'al tevasseru beḥuzot 'Ashqelon . . .* ("Do not declare in Gath, do not bear news in the outskirts of Ashkelon . . . !"—II Sam. 1:20). This overlay of the king's gesture of refusal with a moment from the hushed-up crime and a moment from the king's farewell to his confederate past makes clear to us the wider arc of changes in Israel that have conditioned his avoidances. Several clear warnings have not enabled the king to see the extent to which he has acquired the executioner's touch even in his pliant shrugs and retreats. The refusal is Absalom's pretext for a suggestion to which he knows the king is all too used to acceding: to send a proxy. Only in his momentary hesitation ("The king said . . . 'Why should he go with you?'") does he entertain a flash of insight about the meaning of such "representation." And the moment passes.

NABAL AND ABIGAIL

Non idem licet mihi
quod iis qui nobili genere nati sunt,
quibus omnia populi Romani beneficia
dormientibus deferentur.

Cicero, *Verrines*
II.5:180

During the days of David's flight from Saul, he had pursued for a time something of a freebooter existence, conducting forays against the Philistines independently of Saul; living, apparently, at least partly by aid from the populace; and, in general, trying to stay a step or two ahead of Saul. The traditions do not represent the period as one of open war between the house of Saul and that of David, as seems to have been the case after Saul's death (see II Sam. 3:1), but the fugitive phase of David's career seems to have attained the character of a social *movement* somewhat early on: "There gathered themselves to him all persons in distress, and everyone with some debt, and everyone embittered of spirit. He became their chieftain [*sar*]. There were with him about 400 persons" (I Sam. 22:2)—and the merits of such "movements" were not appreciated by all: "Nabal answered the servants of David, and said: 'Who is David, and who is the son of Jesse? Nowadays, the servants have multiplied who are breaking away from their respective masters!'" (ibid., 25:10). Nabal is not just being obtuse, his reputation for foolishness (25:25) notwithstanding. As a rich Judean and a Calebite, he can speak patronizingly of David and his eclipsed clan, despite David's pan-Israelite fame.[59] Nabal's scornful dismissal is well aimed at an easily imagined weakness of David's ostensible movement: it is a revolt of the underclass, of servants and younger sons, and David himself is a rebel against his "master" Saul. The situation portrayed is one in which David, in flight from Saul, seeks to live by the patronage of the Judean populace, due him partly as a known hero in "YHWH's wars" (see Abigail's words in 25:28) and partly as a bestower of more specific kindnesses and protection. The extent to which David's activity could be seen as a protection *racket* by those unappreciative either of his reputation or of his presence in the area should not be taken simply as the measure of Nabal's benighted cynicism. This is the first recorded protest in the narrative against Davidic taxation. In the absence of definitive sovereignty in eleventh-century Palestine, "protection" may, in any case, have been a commodity in demand, easily sold or bartered, and perhaps at times easily forced on its recipients. Nabal, apparently, considers himself adequately defended without it. As it turns out (14–17), David's behavior toward his intended clients is, indeed, scrupulous and above board in all respects, although a serious clash that could adversely affect both David's reputation and his personal welfare is narrowly averted by the eloquent intercession of Nabal's wife Abigail.

The sequence of actions is important here, and the textual subtleties worth noting. David first presents his case via messengers:

> "Say to them: 'Viva! [text obscure] May you be at peace, your household at peace, and all that you have at peace! And now, listen, for you have sheepshearing. Now, the shepherds of yours were with us. We did not abuse them. They have found nothing missing all of the days they were in Carmel. Please ask your youths and they will tell you. Let the youths find favor in your eyes, since we have come at a special time. Please give us whatever your hand may find for your servants and for your "son," for David.'" (25:6–8)

While the address is never quite free of the suspicion of godfatherly practice, David represents himself as a *"son"* of his intended patrons, and the threefold repetition of the word "peace" (*shalom*) in verse 6—despite its being compromised by the later narration's similarly threefold use of the term in David's salutation of Uriah the Hittite in II Sam. 11:7 ("David inquired after the welfare of the battle, etc.")—must be taken as a serious oath, sincere of intention, and signifying David's good faith toward the household of Nabal.

Nabal's contemptuous refusal (25:10; see above) is then received by David without a word of comment, David preferring instead the impulsive battle parley associated with charismatic heroes,[60] a gesture of a sort at which David's son Absalom, some space of text hence, will excel: "David said to his men: 'Strap on each man his sword!'—and each man strapped on his sword, and David, too, strapped on his sword. About 400 men followed David up, 200 stayed encamped" (ibid., 13). One notes here the importance of the phrase " . . . and David, too, strapped on his sword." David's involvement in an action of unjust retaliation against Nabal is described both by agency ("400 men") and by person (" . . . and David, too . . ."). At this particular point, David is rushing headlong into a disaster of his own making—not coincidentally, a parry in the confederate-style politics of retaliation—and here, appropriately, the scene breaks off and shifts to another locale. For at that very moment, as David is apparently flying off the handle, a servant boy is describing to Abigail the care and restraint with which David and his servants had treated the sheep and herders of Nabal's, speaking in figures of pastoral and psalmody ("... a wall [*homah*] they were around us both night and day ..."). Abigail then wordlessly hastens preparations and intercepts David (18–20). The narrative syntactical peculiarity of the verse that follows suggests that David is speaking his complaint not to Abigail directly but to his own men, or, better, to the air—a measure of his stormy preoccupation and precipitous momentum. David, who in other situations is the consummate pauser and pronouncer,[61] here is shown cooking up his reasons in a distracted, improvised, and hurried manner as he rushes toward confrontation, and his language is notably blunt, colloquial, and crude:

> ... Now, David had been saying: "Why, for nothing I've guarded all that belongs to this guy in the wilderness! And nothing turned up missing among all that he had, yet he returns me evil for good! So may God do for the enemies of David, and so may He add [against me] if by daybreak I leave untouched of all that is Nabal's so much as one who pisses against a wall!" (Ibid., 21–22)

Abigail's obeisance, in any case, is scrupulously courteous and sympathetic:

> She fell upon his feet and said: "On me, myself, milord, fall the blame! Please let your maidservant speak into your ear, listen to the words of your maidservant! Do not let milord pay attention to this worthless man, to Nabal. As his name is so is he. His name's Nabal [fool] and foolishness is with him. As for your maidservant, I haven't seen the youths of milord, whom you had sent. So now, milord, as YHWH lives, and as your soul lives, YHWH has restrained you from entering into bloodshed were your hand to seek redress for you. So now, like Nabal may your enemies be, and all who seek evil for milord. So now, let this gift [*berakhah*] which your servingmaid has brought be given to the youths who go about at milord's feet. Forgive the misdeed of your maidservant, for YHWH will surely make for milord an enduring house, for milord fights YHWH's battles, and no evil has been found in you in all your days.
> "And should any human being [*'adam*] rise up to pursue you, and to seek your life, let milord's soul be bound up in the bundle of the living [*ẓerurah biẓror haḥayyim*], with YHWH your God; as for the souls of your enemies, may He fling them away as from the hollow of a sling. May it come about that YHWH do for milord according to all that He spoke, bringing goodness upon you. May He command you to be a prince [*nagid*] over Israel. May this not be cause for faltering in you or for hesitation on the part of milord, that you might [thereby] shed blood gratuitously, or lest milord act as his own savior. May YHWH do well for milord, and may you remember your maidservant." (Ibid., 24–31)

Yet David, who is otherwise eloquent with a threefold beatitude ("Blessed is YHWH God of Israel who has sent you toward me this very day, and blessed is your reasoning, and blessed are you who have prevented me from entering into bloodshed should my hand act on my own behalf!"), insists on repeating to her the original crudity, curiously reaffirming the very threat he sees her to have forestalled: " . . . But now, as YHWH lives, the God of Israel has restrained me from harming you, for had you not hurried along coming toward me, surely there would not remain of Nabal's by the break of day so much as a single one who pisses against a wall!" (ibid., 34).

There is a curious kind of standoff in this story, in which both David and Abigail agree (26, 33–34) that he has been providentially saved from committing acts he would regret, and David accepts her plea and gift (35), though he does not otherwise concede regret about the rashness of his anger or mitigate the harshness of his evaluation of Nabal. He now anticipates divine vindication, as in chapters 24 and 26, and, sure enough, it comes:

> Abigail came to Nabal, who, just then, was having a party in his house. He was in a good mood because he was exceptionally drunk. So she didn't tell him anything at all until break of day. It came about that when the wine wore off on Nabal, his wife told him of these things. His heart died inside of him, and he became like stone. About ten days later, it happened that YHWH struck Nabal and he died. (Ibid., 36–38)

The story is flanked by traditionary doublets (I Sam. 24 and 26) that have certain points in common with it.[62] Both bodies of material are concerned with the problem of military self-help. Both make use of the *Leitwörter* "good" (*ṭov*) and "evil" (*raʿ*). Both show David stopping just short of acting on his own behalf, an option that would have harmed his welfare and name, and awaiting vindication from without, by the hand of YHWH. Yet in another respect the two bodies of material seem diametrically opposed: the doublets show David *teaching* the restraint of the saintly: the Nabal/Abigail episode shows David being *taught* such restraint by the intervention of a sagacious woman. I Sam. 24–26 thus form a kind of traditionary garland, most analogous perhaps to that of Gen. 15–17. In a sense, I Sam. 25 is an inverse situation not just to that of the doublets but also to that of II Sam. 11. In the latter, David, at the pinnacle of his power, is *imperiled* by a woman, whose character and motives remain unknown; in the former, David, at the nadir of his power, is *saved* by a woman, whose character is amply drawn and finely articulated.

The triad is still more significant when we consider the change that is being described in David's relation to Saul, to the Israelite league, and to his home territory of Judah. The wealth and power of the Calebite Nabal signify an obstacle to David's foothold in Hebron and, accordingly, in Judah. The defeat of Nabal and the winning of Abigail signify a turning point in David's Judean fortunes, his later Philistine alliance notwithstanding.[63] The last verse of chapter 25—Saul's giving away of Michal to another suitor, Palti, son of Laish of Gallim, thus a reneging on a promise Saul once made to David—signifies David's further estrangement from the house of Saul, and thereby from the north. It appears from I Sam. 22:1–2 (" . . . and his brothers and his whole father's house heard, and went down to him there. There gathered themselves to him all persons in distress, etc.") and from Nabal's taunt (" . . . and who is the son of Jesse? . . .") that not only David's fortunes are in eclipse but also those of the house of Jesse. Had the situation not improved for David in Judah, he would have become a full exile from both regions, and possibly have faded into political obscurity long before his prime. The role of divine providence at this juncture is thus critically important to the unfolding of David's destiny, and it is signally important that here, as at numerous other junctures in biblical history (Gen. 3, 16, 27, 29–31, 38, Ex. 1–2, Josh. 2, I Sam. 1, etc.), the key assertive character is a woman.

Biblical narrative's penchant for surprise factors and sudden reversals is intimately tied to the pivotal role of women in the action. This is not just because Israelite women are freer and less subordinate than their Canaanite counterparts (as the end of Deborah's song suggests)—for, indeed, as the case of Rahab the harlot shows, the most exploited and degraded women sometimes have the most opportune vantage point on men's vulnerabilities, and the non-Israelite women rack up a good score in fighting YHWH's wars. But the woman's terrain in general in the Hebrew Bible, being an entity alluded to only by metonymy, remains an unknown and unacknowledged domain that lives in a complicated but often unspecified truce with the male world, which, at times may amount to very creative and destructive collaborations. Biblical women at times wield a balance of power, whatever other ways men are represented influencing the course of things. But it is the women's role in divine plan that most interests the narrator: the particular way that their placement and presence affect the unfolding of history and satisfy the purposes of a deity who is contemptuous of the trappings of status and caste that prevail in the world; who delights in upheaval, and who restlessly juggles the fortunes of persons and nations in an effort to right the moral balance in the land—a land that, by an immanent justice of its own, exacts its tithes and Sabbaths sooner or later. And it is the *songs* of women (Ex. 15:20–21; Judg. 5; I Sam. 2, 18:7, etc.) that pronounce a theory of biblical history. Its motions are those of mischief, cunning (Hegel's *List der Vernunft*), the wiles of a kind of guerrilla divinity:

> Yea, a crafty God is YHWH;
>   by Him much mischief is contrived,
> The bows of mighty men are smashed;
>   they that stumble have grown strong,
> Those sated with food are hirelings;
>   the hungry are [hungry] no more
> The barren woman has borne seventy;
>   the mother of many is forlorn,
> YHWH causes death and causes life;
>   brings down to Sheol and raises up,
> YHWH disinherits and makes wealthy;
>   humbles as He elevates,
> Raises the pauper from the dust;
>   from dungheaps lifts the destitute,
> To seat them among princes,
>   vouchsafes them the Throne of Glory!
> Truly, YHWH's are the world's extremities,
>   on which He founds the world!
>   (Ibid., 2:3b–8)

We find a great leveling of class and caste, the unblindered causality of the warrior and the "new man," but an illusory crucible of change, in which no human victor can remain resplendent for very long, in which new must yield to newer, and which, viewed from the yonder end of the human life-cycle, takes on a different visage entirely:

> Vanity of vanities, said Koheleth,
>   Vanity of vanities, everything is vanity!
> What advantage has a human being ['adam] in all his toil
>   That he may toil beneath the sun?
> A generation comes, a generation goes,
>   and the land abides forever.
> The sun may arise, and it may set,
>   And to its destination it aspires
> And there it shines,
>   It wanders to the south,
> And rounds back to the north,
>   And round and round the wind blows
> And on its rounds the wind returns.
>
> All streams flow into the sea,
>   And yet the sea is never full.
> Unto the place the rivers flow,
>   There they turn their flowing back.
> All things wear out,
>   A person ['ish] never has enough to say
> The eye is never satisfied with seeing,
>   And the ear is never filled by what it hears.
> That which was is what shall be,

And what was done is what will be done.
There is nothing new beneath the sun.
(Eccles. 1:2–9)

Is there not a strangely kindred vision shared by the fruiting woman and the withering old man? Heraclitean change and Parmenidean stasis are two aspects of the same historical reality. The folly of human presumption is stressed in both circumstances. But we misread the weight and relation of these textual moments if we fail to grasp the political argument that unites them—if we discern only the exultation of *ressentiment* in the one or the shrug of quietism in the other. Nor have we here the transmoral masque of the *Bhagavad Gita*'s glittering tapestry. Only the gnarled strophes of Job 38–41 approach the lineaments of that frightening possibility. And much the same exegetical intelligence that turns the whole of Ecclesiastes into a casuistic clause (an "if" leading to a very consequential "then . . ."), by the penning of the final two verses:

The end of the matter, all things being heard,
    fear God, and keep His commandments,
for this is the whole of human life [*kol ha 'adam*]:
    that every creature of God he brings in judgment
For each hidden deed, be it good or bad [*'im ṭov we'im ra'*].
(Eccles. 12:13–14)

likewise places, at the end of Job, after the voice "from the whirlwind" (38:1ff.), a revisionary epilogue (Job 42), which, in a subdued and "orthodox" manner, reaffirms the contours of the ordinary, and re-establishes the continuity of the generations. The radicalism of this apparent orthodoxy rests in the species consciousness on which it is founded, and in the revisionary self-confidence with which it effects its transcending discourse. The project of culture as such is at stake here, as it is through all of Genesis through Kings. David's providential rescue from the pride of the young is in its own way a step in the direction of a more focused and responsible politics, and so a major stride in the Israelite cultural endeavor. Unfortunately, it will not shield him from the cupidity of middle age, even though the chain of events precipitated by that cupidity will ultimately lead to a dynasty, in whose protective shade literacy as such, alphabetic and traditionary, will flourish.

ABSALOM

GLOUCESTER . . . Ah, dear son . . . ,
The food of thy abusèd father's wrath,
Might I but live to see thee in my touch,
I'd say I had eyes again!
                    (*King Lear*, IV, ii, 23–26)

Unlike the depraved Amnon, Absalom seems better predisposed for the royal mantle that has not yet been extended. He is a protective, reassuring, decisive brother, capable of self-discipline (or deceit) in regard to his feelings, whether of rage or of hatred (13:20–22)—and he is a patron of, or notable among, the sheepshearers of Ephraim (23ff.), therefore in contact with the pastoral past that the king has left behind. One thinks of a kind of "bonny prince," clad in shepherd's garb or military linen as befits the occasion of the particular ceremony of state he or the royal court has contrived, eye and ear ever attuned to the symbolic significance of public acts, aiming for strategic ties with the rustics and ethnics of the realm. Absalom, despite being born in David's years of being king at Hebron, is a child with a court education. His mastery of the grammar of pageant and orchestrated nostalgia show him to be so. He cultivates a certain narcissism centered in the hair, weighing in his annually shorn locks at two hundred shekels of the royal weight (14:25–26). If he is a type of David, it is a particularly hollow and romantic version, laden with posturing and public relations, and markedly heavy on the visual and superficial. (Remember that YHWH sees "not as a man sees: man sees only what is visible; YHWH sees into the heart" [I Sam. 16:7].) Absalom, anyway, knows how to affect the provincial touch. He is able to base it on his pre-Jerusalem birth (II Sam. 3:3), and he exploits both birth and bucolic affectation for his eventual, so to speak, candidacy.

He betrays an unexpected fuzziness of attitude, however, in the first words he speaks (his first altogether in the Hebrew Bible, 13:20): "Was your brother Am(i)non with you? Now, my sister, quiet down, *he is your brother*. Don't take this to heart." Is he encouraging her to think that Amnon's consanguinity should be considered *good* news? More likely, we are getting a spontaneous outpouring of stroking words, cooings of reassurance handed out at random by a brother himself quite distracted by his own whirlpool of thoughts and emotions. Or is he, in fact, quite lucid?

One finds it strange, anyway, that Absalom is capable of smoldering against his brother Amnon for two full years while speaking circumspectly (22–23). But much else about Absalom goes unelaborated. His sense of priorities is always presented slightly askew. When the king refuses his invitation to attend a sheepshearing festival, Absalom presses him, at first to no avail. And, rather than acquiescing, Absalom suddenly and, it seems, quite spontaneously suggests that the king send Amnon. David's firstborn is here pointedly spoken of as "my brother"—Absalom knows royal etiquette well enough to refer to the son of his father by a different mother by a term implying full consanguinity, or at least blurring the dissanguinity, in deference to the king's fantasy of the peaceable household fully united behind the living monarch. (When the king later, out of parental anxiety, expresses concern for "the lad Absalom," he is similarly telegraphing his sense of the particular grip he has, and expects to have for a long while, upon the throne and the kingdom.)

So Absalom's demand for the substitution must come under scrutiny. Is this first clear sign of a plot on Amnon simply the fruit of Absalom's two-year nursed grudge ("for he hated Amnon for having raped Tamar, his sister"), or is it a substitute expression of a deeper grudge or plan? Now, as to the matter of plan, it will be clear from the later slogan of Absalom's rebellion, "Your words are good and proofworthy; you have no hearing with the king" (15:3), that he will sell his candidacy for the throne on the basis of a claim to more personal, or at least more rapid, justice. He will tap the memory of confederacy and of judges in the gate. A distinct logic begins to manifest itself in the king's household as early as chapter 13: Amnon, parody of an Egyptian prince, is counterbalanced by Absalom, parody of an Ephraimite or Bethlehemite shepherd—two contradictory strands of the king's own identity. But is this a genuine rift between father and son over state policy and philosophy of justice? Or is it a particularly *visual* manifestation, an *emblematic* campaign for "the hearts of all Israel"? Are there clues to the larger dimensions of Absalom's strategy even before Absalom is introduced?

The clue, if it is such, is found in Jonadab. He appears but twice in the story, and is never heard from again (13:3–5, 32–33)—as if sandwiching the story's events, and thus framing it under the rubric of the scheming courtier, both ubiquitous and ubiquitously disappearing (is he receding as a planner or as a victim? Is he a major strategist or a pawn? Is his own blood kinship a factor or an accident?). Never, at any point, is the exact nature of Jonadab's functional relation to Absalom clarified. Yet *narratively* (or rather, if you will, exegetically), his function seems clear enough: to convey a suggestion of some *other* meaning to Absalom's blood feud, one in which Absalom's role is considerably more calculating and more sordid than his public self-presentation conveys—to the extent of even *sending* Tamar, via the agency of Jonadab and David, into the bedchamber of the rapist. Were this the case, as one historian suggests,[64] then we have, as historians have been accustomed to assume, a genuine "succession" plot. The point to remember is that our awareness of such a plot (in two senses of the term "plot": conspiracy and story line) is mediated almost exclusively by the presence of Jonadab in the narrative, and by very little else prior to 15:1ff. If the "succession" connection is a thin reed, it is by no means flimsy—it is supplied in a manner typical of biblical storytelling: the parenthesis. So, while the reader's knowledge of the larger dimensions to the events of II Sam. 13 is contingent on the closing of the parenthesis at verses 32–33, the process forces a rereading of Amnon's demand for a substitute to the king: it appears, in hindsight, as the start of an act against the throne itself. The rebellion of Absalom does not begin at 15:1 but at 13:27 ("In that case, let my brother Amnon come with us"), if not some time before. In attacking the king's firstborn, Absalom is simultaneously attacking the person of the king (by the standard of royal ideology to which Absalom stands at least *formally* opposed) and reaffirming the fluidity of kingly charisma, its ability to cut across the bounds of primogeniture, as in the divinely orchestrated chaos of certain royal psalms (e.g., 2:7: ". . . this day I have begotten thee . . .").

Or is it a grudge? Lest we be too quick to see only political cunning in this "new man," our text hints of Absalom's more voluptuary and court-determined nature—but in this instance, only belatedly, and this time outside the bounds of chapter thirteen, *after* Absalom has been brought home from exile, and still before the more explicit revolt:

> There was no man more handsome than Absalom in all Israel, in [the people's] emphatic admiration. From the sole of his foot to the crown of his head, there was not a blemish on him. When he cut his hair, as he was wont to do from year to year—for it grew heavy and he'd shave it off—the hair of his head weighed two hundred shekels of the royal weight.
> There were born to Absalom three sons and one daughter. Her name was Tamar. She was a beautiful woman. (14:25–27)

The picture of Absalom as a kind of Nazarite showpiece, a Samsonlike strutter, or, indeed, in his submitting himself to the shears, a logo of the sheepshearers, returns us again to the visual standard (". . . no man more handsome . . ."). This is followed by the crudest of genealogical notices, bearing not even the names of Absalom's alleged sons, but highlighting the daughter—not only by giving her name, but by again adding data of the visual standard ("She was a beautiful woman"), information that harks back, as well, to the description of the elder Tamar ("a beautiful sister," 13:1) and of Bathsheba ("The woman was very beautiful in appearance," 12:2). That she is named *Tamar* is odd enough, but its significance is confused by the absence of any clear indication of whether the younger Tamar was born before or after her namesake aunt was raped. If after (which the positioning of the notice encourages us to assume), the naming seems to reflect Absalom's desire to rekindle his sister's lost honor (or to neutralize his possible role in her dishonor). If before, another kind of desire could be in evidence, however sublimated its expression. Once again, we think of his words to his violated sister: "Now, my sister, quiet down. He is your brother; don't take this to heart." If the rape of Tamar was a political plot (and even, given David's agency, a political blackmail), it was not exclusively guided by political logic. Whether or not Absalom created the dishonor he avenges, his avenging is sincere, and bears the animus of one ruthlessly suppressing his own hidden longings. So, at any rate, we are encouraged to wonder by the odd non sequitur on Absalom's daughter "Tamar."

But then, the reference may rest on something much simpler and less psychoanalytic in nature: "Tamar," after all, is the name of the dynastic mother (Gen. 38) of the Judahite line of Peretz, from which both David and Absalom have sprung. In naming his daughter "Tamar," Absalom may be expressing his own ambition to be a dynastic founder—despite the fact that the course of action he later pursues (15:1ff.) would, if successful, render dynastic succession (understood as the choice by the dynastic *father* of his heir) virtually meaningless, by leaving the throne perpetually vulnerable to charismatic challengers and younger sons.

THE IMPERIUM

Anyone who has followed events in modern Lebanon knows how a system of blood vengeance (if, indeed, it can be called a "system") can wreak havoc with the independence and sovereignty of a territorial state. It is not far off the mark to say that an analogous problem plagued the land of Canaan (including the area that is now Lebanon) in the days of the tribal settlements, when, according to the rubric of Judges 21:25 (the book's final sentence), 'ish hayyashar be'eynaw ya'aseh ("each one did what was right in his own eyes"). The book of Judges itself is our best source for understanding this condition, especially the final three chapters, which describe an event of intertribal justice that came perilously close to wiping the tribe of Benjamin (not coincidentally, the tribe that produced Israel's first king) off the map. Israel, to be sure, was not at this point a sovereign state, in the sense that it was to become under Saul, David, and Solomon, but the corrosive effects of later internecine warfare were clearly in mind for the author of Judges, and the summary statement, in beginning with the words bayyamim hahem (in those days . . .), must surely have been spoken with some irony.

Against such a background must we understand David's reaction upon learning of Joab's murder of Abner:

> Abner returned to Hebron, and Joab drew him aside into the gateway to speak with him privately. But he struck him through the fifth rib, and he died—for the blood of Asahel, his [Joab's] brother.
>
> When David heard about it, he said: "I and my kingdom [mamlakhti] are innocent before YHWH forever from the blood of Abner son of Ner. Let it fall upon the head of Joab and upon his entire paternal household! May Joab's house never lack one with a bodily discharge, or a leper, or one leaning on a cane, or one who falls by the sword, or one who lacks bread!"
>
> Joab and Abishai had killed Abner because he had killed Asahel their brother at Gibeon during the battle.
>
> David said to Joab and to all the people who were with him: "Rend your garments! Put on sackcloth and mourn before Abner!" And King David walked behind the bier.
>
> They buried Abner in Hebron. The king raised his voice and wept over the grave, and all the people wept. David made lamentation over Abner, saying:

"Should Abner die like a fool?
Your hands were not bound,
your feet were not fettered,
As one falls before the wicked, so you fell."
(II Sam. 3:27–34)

Such a roundly emphatic and definitive curse as David directs at Joab must sound strange coming from one who maintained throughout his career such an intimate and interdependent relation to Joab and Abishai. The text, we note, goes out of its way twice to indicate that Joab had a clear motive and possibly even legal ground for doing away with Abner. Indeed, at no point in II Sam. 3 is mention made of any more pragmatic motive for the killing, such as the elimination of a rival for the army command. It is significant, to be sure, that David had carried on negotiations with Abner during Joab's absence, and, while we might possibly surmise that Abner's promise to deliver Israelite support was in exchange for some personal perquisite, David in fact makes no such promise. The denunciation voiced by David, in any case, is less concerned with the motivations of Joab than with the task of exempting David's imperium (*mamlakhah*) from embroilment in the feuds among clans and tribes.[65] We thus find here another definitive moment in the formation of royal and national institutions, and what is principally at issue is the legality of Joab's action. David is not just denouncing the wickedness of Joab (vehement as his declaration waxes), but is declaring the illegality of the blood feud. As king and chief justice, David will serve as policeman over the feuds and conflicts that arise in his kingdom, and will seek to dispense justice in proportionate measure for the wrongs committed between one faction and another. A crime against a given party will thenceforth be construed as a crime against the *crown* and *state*. This scene is essential for our understanding of the various "adjudication" scenes that abound in the court history—one thinks of Nathan's "rich man/poor man" parable (II Sam. 12:1ff.), the alleged plight of the woman of Tekoa (14:2ff.), the dispute between Ziba and Mephiboshet (16:1ff. and 19:24ff.), and, beyond the borders of the court history, Solomon's case of the two prostitutes who claimed the same baby (I Kings 3:16ff.).

Imperial justice is, of course, "Solomonic," in our conventional sense of the term: it is invariably inexact and compromising, a form of averaging that shears persons and property, as the case of Ziba and Mephiboshet best demonstrates. There, one of the two plaintiffs has to be lying, and, while one certainly feels more sympathy for Mephiboshet, finds his explanation plausible, and applauds his self-effacing response to the verdict, it is essential that neither David nor the reader know the full truth. The end result is that each plaintiff is given one-half of Saul's estate, and therefore that the wicked man, whichever of the two it is, has reaped unjust profit.[66]

Solomon, on the other hand, does seem to improve on his father's rough judicial style. Faced with an apparently irreconcilable dispute (the harlots' claims), he wields the judicial process in a manner calculated to flush out the truth. What Solomon is unable to control, however, is a recrudescence of the regional feuds and rivalries that will, after his lifetime, "divide the baby"—namely, the Solomonic kingdom itself.

David, in any case, formulates the policy of a united Israel before such a union was realized in fact. That a blood feud exists between the two parallel military commanders cannot be seen in isolation from the factors that divide the polities they represent. And David's very attempt to rise above the retaliatory passions of the blood feud will be a policy keenly put to test in the violence that will erupt within his own household, with Absalom's murder of Amnon. Absalom's action arises in the king's apparent failure to dispense the impartial justice he had earlier claimed to be the prerogative of the crown; and it is a tangible attack on the system of justice that the crown represents. It is fitting, then, that when Joab, through the hired actress-diplomat from Tekoa, seeks to warn David of the burgeoning dangers of the blood feud within his household, he gives her language reminiscent of—or anticipatory of—the primordial fratricide recorded in Genesis:

> "Alas, I am a widowed woman. My husband has died. Your servant had two sons, but the two of them were quarreling in the field, with no one restraining them, and the one struck the [other] one and killed him. And behold, the whole family has arisen against your servant, and they have said 'Give us the one who struck his brother, and let us kill him for the life of his brother whom he had slain, and also let us destroy the heir.' They would extinguish my glowing coal who remains, without providing my husband a name and remnant on the face of the earth!" (II Sam. 14:5–7)

> Cain spoke to Abel his brother, when the two of them were together in the field, and Cain rose up against Abel his brother and slew him. . . . Cain [later] said to YHWH: "My sin['s punishment] is greater than I can bear. Behold, you have driven me out this day from the face of the earth. From Your presence I shall be hidden, and I'll be a wanderer and wayfarer in the world. Whoever finds me will slay me!" YHWH said to him: "Therefore, whoever kills Cain will be avenged sevenfold!" and YHWH placed on Cain a sign so that whoever found him would not strike him. (Gen. 4:8–15)

And, indeed, we know what became of that restraining legislation through the erosion of time:

Lamech said to his wives:
"Addah and Zillah, listen to my voice,
O wives of Lamech, hearken to my utterance!
For I have killed a man for wounding me,
A boy for having injured me!
Truly, if Cain was sevenfold avenged,
Then Lamech seventy and sevenfold!"

(Ibid., 4:23–24)

THE SONS OF ZERUIAH

The arms of others either fail, overburden, or else impede you.
Machiavelli, *The Prince*

Joab first appears in the Davidic history, in name only, as the brother of Abishai, son of Zeruiah, in I Sam. 26:6. The text seems to take for granted that the reader knows who Joab is. The situation in which the narrator introduces the name is, as the reader eventually learns, typical of David's numerous interactions with Joab and his kin (II Sam. 3:28ff., 16:9ff., 19:22ff.), who are repeatedly shown urging the king toward, or embarking on, a precipitous course of action that David chooses to resist or oppose, coupling his refusal (in the latter two instances) with a denunciation of the seemingly coarse and contentious style of the "sons of Zeruiah." The name "Zeruiah," a common type of Yahwistic theophoric, is not, at first glance, necessarily a woman's name—indeed, the syntax of I Sam. 26:6 even leads us to think that "Zeruiah" is Joab's *brother*. It is not until II Sam. 2:18 that we are informed of their correct relation ("The three sons of Zeruiah were there—Joab, Abishai, and Asahel; and Asahel was swift on his feet like one of the gazelles of the field"), and not until 17:25 that Zeruiah is indicated to be a woman, and nowhere in the Davidic history do we learn that Zeruiah is in fact David's *sister*, as I Chr. 2:16 informs us—which, if correct, makes Joab, like Jonadab, a nephew of David's.

II Sam. 17:25 ("Absalom put Amasa over the army in place of Joab; Amasa was the son of a man by the name of Jithra the Israelite [Septuagint: Ishmaelite], who had entered into sexual relations with Abigal [I Chr. 2:16: Abigail], daughter of Naḥash, sister of Zeruiah, Joab's mother") is itself an odd non sequitur, in a manner typical of biblical narrative. Here, it occurs amid preparations for the civil war between David and Absalom. It follows upon the mention of Absalom's replacing Joab as head of the army with Amasa, a rival to Joab in two circumstances, here and after the civil war (19:14), when David again proposes, like Absalom, to make Amasa head of the army in place of Joab. Whatever the exact meaning of the genealogical digression in 17:25 (from "Amasa was a son

164

of . . ." onward), its function within the narrative seems clear enough: to show that Absalom, like David, knew how to exploit apparent familial rivalries among his subordinates, and that some sort of domestic turbulence may underlie this apparent rivalry between Joab and Amasa—though, in other respects, the "sons of Zeruiah" are shown to be an exceptionally close-knit and mutually loyal bunch. The verse leaves unclear whether Amasa is the child of Jithra *and* Abigal, or only of Jithra by another marriage. And especially perplexing is the one nongenealogical element in the passage: Absalom's replacement of Joab with Amasa. When and why did this occur? When the open struggle broke out (Joab, say, remaining loyal to David and going into exile with him)? Or after some rift between Joab and *Absalom* that led to Joab's removal from command, *after* David's flight? If we could understand whether Absalom was replacing a *dissident* or a *loyalist* Joab, we would understand a great deal more about Joab and the civil war alike.

Joab, in fact, disappears from the text altogether between 14:33 and 17:25, precisely during the initial unfolding of Absalom's rebellion, and he resumes an active role in the narrative only in 18:2, where he has apparently joined the fugitive King David at Mahanaim, and is reappointed by David, this time over a *third* of the army—a significant reduction of his former power—now sharing the command with his brother Abishai and with Ittai of Gath (the latter a staunch loyalist to David who seems to enter the picture as a check on the power of the surviving sons of Zeruiah). Because Joab is present through so much of the court history—indeed, second only to David and Absalom in frequency of reference, and surpassing Absalom in *range* of textual space occupied—we are perhaps surprised to find him conspicuously *absent* from the scene of David's flight from Jerusalem (15:14ff.), where key figures among David's supporters and detractors appear and recede in turn (in a manner exactly parallel to the scene of David's return procession in 19:16ff., where certain of the same figures return to the scene in more or less the reverse order). Is Joab with David? Or is he, as chief military commander, watching over his command post, as his duty to the king—to *David*—demands. Or is he, like Hushai, a plant within the camp of Absalom, seeking to sabotage the rebellion according to previous arrangements with David? Or does he, for a time (until the failure of the rebellion becomes evident to him), throw his lot in with Absalom? The text leaves all of this unclear.

We know, to be sure, that Joab's brother Abishai (whose sib loyalty David appears to recognize, in referring to "the sons of Zeruiah") stays with David throughout and beyond the rebellion, and we may thus assume either that Joab is counted among the loyal or that David knows, as does Absalom, how to exploit intrafamilial rivalries to neutralize any disloyalty. Joab, in any case, does reenter the service of David in 18:2ff. with greatly reduced responsibilities, and is clearly resented and distrusted by David throughout most of their long association, to the extent of David's *vowing* to Amasa in 19:14 to place him in Joab's position. Yet David remains curiously docile before Joab in two instances where we might expect behavior to the contrary. First, he does not protest when Joab, contrary to David's express orders, kills Absalom. (Indeed, there is in fact no textual indication that David even *knows* of Joab's role—an ambiguity we shall return to.) Second, he remains docile when Joab, asserting the reasons of state security that demanded Absalom's death, accuses David of grave discourtesy to his supporters and friends—the words are extraordinarily frank and represent Joab's only open rebuke of the king throughout the entire Davidic history:

> Joab was told: "Behold, the king is weeping. He mourns over Absalom." Victory became on that day mourning, for all the people, for the people heard on that day as follows: the king is saddened over his son. The people stole away on that day to return to [their] town[s], as a disgraced people steals away in their flight after a battle. The king hid his face. The king cried out in a loud voice: "My son, Absalom, Absalom, my son, my son!"
>
> Joab came to the king at his residence, and said: "You have put to shame today the faces of all your servants who have saved your life today, and the lives of your sons and daughters, and the lives of your wives, and the lives of your concubines—loving your enemies and hating your friends! For you have declared today that you have no ministers and servants—truly, I know today that were Absalom living, and all of us dead today, then would it be proper in your eyes! So now, rise, go forth, and convince the people, for I swear by YHWH that if you don't go forth, no man will remain with you overnight, and this will be worse for you than all of the evil that has come upon you from your youth until now!" (19:2–8)

It is clear that Joab—a man well regarded among the professional standing army and officer ranks, and intertwined in family connection to David's and to various other Judahite families—is an unwanted linchpin of David's precariously ruling coalition. David's carping at "the sons of Zeruiah" has a peculiar ring of powerlessness about it, and hints of complicated infighting between David and his chief allies, the exact nature of which remains unknown.

Two chief interpretations of Joab's character are thus possible, and modern investigation has, indeed, adduced opposed hypotheses. For Schulte, who sees the court history as arising in the milieu of the Adonijah rebellion and its aftermath (I Kings 1–2), and who sees a close connection between Joab, Abiathar, and Jonathan ben Abiathar (the latter the presumed author of the court history), Joab is a sympathetic figure—decisive when the king is vacillating; loyal to David throughout his reign and the interregnum; active where the king is sedentary; performing the work that the king finds odious (II Sam. 11:14ff.) and deferring to the king where credit is to be claimed for victories (ibid., 12:26ff.); and, in general, devoted to the civil peace, or at least, like any good Machiavellian courtier, devoted to the economy of violence (cf. II Sam. 20:20).[67]

For Israeli historian Abraham Levanon, on the other hand[68]—in a highly speculative but also highly interesting study of Joab's career— Joab does, indeed, part ways with David for the first half of Absalom's rebellion, staying in command of the army in Jerusalem and remaining, at least formally, in Absalom's service, until Absalom, by preferring Hushai's planted counsel over Ahitophel's, seals the doom of the rebellion. Levanon, like Schulte, retains a certain admiration of Joab, and concedes that his service to David in most other respects was true. But he includes Joab among the schemers against Amnon, sees him as a co-conspirator with Absalom (thus explaining his murder of Absalom as an attempt to cover up his own involvement in the coup), and holds Joab responsible for scuttling, much earlier in the history, the effective merger of the courts of Saul and David under David's leadership, which David had intended by bringing Abner into his court, for Joab, seeing Abner as a rival for his army commander's job, had killed him (II Sam. 3:22ff.). Indeed, according to Levanon, virtually any movement of rapprochement between Israel and Judah was a threat to the prerogatives of the sons of Zeruiah, and opposed by Joab. And Joab's ruthlessness, like that which David alleges of the sons of Zeruiah in general, Levanon sees as his most distinguishing trait.

Levanon also sees Joab's role in the killing of Uriah as a personal favor aimed at restoring Joab's army command. Whether II Sam. 10:14 and 17 ("Joab returned from attacking the Ammonites, and came to Jerusalem . . . David . . . assembled all Israel, and crossed the Jordan . . .") actually mean that Joab was removed from his command is very much a matter of debate, and highly unlikely in the light of 11:1 (" . . . and David sent Joab, and his servants with him, and all Israel, and they devastated Ammon . . ."). But, while Joab is never explicitly counted among David's enemies, the nature of his loyalty is never fully clarified, and at least the possibility exists that he knows how to exploit his proximity to the throne for personal ends.

It is curious, at any rate, that in David's deathbed instructions to Solomon to have Joab killed, David cites as his reason neither Joab's murder of Absalom nor Joab's blunt reprimand of the king over his private grief, but rather Joab's murders of Abner and Amasa:

> " . . . And also you know what Joab son of Zeruiah did to me, what he did to the two commanders of the army of Israel, Abner son of Ner and

> Amasa son of Jether: he killed them, shedding the blood of war in
> peacetime, putting blood of war on his girdle about his loins and on the
> sandals of his feet. So act in accordance with your wisdom, and do not
> let his white hair go down to Sheol in peace."

The irony of these words is that throughout the remainder of his service to King David (the question of his role in Absalom's rebellion aside), Joab served the king with exemplary restraint. He judiciously stepped aside after subduing Ammon so that David could take credit for the conquest (12:26–31); at no point does he seem to have engaged in violence for its own sake; his employment of the "wise woman" of Tekoa was (at least, to judge from the woman's words) aimed at preventing the bloodshed and civil war that might result from Absalom's indefinite banishment; Absalom's burning of Joab's fields went unpunished (at least until the cloak of war could again disguise his revenge); and Joab was willing to cut short his mission against the town of Abel-Beth-Maacah in exchange for the head of the rebel Sheba ben Bichri. Surely, it could be said that Joab applied well the lessons he had learned. And against Abner, at least, he had an arguable case—but here we see the crux of David's anger at Joab: that the latter both contravened Davidic policy and committed a murder that was politically inconvenient to the king. Twice during David's career, David's effort to merge the feuding regions by incorporating the military leader of the opposed side into his court was forestalled by Joab. In opposing the *union*, Joab in effect was opposing David.

What is clear from these considerations is that the relation between David and Joab is a continuing issue throughout the entire court history, and that the vicissitudes of this relation are a sensitive indicator of David's overall power, or lack of it. The intertwined fortunes of David and Joab are, in a sense, a chief hidden problem of David's reign. For the king's shifting ability to exploit or dispense with the services of a key Judean family ("the sons of Zeruiah") serves as a guide to the success or failure of the king's pan-Israelite ambitions. How universal can his reign be? How parochial must it remain? These are the questions posed by the presence of Joab in the story. And again, David's relation to an agent is the theme chiefly at issue: to what extent does the king's reliance on agents create dependencies and vulnerabilities that in some sense cancel the apparent gains wrought by contracting the agent relation in the first place?

Yet Joab is not just significant in terms of the power he has over David. His moments of powerlessness tell us much, as well. Two such glimpses of Joab are especially important to our understanding of him and of his relation to David.

The first is the odd, folkloric *traditum* of II Sam. 24, where David, "incited" by YHWH to number Israel in a census, commands Joab to carry out the census, evoking vigorous but ineffective protest from the latter: "May YHWH your [*sic*] God add on to the people this way and that [*kahem wekhahem*] a hundredfold while the eyes of milord the king look on [*ro'ot*]. But why does milord the king wish this thing [*baddavar hazzeh*]?" (24:3). Laden with key words, this brief moment of open, if subdued and courteous, disagreement with David preserves almost emblematically the full complexity of their relation as understood by the remainder of the traditions on them: Joab is the reluctant executor of an order of the king's that serves a plan of YHWH's that will lead to a punishment of Israel (a "second" example of a pattern begun in 21:1ff.); David, for his part, is driven by an unquenchable mania to undertake this ominous and institutionally subversive venture, and later (v. 10) he is overwhelmed by guilt over his decision to do it, which, indeed, the Chronicler, from a latter-day perspective, saw fit to label the work of Satan (I Chron. 21:1).

As if in token of the ambiguous divine involvement in the events of II Sam. 24:1ff., YHWH takes the unusual step (if one appropriate to a folktale) of offering David a *choice* of punishment to befall Israel. The prophet Gad declares the alternatives: seven years' famine; three months' flight by David from pursuers; or three days' pestilence (*dever*) in the land. David, rejecting the one option that explicitly entails his own personal distress, chooses to rely on the mercies of YHWH, over the mercies of a human antagonist. This effectively throws the final choice back to YHWH, who sends a plague by the hand of an angel/agent (*mal'akh*). Agency has somehow gone haywire, and by this point in the story, Joab's conflicted role in the affair has been absorbed into a wider tableau of divine and human collaboration. That Jerusalem is miraculously spared the affliction (cf. also I Chron. 21:15 ff.) is a traditionary datum with two thoroughly opposed resonances: one is that the land has been made to suffer for deeds that emanated from Jerusalem; the other is that the slayer was turned from the city at the site of the future Temple.

The miraculous deliverance of Jerusalem and the house of David at the last moment is told again in II Kings 18:13–20:21. There, the invasion of King Sennacherib, the conqueror of Israel, is aborted by the prayer of King Hezekiah. Through the prophet Isaiah, the downfall of Sennacherib is foretold, and the safety of Jerusalem is affirmed. A *mal'akh* slaying in the night destroys 185,000 of the encamped soldiers of the Assyrian invader, forcing his retreat back to Nineveh, where, in the temple of his god Nisroch, he is slain by two of his sons. Hezekiah's prayer also averts his own mortal illness "on the third day," whereupon he is to go up "to the house of YHWH." Abraham, one recalls, spotted Mt. Moriah "on the third day" of his anguished journey from Beersheba. Hezekiah is granted fifteen more years of life, but his last recorded act is a welcoming of a Babylonian delegation, who are shown all the storehouses and artifacts of his palace in the minutest detail, whereupon Isaiah prophesies the Babylonian invasion. In an almost complacent relief, Hezekiah remarks that YHWH's word, by sparing his generation, is fair.

To return to Joab: It seems no accident that his name is associated with this complex of symbols—disease, a slaying angel, a house of divinity, deliverance on "the third day," turning of the gentile back from Jerusalem, the sedentary king. I Chron. 11:6 connects Joab with the first inroads against Jebusite Jerusalem, and 11:8 with the rebuilding of the city around Millo and the City of David. If Joab's key role in the traditions about the taking of Rabbat-Ammon (II Sam. 11–12; I Chron. 20:1–4) is added into the overall picture, one is struck by how much of his destiny was tied up with the life of capitals, fortresses, and sanctuaries. That the volatile and ethically confusing play of agency and delegation in II Sam. 24 culminates in the strange events at the threshing floor of Araunah, indirectly connects Joab with the etiology of the Temple and recalls the grim etiologies of the sacred that punctuate the wilderness traditions (Ex. 32; Lev. 10; Num. 16; etc.). Two key pillars of the Solomonic bureaucracy—the census and the house of YHWH—are thus established in II Sam. 24. Joab's "powerlessness" in this text is suggested not just by his failure to sway the policy of David, but by the ever-widening arc of divine purpose that dwarfs his reluctant services.

Our other glimpse of the "powerless" Joab is the scene that records his death, and this, too, is illuminated by the complex of assoications I have outlined above. It is appropriate that Joab, upon hearing of the death of his protégé Adonijah, by order of Solomon, should flee to the "tent of YHWH" for sanctuary. This ploy does not avail him, however, and what began as an appeal for safety ends as a gesture of civil disobedience: "No, rather I shall die here"—a declaration that momentarily holds off even that unstoppable executioner Benaiah son of Yehoiada, while he seeks counsel from Solomon. It is worth noting that Joab's flight was prefaced by an unusual introjection of the narrator as to his motive: " . . . for Joab had taken the side of Adonijah, though he had not taken the side of Absalom" (I Kings 2:28). This affirmation of Joab's *past* loyalty during the revolt of Absalom is our only narratorially asserted information as to Joab's otherwise ambiguous and murky relation to those events, and oddly it comes at a time when it is too late to do him any good. (One might similarly compare the technique of delayed vital information in connection with Uriah in II Sam. 23:39, the verse that immediately precedes the "pestilence" pericope.) Joab, at any rate, who had done so much for the peace of YHWH's tent, now dies within its shelter, as if to make his own demise a kind of Tabernacle offering, whatever else the noisily vacant pronouncement of Solomon might make of it. Or is it a Tabernacle shaming? Joab, who had done so much *against* the union of Israel and Judah, and who is so closely allied to legends and history that underscored their separate destinies, here makes sure that his blood stains the Tabernacle that symbolized their unity—or was the ghost of their unity—before its house of cedar is built. Even in demise, Joab remains in the insistently double identity of the unaccommodated man of the field, hinging his historical significance on the fickle revisions of historical hindsight. The last thing said of Joab in the court history is appropriately double: that "he was buried at his house [x], in the wilderness [y]" (2:34).

" . . . THIS WAY AND THAT . . ."

"Here's another nice mess you've gotten me into."
                                        Mr. Hardy to Mr. Laurel

When David learns of the death of Uriah the Hittite, member of his brethren Israel, a death concocted through the agency of David's army commander, Joab, by command of David himself, the following words ensue: "David said to the messenger: 'Don't let this thing be evil in your eyes, because the sword eats this way and that. Strengthen your battle against the city and destroy it! Encourage [Joab]'" (II Sam. 11:25).

At the point in the story that this occurs, we readers know about David's involvement in the death of Uriah, so these words must strike us as the grossest kind of cynicism, in which appeal is made to the order of things, to a transcendent causality, to the natural way of indiscriminate destruction in wartime, as a cloak for a death we know all too well was premeditated, and which wrought, in consequence of its complicated logistics, the deaths of numerous Israelite soldiers with no relation to the private intrigue at all. We could call this a "lie," plain and simple, were it not for the fact that it suggests something even more damaging and far-reaching—a type of lie that reshapes its perpetrator. It is partly *believed* by the perpetrator, and seems to draw its strength and plausibility from the fact that its contours sit easily on the speaker's lips, that the words sound natural, that they are perceived as appropriate and in some sense *usual* utterances for one in his position. What is curious here is that David's imagined recipient is not in fact Joab, whom David knows to be fully cognizant of his, David's, true reaction to the news, but something like a *public* eye[69]—his courtiers, the army, the people, or perhaps simply the eyes of history—for whom the fate of Uriah and his household will somehow have to wash, in time to come. It is perhaps to David's credit that he exercises this much compunction about his act of treachery, but it is important to note that David's violence to Uriah is here not just twofold, as it had been until now—an assault on Uriah's marriage and on his physical person—but now threefold. For Uriah is now erased even from the public memory. The king issues no eulogy of those who have

172

fallen, though that might perhaps have improved his case in the eyes of any interested onlooker. He offers no statement—as he had, lavishly, for his beloved comrade Jonathan—about the meaning of their lives, or the pain of their loss. He only chalks it up to blind chance on this cruellest of arenas. This chilling and revealing form of historical editing—an editing on display, as it were—is the biblical text's curious way of commenting on a kind of historicizing *manqué*, on a failed scripture, one that in the light of further events fell short of the definitive record it purported to be. The self-destructive dimension of David's act lies in its erasure of the perpetrator as well as the victim. David, by his own self-editing, ceases to be the deeply sentient respondent to the woes of war he had shown himself to be at the beginning of II Samuel. He now prefers to be the strategist, the manager from afar, a kind of Faustian technician of war busily tinkering with the channels of power he otherwise so freely wields. David the soldier, in retreat from soldiering at least since his elegy for Jonathan, has fully withdrawn behind the mask of David the king.

A lie to oneself—Sartre has given this the curious oxymoron of a name, "bad faith"[70]—how can such be possible? How can faith be bad and still faith? How, indeed, can a person truly *lie* to himself? Does it involve forgetting, as if painful and offensive information could simply fade from consciousness? Is there a kind of narrowing of one's vision, as one would squint into a glaring sunlight? Or is there a knowing concealment of what one knows, as if before the tribunal of an outside observer—courtiers, armies, history . . . us?[71]

David's behavior as king bears useful analogies to certain matters discussed in Stanley Cavell's fine essay on King Lear.[72] Cavell's prose grows murky precisely where he departs from the text to extrapolate on the consequences in ordinary human experience of an essentially bad-faith process. But in showing that the king's experience is above all something quite ordinary and human, he treats the text in a thoroughly convincing way. No character in Shakespeare's play comes off unscathed: all are implicated in the actions that lead, among other things, to the exiling of children, the blinding of a father, the exiling of a king by his children, and, eventually, the shattering of the civil peace. What Hannah Arendt, in another context, called "the banality of evil" is here revealed in its hideous ordinariness. Cavell holds that the manifestation of love between kin entails a revealing of oneself, of one's own need and capacity for love. The key emotion involved in the withholding of love is *shame*—the desire to cover up oneself, one's body, one's emotions and needs, one's presence to another. "For otherwise," says Cavell, the kin who confront each other "are simply two human beings in need of one another, and it is not usual for parents and children to manage that transformation, becoming nothing more, but nothing less, than unaccommodated men" (Cavell, 285).

It is this apparently universal cruelty, inhabiting the motives even of the play's most wronged characters (Cordelia, Edgar, Gloucester), that links all "to the sphere of open evil" (Cavell, 283)—and, in so doing, shows us "how radically implicated good is in evil" (ibid.). Lear's behavior "is explained by—the tragedy begins because of—the same motivation which manipulates the tragedy throughout its course, from the scene which precedes the abdication, through the storm, blinding, evaded reconciliations, to the final moments: by the attempt to avoid recognition, the shame of exposure, the threat of self-revelation" (286).

Let me, in any case, try to apply these considerations to the situation of King David. David's selective self-sequestration, his minimal involvement in the affairs of his house, his withholding of the approval of his appearance, his dotage on the wrong children, his refusal to discipline his children in general, his avoidance of a definable position, his avoidance of reconciliation—are they not in some sense, like Lear's, effects of the shame of exposure, the blindness to one's own flawed being, and the inability to disclose oneself to another that flow from *correct* performance of the kingly office?[73] "Families, any objects of one's love and commitment, ought to be the place where shame is overcome. . . . but they are also the place of its deepest manufacture" (Cavell, 286). Of all households, the king's is most vulnerable to shame. The king's body eternal and his body temporal jostle together uncomfortably. His house, a mirror of the polity, bearing the contradictions of the body politic, manifesting the marriages of political convenience, is a veritable hothouse of shame. Its denizens are most alien to one another, most in need of love, most given to conspiracy and betrayal, and most prone to feign and conceal.

One curious feature of the Davidic history as a whole, beginning as far back as I Sam. 16, is the apparent disjunction between David's own father's house (the house of Jesse) and the one he himself forms. Indeed, the house of Jesse seems mysteriously to fade away quite some time before the house of David is fully constituted. The last mention of it is I Sam. 22:3–4, when David's rallying of the discontented of the land necessitates the removal of his parents to the protection of their distant kinsman, the king of Moab. Yet the same king is next mentioned (II Sam. 8:2ff.) as a conquered enemy of David. There is a strange textual silence here as to what actually became of David's parents in the interim. Jewish sources (see Rashi, Radak to 8:2, based on Num. R. 14:1) actually suggest that the Moabite king had indeed killed them—making David indirectly responsible for their deaths by an act undertaken precisely at the inception of his political career—the open defiance of his political "father," Saul. This linking of political engagement with familial endangerment strikes at the heart of the tragedy of I/II Samuel and I Kings 1–2. Yet curiously, the house of Jesse suffers an even greater oblivion—disappearance from the historical record. Bad faith of a rather fundamental sort! They are not even accorded the dignity of an obituary—a sort of rough justice, one might note, for the near-concealment of David by Jesse and his older sons that preceded David's emergence into the historical record in I Sam. 16.

This mutual anonymizing of David and the house of Jesse underlies David's precocious yet apparently belated emergence into public life. Whatever the motives at play, a part of David himself remains hidden. His precise relation to the house of Jesse, perhaps the most formative factor in his private personality and public self alike, remains shadowy. The deep silence in the tradition about the rise and fall of the house of Jesse sits like a kind of scotoma, a cognitive emptiness or scar, on the textual portrait of David—as if David himself had somehow played a role in this lacuna, and as if shame had strangled the words.

The text, nonetheless, tells us enough. The parade of Jesse's sons before the prophet Samuel, who, forewarned by YHWH, rejects each in turn until David, as an afterthought, is summoned and chosen as *nagid*, paints, with an emblematic clarity, the priorities of Jesse (I Sam. 16:6–13). Significantly, only the three eldest sons are named in the pre-exilic tradition (cf. 17:12–14; but contrast I Chron. 27:18). David speaks no words either in this scene or in the next traditionary block (16:14–33), where, summoned by Saul, David is engaged on a regular basis to play his famous lyre to soothe the emotionally ailing king. David's home career and field career are here meaningfully juxtaposed. The same personal qualities and apparent divine favor that will permit him to escape the anonymity of his father's sheepfolds will eventually put him on a collision course with his adoptive patron, Saul, but for the time being he wordlessly distinguishes himself in both settings. The simultaneous declines of the houses of Jesse and Saul are here foreshadowed in a muted and elliptical manner.

The household founded on primogeniture, one could say, is an enshrinement of a particular moment in the life history of the father, and as such is an irrational and contingent construction.[74] Elder sons tend to be favored because their birth typically coincides with the rise or zenith of the father's physical strength, sexual vigor, fortunes, and societal participation. It is essentially at this point that the father's sense of generational closure is (erroneously) completed, and here—perhaps, as in Gen. 21, up to the birth or weaning of the second child—that his particular notion of inheritance is first formulated. I say "first," because there is often a second—and the transition from the one to the other is the stuff of generational crisis that in the Hebrew Bible stands for historical change. The father's narcissistic projection of his own moment of triumph into the indefinite future is bound to clash with the imperatives of time and the rationality of talent—the "cunning of reason." And he often enters into his second and subsequent begettings ill prepared for the buffetings his paternal glory will suffer. He carries with him the frozen moment of his primogeneration, the moment when he, godlike, bestowed life *ex nihilo,* basking in the sunlight of his power and plenty, and pronouncing by this genetic utterance the meaning of his own fair life, so soon to dissipate.

The firstborn, for his part, remains a caricature of the father's arrested development—idle, pampered, dandified; bred, perhaps, to know the symbols of the household's life and language, but lacking true instruction, his relation to those around him remaining shapeless and fantasy-laden. The latter-born, for their part, have the misfortune of being born, not into a commonwealth of sons, one governed by an eye for the heart, but into a competitive aggregate, an improvised and rudderless mixed multitude scrambling for whatever blessings of paternal grace sift down by chance, caprice, error, or weakness.

Is Jesse's apparent sin of omission, with the bad faith it implies, all we are meant to know of the relation of David and Jesse? Is there, indeed, a "story of Jesse"? The story of Jesse, like all else in biblical narrative, is the sum total of the words about him. There are dangers to reading too much into a text that speaks so sparingly, but when sparse words are the only story we have, we must make what we can from what we are given. The words are, after all, what the makers of the text chose for us to know about Jesse, so the burden of interpretation is not to be skirted. We know, of course, from the poetic tradition, resonances of a very different sort to the expression "son of Jesse," but in the Davidic history it is a term laden with tension and claustrophobia. By the time we reach Nabal's shortsightedly contemptuous dismissal of "the son of Jesse" in I Sam. 25, the term has been taken through a variety of contexts that collectively portray David's exit from the house of Jesse, and, more than this, an archetypal moment in the history of fathers and younger sons, the emergence of the historical actor. It is a moment that must be apprehended both in its most resoundingly paradigmatic and in its most embarrassingly interpersonal dimension. If we must dig a bit to reach the latter (unlike, say, *King Lear,* where the rich self-expression of the characters allows their competing subjectivities to come alive more at the surface of the text), it is no less present than the former.

I Sam. 17, the famous tale of David and Goliath, details this leaving of the father's house in a complex and delicate manner, heavily dependent on key words and gestures, and intertwining several stories at once. The culmination of the narration is the landing of the rock at its target in 17:49, a moment of gasping awe and astonishment, at least for the characters witnessing the event, so much so that it seems as if the story existed only for this moment. Yet it is the long deadlock that precedes this exhilarating outcome, and the politicking, bickering, gossip, and consternation that plague the camp of Israel, that carry the real thematic weight of the story. Against this harried and paralyzed background, David moves with such calm certainty and quiet elegance that we are apt to construe his action as unilinear and single-minded. This is not quite the case, as we find on closer reading, for the resistances and temporary turmoils that punctuate David's progress, and the stages of improvisation by which he perfects his pan-Israelite message, convey a more convoluted sense of his otherwise rapid and precocious maturation. I shall explore this set of events by concentrating on certain clusters of key words and themes.

Abandoning. Three times within a short space of text the verb *naṭosh* (leave behind/leave in the hands of someone else) occurs: "[David] left the sheep with a keeper . . ." (17:20); "David left his baggage with a baggage-keeper" (22); and "[Eliab] said: 'Why have you come down here? With whom have you left the sheep?'" (28). The gesture has several overtones of significance to the plot: delegating (the first time David is shown relying on the assistance of an aide or hireling), abandoning (David never resumes care or dispatch of the items in his charge; his father's instructions in vv. 17–19 are, arguably, not obeyed to the letter), disencumbering (three times in the story, David rids himself of burdens: the sheep; the baggage of Jesse's errand; the cumbersome armor of Saul). In a broader sense, of course, it is the whole structure of primogeniture and patriarchal obligation that David sheds, as well as obsolete and inefficient weaponry. The verb *naṭosh* has other resonances in I/II Samuel: "The war spread/got out of hand/was [fought] with abandon" (I Sam. 4:2); "Your [Saul's] father has abandoned the matter of the asses" (10:2); " . . . for YHWH will not abandon His people" (12:22; whereas kings might!); " . . . and behold, [the Amalekites] were spread out [*neṭushim*] over the whole area . . ." (30:16); "[The Philistines] spread out [*wayyinnaṭeshu*] into the Valley of Rephaim" (II Sam. 5:18, 22). The connection between abandoning or delegating on the one hand, and the unchecked spread or burgeoning of enemy forces or other disruptive powers on the other, is to become a painful and pressing problem of David's later reign. Yet in I Sam. 17, David's abandoning of the inessential is allowed to appear as an unprecedented improvement. That anonymous hands stand ready to assume David's delegated burdens is perfectly in harmony with his later style of kingship, even though he is here but a boy, and as yet unproven.

Doing/being done. Man. Word/thing. As David nears the battlefront, Israelites are standing in dismay and discussing the unassumable chal-

lenge. The word *'ish* (man) is curiously abundant here (esp. vv. 23–27)—
we are in the realm of unaccommodated man, the field of naked engagement, of agon and championship. The norms of fathers' houses fade
here, where doing supplants being. Indeed, so out of the "ordinary" is
this realm that there is almost a fairytale quality to the gossip David
overhears: the king has offered his daughter in marriage to the champion who defeats the challenger. (That the king himself will not engage
the challenger seems taken for granted; it is a job, apparently, for
younger men and aspiring courtiers.) At this moment, David chooses to
utter his first words in the Davidic history: "What will be done [*mah
ye'aseh*] for the man who will strike down this Philistine and remove the
insult from Israel, for who is like this uncircumcised Philistine who has
insulted the troops of the living God?" This floridly pious epithet for
Israel stands in bald contrast to the worldly ambition apparently kindled
in David at this moment ("What will be done for the man . . . ," which, to
be sure, could be read: "What *could* be done for the man . . ."). As if by
instinct, he has struck upon the theological *mot juste* that will pluck the
heartstrings of Israel. The musician starts to compose his theme. He is
answered—by someone—as follows: "Thus will be done [*ye'aseh*] for the
man who will strike him down" (27). He has already begun to ride the
foamy currents of news and political talk, and the informant is appropriately anonymous. But at this moment David is interrupted by his older
brother, Jesse's firstborn:

> Eliab, his older brother, heard him talking to the men. Eliab grew
> angry, and he said to David: "Why have you come down, and with
> whom have you left that little herd of sheep in the wilderness? I know
> your treachery and the badness of your heart [*sic*]. You came down to
> see the war!"

David, for a highly revealing split second, breaks character. After
having dwelt in his imagination on the fruits of manhood, he momentarily becomes a small boy again: "What have I done [*meh 'asiti*] now? It's
only talk [*halo' davar hu'*]." As if by reflex against the voice of his
domineering and belittling older brother (". . . that little herd . . ."),
who, like Jesse, is blind to matters of the heart (cf. 16:7), David adopts a
familiar and no doubt habitual defensive posture, and, notably, the
gesture is one of bad faith: a retreat and self-exculpation, appealing to
the empty and inconsequential ways of small talk, as a cover for the idea
coming to birth within. But at this moment, David advances one step
further toward independence, almost as if by a fever of distraction, but a
concrete and consequential step nonetheless: "He turned away from him
toward another man, who told him . . ." (30). Meanwhile, Saul, anony-
mously informed of the presence of the newcomer, summons him,

whereupon David, baring his true intention for the first time, says: "Let no man's heart [*lev ha 'adam*] be in dismay. Your servant will go and fight with this Philistine." *'Ish* has parted ways from *'adam*, and now proposes to protect the latter.

Servants/slaves. The champion ritual proposed by Goliath (8–10) stipulated that the people of the vanquished champion would become the servants—or slaves—to the people of the victor. But indeed, he already has called the Israelites "servants of Saul" (*'avadim lesha'ul*), a term that hovers between the meaning of "servants" and "slaves," and thus between seeming a Philistine misconception (surely Israelites are more than slaves to a king!) and seeming an astute observation of historical reality (Israelites have indeed ceded back at least a part of their independence from masters). In fact, one of the benefits promised by Saul to the paternal household of the victor against Goliath is tax exemption. The actual words (v. 25) seem more radical and far-reaching: " . . . his father's house [King Saul] will make free in Israel [*ya'aseh ḥofshi beyisra'el*]"—calling to mind Samuel's warnings of the servitude kingship would bring. David, however, seems to steer a middle course before Saul, neither fawning before him as a slave nor departing from deferentiality: " . . . your servant is a shepherd. . . . your servant struck. . . ." But at the moment when YHWH's protective relation is affirmed, "your servant" disappears and David speaks in the first person to the free: " . . . He will save me . . ." (37).

At this point, David's demeanor could be understood as the innocent zeal of a plucky lad, as it certainly had registered in the memory of the tradition. But, understood another way, his words come to appear as a subtle revision in the politics of Yahwism, for they are accompanied by a repetition of the theological flourish he had somewhat experimentally uttered in the crowd: "Your servant struck down both lion and bear, and this uncircumcised Philistine will be like one of them, for he has insulted the troops of the living God." At the same moment, David's line changes from Elohist to Yahwist: "YHWH who has saved me . . . He will save me. . . ." The deliverance of YHWH is perhaps not just from lion and bear, but from the provincial grip of Judah (a "lion's whelp" in Gen. 49:9) and from the suffocating hyperplenitude of an overpopulated father's house—"bereaved bear" will later be used (II Sam. 17:8) as a simile for an angry father (David himself!) coming after a rebellious son.

When David confronts Goliath directly, at any rate, the Yahwist manifesto is now perfected, and, as in David's later piety for "YHWH's anointed," it displays a truth that has somehow always existed. The Israel here is not a servant of any mortal: it is the martial Israel of the wilderness days, the troops of the living God. These are David's first words before a pan-Israelite audience, perhaps his ripest and ideologically purest formulation of a vision of Israel. David now shows what "only talk" can do:

> "You come against me with sword and spear and javelin, and I come against you in the name of YHWH of the [celestial] armies, God of the [terrestrial] troops of Israel, whom you have insulted. This day YHWH will deliver you into my hand, and I will strike you down and remove your head from you, and give the corpses of the camp of Philistines this very day to the birds of the sky and beasts of the field, and all the land [or: world] will know there is a God for Israel; and all this community [lit.: congregation] will know that not by sword or by spear does YHWH save, for the battle is YHWH's, and He has given you into our hands!" (45–47)

This self-conscious archaizing depicts wholly the Israel that Israel would like itself to be, and it takes Israel out of the domain of ineffectual politics and imperfect self-defense into the transcendent realm of Exodus typology and the freedom of slaves redeemed, a freedom they apparently taste sufficiently to rally courageously in battle and pursuit against the Philistines after David's miraculous strike (see vv. 48–53). Significantly, the troops of Saul, who have been referred to throughout the story as "Israel," now are called "Israel and Judah" (52), for David (or rather YHWH) has expanded the fame of his tribe and region, and, appropriately, David brings his trophies to a marginally Benjaminite town that will eventually stand for the unity of Judah with Benjamin-ruled Israel: Jerusalem.[75] When David approaches Saul from afar, bearing the head and weaponry of Goliath, Saul asks "Whose son is this lad?" (This detail conflicts with the "musician" pericope of 16:14–23, and possibly with the earlier scenes of chapter 17, where Saul seems, at least in vv. 31–40, to have been adequately introduced to David; we must therefore understand the present passage to comprise a variant tradition of the initial acquaintance of Saul and David.) Saul's aide Abner is unable to answer this question, and Saul repeats it to David himself—significantly, Saul does not ask the lad his own name (provided we can place the comma after *dawid,* and not after *wayyo'mer*)—only his patronymic. And David, sweetly fork-tongued and recalling perhaps the "servant" taunt of Goliath, answers: "The son of your servant Jesse the Bethlehemite." In other words: I who am free am the son of one who serves, of one who has not understood his freedom. The least significant son of Jesse has become the author of Jesse's significance. *Ben-yishai* (the son of Jesse) has become, by shedding and streamlining, *'ish* (man)—the kinless adopted son of the living God (cf. Ps. 2:7). But then, this subliminal unhumility, through the power of "only talk," can easily masquerade as soldierly earnestness and deferential alacrity, as if to say: at your service, *sir!* The full trajectory of David's migration shows him to have found a new freedom—though not yet careless abandon—amid the mercurial politics of the field, where the tongue can rewrite the past and where the sword eats this way and that. The cultural moment that Lévi-Strauss, reflecting on the fortunes of the house of Cadmus, would call "the undervaluing of kinship" is nowhere portrayed with more economy and condensation.

GOOD AND EVIL

Were it not for the evil impluse, no man would build a house, or
marry a woman, or beget children, or engage in business.

Gen. Rabbah 9

The oppositional set "good and evil" appears frequently in the Hebrew Bible, especially in prophecy and psalms, to refer to the domain of moral choice (Isa. 5:20, Am. 5:14, Mic. 3:2, Ps. 34:15, 37:27, Eccl. 12:14, etc.), or, rendered as feminine nouns *ṭovah/ra'ah*, to refer to a concrete human or divine action, either beneficial or injurious (Num. 24:13, I Sam. 24:20, Jer. 21:10, 39:16, Am. 9:4, Ps. 35:12, 38:21, 109:5, Prov. 13:17, etc.), usually stated with regard to action in recompense, earned or otherwise, either for specific deeds or for a pattern of behavior by an individual or a group. In I Samuel, the words "good" and "evil," either as a pair or separately, seem to be used motivically to an increasing degree as the book progresses (11:10; 12:23, 25; 14:36, 41; 16:14, 15, 16, 23; 17:28; 18:8; 19:4 [twice]; 20:7, 9, 12, 13; etc.), and are especially prominent in the three stories dealing with David's decision to pursue or not pursue retaliatory action against his enemies (24:5 [vb. *yîṭav*], 12, 18, 19, 20 [twice], 25:8, 15, 17, 21, 26, 30, 34, 36 [vb.], 37, 39; 25:16, 18, 21 [vb.]). What unites most or all of the foregoing examples is that they are reasonably clear in context, calling forth associations that are readily present to the reader within the framework of religious tradition, common sense, or the plain meaning of the narrative or paraenetic line.

This is not quite the case for the contrast "good/evil" in the Davidic court history and the beginning of the Solomon story (II Sam. 13:22, 14:17, 17:14, 19:35, and I Kings 3:9), where, with the possible exception of 17:14, the usage is murky, idiosyncratic, and polysemous, operating in ways contrary to the plain sense of the narrative. Because the contrast appears five times within a fairly short space of text, one may well inquire whether their meanings are interdependent and cumulative in character, and must, therefore, be studied as a sequence, whose relation to the overall development of the narrative must be clarified.

We have seen that following the rape of Tamar, the narrator records that the king "was very angry" (13:21) about the event, and then, as if by way of contrast, that Absalom "did not speak with Amnon either ill or good" (*lo' dibber Avshalom 'im 'Amnon lemera' we'ad ṭov*), and then adds, by way of gloss (as if one were necessary), "for Absalom hated Amnon for having raped Tamar his sister." The narrator, in other words, seems to have jumped a beat, leaving us with a rather convoluted thought that requires unpacking. How is this apparently feigned neutrality on Absalom's part illuminated by a statement that Absalom hated Amnon? Does the particle *ki*, which we usually translate by "for," serve a function that is explanatory ("because"), chronotropic ("when/while"), exclamatory ("[yet] truly, . . ."), or adversative ("whereas/when in truth . . . ," with the sense of *ki 'im;* cf. Gen. 18:15)? If we recall a place in the court history where Absalom *does* speak good or evil—in this case, "good"— namely, in the phrase that characterizes his approval of plaintiffs' demands ("Your words are good and proofworthy; you have no hearing with the king," 15:13), we might reasonably surmise that to speak "good or ill" with someone is to enter into a diplomatic exchange that is (from Absalom's standpoint) useless, ineffectual, or below the dignity of one who perceives clearly the proper (and traditional) mode of redress, namely, nonverbal revenge. On the face of it, the notation marks clearly a sharp difference in attitude between David and Absalom toward the handling of the rape of Tamar, which, as we have seen, delineates two wholly different styles of public life and political behavior.[76]

It should be stressed, however, that the respective positions of both David and Absalom are clouded by less-than-honorable motives: it is possible that David withholds any more than verbal castigation of Amnon because he is trying to cover up the scandalous incident; and it is possible that Absalom shuns a *merely* verbal solution because he plans a reprisal that will, not coincidentally, help clear the way to his own succession. One way or another, it is clear that the difference in response to the rape of Tamar reveals more or less characteristic postures of David and Absalom, and that to speak "good or ill" suggests (at least to Absalom) a path of nonaction, ineffectual action, or "courtly" action, which the activist Absalom finds intolerable. The contrast "good/evil," clear enough in context as meaning little more than "a visible and definitive reaction," may thus serve as a touchstone of the nature of court life— where moral outrages can be made a matter of verbal negotiation or dispute, but their redress can, for reasons of state, remain unattended. This supposition will be strengthened if the subsequent occurrences of the motif also bear associations with the theme or problem of court life.

The woman of Tekoa, appearing on behalf of Joab to deliver a surreptitious message concerning the exile of Absalom, refers to David's great wisdom as monarch: " . . . for, as an agent of divinity, so is milord the king, understanding [lit. 'hearing'] good and evil [*lishmoᵃᶜ haṭṭov wehara'*]. . . . Milord is a smart man, with wisdom like the wisdom of an agent of divinity, to know everything that is in the land." Here the expression in its context seems to be a pointed reference to the king's position as a court monarch, standing watch over, rather than taking part in, the affairs of the land. In that the epithet is uttered in the context of a warning that the king's failure to deal properly with the matter at hand (i.e., to protect Absalom from blood avengers) is out of character with his chosen role as policeman over blood feuds, here we have a usage consistent in thematic resonance to that of the preceding example: the king must administer justice in a way that will call a halt to private reprisals, even if this involves a compromise in the justice meted out to the specific offender (Absalom). Ironically, for the king to take action on this plea is to *withhold* or *restrain* action on Absalom's case, which itself had been precipitated through a "courtly" temporizing on the king's part.

In her speech before the king, the woman of Tekoa indirectly predicts that failure to protect Absalom will lead to civil strife. (So, at any rate, we might make of her references to blood reprisal in her own fictitious "family," and of the particularly florid metaphor of death in 14:14, by which she seeks to contrast the perishability of the human social order—"like water poured out upon the ground" inevitably suggests blood-shed—over against the enduring intention of God to punish those who contribute to civil disorder.) We eventually learn that there is in fact no course the king can follow that will *not* lead to an outbreak of civil strife, given the positions, temperaments, and inclinations of the respective antagonists, and given the social and political structure that the king has labored to establish. Joab, whose words the woman speaks, knows this all too well. For all of the king's effort to place himself above blood feuds and private vengeances, to gain a vantage point over the "good and evil" afoot in his kingdom, the king has failed to control that which is afoot in his own house. "To understand [or, like a spymaster, to hear] good and evil" thus stands as an ironic epithet for the position of the king, and a symbol not of his power but of his powerlessness. Again, the motif helps to characterize court life.

In 17:14, the usage seems to shift significantly. Here, to be sure, the setting is that of a royal court, but this time it is the counter-court of Absalom. He and his advisors are deliberating the plan of Ahitophel: whether, as Ahitophel suggests, to fall upon the fugitive David immediately, while he is weak and unguarded; or whether, as Hushai suggests, to raise a national militia against David and his followers. It is never clear what hesitation or failure of nerve in Absalom (whatever the motives of "all the men of Israel" who are of one will with him here) bends him to prefer the more costly and cumbersome strategy of Hushai to the far simpler and more practical plan of Ahitophel. Indeed, at that moment— the dead center of the court history from a structural and conceptual standpoint—causality is removed from the human actors altogether, and the oppositional set "good/evil" acquires a new meaning:

> Absalom and every [fighting] man of Israel said: "Better [*tovah*] is the advice of Hushai the Archite than the advice of Ahitophel." Now, YHWH purposed to nullify the good [*tovah*] advice of Ahitophel, so that YHWH could bring upon Absalom evil [*ra'ah*].

In the divine perspective, in other words, as is not the case for the human actors, all is clear: Ahitophel's advice is known to be good (i.e., practical, effective), and the consequences of Hushai's advice are known to be bad (i.e., disastrous). The blind and erroneous judgments of a human court further the more complicated strategies of the divine court. The story at this point returns us to the questions of human and divine causality that had dominated I Sam. 24–26—again, a narrative counterpart to the theodicic themes of the psalmist, but told in the midst of a story otherwise of a far less faith-saturated perspective. II Sam. 17:14 is one of just three places in the Davidic court history that divine intervention is mentioned by the narrator, speaking of YHWH's plan, and not by YHWH himself.[77] The remainder of the history records almost exclusively the acts and intrigues of the human characters. The rare, sudden, and fleeting shift to a transcendent realm does not seem to have as its basis a theodicic motive per se: biblical narrative in general takes for granted that human players enact divine providence, so one wonders why it needs to be said here, and by a narrator speaking *of* God rather than, as is more generally the case, by God speaking as *quoted* by the narrator. A statement this parenthetic and anticlimactic seems less to have God as its point of reference and more the human actors, and, most of all, the absent David: this is *his* moment of greatest vulnerability, *his* moment of greatest contingency, and, as in his yielding to the plea of Abigail in I Sam. 25, the turning point in his fortunes. At the moment of silence just preceding II Sam. 17:14, no human actor—least of all Hushai, who is at this point as vulnerable as David—can help the fugitive king. If Absalom's decision is the fruit of a momentary hesitation, we find here material for fruitful speculation on the relation between divine providence and the hesitations of the wicked. "Good and evil," at any rate, do not appear here as an opposition after all, but as a kind of internal bifurcation: what people judge good may bring them evil; what might have brought them good would have entailed the triumph of evil.

The clumsiness and vertiginous relativism of human value judgments are set in contrast to the clarity, subtlety, and comprehensiveness of YHWH's.

Following the successful suppression of Absalom's revolt and the death of Absalom, the king proceeds home to Judah to reclaim power (II Sam. 19:12ff.). On his way, he is portrayed dealing with numerous groups and individuals whose cases represent various postures of loyalty or disloyalty displayed toward him during the rebellion. His treatment of a former enemy Shimei ben Gera (a fiercely pro-Saul northerner, who had cursed the king roundly on the latter's departure into exile, 16:5ff.) is scrupulously fair (although it offers him yet another opportunity to chide publicly the "sons of Zeruiah" for their zeal against the man): the king now gives Shimei his oath of protection (which is not, we learn eventually, binding upon his heir Solomon). This incident is followed by the case of Ziba and Mephiboshet, on which I shall not elaborate, having dealt with it in another discussion, where we have considered the inexact and compromising nature of royal justice.[78] The king then turns toward Barzillai the Gileadite, who had shown him loyalty and hospitality during his transjordanian exile. David invites the old man to come dwell with him in Jerusalem. Barzillai's reply again picks up the motif of "good and evil":

> "How many years of life have I that I should go up with the king to Jerusalem? I am presently eighty years old. Would I know good from evil [*ha'eda' beyn ṭov lera'*]? Could I, your servant, taste what I eat or drink? Could I still listen to the sound of men and women singing? Why should your servant remain a burden to milord the king?" (19:35–36)

As commentators have noted, Barzillai's statement in context means simply: I do not have the refined palate for court life; I am too old, and I am a simple man of the country. "To know good and evil" thus means here something like: to have one's physical senses in working order.[79] The statement is innocently meant, and accepted by the king as inoffensive, but the reader cannot ignore the narrative context which gives "to know good from evil" a deeper, more manifold meaning. Barzillai, not coincidentally, picks up actual and implied motifs of the David/Bathsheba episode (eating, drinking, leisure, amorous dalliance), such that his words amount to a ringing rejection of court life. Again, we find a character stating that "knowing good from evil" is a faculty indigenous to court life, and, more specifically, applicable *par excellence* to the king. The casualness of the statement contrasts with the growing scope of expense in human lives and ruined families that has been entailed in the creation of royal institutions. Barzillai unintentionally states with consummate conciseness and clarity the *reader's* cumulative nausea. The effect is richly enhanced by the unassuming nature of the old man's remarks, and by an even more paradoxical effect: the king's gracious concurrence in the judgment.

The final statement of the motif occurs outside the framework of the alleged "Succession Document," yet can best be understood as closely related to it in theme and import. Following Solomon's final consolidation of his power (I Kings 2:46, which is believed to conclude the "Succession Document"),[80] a new phase of the narrative begins, namely, the account of Solomon's reign. That this material is markedly different in tone and content from what has preceded it is what has led modern exegetes to see a major compositional break at 2:46: "And the kingdom was secured in the hands of Solomon." The scene that ensues, however, must be examined more closely. The reader knows all too well the ruthless deeds that have made this statement possible: the execution of Adonijah, Solomon's elder brother and rival contender for the throne; the dispossession of Abiathar the priest, an ally of Adonijah's; the murder, in the sanctuary of YHWH's tent, of Joab; and the execution, on grounds of a trivial technicality, of Shimei, the man whom David had previously sworn to withhold from harm. (The details of I Kings 2:36–46, especially 39–41, suggest that Shimei's violation of the ban on his activities was rigged: anonymous informants guide Shimei, in search of his runaway slaves, to a spot, the Philistine town of Gath, where the local royalty has had a long-standing relationship to Jerusalem, and where other anonymous informants spot Shimei's illegal presence and report it to Solomon.) Each enemy of Solomon, real or imagined, is dealt with in turn. All except Abiathar are brutally struck down. Each event is accompanied by a characteristically Davidic litany of disclaimer, by which Solomon swears his own innocence and good intentions (compare II Sam. 1:14–16, 3:28ff., 4:9ff.), repeats his father's abstracting perception of the rights and wrongs involved, declares a curse on the head of the "guilty" party, then orders his ubiquitous henchman Benaiah son of Jehoida (a sinister thug who out-Joabs his predecessor) to strike the hapless victim. Thus is the throne "secured." The text then proceeds (3:1ff.) to record two curiosities that help characterize this transitional period: first, it is noted that Solomon has concluded a marriage alliance with the Egyptian Pharaoh (as if undoing the Exodus, a pattern we found operating in the Abraham cycle); second, that a building project is under way to establish a permanent "house of YHWH" and city wall for Jerusalem—unmistakable signs of the neo-Canaanite institutions arising full-scale in the land of Israel. The "high places," to be sure, have not yet been closed down, and it is while sacrificing in the great shrine of Gibeon that Solomon receives a dream-visitation of YHWH, and is told to ask for whatever he wants. Solomon's reply:

> "You have shown great kindness for my father David, just as he has walked before you in truth, justice, and uprightness of heart. You have held great love for him now, in giving to him a son who sits this day upon his throne. And now, YHWH my God, you have given dominion to your servant, in place of David, my father. I am but a young boy. I know not going out or coming in. And your servant is in the midst of your people whom you have chosen, a great people that cannot be counted or listed on account of its great size. May you give your servant an understanding heart to judge your people, to discern between good and evil [*lehavin beyn ṭov leraʿ*], for who could be able to judge this cumbersome people?" (I Kings 3:6–9)

Whereas the epithet "speaking/hearing/knowing good and evil" had been applied to David's court as an ad hoc characterization, by indirection, of David's complicated and compromised position as court monarch, Solomon now appropriates it to his own vision of the monarchy, indeed, as its seal and symbol. We must consider, in this connection, YHWH's reply:

> "Because you have asked for this thing [*haddavar hazzeh*], and have not asked for long life for yourself, nor . . . wealth for yourself, nor . . . the life of your enemies, but have asked for discernment to understand what is just, behold: I have done as you have asked . . . : I have given you a wise and discerning heart, like none before you or after you." (Ibid., 11–14)

It is under the rubric of such proverbial wisdom that we are to know the legendary King Solomon, master of the orders of Creation. The return of an echo of bygone transgressions of the house of David ("this thing," a leitmotif of the Davidic court history) suggests how complete has been the rewriting of history. So delicate a brushstroke of irony shades a majestic and imposing royal amnesia. The cornerstone of an eternal dynasty has been laid, and the bodies of its enemies and victims cemented in. "To discern between good and evil," in the context of what has come before it, now comes to mean: to proclaim the general good and forget the particular evil. It is the bad faith that sustains all statecraft of a "cumbersome people."

THE GARDEN

We are not just sinful because we have eaten from the Tree of
Knowledge, but also because we have not yet eaten from the Tree
of Life.

—Kafka

Much has been said about the "wisdom" influence in the court history,
and I will not attempt here to assess this question in any detail.[81] My
views on the matter can be summarized by the simple observation that
products of a literate culture—indeed, efforts to sustain an oral or
written culture altogether—are, by definition, "wisdom." To look for a
"wisdom" *genre*, or for hallmarks of a "wisdom" *style*, is simply to add to
the fund of fruitless abstractions of which—if I may be indulged this
momentary fit of cantankerousness—Ph.D. dissertations and publish-or-
perish articles are made. It is well known that a long, rich, and ramified
scribal tradition connects, say, the Hellenistic world (and Roman, and
medieval, and even modern worlds) with the very dawn of civilized
culture,[82] and that certain myths, character types, and philosophical
projects have tended to recur again and again across chronological,
geographic, and linguistic boundaries, such that their recurrence in this
or that literate culture should occasion little surprise. I would like to deal
here with two closely intertwined motifs from the vast sea of ancient
"wisdom" that bear particular relevance for our understanding of the
Davidic history: the notion of paradise and the notion of generational
continuity.

In my chapter on the Garden story, I explored the connection between
these two notions. I tried to show that the story as a whole is modeled on
the human life-cycle, and that the "paradisic" state could be seen as a
particular moment in this cycle. Our own contemporary culture, to be
sure, in romanticizing childhood, has tended to apply the paradise metaphor most often to the *earliest* years of life, when one enjoys the protection of parents, the security of sustenance, and the almost unlimited
diversions of play. In the Garden story, on the other hand, the paradisic
moment seems rather to be the period of human life *after* the dependent

189

state of childhood (with its attendant terrors and insecurities) is ended ("Therefore does a man leave his father and his mother, etc. . . .") and *before* the interdependent state of adulthood begins, before the hard tasks and choices involved in providing for a new generation (" . . . in suffering you shall bear children . . . ," " . . . by the sweat of your brow you shall eat bread . . .") have beset the maturing person. This omnipotential state, when one feels the full strength of one's body and mind, when one is the most independent and most mobile, when one contracts alliances and friendships most freely—this phase of life is, in the symbolic schema of the Garden story, the time of "paradise."

Mankind's loss of Eden, as I tried to show, could be read both mythically and allegorically. In the mythic mode, the reader is encouraged to dwell wistfully on the lost pleasures of a sequestered realm, where nourishment grows on trees and waters bubble up from underground, where the blissful inhabitants perform the token labor of royal stewardship on behalf of the divine court, and where their continued security hinges on their unquestioning obedience to divine will. From the Sumerian Dilmun to Spenser's "Bower of Blisse" to television's "The Love Boat," the lineaments of the sacred enclave shift and change to suit the prejudices and utopian yearnings of each culture, but the paradisic vision seems rooted in psychological and anthropological factors that remain more or less constant. The sense of loss of a state of higher perfection seems a fairly universal topic of fiction and myth. Where cultural expressions of this sense differ is in the allegorical uses to which the notion of "paradise" is applied. Spenser, for example, made his "Bower of Blisse" part of a vast, complex fabric of temptations and perils through which the Christian virtues had to make their precarious way, along an arduous path of trial and service, that in itself, like the unfinishable *Faerie Queene*, had no proper end. It was not a place where one would want to stop off for very long—

> The painted flowres, the trees vpshooting hye,
> The dales for shade, the hilles for breathing space,
> The trembling grouses, the Christall running by;
> And that, which all faire workes doth most aggrace,
> The art, which all that wrought, appeared in no place.
>
> One would haue thought, (so cunningly, the rude
> And scorned parts were mingled with the fine,)
> That nature had for wantonesse ensude
> Art, and that Art at nature did repine;
> So striuing each th'other to vndermine,
> Each did the others worke more beautifie;
> So diff'ring both in willes, agreed in fine:
> So all agreed through sweete diuersitie,
> This Gardin to adorne with all varietie.

—yet the discovery of temptation is an essential exploration of "the garden of the self," a process in fact necessary to life and growth.[83]

In the allegorical mode, then, the Garden story ends up meaning something very different from what its mythical sense purports. If allegory is thought of as the use of the unfamiliar to portray the familiar, we see that the story, like a great number of similar stories in antiquity, accounts for the "origins" of life as we know it. These "origins" are not matters of historical genesis, in the manner of, say, an account of the origins of the English revolution, or the origin of iron smelting, or the origin of primates—rather, they are noetic origins: the falling into place of the premises and conditions of a certain awareness that is typically repeated in every human lifetime. On the other hand, such noetic transformations can be pressed into the service of historical explanation and political knowledge.

The human population of the biblical "Garden," by the reasoning set forth in this study, was a form of political commonwealth. The Garden story describes the coming into being of that commonwealth's self-conscious maturity. That the process involves disobedience and sin seems to be more or less taken for granted, since it is a condition of human freedom that wrong choices will at times be made (the complicated structure of atonement ritual in biblical law reflects a recognition of the inevitability and normality of sin), and the knowledge thereby gained, whatever suffering it occasions, is a knowledge from which there is no turning back. It represents a decision to live in cooperation with a successor generation; it involves give and take; it involves negotiation; as such, it demands compromises on strict justice. The greater the complexity of the social tableau, the greater the reign of injustice. Such is "knowledge of good and evil": knowing the qualified immortality of procreation (for this is the prospect tradition affords for someone *this* side of the Garden's gates) entails certain profound changes in human social organization, changes that bring their necessary share of conflict, mishap, and tragedy.

The growing interdependence of the first man and woman serves as an admirable metaphor of the nonsexual alliances that are typically the stuff of political existence—and while there is certainly a difference between a sexual and a nonsexual alliance, or between the domestic and public dimensions of social interaction, there is a certain dialectical relation between the respective domains that shapes one's political choices differently at different phases of the life-cycle. A householder and parent will see life in the political realm differently from a "young Turk" or *'apiru* freebooter—not that the latter is always a bachelor or nonparent, but that in the main one who is conscious of providing for and transmitting culture to a successor generation will be predisposed toward a stable and noncharismatic style of politics, and a concern for the institutions of tradition, education, law, practical arts and sciences, in short, all that fosters continuity and cultural survival. The *loss* that this entails, to be sure, is tangible: conspiratorial unanimity gives way to dialogue and consensus; apodictic certainty gives way to casuistry; justice is less absolute and more prone to averaging and compromise; and leadership tends less to guide and inspire than to represent, instruct, and preside. Yet all of these changes are necessary to the continuance of life and the preservation of social order. Were the losses not tallied, such order would amount to an oppressive complacency. Were the losses not incurred, there would be no framework in which gain or loss could be weighed at all. As in the formulation of Hobbes, life would be "solitary, poor, nasty, brutish, and short."

In the Abraham cycle, as I have tried to show, a further elaboration of the Garden paradigm can be seen. Abram and Sarai (for these are the names of Abraham and Sarah prior to their reaching true parenthood) appear on the scene as "sibling" mates, as wanderers with initially few personal ties to the lands that receive them. As they grow progressively more intertwined with the life of Canaan, progressively more sedentary and tied to urban centers, certain changes occur within their household that pertain to their foothold in the future. As for Adam and Eve, the steps toward a temporal commonwealth, toward a cross-generational system of culture (and there is no culture that is *not* "cross-generational"), involve unforeseen hardships, tragic dispossessions, and trials of faith. Paradoxically, whereas for the first human couple the state of innocence was sedentary and the state of knowledge nomadic, for Abraham and Sarah the reverse is the case—yet the cycle's symmetrical structure, the story's asymmetrical departures, and the language's motivic echoes establish a typological congruence between the Garden story and Gen. 12–25.

When we turn from legendary history in Genesis to political history in II Samuel, we are struck by intertextual affinities and common thematic preoccupations, which should undermine somewhat the source-critical picture shaped by Noth's *Überlieferungsgeschichtliche Studien* (1943), which drew a line severing a "Priestly" edited Tetrateuch (Gen.–Num.) from a "Deuteronomistic" history (Deut.–Kings). But there is no need to advance any new hypotheses concerning biblical source history—the intertextual relation is there whatever our view of the sources, and the traditionary affinities between David and Abraham are, in any case, well known, as are the "wisdom" affinities of Gen. 2–3 and II Samuel. When we add into the picture the web of verbal and motivic correspondences among the three texts, we clearly seem to have the apex, midsection, and base of a kind of traditionary pyramid. If, for present purposes, we set aside the question of this material's relation to the Exodus, settlement, and confederate traditions of Exodus through I Samuel, we find a consistently unfolding argument about the problem of generational succession. The three texts deal with Ur-history, legendary history, and history, respectively. The final stage (prior, that is, to the history of the divided kingdom) unfolds a detailed political argument, accounting for the foundation of the monarchy and its attendant radical redefinition of the entity "Israel"; supplying a critique of the social, religious, and political contradictions of the evolving nation; and setting the newly synthesized institution of dynastic monarchy against an anthroposophy of the human life-cycle, in which personal and political senescence are put into provocative analogy.

How, then, does the Garden paradigm affect our understanding of the Davidic history, and especially of the court history?

The ideology of kingship is, as noted numerous times in this study, closely bound up with a mythology of paradise, garden, temple, and sacred enclave. The king, as the worldly vassal and representative both of a patron deity and of a human body-politic, is a sacred being, whose safety and well-being are the unifying concern of the whole social order. One thinks of David's call to the elders of Judah to escort him back to his protected enclave—the gesture is jarring when set against the confederate ideology of minimalist kingship, and against David's own youthful career:

> King David [*sic*] sent to Zadok and to Abiathar the priests, saying: "Speak to the elders of Judah, saying, 'Why are you the last to return the king to his house, when the word of all Israel has come to the king [to return him] to his house? You are my brothers, my bone and flesh are you. So why should you be the last to return the king?'" (II Sam. 19:12–13)

The king's chief task is to receive protection and public acclamation. An aura of ritual narcissism surrounds his person, and the threats to his security are represented psalmodically as—the felicitous term is Baruch Halpern's—a kind of cosmic paranoia. The king is, in his turn, a steward of a sacred realm (temple, holy city, omphalic mountain), whose stewardship is contingent on a favorable relation between him and the patron deity. The king's personal peace and safety are essentially synonymous with the peace, safety, independence, and sovereignty of his realm. And well might it be so, for the very motivation to protect and care for a sovereign dynast can only arise in the *people's* willingness to see in the king a symbol of the unity and continuity of the body politic—a unity that transcends blood ties, regional loyalties, differences in social custom, dialect, and perhaps even language.

David, of course, seems to have made a long, slow, and troubled transition from activist to sedentary monarch. The decision to "go indoors" seems to have been made as early as II Sam. 7 (" ... when the king sat in his house, etc. ...."), but a definitive doctrine of royal sequestration does not seem to have been formulated until II Sam. 21:15–17—not coincidentally, during a resurgence of the very same hostile population whose incursions had created the need for monarchy in the first place:

> There was another war between the Philistines and Israel, and David, and his servants with him, went down and fought the Philistines, but David grew weary, and Ishbi Benob ... tried to attack David. Abishai son of Zeruiah aided him [David]: he struck the Philistine and killed him. Thereafter, David's men swore an oath to him, saying: "You shall not go forth with us to war anymore. You must not extinguish the light of Israel."

This fragmentary episode could have occurred at almost any point in David's royal career, but the detail of David's growing "weary" makes placement of the event in David's old age most appropriate. As a parallel to the king's earlier sequestration in 7:1ff., the episode supplies a closure of traditionary sandwiching, of a type we are familiar with from other biblical narratives, serving the etiological function of summing up David's long struggle to establish a sedentary and transtribal court.[84]

As noted, the doctrine of royal sequestration stands in sharp contrast—at least in its biblical application—to the earlier, confederate ideology of prophetic/charismatic leadership, despite the fact that in certain respects the two models of leadership overlap in their use of common Near Eastern typologies. The interplay of divine warrior and council god in Near Eastern mythological texts suggests that these two moments of kingship—the king resplendent in his battle regalia rallying and leading the troops ("going out and coming in"), and the king as venerable presider of palace council or law court (compare a similar polarity in Dan. 7:9–14)—express complementary phases in the history of most nations. What is striking about the biblical application of the polarity is its complete interfusion with a moralist skepticism, its subjection of the king and his household to close personal scrutiny, and its calling of the king to strict account for lapses in his kingly obligation (in itself a widespread commonplace in Near Eastern lore of kingship) as guarantor of justice.[85] This unique set of traits seems to be rooted in the Bible's distinctive manner of traditionary dialectics, its use of a deviously laconic prose narrative, woven from discrete *tradita*, to conceal an elaborately syllogistic accounting of political evolution.

Because the king represents—that is, signifies—the body politic, his moral health is an indicator of the people's. His progress, the vicissitudes of his fortunes, his quest for divine help, are represented as those of

"Everyman." Georg Lukács has argued that a concern for a literature of "the human condition"[86] reflects a particular moment in the evolution of bourgeois culture, and it is not unreasonable to perceive an analogous moment in the evolution of monarchic society in Israel. The king's "Everyman," like the king's justice, is a product of averaging and metaphysical fantasy. The patent absurdity of the king's embodying the experience of all social classes (the *hieros gamos* of the Song of Songs achieves a sharper articulation of class polarity in Israel than do the Psalms) is, however, rarely a problem to the members of the body politic that sustains royal institutions. The book of Psalms, after all, remains one of the most widely read works of devotional literature—and it merely begs the question to object that this universality is rooted in the book's typological anticipation of the Christ: how, after all, did the myth of the Christ establish itself if not on the foundation of a millennia-long pagan tradition of sacral kingship? The king's function as a body paradigmatic makes the psalmodic lore an anthroposophy and basileosophy in one. The biblical "Adam" is crowned as viceroy of Creation (Gen. 1:28, Ps. 8:6–9), and the corporate self he embodies is the corporate self assumed by the king in coronation. All of the mythological hallmarks of royal ideology are found in Gen. 1–3 (I here use the categories of Engnell):[87] creation in the divine image; reception of divine breath; declaration of man's rulership; establishment of a garden sanctuary and installment of the human being as divine gardener; the presence of "Waters of Life" and a "Tree of Life"; the motif of guardian service of a priestly sort (*le'ovdah uleshomrah*); mention of precious stones; investiture; giving of names; *hieros gamos;* opposition of man and serpent (chaos).

But the king in his "Garden" is, like the primordial human being, subject to test, change, and decay. His subordinate relation to his installant, his patron deity, can never be forgotten, or disaster will ensue. Ezekiel's oracle against the prince (*nagid*) of Tyre reads almost like an inverse psalm: YHWH God promises the very disasters amid which the psalmist customarily begins his plaint:

> "Because your heart was proud,
> and you said 'A god am I,
> in the seat of God sit I,
> at the heart of the seas,'
>
> "Yes wiser are you than Dan[i]el,
> in every mystery none can approach you,
> in your wisdom and understanding you grew rich,
> you put gold and silver in your palaces,
>
> "In your abundant wisdom and your commerce,
> you increased your wealth, your heart grew proud of it,

Therefore"—so says God YHWH—
"because you thought your heart the heart of God,

"Therefore, behold, I bring against you
strangers, the most ruthless of nations.
They will unsheathe their swords
against the comeliness of your wisdom,

"They will trample on your splendor,
to the pit they will bring you down,
you'll die the death of one slain in war,
in the heart of the seas."

(Ezek. 28:6–8)

And against the king (*melekh*) of Tyre, the oracle conjures the imagery
of the sovereign denizen of . . . yes, the Garden of Eden:

"You were the seal of perfection,
full of wisdom, flawless in beauty,
in Eden, garden of God, you were,
all precious stones were your adornment:
carnelian, chrysolite, and diamond,
beryl, lapis lazuli, and jasper,
sapphire, turquoise, and emerald,
and gold. Your drumwork and your flutings
were set down for you the day you were created,
an anointing cherub covering your head.
Upon the holy mount of God you were,
amid stones of fire you walked about,
perfect were you in your ways,
from the day you were created
till your perverseness was discovered.
In your abundant commerce you filled yourself
with violence, you sinned—and I
shall make you fall from the mount of God,
with protective cherub [drive you]
from the firestones. . . ."

(Ibid., 12–16)

Both the *nagid* and the *melekh*—representing essentially the prewar
and postwar phases of the same office—are accused of an over-lively
involvement in commerce, and above all, of mistaking their divine vice-
royship as divine status. The king is virtually represented choking himself with the encrustations of royalty, of primping, preening, and
cultivating a handsome look, of imagining himself a god. He is schooled
in the civilized arts, and perhaps knows (or serves as patron of those who
know) the nature of the elements, the arts of tincture and antimony, the
properties of roots and herbs, the cycles of the sun and moon and stars
and constellations, the guileful arts of magic, music, and the inditing of

odes. These domains of human knowledge are classically associated with the primeval history (Gen. 1–11), and it is Solomon more than David, or Solomon's stylized projection, Koheleth (Ecclesiastes)—the latter's words constituting tropes of an aristocratic *Weltschmerz* that places king and prophet in surprisingly close agreement on the vanities of the material and phenomenal worlds—who domesticates these treasures for Israel.

King David and his son King Solomon looked northwest, to their friends and allies in Tyre, and in other parts of the Phoenician shore—to the remnant of "Canaan"—for building timber, for craftsmen's services, and for kingly paradigms. While David and Solomon were concentrated on building a national entity of a very different type from that of freeport city-state kingship, they borrowed from Phoenicia mythologies of kingship that transcended even differences of social system: poetic types that were protean and adaptable, and that insinuated themselves, as it were, via psalms (those "of David" and of others), into the worship and liturgy of a culture (here including the postexilic and postbiblical Judaism of scribes, sages, pharisees, and rabbis) otherwise so self-consciously aware of its anti-Canaanite legacy.

In the Garden story, the human life-cycle, and thus the story's anthroposophy, is shaped by the narrator's changing designations for "man"—*adam* (human being) and *'ish/'ishshah* (man/woman). These terms—poetic pairs of the Ugaritic type in psalms and prophecy—correspond roughly to the phases of dependence/independence/interdependence in the human life span: the "independent" phase, representing the transitory freedom of young adulthood, after the leaving of a parental household and before the establishment of a new parental household, is represented by the terms *'ish/'ishshah;* the "dependent" and "interdependent" phases, sandwiching the story's central segments, are represented by the term *'adam.* While it is *'ish* and *'ishshah* who inaugurate the conjugal and procreative bond, it is *'adam* who faces the consequences and pays the bills. While *'ish* and *'ishshah* are more powerful and capable than their children (who are yet in the initial *'adam* phase of their lives), the middle-aged *'adam* feels the push of competitive pressure from his maturing offspring (who are now *'ish*), and experiences the interplay of conflicting wills that his household has become. This paradigm serves well for the interpretation of both Genesis and II Samuel, where family relations are most brought to the fore, and where a perpetual discontinuity between the respective orientations of parents and children plagues domestic tranquility and generational succession.

> Listen, my son, to the moral instruction [*musar*] of your
> father,
> And do not spurn the teaching [*torah*] of your mother. . . .
> (Prov. 1:8)

The instructional situation of Proverbs, where the "Solomonic" parent exhorts his child, in seemingly endless variations, to follow in his parents' ways, is a model of generational continuity. It depicts an ideal schema of cultural transmission that presupposes a civil peace and intergenerational accord. Yet its very hortatory tone presupposes the possibility of generational dissonance. The handing-on of historical experience to a successor generation is a desideratum that lies at the heart of the Exodus tradition (has to, or there would be no Exodus "tradition" at all): "You will keep this day [Passover] throughout your generations, as an everlasting statute" (Ex. 12:17). "And you shall tell your child on that day, saying: 'For the sake of this [present observance], YHWH acted for me when I went out from Egypt'" (ibid., 13:8). Yet within the Bible's continuous narrative, no generation is ever extensively represented *teaching* its successors. In every generation, the culture squeaks through, its survival a perennial miracle, its contingency a perpetual threat. We see this better if we look at the Hebrew Bible in terms of its main types of discourse, which, for present purposes, we can see as: narrative, poetry, genealogy (or other forms of archival listing), and law. The latter two modes presuppose institutions of generational continuity—a society with judges, magistrates, counselors, scribes, and teachers, with a system of education and jurisprudence, with a sufficient measure of cooperation between parent and child to sustain the commonwealth in time that is Israel. Narrative and poetry, on the other hand, portray an undercommunicating and miscommunicating social milieu, in which generational discord is the norm, and the possibility of total rupture and cultural death is an ever-present threat. Narrative and poetry record the exceptional; genealogy and law record the (desired) norm. The terrors of the former (where the only rescue is by the divine hand) are invoked to justify the premises for the latter (where people, by an act of will, forge the conditions of their survival).

We see, in any case, that the "Garden" paradigm represents two somewhat overlapping and conflicting situations in the Davidic history. David's halcyon days, his period of freebooting, conquest, heroism, pristine virtue, and popular acclaim, which follow him into his pan-Israelite kingship at least as far as II Sam. 7, are a form of "Eden"—an Eden memorialized (and for all practical purposes, laid to rest) in the protected sedentary enclave he creates for himself at that point out of Jerusalem, the City of David, now transformed into an "Eden" in a new sense, that of Near Eastern sacral kingship. But the very establishment of a Canaanite-style sacred grove marks the beginning of David's fall from youthful vigor and freedom of movement. His amorous dalliance with the wife of Uriah the Hittite, an episode redolent with the motivic echoes of the Garden story, is both occasioned by the institutional changes wrought by David and a first step in the process that will lead to dynastic succession by a scion of his partner in adultery. The full consequences of David's actions, however, do not flourish until the generation of off-spring—accumulated, often for reasons of state, in the pre-Jerusalem and early Jerusalem days—approach sexual maturity. (When Absalom rebels, his principal public gesture of rebellion is the appropriation of his father's concubines.) Then the "Garden" becomes a hornets' nest, and the king's artificial *pax imperii* is shattered.

The apparent conflict in II Sam. 7 between "conditional" and "uncon-ditional" divine blessing matches a pattern I have shown to operate in the Abraham cycle, which, in Gen. 15 and 17, respectively, presents conflicting views of the Abrahamic covenant. This pattern can be found, as well, in the Garden story's opposition between a "Tree of the Knowl-edge of Good and Evil" and a "Tree of Life." Indeed, both senses of covenant lived on in postbiblical Judaism as complementary domains in the national and religious experience of the Jew: the "conditional" view oriented to everyday reality, to matters of law, justice, and ethics; the "unconditional" view to utopian reality, to matters of hope, dream, and prayer. The uneasy coexistence of the two senses of Israelite covenant was already shaped by the literary and traditionary montage that runs, its thematic alternations calibrated with a sonatalike dexterity, from Genesis through Kings.

Who, then, is saying all this?

·EPILOGUE·

THE NATURE OF AN ALLEGORICAL RELATION

Verbally, we can make "one tree" into "five thousand trees" by merely revising our text, whereas a wholly different set of procedures would be required to get the corresponding result in nature.

—Kenneth Burke

Through [a] series of encapsulations, . . . to create an "absolute" novel that, as in Einstein's theory of relativity, contained its own observer within the field of observation.

—Theodore Ziolkowski
on Hermann Broch's
The Sleepwalkers

Who, then, has orchestrated these voices and moments we have come to know as the biblical narrative tradition, and why? Alas, this question, so familiar to generations of modern critical scholarship, is the least critical of questions, and, at least as far as exact persons and dates are concerned, unanswerable. We are immeasurably closer to the *intelligence* of the biblical composition than to its source of authorship. All we have is the text, and so the questions we must pose are questions about the properties of the text. In this light, we may legitimately ask: in what sense, then, does the Hebrew Bible offer us an "allegory?" My introductory essay, "Preliminaries," attempted to answer that question in the light of the relevant literary theory, but let me here specify a slightly different angle on the same problem, making use of the insights afforded by the body of this study.

I have argued and, I hope, demonstrated that the highest forms of the mode represent allegories not "of" something extratextual but rather "in" something textual. The relation of an allegorical text to its referent is not that of a simple one-way encodement, such as we might expect in a one-for-one vulgar allegorizing of the sort that has given allegory a bad name. Allegory is essentially the experience of polysemy, and its basic materials are signs, words, and texts. To speak of allegory is to speak of a manifold and convoluted system of relations, one that is volatile and reversible. Allegory is that which shows—or hints of—the relation between signs, words, and texts, a relation only fully fused in the experience of reading, and fused in a manner that induces or encourages further reading. The allegorical sign thus always points away from itself toward an "other." An allegorical reading is never fully completed, and the allegorical relation is never airtight. It may suit our convenience to take the Garden story as an allegory "of" the events in the Abraham cycle or the Davidic history. But the three texts mean what they mean both independently and simultaneously. It is thus the system of thought "in" which the texts are embedded that it is the task of an allegorical interpretation to discover.

Taking the Garden story, at least initially, as our principal frame of reference, let me try to summarize the ways in which an allegorical correspondence between the story and its related materials is possible. While I run the danger of repeating points made in the preceding chapters, I stress that we are now leaving behind practical criticism and returning to the domain of theory. The correspondences are here listed in an ascending order of complexity and difficulty.

1. *Verbal.* I have pointed out specific correspondences of words and verbal motifs between the Garden story and its related texts: "see," "eat," "know," "this [thing]," "good and evil," "agent," "man," "human," etc. A great many correspondences of this nature are possible, but I have tried to restrict myself to the most persistently repeated examples. The operation of what Buber and Rosenzweig called *Leitwörter* within individual stories has long been recognized by biblical scholarship. Establishment of verbal correspondence *between* stories, and between story cycles, is more difficult to prove conclusively, but if we have two bodies of material, such as the Garden story and Davidic history, where the same set of verbal motifs occupies a principal position in the narrative, we have reasonable grounds *prima facie* for establishing a correspondence. Provided further relations can be substantiated, it is a reasonable supposition to say that one of the texts has influenced the composition of the other, although we are not able to determine, on grounds of verbal correspondence alone, the direction of the influence.

2. *Motivic or gestural.* Much of the analysis I have offered has attempted to freeze the narrative action at selected points, much the same way one might stop a motion picture at an individual frame in order to study the nature of an action or gesture, and to affix more or less characteristic forms or postures in which characters are portrayed—thus: kin repudiation; kin recognition; temptation; reliance on agents; child sacrifice or endangerment; rationalization or denial (what I have called "bad faith"); shifting of blame; change of loyalty; exile; sibling rivalry; etc. While there are grounds for arguing that compiling catalogues of such motifs and gestures merely cites features common to a wide spectrum of biblical literature, and possibly all literature, no narrative analysis would be possible without their specification, and we would, in fact, thereby narrow the field of speculation considerably. We would, in other words, pinpoint the concerns that animate and unify the set of texts presently under investigation; and to point out that there are other texts that fit the pattern is not to belie the relation but to extend it. It can be argued with reasonable certainty that the gestural relations cited above and in the preceding chapters represent a cluster of themes most characteristic of the respective bodies of biblical material under focus here. This can be said even if theories of composition and redaction remain undetermined. One hopes, of course, that specification of these relations would help to clarify (outside the borders of this work) some of the literary-historical issues, but the presence of shared gestures or motifs does not, in itself, provide the basis for literary-historical judgments, only a kind of intertextual complicity that may lend supportive probability to one or another such judgment.

3. *Redactional.* At the end of chapter 2, I suggested that in each of the patriarchal cycles, the major outlines of the Garden story and its after-math are repeated. Indeed, we find that each protagonist, literally or figuratively:

    a. leaves behind homeland and home kin
    b. suffers scandal via a woman, and exile from adopted home
    c. allows one son to be preferred
    d. experiences the "death" of the favored son
    e. sees a son exiled

This pattern suggests that the redactional relation between the Garden story and the remainder of Genesis is carefully wrought and bespeaks a unified set of thematic concerns, which we may, for all practical pur-poses, term a unity of composition. Impression of this unity is strength-ened, rather than weakened, by pointing out the difficulties of corre-spondence or the weakness of some of the analogies. This only indicates that Genesis was a weave of sources and traditions, whose redactional unification under the rubric of the Garden story is all the more impres-sive. The rhetorical force of this redactional correspondence is difficult to assess, and correct judgments hinge upon the establishment of a distinct logic to the overall pattern, but apprehending the pattern itself is prerequisite to such conceptual understanding. Clarifying the Garden story's relation to Genesis is, however, only a step in the direction of establishing it as political allegory, since our principal political frame of reference (not quite the same thing as our *referent*) is the wider arc of biblical history that culminates in the Davidic history. We find, in fact, that the correspondence, with some slight differences of emphasis (ap-propriate to an *originator* of the analogy), carries into the Davidic history, where the protagonist:

    a. repudiates kinship and tribal origin as operative principles of
       public life
    b. suffers scandal via a woman, and eventual exile from his adopted
       home
    c. allows more than one son to be preferred, doted upon, or under-
       disciplined
    d. experiences the death of the initially favored sons
    e. sees a son exiled

It should be stressed that these correspondences do not conform to the time-line of the Garden story, nor do they need to: as I have argued in "Preliminaries," following Paul de Man, allegory is pseudochronic in exposition, precisely a rearrangement of the sequence of elements in the referent, or a temporalization of basically synchronic images or insights. Indeed, we have no guarantee that the temporal arrangement of the Davidic history is any more "historical" than that of the Garden story or of the book of Genesis; in some respects, in fact, it reveals a sequence as abstract as any in the more legendary portions of the Bible. Restricting ourselves to scenes that express the last four elements above (i.e., to the intrafamilial portions of the narrative), we find that the arrangement of the elements is basically symmetrical (fig. 4).

FIG. 4

a   David/Bathsheba and the birth of Solomon
  b   Death of Amnon
    c   Absalom's exile
      d   David/woman of Tekoa
    c' David's exile
  b' Death of Absalom
a' David/Bathsheba and the succession of Solomon

If we express the same sequence more abstractly, we obtain the symmetrical array of fig. 5, which pulses like an obsessive conundrum throughout the court history.

FIG. 5

a   A woman influences affairs of state
  b   A son is killed
    c   An exile occurs
      x   A woman influences affairs of state
    c' An exile occurs
  b' A son is killed
a' A woman influences affairs of state

The remaining material of the Davidic history (from I Sam. 16 to I Kings 2) consists of the "affairs of state" affected by the king's domestic problems. The idyllic phase of David's career, representing, paradoxically, his period of minimal political power, culminates in the establishment of the Davidic "house," in several senses of the term, in II Sam. 7. Up to this point, David is represented (a) repudiating the influence of women (II Sam. 1:26, 6:20ff., though I Sam. 25 shows his career being saved by a woman's intervention); (b) accumulating sons and daughters (3:2ff.; cf. 5:13ff.); (c) establishing a home base (5:6–7:29, with its corollary of foreign victories in II Sam. 8). These are the same three areas tested in the symmetrical cycle described above. Why these areas are important will be explored momentarily; for the present it suffices to note that they form areas of interest to a redactor, and reveal a close affinity with the thematic concerns of Genesis.

4. *Structural or conceptual.* A set of redactional preoccupations does not in itself constitute meaning. Assuming that the foregoing correspondences between the Garden story and its intrabiblical analogues hold up, we are left with the task of determining the point of the parallel—or, to use rabbinic language, the *nimshal* that gave rise to a *mashal.*

If we rephrase the three areas tested in the chiasm outlined above, we can obtain three principal propositions that the story submits to critical examination, each characterizing in some way the contradictions of the Davidic kingdom:

    a. that adoptive fraternal bonds suffice

    b. that one will live forever, accumulating infant children indefinitely

    c. that one's home base is permanent and unconditional.

To comment on each in turn:

a. *Fraternal bonds.* David begins his career as youngest of eight sons (I Sam. 16:10–11), who can hope for little personal advancement within the scope of his familial bonds. David's entry into public life is established through a sort of divinely ordained coup in the protocol of family authority (ibid.; cf. 17:28ff.) and through a series of adoptive relations, first with the entourage of Saul (16:14ff.), then with the discontented of the land (22:2ff.). His first association is idealized in his quasi-fraternal attachment to Jonathan, Saul's son. The two carry on an embattled friendship that cuts across the lines of family loyalty, and later, after Jonathan's death, David sings the praises of a former comrade-in-arms whose love was "more wondrous than the love of women" (II Sam. 1:26). David's life as a freebooter cultivating the loyalties of the countryside inhabitants through personal favors, is idealized in the story of Nabal, whose wife (possibly also a half-sister of David) renders David fraternal assistance against her husband's wishes, and later, after Nabal's death, enters the household of David as David's wife.

It is not clear when David's relation to his rootless allies ceases to be one of *primus inter pares* and becomes one of entrepreneur and employees, but it is certain that the early chapters of II Samuel attempt to drive home the point of the change: the king-to-be is shown to be embarked on the impersonal course of institution-building; he denounces those who have killed members of the rival ruling family in hopes of courting his personal favor (1:6ff., 4:9ff.) and he repudiates those such as Joab who have allowed fraternal loyalties to soil his reputation and political standing. David's choice to embark on the path of building power leads him to exploit the services of, and rely increasingly upon, expendable underlings whose services go unacknowledged. It is at this stage that he becomes a man of leisure, and vulnerable to the corruptions of court life. David, who had idealized his relation to a male comrade-in-arms and who had entered into marriage alliances (such as that with Abigail) of sympathy and fraternal affinity, now succumbs to uxoriousness and to the reckless, haphazard political conduct it entails and symbolizes.

b. *Living forever.* The Garden story, we have seen, is modeled on the human life-cycle. The Davidic history represents the life-cycle catching up with the king. David's pattern of multiple marriages and manifold progeny proclaims his seemingly eternal youth and potency (cf. I Kings 1:1–4 for the contrasting image) only so long as the children remain infants; when they mature, they become a time-bomb, threatening the king's rule and the civil peace alike. The king's blindness to his own mortality leads him to neglect the question of succession and the educational policy that this entails. He hoards the competence to govern, and as such fails to recognize his own expendability under the terms of the life-cycle (cf. Gen. 6:3) and the divine plan. His usefulness to Israel, in other words, is limited by his inability to establish continuity with, and transmission of knowledge to, the next generation. The importance of this theme in the Davidic history should, I believe, help to account for its primary position in the book of Genesis—in the Garden story and its typological parallels in the patriarchal cycles.

c. *Home base.* David's making of Jerusalem his capital is an expression of his aim to establish a center for a divided and diverse nation. Jerusalem is the tactical center of David's monarchy, and it eventually evolves into the seat of a permanent dynasty and centralized cult of worship. But it also threatens to drive a wedge between the monarchical present and the confederate past. The Davidic history wavers uncertainly, so it seems, between two ideologies of kingship, both stated by the prophet Nathan: the first (II Sam. 7:1ff.), initially paying lip service to the notion of a wandering tabernacle, ends up promising an eternal dynasty and a permanent tabernacle; the second (12:7ff.) reaffirms the conditionality of David's rule and, by implication, the permanence of confederate standards. It is not surprising, then, that a considerable weight of thematic interest in the court history centers on the struggle of David to hold onto Jerusalem. The vicissitudes of David's home base serve to call into question the value or merit of a capital city to the formerly diffused and decentralized Israelite confederation. This question, I maintain, is at issue symbolically in the Garden story, where the protagonist's hold on a piece of divinely mandated territory is hinged conditionally on obedience to divine will. There, the contrast between enclosed space and open field supplies the principal symbolic structure. The Garden is a "court," but the open field is a seat of forgotten lines of kinship between man and soil, man and beast. The Davidic court is a "garden," and the battlefield the seat of forgotten lines of kinship between king and tribes.

Typology and verbal texture alike play a role in this level of allegorical correspondence: in the Garden story, the field is where bread (*leḥem,* the fruit of struggle; see Gen. 3:18–19) is made; in the Davidic history, it is where war (*milḥamah,* the expression of struggle; cf. II Sam. 11:7) is made.

We seem to return again and again to one and the same *nimshal:* the "fall of humankind" in the Garden supplies a model for understanding the fall into sordid reality of the once-idyllic kingship of David. But this distilled "message" refuses to sit still for very long. It is rife with conceptual puns that encompass the epigenetic development of the human person, the unfolding progress of the human household, and the historical evolution of the body politic. We are thus dealing also with a story that has a hidden, or at least understated, protagonist: confederate Israel herself. Accordingly, I have chosen to designate a fifth and final level of allegorical correspondence, which I shall call the "negative."

5. *Negative.* In "Preliminaries," I attempted to show how the deceptive strategy of Nathan's parable in II Sam. 12:1ff. is partly designed to displace interest onto a false villain. This process we have found at work also in the Garden story, where we see the buck passing from man to beast and back to man (Gen. 3:14–19)—a pattern reinforcing the insight that we cannot shift responsibility to others but must bear the consequences of our actions. David is generally portrayed as scrupulous even in villainy, in the sense that he is able, at several points in the narrative, to claim responsibility for his own misdeeds, most notably after Nathan's rebuke, and again in a qualified way after the audience with the woman of Tekoa. One area of his life, however, remains closed to his scrutiny, even to his dying day: his reliance on agents and underlings to accomplish his political dirty work, a principal mark of his style of statecraft. This problem is expressed above all in his relation to his loyal lieutenant Joab, toward whom he never utters a kind word, and whom he cold-bloodedly orders killed (I Kings 2:5ff.) for "putting . . . blood upon the girdle at his loins and upon the sandals on his feet" (a strange recollection of the Passover motifs articulated in Ex. 12:11), namely, for allowing private vengeance to stain the sanctity of the throne. Yet this same man has repeatedly served the king well, helping him out of scandal, forestalling a costly blood feud, and, more than once, saving his life. Joab is David's blind spot, and it is interesting that the charge upon which David condemns him is Joab's least characteristic act, and not the act that had in fact caused the king the most personal grief—the murder of Absalom, contrary to the king's express orders. The king is willing to claim tacit responsibility for destroying a son; he does not wish, however, to admit that Joab is anything more to him than a volatile underling whose private ambitions must be kept in check—rather than a chief

mainstay of his kingdom. To do so would both call his own power into question and place in his lap a bloodguilt more monstrous than the one that he publicly repudiates.

Yet the very centrality of this problem—the king's reliance on agents—only begs the question of a still more fundamental problem: the people's reliance on a king. Whatever comes under close scrutiny in the life and career of David both deflects and reflects what has come about in the nation as a whole. Without this broader dimension of the problem, the story would remain but an engrossing and misleading melodrama, falling somewhat short of the radical and far-reaching cultural program embodied in the Hebrew Bible as a whole. The allegorical strategy involved here is the deceptive potential of text as such—the text's propensity for negative meaning, for secret sharers, as it were, that dwell behind the purported subject as a subversive presence. The devices of symmetry and traditionary parenthesis that we have explored in the present work enhance this potential by shaping a relentlessly self-transcending story. Such an esoterism is rooted in the traditionary venture undertaken by the makers of the Hebrew Bible: traditionary literacy in Israel demanded the intricate and partly unconscious cooperation of the many sectors of Israelite readership. Perhaps the majority of that readership knew of Israel's national sovereignty and Davidic kingship only as a nostalgic memory and dream—as a "paradise" lost. Its sanctity and honor had to be preserved even as its weaknesses, fallacies, and contradictions were anatomized. The nakedness of the parents, come uncovered by its own accord, had to be recovered by the children walking backward with their eyes averted. The canaanitish myths of kings and gardens, so essential to the style of kingship of David and Solomon, required their moment in the sun. All is placed with care before our eyes, then gathered to its place of rest within the larger fabric of tradition. And behind this masque of time's progress remains a voice—quiet, neutral, and respectful—our one constant throughout the entire literature of the Hebrew Bible: the anonymous traditionary voice that underlies all voices, human and divine, under whose rubric books begin and end, things are brought to pass, persons are made to speak. This steadying but negative presence, whose humbly playful marshalings of perspective must always be read with an attentive eye, and whose silence is the silence of a text, could easily be mistaken for "tradition" were we to lose sight of the open-ended and visionary task that tradition formation must be. Here we approach the "who" of biblical composition, who is so near and yet so far. It is perhaps appropriate to view this presence as a "we," for that is the corporate selfhood to which it summons—an "Israel" self-aware, self-sovereign, rationally navigating, sadly wise; an Israel capable of civilized disputation, mutual aid in time of need, and proportionate justice at all times. Yet in answering that summons, we sacrifice our neutral perspective as critical exegetes or theorists—not necessarily because we have thereby become existentially or religiously *engagés,* but because we have come to participate in the paradoxical dilemmas experienced by the wielders, mediators, and interpreters of power. In so doing, we come to understand why the text stands in the service of something that cannot be represented. Our dilemma as critical exegetes or as theorists begins on the far side of this knowledge.

ABBREVIATIONS

AAR	American Academy of Religion
AJSL	*American Journal of Semitic Languages and Literatures*
ANET	*Ancient Near Eastern Texts*, ed. James A. Pritchard
ANVA	*Avhandlinger utgitt av det Norske Videnskaps-Akademi* (Oslo)
AOS	American Oriental Series
BAR 3	*The Biblical Archaeologist Reader* 3, ed. Edward F. Campbell, Jr., and David Noel Freedman (Garden City: Doubleday/Anchor, 1970)
BASOR	*Bulletin of the American Schools of Oriental Research*
BDB	Brown, Francis, S. R. Driver, and C. A. Briggs, eds., *Hebrew and English Lexicon of the Old Testament* (Oxford: Clarendon, 1907, 1966)
BiKi	*Bibel und Kirche* (Stuttgart)
BK-1	*Biblischer Kommentar I, 1: Genesis 1–11* (Neukirchen-Vluyn, 1974)
BK-2	*Biblischer Kommentar I, 2: Genesis 12–50* (Neukirchen-Vluyn, 1981)
BMMLA	*Bulletin of the Midwest Modern Language Association*
BZAW	Beihefte zur *Zeitschrift für alttestamentliche Wissenschaft*
CBQ	*Catholic Biblical Quarterly*
CHB	*The Cambridge History of the Bible*, ed. Peter R. Ackroyd, 3 vols. (Cambridge: Cambridge University Press, 1970)
CJT	*Canadian Journal of Theology*
CR	*Centennial Review*
DBS	*Dictionnaire de la Bible, Supplément*
EJ	*Encyclopedia Judaica*
ELH	*English Literary History*
EThL	*Ephemerides Theologicae Louvanienses*
FMLS	*Forum for Modern Language Studies*
FRLANT	Forschungen zur Religion und Literatur des Alten und Neuen Testaments
Ges.-K.	*Gesenius' Hebrew Grammar*, ed. E. Kautzsch, 2d ed. (Oxford: Clarendon, 1910, 1974)
HES	Harvard English Studies
HKAT	Handkommentar zum Alten Testament
HSM	Harvard Semitic Monographs
HTR	*Harvard Theological Review*
HUCA	*Hebrew Union College Annual*
ICC	International Critical Commentary
IDB	*Interpreter's Dictionary of the Bible*
IDB Supp.	*Interpreter's Dictionary of the Bible*, Supplementary volume (Nashville, 1976)

JANES	*Journal of the Ancient Near Eastern Society* (Columbia University)
JAOS	*Journal of the American Oriental Society*
JBL	*Journal of Biblical Literature*
JJS	*Journal of Jewish Studies*
JSOT	*Journal for the Study of the Old Testament*
JSS	*Journal of Semitic Studies*
KHC	Kurzer Hand-Commentar zum Alten Testament (Tübingen)
NJPS	The New Jewish Publications Society Bible translation
NRTh	*La nouvelle revue théologique*
PAAJR	*Proceedings of the American Academy of Jewish Research*
PL	*Patrologia latina,* ed. J. Migne, 221 vols. (Paris, 1844–64)
PT	*Poetics Today*
REJ	*Revue des études juives*
RHPhR	*Revue d'histoire et de philosophie religieuses*
RSR	*Recherches de science religieuse*
SAT	Studien zum Alten Testament
SBL	Society of Biblical Literature
SBLMS	Society of Biblical Literature Monograph Series
SBT	Studies in Biblical Theology
SGV	Sammlung gemeinverständlicher Vorträge und Schriften (Tübingen)
SVT	Supplements to *Vetus Testamentum*
SWI	Studies of the Warburg Institute
TDNT	*Theological Dictionary of the New Testament,* ed. G. Kittel and G. Friedrich
TDOT	*Theological Dictionary of the Old Testament,* ed. G. J. Botterweck and H. Ringgren
ThB	*Theologische Blätter*
ThZ	*Theologische Zeitschrift*
TTKi	*Tidskrift for Teologi og Kirke*
TWzAT	*Theologisches Wörterbuch zum Alten Testament,* ed. G. J. Botterweck and H. Ringgren
UF	*Ugarit-Forschungen*
VT	*Vetus Testamentum*
YFS	*Yale French Studies*
ZAW	*Zeitschrift für alttestamentliche Wissenschaft*
ZBK	Zürcher Bibelkommentar (Zürich)

NOTES

Preface

1. "Kingship vs. Kinship: Political Allegory in the Bible—A New Reading of Gen. 1–3 and Related Texts." Copyright, 1979, Ann Arbor: University Microfilms International.

2. Throughout this work, "traditionary" means: of or pertaining to the form or content of a tradition. "Traditional" means: in a manner or form suggested or dictated by tradition.

3. For a more concise exposition of my views on this matter, see the following of my articles: "Meanings, Morals, and Mysteries: Literary Approaches to Torah," *Response: A Contemporary Jewish Review* 9:2 (Summer 1975), 67–94; "Biblical Narrative," in Barry W. Holtz, ed., *Back to the Sources: Reading the Classic Jewish Texts* (New York: Summit/Simon & Schuster, 1984), 31–81; "Biblical Tradition—Literature and Spirit in Ancient Israel," in Arthur Green, ed., *Jewish Spirituality from the Bible through the Middle Ages,* World Spirituality: An Encyclopedic History of the Religious Quest, Vol. 13 (New York: Crossroad, 1986), 82–112. Cf. also Robert Alter, *The Art of Biblical Narrative* (New York: Basic Books, 1981), 19–20, for comments on the first article cited above.

Preliminaries

1. Hermann Gunkel, *Genesis*, HKAT, 5th ed. (Göttingen: Vandenhoek & Ruprecht, 1922); Benno Jacob, *Das Erste Buch der Tora: Genesis* (Berlin: Schocken, 1934; reprint, New York: Ktav, 1974). For a general account of the modern research on Gen. 2–3, cf. discussion and extensive bibliography by Claus Westermann, *Biblischer Kommentar I, 1: Genesis I–XI* (Neukirchen-Vluyn: Neukirchner Vlg., 1974; henceforth, BK-1), 245–49. Concerning premodern exegesis, cf. F. R. Tennant, *The Sources of the Doctrines of the Fall and Original Sin* (1903; reprint, New York: Schocken, 1958); Arnold Williams, *The Common Expositor: An Account of the Commentaries on Genesis 1527–1633* (Chapel Hill: University of North Carolina Press, 1948), 65–93; Louis Ginzberg, *The Legends of the Jews*, Vol. 1 (Philadelphia: Jewish Publication Society, 1909), 49–102; Vol. 5 (1937), 245–49.

2. Cf. Gunkel, *The Legends of Genesis*, trans. W. H. Carruth (1901; reprint, New York: Schocken, 1970), 2.

3. Wellhausen himself should perhaps be exempted from this judgment, as his *Prolegomena to the History of [ancient] Israel* (1878; reprint, New York: Meridian, 1957; Gloucester: Peter Smith, 1973) are a model of clarity and persuasion that may have done more for the "Documentary Hypothesis" than his more

analytic and technical *Die Komposition des Hexateuchs und der historischen Bücher des Alten Testaments,* 4th ed. (Berlin: de Gruyter, 1963).

4. On form criticism in general, cf. Claus Koch, *The Growth of the Biblical Tradition: The Form-Critical Method,* trans. S. M. Cuppitt (New York: Scribners, 1969). On traditiohistorical study, cf. Douglas A. Knight, *Rediscovering the Traditions of Israel: The Development of the Traditio-Historical Research of the Old Testament, with Special Consideration of the Scandinavian Contribution,* SBL Dissertation Series 9 (Missoula: Scholars Press, 1975). On broader philosophical and theological questions arising from study of biblical tradition, cf. idem, ed., *Tradition and Theology in the Old Testament,* with contributions by Walter Harrelson, Helmer Ringgren, et al. (Philadelphia: Fortress Press, 1977).

5. Gunkel, *Genesis,* 5, 6, 10, 27. Except where indicated, all translations in excerpted quotations are my own.

6. J. G. von Herder, *Vom Geist der Ebräischen Poesie,* ed. J. G. Müller (Stuttgart, 1827); cf. idem, *Reflections on the Philosophy of History of Mankind,* ed. Frank E. Manuel (Chicago and London: University of Chicago Press, 1968), 119–64. On Herder's influence in biblical criticism, cf. Gunkel, "Ziele und Methoden der Erklärung des Alten Testaments," in idem, *Reden and Aufsätze* (Göttingen: Vandenhoeck & Ruprecht, 1913), 22. See also Bernhard W. Anderson, "The Traditio-Historical Approach," introduction to Martin Noth, *A History of Pentateuchal Traditions,* trans. B. W. Anderson (Englewood Cliffs: Prentice-Hall, 1972), xviii/ff.; Herbert F. Hahn, *The Old Testament in Modern Research* (Philadelphia: Fortress Press, 1954, 1966), 119ff.

7. See Hans W. Frei, *The Eclipse of Biblical Narrative: A Study of 18th and 19th Century Hermeneutics* (New Haven and London: Yale University Press, 1974), 183–201.

8. Wellhausen's indebtedness to Hegelian theologian Wilhelm Vatke's *Die Biblische Theologie wissenschaftlich dargestellt* (Leipzig, 1866) is acknowledged in the introduction to the *Prolegomena* (Engl. ed., 4, 10, 12–13). On the reign of Hegelianism in nineteenth- and early twentieth-century biblical scholarship, cf. George E. Mendenhall, "Biblical History in Transition," in G. Ernest Wright, ed., *The Bible and the Ancient Near East: Essays in Honor of William Foxwell Albright* (Garden City: Doubleday, 1971; reprint, Anchor Books, 1965; citation from this ed.), 25–58. esp. 32–33. Cf. Albright's own work, *From the Stone Age to Christianity: Monotheism and the Historical Process* (Baltimore: Johns Hopkins University Press, 1942; reprint, Garden City: Doubleday/Anchor, 1957), 82–126. For a more detailed treatment of Wellhausen's relation to Hegel and Vatke, see Lothar Perlitt, *Vatke und Wellhausen,* BZAW 94 (Berlin: de Gruyter, 1965).

9. One sees this notion expressed most freely, perhaps, from the vantage point of New Testament criticism. See, for example, the chapter on "Jewish Legalism" in Rudolf Bultmann, *Primitive Christianity and its Contemporary Setting.* For a sample of a similar bias in Old Testament criticism, cf. Robert H. Pfeiffer, *Introduction to the Old Testament* (New York: Harper & Row, 1948), 207–209 (on the "Priestly" source). Compare the useful corrective remarks of Peter R. Ackroyd, *Exile and Restoration* (Philadelphia: Westminster, 1968), 1–16, and Joseph Blenkinsopp, *A History of Prophecy in Israel* (Philadelphia: Westminster, 1983), 14f.

10. For a classic analysis of the intellectual trends and models in nineteeth-century biblical studies, see Albright (cited in n. 8, above), loc. cit.; cf. Mendenhall (also cited in n. 8), loc. cit.

11. Gunkel, *Genesis,* 27.

12. Cf. Gunkel, *Legends of Genesis*, 15–16, 37ff., 123ff.; Noth, *History of Pentateuchal Traditions* (see n. 6, above), 1–2:

> ... the decisive steps on the way to the formation of the Pentateuch were taken during the preliterary stage, and the literary fixations only gave final form to material which in its essentials was already given. ... The Pentateuch ... does not have an "author" in [any strict sense of the term]. ... Even the original writers of the so-called sources of the Pentateuch, from which the whole was finally compiled, cannot be regarded as "authors" ... however effective and significant their work may have been. To be sure, they did not give them the basic form. This basic form did not finally emerge as the later consequence of a substantive combination and arrangement of *individual* traditions and individual complexes of traditions. Rather, this form was already given in the beginning of the history of the traditions in a small series of themes essential for the faith of the Israelite tribes.

A direct line of evolution in O.T. form criticism can be traced from the formulation by Gunkel cited in n. 11, through the German tradition historians Alt, Eissfeldt, von Rad, Noth, and Westermann, to the extreme position formulated by Engnell and the Scandinavian schools discussed by Knight, *Rediscovering*, 217–399. Cf. C. R. North, "Pentateuchal Criticism," in H. H. Rowley, ed., *The Old Testament and Modern Study* (London, Oxford, and New York: Oxford University Press, 1956), 48–82, esp. 59–70. Also, Johannes Pedersen, "Passahfest und Passahlegende," ZAW 52 (1934), 161–75; idem, *Israel, Its Life and Culture*, I–II (Danish: 1st ed., Copenhagen: Povl Brunner, 1926; Engl. ed., London: Geoffrey Cumberlege, 1940) and III–IV (Danish: 1st ed., Copenhagen: Brunner, 1934; Engl., 1940); Ivan Engnell, *Gamla Testamentet. En traditionshistorisk inledning*, I (Stockholm: Svenska Kyrkans Diakonistyrelses Bokförlag, 1945); idem, *A Rigid Scrutiny: Critical Essays on the Old Testament*, trans. John T. Willis, with Helmer Ringgren (Nashville: Vanderbilt University Press, 1969), esp. 3–11, 50–67.

13. Gunkel, *Legends*, 123–44.

14. See Gunkel, *Genesis*, 1–4, 25ff.; Westermann, BK I, 255ff.

15. See esp. Noth, *History of Pentateuchal Traditions*, 46f. Gerhardt von Rad, *The Problem of the Hexateuch, and Other Essays*, trans. E. W. Trueman Dickman (London: Oliver & Boyd, 1966), 1–78 [1938], while placing stronger emphasis on literary factors than Noth, nevertheless sought to reconstruct the "confessional" history recited at pan-Israelite tribal festivals in premonarchic times, where bards may have played a role.

16. Cf. Frei, who argues that Herder viewed biblical writings as "historical" or "history-like," and not as myths or allegories, but wavered between viewing this historical character as a factuality of historical reportage and as a realism of spirit or outlook (*Eclipse of Biblical Narrative*, 191).

17. Cf. Thorkild Jakobsen, "The Cosmos as a State," in Henri Frankfort et al., *Before Philosophy: The Intellectual Adventure of Ancient Man—An Essay on Speculative Thought in the Ancient Near East* (Baltimore: Penguin, 1949, 1963), 137–99; Harry Berger, Jr., "Naive Consciousness and Cultural Change: An Essay in Historical Structuralism," BMMLA (Spring, 1973), 1–44; idem, "Outline of a General Theory of Cultural Change," *Clio* 2 (1972), 49–63. The functionalist and structural-functionalist sociology of religion found in the work of W. Robertson Smith, James G. Frazer, Emile Durkheim, Marcel Mauss, Max Weber, S. H. Hooke, et al. might be relevant in this context. Gunkel routinely uses the

designation "der Mythos" to describe Gen. 2–3. Cf. Hahn (cited above, n. 6), 44–82, 157–84.

18. Gunkel, *Genesis,* 32–33.

19. Cf. esp. George E. Mendenhall, "The Hebrew Conquest of Palestine," BAR 3 (1970), 25–53; idem, *The Tenth Generation: The Origins of the Biblical Tradition* (Baltimore and London: Johns Hopkins University Press, 1973), and Norman K. Gottwald, *The Tribes of Yahweh: A Sociology of the Religion of Liberated Israel, 1250–1050* B.C.E. (Maryknoll: Orbis, 1979). What is surely by now known as "the Mendenhall-Gottwald hypothesis"—namely, that Israel originated in an indigenous "peasant revolt" in Canaan—has at present a lively debate and polemics, which will probably not be settled by Baruch Halpern's otherwise worthwhile *The Emergence of Israel in Canaan* (Chico: Scholars, 1983), which, taking a position contra "peasant revolt," offers a study of the era of waning Egyptian power in Canaan, and of the wave of successor states (including Israel) that filled the power vacuum.

20. Cf., in addition to Jacob, Umberto (M. D.) Cassuto, *The Documentary Hypothesis and the Composition of the Pentateuch,* trans. Israel Abrahams (Jerusalem: Magnes Press, 1941); idem, *From Adam to Noah: A Commentary on Gen. I–VI, 8,* trans. Abrahams (Jerusalem: Magnes, 1961, 1972); idem, *From Noah to Abraham: A Commentary on Gen. VI. 9–XI. 32,* trans. Abrahams (Jerusalem: Magnes, 1949); idem, *A Commentary on the Book of Exodus,* trans. Abrahams (Jerusalem: Magnes, 1951); idem, *Biblical and Oriental Studies, Vol. 1: Bible,* trans. Abrahams (Jerusalem: Magnes, 1973); M. H. Segal, *The Pentateuch: Its Composition and Its Authorship and Other Biblical Studies* (Jerusalem: Magnes, 1967). Working within the assumptions of documentary criticism, Yehezkel Kaufmann has issued the most serious challenge to Wellhausen's Documentary Hypothesis by questioning the alleged dating of the "Priestly" material of the Pentateuch, and proposing its extreme antiquity, in *Toldot ha'emunah hayyisra'elit* (History of Israelite religion), 8 vols. (Tel Aviv: Bialik Institute/Devir. 1937–56). See English abridgment: Y. Kaufmann, *The Religion of Israel,* trans. Moshe Greenberg (Chicago and London: University of Chicago Press, 1960). Kaufmann's conclusions have been supported more recently by Gershon Weinfeld, "Pentateuchal Criticism," EJ (1972). Certain other scholars and translators, e.g., Martin Buber and Franz Rosenzweig, *Die Schrift und ihre Verdeutschung* (Berlin: Schocken, 1936); Buber, *Werke,* II: *Schriften zur Bibel* (Munich: Kösel Vlg., 1964), have conveyed a studied indifference to source criticism. Cf. Rosenzweig, in a letter to Jacob Rosenheim (April 21, 1927): "If Wellhausen's theories were correct . . . our faith would not be shaken in the least" (Rosenzweig, *Briefe,* ed. Edith Rosenzweig [Berlin: Schocken, 1935]). In the same spirit, Rosenzweig half-jokingly proposed that the scholarly designation "R" (*Redaktor*) be understood as the Hebrew honorific *Rabbenu* (our teacher). For a useful recent overview of the role of Jews in biblical studies, cf. S. David Sperling, "Judaism and Modern Biblical Research," in L. Boadt, H. Croner, and L. Klenicki, eds., *Biblical Studies: Meeting Ground of Jews and Christians* (New York: Paulist/Ramsey/Stimulus, 1980), 19–44.

21. This is not to suggest that biblical studies are fully dependent on parallel developments in the world of literary scholarship, Cassuto's remarks to this effect (*Documentary Hypothesis,* 5–14) notwithstanding. It is not unreasonable, however, to assert that developments in the latter domain can greatly enrich the former. On the interpenetration of biblical and literary studies, compare, among more recent works, Robert Polzin, *Biblical Structuralism: Method and Subjectivity in the Study of Ancient Texts* (Philadelphia/Missoula: Fortress/Scholars, 1977; idem, with

Eugene Rothman, eds., *The Biblical Mosaic: Changing Perspectives* (Philadel-phia/Chico: Fortress/Scholars, 1982; also, Robert Alter, *The Art of Biblical Narra-tive* (New York: Basic Books, 1981). Among earlier discussions of this matter, cf. A. Alonso-Schöckl, "Hermeneutical Problems of a Literary Study of the Bible," SVT 28 (Edinburgh/Leiden: E. J. Brill, 1975), 1–15; J. P. Fokkelman, *Narrative Art in Genesis* (Amsterdam: Van Gorcum, Assen, 1975), 1–8. Erich Auerbach's groundbreaking essay "Odysseus' Scar," in idem, *Mimesis: The Representation of Reality in Western Literature*, trans. W. Trask (Garden City: Doubleday/Anchor, 1957), 1–20, remains relevant in this context.

22. Jacob, *Das erste Buch*, 76, 134, 952.

23. Ibid., 102ff.

24. Ibid., 107; cf. 105, 125–26.

25. Ibid., 112–13.

26. Ibid., 116.

27. Among many sources on this matter, cf. William Empson, *Some Versions of Pastoral* (1935; reprint, New York: New Directions, 1974); Erwin Panofsky, "*Et in Arcadia Ego:* Poussin and the Elegiac Tradition," in his work *Meaning in the Visual Arts* (Garden City: Doubleday/Anchor, 1957); Harry Berger, Jr., "The Renais-sance Imagination: Second World and Green World," CR 9 (1965), 36–86; idem, "Andrew Marvell: The Poem as Green World," FMLS 3:3 (July, 1967), 290–309; idem, "Conspicuous Exclusion in Vermeer: An Essay in Renaissance Pastoral," YFS 47 (1970), 243–65.

28. On allegory in general, the following sources have been consulted: C. S. Lewis, *The Allegory of Love: A Study in Medieval Tradition* (1936; reprint, New York: Oxford/Galaxy, 1958), esp. 44–111; Edwin Honig, *Dark Conceit: The Making of Allegory* (1959; reprint, Hanover and London: University Press of New England, 1982); Harry Berger, Jr., *The Allegorical Temper: Vision and Reality in Book II of Spenser's "Faerie Queene"* (New Haven and London: Yale University Press, 1957; reprints Hamden: Archon, 1967); Northrop Frye, *Anatomy of Crit-icism: Four Essays* (Princeton: Princeton University Press, 1957, 1973), 89–91 et passim; idem, "Allegory," in Alex Preminger, ed., *Princeton Encyclopedia of Poetry and Poetics* (Princeton: Princeton University Press, 1965; rev. 1974), 12–15; Walter Benjamin, *The Origins of German Tragic Drama*, trans. John Osborne (London: NLB, 1977), esp. 159–235; Angus Fletcher, *Allegory: The Theory of A Symbolic Mode* (Ithaca and London: Cornell University Press, 1964); Georg Lukács, *Realism in Our Time: Literature and the Class Struggle* (New York, Evanston, et al.: Harper & Row, 1964), 17–46; Paul de Man, "The Rhetoric of Tem-porality," in Charles S. Singleton, ed., *Interpretation: Theory and Practice* (Bal-timore: Johns Hopkins University Press, 1969), 173–209; Don Cameron Allen, *Mysteriously Meant: The Rediscovery of Pagan Symbolism and Allegorical Interpretation in the Renaissance* (Baltimore and London: Johns Hopkins University Press, 1970); Maureen Quilligan, *The Language of Allegory: Defining the Genre* (Ithaca and London: Cornell University Press, 1979); Stephen J. Greenblatt, ed., *Allegory and Representation: Selected Papers from the English Institute, 1979–80* (Baltimore and London: Johns Hopkins University Press, 1981); Morton Bloomfield, ed., *Alle-gory, Myth and Symbol*, HES 9 (Cambridge, Mass., and London: Harvard Univer-sity Press, 1981). The last two anthologies are discussed at length by Joel D. Black, "Allegory Unveiled," PT 4:1 (1983): 109–26.

29. Cf. Frye, *Anatomy*, 90; idem, "Allegory," 12. Frye speaks of "simple" or (in *Anatomy*) of "naive" allegory, in contradistinction to "complex" allegory, the latter with more political and historical themes and more of an ironizing tone.

30. So esp. Quilligan, *Language of Allegory*, 25–26, 29–32, Cf. Frye, "Allegory," 13 (col. 1). Honig, *Dark Conceit*, 19–27, elaborates on the priestly and institutional basis of allegoresis (without using this term) and on the critical role allegorizing interpretation plays in the formation of tradition around a traditional book: "Whether taken devoutly or as an exercise in exegesis, the practice of systematizing myths seems essential to establishing their character in the traditional book. What is true of the Homeric poems may also be said of every great work of similar scope: the Bible, the *Aeneid*, the *Commedia*. They become traditional by attracting widely predicated systems of interpretation and belief."

31. See, for example, Jean Seznec, *The Survival of the Pagan Gods: The Mythological Tradition and Its Place in Renaissance Humanism and Art* (Princeton: Princeton University Press, 1953; hereafter, *Survival*), 84–87, who bases his discussion in part on Paul Decharme, *La critique des traditions religieuses chez les Grecs, des origines au temps de Plutarch* (Paris, 1904); Gilbert Murray, *Five Stages of Greek Religion*, 3d ed. (Boston: Beacon Press, 1951), chap. 4, and Roger P. Hinks, *Myth and Allegory in Ancient Art*, SWI 6 (1939). Cf. F. E. Peters, *The Harvest of Hellenism: A History of the Near East from Alexander the Great to the Triumph of Christianity* (New York: Touchstone/Simon & Schuster, 1970), 446–79; Emile Bréhier, *The History of Philosophy: The Hellenistic and Roman Age* (1931; trans. W. Baskin, Chicago and London: University of Chicago P., 1965), 10–12; Honig, *Dark Conceit*, 28–31. Relevant primary texts (cited by Seznec) include Heraclitus, *De allegoriis apud Homerum* (Venice, 1505), Phornutus, *De natura deorum* (Venice, 1505), and Sallust, *De diis et mundo*, ii and iv—texts all late Hellenistic in origin. Saul Lieberman, "Rabbinic Interpretation of Scripture," in idem, *Hellenism in Jewish Palestine*, 2d ed. (New York: Jewish Theological Seminary, 1962), 47–82, describes the relationship of rabbinic exegesis of Scripture to late Hellenistic Homeric allegoresis. Cf., in general, Henry A. Fischel, ed., *Essays in Greco-Roman and Related Talmudic Literature* (New York: Ktav, 1977), and sources on Philo cited below, n. 60.

32. So, for example, Heraklides (*sic*), cited by Seznec, *Survival*, 84, n. 2: "If Homer were not speaking in allegorical terms, he was guilty of the greatest impieties." Cf. Xenophanes in Plato's *Republic*, X: "Homer and Hesiod have ascribed to the gods all deeds that are a shame and a disgrace among men: thieving, adultery, fraud."

33. Quilligan, *Language of Allegory*, 67–69, sees the literal (which she characteristically understands as "letteral") meaning as something essential to an allegoric mode: " . . . the poet [here Langland] insists that the reader read not less literally but more literally, for, if the reader can no longer follow an imaginary event in his mind's eye, he must look at the words on the page. . . . the allegorist is always at pains lest his text be read as mere metaphor of any sort." This, of course, is not quite the same as granting priority to the *historical* sense of the text (nor are Quilligan's illustrative texts "historical"), but it reinforces the principle that a mimetically plausible "literal" situation must be conjured in the mind's eye as foundation of the reader's experience of allegory.

34. Cf., among others, Herman Hailperin, *Rashi and the Christian Scholars* (Pittsburgh: University of Pittsburgh Press, 1963), esp. 254–60 (and, on Nicholas of Lyra [see my discussion further on], 137–46). Gershom G. Scholem, "The Meaning of the Torah in Jewish Mysticism," in idem, *On the Kabbalah and Its Symbolism*, trans. Ralph Manheim (New York: Schocken, 1965), 32–86, esp. 50–65, offers a valuable discussion of esoteric and "fourfold" meaning in medieval Judaism—cf. Erwin I. J. Rosenthal, "The Study of the Bible in Medieval Judaism," CHB II (1969; 1976), 252–79; also, Wilhelm Bacher, "L'exégèse biblique

dans le Zohar," REJ 22 (1891), 33–46; P. Sandler, "Leva'ayat Pardes," Auerbach
Jubilee Volume (Jerusalem, 1955), 222–35. The allegorical interpretation was also
employed among medieval Jewish exegetes for problematic *aggadot*—see Mark
Saperstein, *Decoding the Rabbis: A Thirteenth-Century Commentary on the Aggadah*
(Cambridge, Mass., and London: Harvard University Press, 1980). On the early
medieval Christian use of the doctrine of fourfold meaning, see Ernst von
Dobschütz, "Vom vierfachen Schriftsinn: Die Geschichte einer Theorie," *Har-
nack-Ehrung: Beitrage zur Kirchengeschichte . . . Adolf von Harnack . . . dargebracht*
(Leipzig, 1921), 1–13—cited by Scholem, op. cit., 52, n. 1. On general background of medieval Christian exegesis, cf. Beryl Smalley, *The Study of the Bible in
the Middle Ages* (Notre Dame: University of Notre Dame Press, 1964, 1978).

35. It is cognate to Gr. παράδεισος and O. Pers. *pairi-daeza*, lit. "enclosing
earthwall," i.e., "garden, garden-sanctuary."

36. The rabbinic legend (Tosefta Hag. 2:4 and parallels) of "the four who
entered Pardes" was, in its earliest context, understood to deal with esoteric study
of Scripture, but the acronymic sense of the term "Pardes" originated in the
thirteenth-century writings of Moses de Leon, Bahya ben Asher, and Joseph
Gikatilla (see Scholem, "Meaning of the Torah," 53ff.), even though a doctrine of
fourfold meaning in general is at least as early as Augustine's *historia, aetiologia,
analogia, allegoria* (cf. Hailperin, *Rashi*, 255).

37. See H. D. Chevel, ed., *Rabbenu Bahya: Be'ur 'al ha-Torah*, 3 vols. (Jerusalem: Mosad ha-Rav Kuk, 5734/1974).

38. Sermo II (PL, vol. 38, col. 30)—cited in Edward A. Gosselin, *The King's
Progress to Jerusalem: Some Interpretations of David during the Reformation Period and
Their Patristic and Medieval Background*, Humana Civilitas: Sources and Studies
Relating to the Middle Ages and the Renaissance, vol. 2, Center for Medieval and
Renaissance Studies, University of California at Los Angeles (Malibu: Undena
Publications, 1976), 12, 23, n. 6; and in Émile Male, *The Gothic Image: Religious
Art in France in the Thirteenth Century* (New York and Evanston: Harper &
Row/Harper Torchbooks, 1956), 135–36.

39. Saint Augustine, *The City of God* XI.21, trans. M. Dods, with an introduction by Thomas Merton (New York: Random House/Modern Library, 1950),
431–32.

40. These and related matters of biblical authorship are discussed in Talmud
Baba Bathra 14b–15a.

41. This trend goes back to Coleridge's statement that allegory "cannot be
other than spoken consciously, whereas in . . . the symbol the general truth may
be unconsciously in the writer's mind. . . . The advantage of symbolic writing
over allegory is that it presumes no disjunction of faculties, but simple domi-
nance" (*Miscellaneous Criticism*, ed. T. M. Raysor [London: Constable, 1936], 29–
30). Cf. Quilligan, *Language of Allegory* (see above, n. 28), 32; de Man, "Rhetoric
of Temporality," 173–91; and Fletcher, *Allegory*, 13–19, who cites Goethe's
distinction between allegory and symbol in his poetic theory, *Maxims* I, 211
(trans. René Wellek, in *A History of Modern Criticism* [New Haven and London:
Yale University Press, 1955])—see also Honig, *Dark Conceit*, 39–50.

42. Quilligan, *Language of Allegory*, 155, 221, 223.

43. Lukács, *Realism in Our Time*, 40.

44. I quote from the Mander translation of Lukács cited in the preceding note.
Cf. Benjamin, *Origins* (trans. Osborne), 233: "Allegory goes away empty-handed.
Evil as such, which it cherished as enduring profundity, exists only in allegory, is
nothing other than allegory, and means something different from what it is. It

means precisely the non-existence of what it presents. The absolute vices, as exemplified by tyrants and intriguers, are allegories." These estimates of the allegorical vision of German baroque tragedy are perhaps a problematic starting point for generalizations about allegory and its functions in Israelite antiquity, but they are strikingly appropriate to the Bible's vision of human nature and human destiny, as I hope the full course of the present study will make clear.

45. The relation of allegory to irony is explored by de Man, "Rhetoric of Temporality," 191–209.

46. De Man, "Pascal's Allegory of Persuasion," in Greenblatt, ed., *Allegory and Representation* (see n. 28, above), 1.

47. De Man, "Rhetoric of Temporality," 206–207.

48. *Language of Allegory*, 32.

49. Ibid., 28.

50. Culler, *On Deconstruction: Theory and Criticism After Structuralism* (Ithaca and London: Cornell University Press, 1982); see esp. 17–30.

51. Cf. sources cited in n. 21, above.

52. The harshest case, engagingly argued, against literary approaches to the Hebrew Bible has perhaps been put by James L. Kugel, himself no stranger to literary method, in his essay "On the Bible and Literary Criticism," *Prooftexts* 1:3 (Sept. 1981), 217–36. Cf. the exchange of views that followed between Kugel and Adele Berlin, *Prooftexts* 2:3 (Sept. 1982), 323–32. A similarly skeptical point of view, also appealingly argued, is offered by John A. Miles, "Radical Editing: *Redaktionsgeschichte* and the Aesthetic of Willed Confusion," in Baruch Halpern and Jon D. Levenson, eds., *Traditions in Transformation Turning Points in Biblical Faith* (Winona Lake: Eisenbrauns, 1981), 9–31.

53. See Fletcher, *Allegory*, 2.

54. Leo Strauss, *Persecution and the Art of Writing* (Glencoe: Free Press, 1952), 24–25.

55. Ibid., 25.

56. On Philo's relation to rabbinic tradition and methods, and to Palestinian Judaism in general, see Harry Wolfson, *Philo: Foundations of Religious Philosophy in Judaism, Christianity, and Islam*, vol. 1 (Cambridge: Harvard University Press, 1947), 90–93, 95ff. On allegory in Philo, cf. John Dillon, "The Formal Structure of Philo's Allegorical Exegesis," in David Winston and John Dillon, eds. *Two Treatises of Philo of Alexandria* (Chico: Scholars, 1983), 77–84.

57. *De Abrahamo*, 68.

58. See, for example, on the serpent's powers of speech: *Agr.* 22: 96–97. On Philo's relation to "myth," see, in general, Wolfson, *Philo*, I, 32–34. One should keep in mind that, while Philo had recourse to allegorical meaning with fewer reservations than to literal meaning, "no allegorical interpretation of a scriptual story . . . means the rejection of the story itself as fact" (Wolfson, ibid. 126).

59. *De Abrahamo*, 1–2.

60. This is a fundamental tenet of Deuteronomic theology, as, for example, in Deut. 11:13–21, and esp. Deut. 27–28. It is likewise an element in Holiness-Code theology, as, for example, Lev. 26:3–45.

61. *De Abrahamo*, I, 5.

62. *Zekher*, for example, is rendered in the Septuagint to Ex. 17:14 as μνημόσυνον to Deut. 25:19 as ὄνομα, to Ps. 111:4 (LXX: 110:4) as μνεία, to Ps. 145:7 (LXX: 144:7) and Prov. 10:7 (LXX: 10:6) as μνήμη, etc.; *zikkaron* by Septuagint to Ex. 17:14 (first bicolon) as μνημόσυνον, to Eccl. 1:11 as μνήμη, etc.; *'azkarah* by Septuagint to Lev. 24:7 as ἀνάμνησις, to Lev. 2:2,9, etc., as

μνημόσυνον, etc. One notes in any case the cognate relation of most of the above equivalents, and the abundance in both Hebrew and Greek of synonyms on the theme of memorial, mention, memory-trace, and the like. Cf. H. Eisig, "zekher" in TDOT, IV, 64–82, and O. Michel, "μιμνῄσκομαι, etc." in TDNT, IV, 675–83, esp. 679.

63. Moses Maimonides, *The Guide of the Perplexed,* trans. S. Pines (Chicago and London: University of Chicago Press, 1963), II, 27, 60a (Pines, 510)—all citations are from this edition, but I have consulted the Arabic text and Hebrew translation by Joseph D. Kapaḥ, *Moreh Hannevukhim,* 3 vols. (Jerusalem: Mosad ha-Rav Kuk, 5732/1972). Concerning the passage quoted here, cf. Leo Strauss, "Maimonides' Statement on Political Science," PAAJR 22 (1953), 1–16; reprinted in Arthur Hyman, ed., *Essays in Medieval Jewish and Islamic Philosophy* (New York: Ktav, 1977), 164–79.

64. See Maimonides, *Guide,* intro., 2b–8b (Pines, 5–14). Cf. Strauss, "The Literary Character of the *Guide for the Perplexed,*" in idem, *Persecution,* 38–94; also, idem, "How to Begin to Study *The Guide of the Perplexed,*" intro. to the Pines translation, xi–lvi.

65. *Guide* I, 9b–12a (Pines, 17–20). The rubrics for the individual causes in my discussion that follows are my own and serve only for convenience—the reader should refer to Maimonides' actual formulation.

66. Jacob, *Das erste Buch,* 101–102.

67. Compare Umberto Cassuto, *From Adam to Noah* (cited above, n. 20), 139–43:

> . . . in order to make it quite clear that we have here [in the serpent] only a symbol . . . the Torah stressed at the very outset that the serpent belonged to the category of *beasts of the field that the Lord God had made. . . .* The special characteristic that the Bible attributes to the serpent is cunning, and since it does not ascribe any other quality to him, it intends, apparently, to convey that the evil flowing from the serpent emanated only from his cunning. In the ultimate analysis, we have here an allegorical allusion to the craftiness to be found in *man himself.* The man and his wife were, it is true, still devoid of comprehensive knowledge, like children, who know neither good nor bad; but even those who lack wisdom sometimes possess slyness. The duologue between the serpent and the woman is actually, in a manner of speaking, a duologue between her willingness and her innocence, clothed in the garb of a parable. Only in this way is it possible to understand the conversation clearly; otherwise, it remains obscure. . . . By interpreting the text this way, we can understand why the serpent is said to think and speak; in reality it is not he that thinks and speaks but the woman who is aware of it. Nor should we be surprised that he knows the purpose of the Lord God; it is the woman who imagines that she has plumbed the Divine intention—but is quite mistaken!

Cassuto, essentially agreeing with Jacob's stipulations, is the more detailed in his evaluation of the serpent's allegorical properties. Strikingly congruent, in part, with certain propositions about allegory advanced by Fletcher, *Allegory* (see n. 28, above), the two quoted statements suggest the following underlying principles to the art: (1) *allusiveness,* the implication ("actually, in a manner of speaking . . . ," "in reality, it is not . . . but . . .") of frames of reference beyond or behind the text at hand (though still textual), to which the text is seen to allude in a veiled or even deceptive manner; (2) *hierarchical organization,* or what Fletcher, 70–146, appealingly characterizes as the "cosmic/cosmetic" function, implied in the categorical distinction "beasts of the field/man," and in the visual modality of expression ("clothed in the garb of a parable")—cf. Fletcher, 252ff.; (3) *ritual combat* (in the psychomachian "duologue . . . between . . . willingness and innocence")—cf. Fletcher, 147ff.; (4) *reductiveness,* relating an image or action that is *only* this or *actually* that ("actually . . . ," "it is not . . . but . . . ," "Only in this way . . ."), a principle closely related to (5) the *demonic agent,* a character that serves one function only, who embodies, therefore, but one trait or principle ("The special characteristic that the Bible attributes to the serpent is *cunning* . . . ; it does not ascribe any other . . .")—cf. Fletcher, 25–69.

68. This view is suggested by the principle Maimonides states further on (7a), "that the prophetic parables are of two kinds. In some of these parables each word has a meaning, while in others the parable as a whole indicates the whole of the intended meaning. In such a parable very many words are to be found, not every one of which adds something to the intended meaning." One should note in the passage quoted from 6b that the expression "is worth nothing" (*'eyno klum*), though given in Hebrew, in accordance with Maimonides' general practice for quoting from Scripture or rabbinic literature, is not found in the midrashic original.

69. There is, of course, the possibility that Maimonides possessed a different text of the rabbinic statement from the one currently extant (cf. *Motnot Kehunah* to Song Rabbah I, i, 8, which suggests the possibility of alternative versions), or that Maimonides, being unconcerned with presenting any more than an approximation of the original, quotes from memory. But such explanations are at least as conjectural as any attempt to interpret the discrepancy as it stands, and we are left in any case with a distinct difference of emphasis in Maimonides' version, which accords with the general drift of his discussion.

70. One is reminded in particular of the well-known "Hymn of the Pearl" appended to the Christian apocryphal Acts of Thomas. See Robert M. Grant, ed., *Gnosticism: An Anthology* (London: Collins, 1961), 116–22.

71. Cf. de Man, "Rhetoric of Temporality," 191ff.; Fletcher, *Allegory,* 229–30.

72. Cf., among others, Otto Eissfeldt, *The Old Testament: an Introduction,* trans. P. R. Ackroyd (New York, Evanston, and San Francisco: Harper & Row, 1965), 81–87, and Aage Bentzen, *Introduction to the Old Testament* (Copenhagen: G. E. C. Gad, 1967), 167ff. The examples offered in my discussion that follows are by no means to be thought of as representing a single genre, but all in some way present characteristics relevant to our understanding of biblical parable.

73. See Susan Niditch and Robert Doran, "The Success Story of the Wise Courtier—A Formal Approach." JBL 96:2 (June 1977): 179–93.

74. The "parablers," one should note, speak on three levels: as riddlemakers (asking: who can understand this image which is not yet realized fact?); as oraclers (whose oracle is remembered years after it has been realized as historical fact); and as proverbists (coining the byword in the gossip of the nations, the image that has become fate in the discourse of later generations). On the Song of Heshbon, cf. Paul Hanson, HTR 61 (1968), 297–320, and other sources cited by Elias Auerbach, *Moses* (Detroit: Wayne State University Press, 1975), 223, n. 135; cf. 165–66 of that work.

75. See Menaḥem Perry and Meir Sternberg, "Hammelekh bemabbaṭ 'ironi: 'al taḥbulotaw shel hammessapper besippur david uvatsheva' " (The king viewed

ironically: On the narrator's devices in the story of David and Bathsheba), *Hassifrut* (1968): 263–92. My discussion following is based in part on this essay. See also the counterargument of Boaz Arpali, "Zehirut! Sippur Miqra'i" (Caution! Biblical story), *Hassifrut* 2 (1970): 580–97, and the rebuttal by Perry and Sternberg, "Zehirut: Sifrut! Leva'ayot ha'interpretaziah wehappo'etiqah shel ha-sippur hammiqra'i" (Caution: Literature!—On problems in the interpretation and poetics of the biblical story), ibid., 608–63, and subsequent studies by Sternberg, some of which are incorporated, in substance, into his English work *The Poetics of Biblical Narrative: Ideological Literature and the Drama of Reading* (Bloomington: Indiana University Press, 1985).

76. J. P. Fokkelman, *Narrative Art and Poetry in the Books of Samuel, Vol. I: King David (II Sam. 9–20 & I Kings 1–2)* Amsterdam: Van Gorcum, Assen, 1981), 338–41.

I. The Garden Story Forward and Backward

1. See "Preliminaries," n. 36, and its accompanying discussion.

2. Cf., despite his qualifications of the matter, Isaac Heinemann, *Darkhey ha-'aggadah* (Jerusalem: Magnes, 1950), esp. 165–69; also, I. L. Seeligmann, "Voraussetzungen der Midraschexegese," SVT 1 (1953), 150–81; Eduard Nielsen, "The Role of Oral Tradition in the Bible," in idem, *Oral Tradition—A Modern Problem in Biblical Introduction*, SBT 11 (London: SCM, 1954); Renée Bloch, "Midrash," *Supplément au Dictionnaire de la Bible* V (1957), cols. 1263–81; Samuel Sandmel, "The Haggadah Within Scripture," JBL 80:2 (1961), 105–22; Geza Vermes, "The Bible and Midrash: Early Old Testament Exegesis," CHB I (1970), 199–231; Brevard S. Childs, "Midrash and the Old Testament," in J. Reumann, ed., *Understanding Sacred Texts: Essays . . . [for] M. S. Enslin* (Valley Forge: Judson, 1972); Kalman P. Bland, "The Rabbinic Method and Literary Criticism," in Kenneth R. R. Gros Louis, et al., eds., *Literary Interpretations of Biblical Narratives* (Nashville: Abingdon, 1974), 16–23; also, Michael Fishbane, "Revelation and Tradition: Aspects of Inner-Biblical Exegesis," JBL 99:3 (1980), 343ff.

3. On the formation of the Hebrew canon, cf. Ernst Sellin and Georg Fohrer, *Introduction to the Old Testament* (Nashville: Abingdon, 1965), 480–88; Otto Eissfeldt, *The Old Testament: An Introduction* (New York: Harper & Row, 1965), 560–71; G. W. Anderson, "Canonical and Non-Canonical," CHB I (1970), 113–59; Sid Leiman, *The Canonization of Hebrew Scripture* (Hamden: Archon Books, 1978). B. S. Childs, *Introduction to the Old Testament as Scripture* (Philadelphia: Fortress Press, 1970), 46–83, offers a useful critique of the major scholarship. See also Nahum M. Sarna, "The Order of the Books," in Charles Berlin, ed., *Studies . . . in Honor of Edward Kiev* (New York: Ktav, 1971), 407–13.

4. So the sense of Neh. 8:8, assuming that *meforash* means "explained" rather than "distinctly." Cf. J. Weingreen, IDB Supp., s.v. "Interpretation, History of," cols. 436–38.

5. Avot de Rabbi Nathan (A) 15, 61; Sifré Deut. 351. Cf. Avot 1:1.

6. Gunkel, *Genesis* (see "Preliminaries," n. 1), 1–40, esp. 25ff; Rudolf Smend, *Die Erzählung des Hexateuch auf ihre Quellen untersucht* (1912); Johannes Meinhold, "Die Erzählung vom Paradies und Sündenfall," BZAW 34 (1920), 122–31; Otto Eissfeldt, *Hexateuch-Synopse* (1922), 6–8, 3*–5*; Otto Procksch, *Die Genesis übersetzt und erklärt. A. Die Jahwequelle* (1924); Hans Schmidt, *Die Geschichte von*

Paradies und Südenfall, SGV 154 (1931); Joachim Begrich, "Die Paradieserzählung. Eine literargeschichtliche Studie," ZAW 50 (1932), 93–116 (= *Ges. Stud.,* ThB 21, 1964), 11–38; Paul Humbert, "Mythe de Création et mythe paradisiaque dans le séconde chapître de la Génèse," RHPhR 16 (1936), 445–61; Sigmund Mowinckel, "The Two Sources of the Predeuteronomic Primeval History (JE) in Gen. 1–11," ANVA II (1937), 1–84; Paul Humbert, *Études sur le récit du paradis et de la chute dans la Génèse,* Memoirs de l'Univ. de Neuchatel 14 (1940), 1–193; Walther Zimmerli, *1. Mose 1–11. Die Urgeschichte I.2 Der jahwistische Bericht* (1943), in ZBK (3d ed., 1967), 107–203; A. Lefèvre, *Bulletin d'exégèse de l'AT,* RSR 36 (1949), 455–80; Robert H. Pfeiffer, *Introduction to the Old Testament,* 2d ed. (New York: Harper & Row, 1953); et al. Cf., in general, discussion and sources cited by Westermann, BK-1 (see "Preliminaries," n. 1), 245–46, 255–69. Because of his invaluable bibliographic survey of the critical discussion of literary and form-critical problems in the Garden story, I shall cite Westermann the most frequently in the present chapter, a matter that should not, I hope, be mistaken for an uncritical reliance on one commentator.

7. See, esp. Gunkel, Begrich, Humbert, and Westermann. On the form-critical and traditiohistorical methods in general, cf. "Preliminaries," n. 4.

8. On a distinction between a "Creation" and "Paradise" story in Gen. 2–3, see Humbert (1936, 1940; see n. 6 above); similar conclusions from a form-critical perspective have been offered by Gunkel, *Genesis.* Cf. also Adolphe Lods, *Israel des origines au milieu du VIIIe sièle* (Paris, 1930), 559. Westermann has proposed that the merger of these stories was effected by infixing "Paradise" material into the "Creation" segment (2:9, 16–17; 2:10–14 being a parenthetic elaboration of separate origin). Westermann bases himself here (for the "Creation/Paradise" distinction) in particular on Humbert, and (for a form-critical perspective) on Gunkel and Begrich. The same commentator, basing himself on the etiological reading of 2:18–24 by Begrich, sees a "creation of woman" segment as a further elaboration of the "creation of man" segment. Still others have argued that the two problematic trees of the story ("Tree of Life" and "Tree of the Knowledge of Good and Evil") were originally the nuclei of independent stories. See K. Budde, *Die biblische Urgeschichte (Gen. 1–12.5) untersucht* (1883), who, however, regards only the "Tree of Life" motif as a later accretion to a basically unified story. Similar conclusions were reached by H. Hölzinger, *Genesis. II. Das Paradies und der Sündenfall,* KHC (1898), 24–45. More literary equality was granted to the two alleged strands by Gunkel, Smend, Meinhold, Schmidt, Eissfeldt et al. A former student of mine, Michelle Snyderman, wrote a term paper advancing a persuasive counter hypothesis: that a "garden" motif and a "*two* trees" motif may have been the originally independent units. In regard to preliterary elements, critics and commentators have been alert to possible etiologies, namings, myths or mythic motifs, epigrams, poetic lines, geographical and natural lore, and the like. One need only consult an erudite commentary such as Westermann's to realize that practically every verse of the Garden story has had an independent history of critical discussion, if not of actual composition or transmission.

9. One should, of course, note here those commentators who defend the basic unity of the Garden story: Budde, Holzinger, Jacob, *Das erste Buch der Tora* (see "Preliminaries," n. 1), 71–134; Joseph Coppens, *Miscellanées bibliques* 25, "L'unité litteraire de Génèse II–III," EThL 27 (1951), 91–99; J. Schildenberger, "Die Erzählung vom Paradies und Sündenfall," BiKi 1 and 2 (1951), 2–46; W. G. Lambert, "Le drame du jardin d'Eden," NRTh 76:9–10 (1954), 917–48, 1044–72; A. Bjørndalen, "Hvem er Adam?" TTki 34:2 (1963), 80–93; Umberto

Cassuto, *From Adam to Noah* (see "Preliminaries," n. 20), 71–177; Ephraim A. Speiser, *Genesis*. The Anchor Bible (Garden City: Doubleday/Anchor, 1964), 14–28; et al. Several recent studies of a structuralist nature would also fall into this category: Jerome T. Walsh, "Genesis 2:4b–3:24: A Synchronic Approach," JBL 96:2 (1977), 161–77; the papers by Thomas E. Boomershine, Robert C. Culley, and David Jobling in *SBL Seminar Papers* (1978), 31–69; and the articles of *Semeia* 18 (1980). These newer sources came to my attention after the main lines of my own study were worked out, and they offer me no cogent reasons for altering my own judgments. My differences with them (especially with Walsh, whose structural judgments approximate in some respects my own) will become apparent in the course of my discussion.

10. Cf. Westermann, BK-1, 256–59; and the sources cited in n. 2, above, and "Preliminaries," n. 4.

11. Cf. sources cited in "Preliminaries," n. 12.

12. Cf. Koch, *The Growth of Biblical Tradition* (see "Preliminaries," n. 4), 57ff.; Childs (see above, n. 3); also, idem, SVT 29 (1977), 66–80.

13. That literary structures in biblical narrative can cut across the boundaries of "documentary" sources is observed, e.g., by Gordon J. Wenham, "The Coherence of the Flood Narrative," VT 28 (1978), 337–48. See also Bernhard W. Anderson, "From Analysis to Synthesis: the Interpretation of Genesis 1–11," JBL 97:1 (1978), 23–39. Michael Fishbane (cited in next note, below), however, views the methods of redactional criticism as compatible with documentary analysis.

14. Michael Fishbane, "Composition and Structure in the Jacob Cyccle," JJS 26 (1975), 14–38. Cf. idem, *Text and Texture: Close Readings of Selected Biblical Texts* (New York: Schocken, 1979). For a similar approach to the Jacob cycle, cf. John G. Gammie, "Theological Interpretation by way of Literary and Tradition Analysis: Genesis 25–36," in Martin J. Buss, ed., *Encounter with the Text: Form and History in the Hebrew Bible* (Philadelphia/Missoula: Fortress/Scholars, 1979), 117–34. It is worth noting that Fishbane and Gammie arrived at similar conclusions working completely independently of one another, as did Wenham and Anderson (see above, n. 13).

15. Cf. Westermann, 263–69; Gunkel, *Genesis*, 26ff., esp. 28–33; John Skinner, *Genesis*, ICC (Edinburgh: T. & T. Clark, 1910, 1963), 90–97; Wellhausen, *Prolegomena* (see "Preliminaries," n. 3), 297ff., esp. 299–308; Jacob, 71–79; von Rad, "The Form-Critical Problem of the Hexateuch" (see "Preliminaries," n. 15), 63ff.

16. The Garden story (Gen. 2:4–3:24) has generally been assigned to a "documentary" source different from and older than that of the Creation story (1:1–2:3 or 2:4a). So maintain the majority of investigators, including Wellhausen, Gunkel, Skinner, Eissfeldt, Pfeiffer, von Rad, Noth, Speiser, et al.; in disagreement with this consensus, see especially Cassuto and Jacob. The majority of commentators also assign 2:4a and 2:4b to the respective sources. I have chosen to read all of verse 4 as belonging to the Garden story—cf. Jacob, 71–75; Cassuto, 96–100 (reading 4a and 4b as a chiasm). I occasionally refer to the Garden story as "Gen. 2–3," by which I mean specifically 2:4–3:24.

17. For an illustration of the ways that form-critical and traditionary factors are relevant to a literary-structural understanding, cf. Koch, 159ff., 171ff., 183ff.

18. In this respect, the criteria established, e.g., by Walsh (see above, n. 9) for determining an element of literary structure seem unduly arbitrary and technical. It seems to me more reasonable to start with the natural divisions that have

been felt by a majority of readers and commentators to express the boundaries between coherent units of thought or action (some of which, to be sure, Walsh has judged correctly), and to proceed from there to a consideration of their interrelationship.

19. Cf. the strictures expressed by Shimon Bar-Efrat, "Some Observations on the Analysis of Structure in Biblical Narrative," SVT 30 (1978), 154–73, esp. 172: "It is definitely undesirable to base the structural analysis partly on verbal elements, partly on elements of technique and partly on conceptual content." This principle, however, cannot be applied rigidly, and Bar-Efrat himself offers examples of analysis that mix verbal and thematic elements. With respect to my own distinction between generic and semantic levels, one must say that generic elements have a semantic dimension of their own (and so, ultimately, a textual meaning) simply by virtue of having a content. For example, Gen. 2:23 is both a form-critical entity ("naming") and, at the same time, a conveyor of a specific name-etymology. Generic identifications are, in other words, themselves motifs, and eventually take their places as such in the story's motivic structure, as my discussion will eventually make clear.

20. On the "synchronic" sense in biblical literature, cf. Jan P. Fokkelman, *Narrative Art in Genesis* (see "Preliminaries," n. 21), 1–8; Robert C. Culley in *Interpretation* 28 (1974), 167–71; M. Kessler in Jared J. Jackson, ed., *Rhetorical Criticism: Essays in Honor of James Muilenberg* (Pittsburgh: Pickwick Press, 1974), 1–17, esp. 1; and the works by Robert Polzin cited in "Preliminaries," n. 21, as well as idem, *Moses and the Deuteronomist: A Literary Study of the Deuteronomic History* (New York: Seabury, 1980), esp. 1–24.

21. On this matter, see Michael Fishbane, "The Sacred Center: The Symbolic Structure of the Bible," in idem and Jehuda Reinharz, eds., *Texts and Studies*, Nahum N. Glatzer Festschrift (Leiden: Brill, 1975), 6–27, and extensive sources cited there.

22. On the non-narrative character of 2:10–14 ("Aufzählung" over against "Erzählung"), cf. Westermann, 293–94.

23. 2:23, 24, and 3:20 are recognized as form critically distinct entities by a wide consensus of commentators. Cf. Skinner, Gunkel, von Rad, Westermann, et al. ad loc. The rhetorical and thematic distinctness of 3:19b (referred to as "3:19c") from what precedes it is recognized by Westermann ad loc., 362–63. The presence of two clauses, 19a and 19b, both introduced by *ki* (for . . .), suggests that one of them is redundant, more likely the latter, more generalized one. Properly speaking, the whole of 14–19 should be isolated as a traditionary "package" of etiological ascriptions. I distinguish 19b on grounds partly of its redundancy, partly of its placement, and partly, as I discuss more fully further on, of its thematic parallel to 2:24. The segment 14–19a is, in any case, a unit sufficient unto itself, whose function is best understood in the light of its relation to the narrative segment that precedes it.

24. On namings, cf. George B. Gray, *Studies in Hebrew Proper Names* (1895); M. Noth, *Die israelitische Personnamen* (1928); Gunkel, *Legends of Genesis*, 27–30; Johannes Pedersen, *Israel: its Life and Culture*, I–II (London: Oxford University Press, 1926), 245–59; Roland de Vaux, *Ancient Israel: Social and Religious Institutions* (New York: McGraw Hill, 1975), 43–46; Raymond Abba, IDB Supp., s.v. "Name." On etiologies, cf. in general Gunkel, *Legends*, 24–36; Brevard S. Childs, "A Study of the Formula 'Until this Day,'" JBL 82:3 (1963), 279–92; idem, "The Etiological Tale Reexamined," VT 24:4 (1974), 387–97; Burke O. Long, *The Problem of Etiological Narrative in the Old Testament*, BZAW 108 (Berlin: Topelmann, 1968); I. L. Seeligmann (in Hebrew), *Zion* 26 (1961): 141–69; idem,

ThZ 18 (see next note), 305–11; John F. Priest, IDB Supp., s.v. "Etiology." Westermann, while noting the generic distinctiveness of 2:23 as a traditionally rhythmic oral formula (314–15), points out that it is more firmly anchored in the narrative than 2:24 (316). Cf. n. 35, below.

25. This phenomenon is more often referred to as "chiastic." On chiasm in biblical narrative, cf. N. Lund, "The Presence of Chiasmus in the Old Testament," AJSL 46 (1930), 104ff.; 49 (1932), 281ff.; and other sources cited by Fishbane, "Composition and Structure" (see n. 14, above); Fokkelman, 22ff., 33 ff., 71ff., 93ff., 236, 240; M. Dahood, IDB Supp, s.v. "Chiasmus." The term "chiasm" is best reserved for a structure of no more than four elements (two pairs), as per the useful terminology of Bar-Efrat (see n. 19, above), 170: "parallel" (a a'), "ring" (a x a'), "chiastic" (a b b' a'), "concentric" (a b x b' a'). I borrow the more general term "palistrophic" from Wenham (see n. 13, above), to refer to any symmetrical formation of four or more elements. The phenomenon of symmetry in biblical literature should also be seen in the light of the well-known principle of "resumptive repetition" or "Wiederaufnahme." See H. M. Wiener, *The Composition of Judges 2:11 to I Kings 2:46* (Leipzig, 1929), and Curt Kuhl, "Die Wiederaufnahme: ein Literarkritisches Prinzip?" ZAW 64 (1952), 1–11. Cf. I. L. Seeligmann, "Hebräische Erzählung und biblische Geschichtsschreibung," ThZ 18 (1962), 302–25, and compare my discussion of etiological parenthesis, toward the end of chapter 2.

26. *Gilgamesh*, Assyrian Tab. I, cols. iii–iv (ANET, 74–75); cf. T. Jacobsen, *Treasures of Darkness: A History of Mesopotamian Religion* (New Haven, 1976), 195–219, esp. 197–99. On the parallel of *Gilgamesh* with Gen. 2–3, cf. Westermann, 336f., and sources cited there. A useful general study of *Gilgamesh* is G. S. Kirk, *Myth: Its Meaning and Function* (Berkeley and Los Angeles: University of California Press, 1973), 132–52.

27. *Gilgamesh*, Assyr. Tab. XI, lines 287–89 (ANET, 96). The parallel is a loose one, and the literary disunity of the epic does not permit a rigorous comparison with Gen. 2–3, but the analogy is striking nonetheless, if only in the light of the *dis*similarities of the two works.

28. Cf. discussions by Jacob, 101–102, and Cassuto, 139–43, where, however, the issue is between a mythical vs. a psychological-moral interpretation of the serpent. On the manifold interpretations of the serpent, cf. discussion and sources cited by Westermann, 322ff.

29. Recognized as palistrophic by Jacob, 112; Cassuto, 159. Cf., however, Westermann's form-critical analysis of the sequence, 349ff.

30. So maintain a majority of commentators, as, e.g., Skinner, 87; Gunkel, 23; Speiser, 21; Cassuto, 171. Cf., however, the alternative reading ("clothes *for* the skin") proposed by Jacob ("Leibröcke"), 123.

31. Cf. esp. Cassuto, 100–104 (to 2:5–6), and 107–108, 114–15 (to 2:8, 10), who distinguishes a fundamental contrast in the story between the two modes of irrigation, springwaters vs. rainwaters.

32. The connection of Gen. 2–3 with rituals of the life-cycle is noted by Westermann, 267; Eissfeldt, *The OT: An Introduction*, 67. I offer, in the discussion that follows, a fuller rationale for understanding the centrality of the life-cycle to the story's unfolding structure.

33. Cf. n. 23, above.

34. Cf. Jacob on the word *luqoḥah*, 99n.; but cf. Ges.-K. § 10h. On the rhythmic style of the verse, and the use of the *Leitwort*, cf. Gunkel, Skinner, Jacob, Westermann, et al. ad loc.

35. Certainty on this matter is impossible, because we are dealing with the

gray area where form criticism and tradition history meet. It is perhaps wiser to think of the verse as something derived from a τόπος that was a part of the inherited stock-in-trade of a narrator—cf. Quintilian's sense of τόποι as "store-houses of trains of thought" (*Institutio oratoria,* 5:10, 20)—i.e., as for Gunkel, of inherited *forms.* Nevertheless, the thought *content* (the etymon *'ish/'ishshah*) is separable from the story, and so possibly a "tradition." Westermann ad loc. actually distinguished *two* discrete forms at work: a "Verwandtschaftsformel" (cf. Gen. 29:14, Judg. 9:2, 3; II Sam. 5:1, 19:13, 14) and a "Namensätiologie"-proper.

36. Cf. sources cited in n. 2, above.

37. So Skinner, ad loc., 68n.; also, Dillmann, Procksch, et al.

38. So Jacob, ad loc., 97; or, reading the *lamed* as *casus pendens* (cf. Cassuto, ad loc.): " . . . and as for. . . ." The subject of the verb *maza'* has variously been construed by commentators as God, the man, or the impersonal: " . . . one did not find. . . ."

39. For a comparative intrabiblical survey of the two words, cf. J. G. Plöger, TWzAT, s.v. *'adam,* and N. P. Bratsiotis, ibid., s.v. *'ish/'ishshah.* It is interesting to note that between Gen. 2–3 and the remainder of the Hebrew Bible, the two words are more or less exactly reversed in (1) relative frequency, and (2) usage. Outside the Garden story, *'adam* is more often "man" in a biological or proverbial context, *'ish* more often "a particular man," in a narrative or casuistic context.

40. Cf., e.g., Jacob's worried remarks on Eve's alleged anatomical "changes" in 3:16 (116; cf. "Preliminaries," n. 26 and discussion thereto). Jacob's main point, on the other hand, is unassailable: that what is new in 3:14–19 is human *knowledge* of the stated afflictions, not the *existence* of them per se.

41. I refer here only to a grammatical resemblance, not necessarily a matter of scientific grammar—if there is folk-etymology, there can also be folk-grammar. On the conception of Eve as *genetrix,* cf. I. Eitan, JAOS 49 (1929), 30 ff.

42. A surprising number of commentators, ancient and modern, have maintained this connection: Gen. Rabbah, Philo, Clement of Alexandria, et al. Cf. sources cited ad loc. by Skinner and Westermann.

43. It may not be necessary to say that b' is only "implied." It should be noted that without 24a, the two phrases 23 and 24b stand in a sequentially parallel relationship (p q p' q'). 24b may thus be appositive to 23, comprising, so it seems initially, a variant tradition of a mythological nature in what is otherwise a folktale. 24a, in this light, seems inserted to avoid confusion as to the subject of *wayyashken* (and He installed) at the beginning of 24b, a confusion that results from the merging of the two variants. Verse 23 thus otherwise quite adequately ends the story, yielding b' in its proper place in the story's motivic structure. It is not necessary, of course, to make 24b "extraneous" to the composition by ascribing to it the character of a mythological "variant." It is equally plausible to say that the author's grammar of composition permitted a parallel appositive (with an "echo" effect) as something compatible with an otherwise cleanly palistrophic structure, thus as parenthetic by virtue not of motivic content but of form. Taken as traditionary variant, however, the whole of 24 (incl. 24a) is plausible in its Masoretic formulation: it is simply the form in which it would have entered the author's inherited stock of narrative tropes or internally exegetical traditions. That editing of more or less unalterable traditional formulations might be involved seems further evident from the fact that as a *fully* intentional composition, the whole sequence (incl. the words of 24a) would have manifested the best diction as follows: "And YHWH God drove out the man

from the Garden of Eden, and sent him forth to work the ground from which he was taken, and He installed at the east of the Garden of Eden the cherubim and the revolving flaming sword, to guard the way to the Tree of Life." This wording again yields two more or less parallel sentences (the latter again appositive to the former), while restoring a more plausible sequence of verb, subject, and object. This formulation is in fact *not* made, and the Septuagint, which routinely adjusts for cleaner diction, did not choose to render it thus, even though it did revise the verses to make "the man" the object of *wayyashken*—indicating that the Septuagint translator did, in fact, sense some difficulty with the diction of his received text, which must have been similar or identical to the Masoretic version and must have become quite fixed long before.

44. Cf. n. 40, above, and further on in my discussion.

45. Cf. discussion by Cassuto cited in n. 31, above.

46. On the question of where to begin the story, cf. n. 15, above. 2:4a, in any case, is parallel to 4:1, and it is a moot point whether these verses stand within or without the borders of the Garden story: they *are* the borders.

47. Cf. Jacob's worthwhile schematic discussion of the formula *'eleh toledot* (These are the generations of . . .), commentary to 2:4 (71–75). One notes, as well, the verbal echo of *'eleh toledot* in the word *watteled* (and she bore) in 4:1.

48. See Gressmann, Schmidt, Gunkel, et al.; cf. discussion and sources cited by Westermann, 328ff., esp. 331–332.

49. Cf., in general, discussions and sources cited by Skinner, 58–59; Gunkel, 7f.; Westermann, 289–92; also, Skinner, 52; Cassuto, 112; Jacob, 86. On the grammatical construction "the tree of the knowledge of good and evil," cf. Ges.-K. §115d. Cf. also Gerhardt von Rad, *Genesis: A Commentary*, trans. J. H. Marks (Philadelphia: Westminster, 1961), 26; Jacob to Gen. 2:17 (92–94).

50. Cf. Ivan Engnell, "'Knowledge' and 'Life' in the Creation Story," SVT 3 (1955), 103–19.

51. See the capable analysis offered by George Buccellati, "Adapa, Genesis, and the Notion of Faith," UF 5 (1973), 61–66.

52. J. A. Knudtzon, et al., eds., *Die El-Amarna Tafeln*, Vorderasiatische Bibliothek 2 (Leipzig, 1911, 1915), 965ff., *Adapa* A, 4 (ANET, 101), and discussion by Skinner, 91–92. Simplistic parallels between *Adapa* and Gen. 2–3 should be avoided. Cf. the strictures in this regard by Theodore H. Gaster, *The Oldest Stories in the World* (New York: Viking, 1952), 85–92, and by Buccellati, op. cit. Adapa is not "tricked" into surrendering immortality, nor, for that matter is the human couple in Gen. 2–3. Protagonists in both stories learn what is already known to those whose knowledge reaches beyond the borders of mortal life: the difference between mortal and immortal life.

53. Jacobsen (see n. 26, above) discerns two principal strands of tradition at work in *Gilgamesh:* one a martial tradition; the other a sacral tradition. In the former, the hero cavalierly disregards death, and strives for immortality conferred by the fame of heroic deeds; in the latter, the hero is anguished by the fact of death and embarks on a quest for immortality that ends when he is led to understand that his immortality hinges on lasting social achievements. Both the epic and (as I suggest further on in my discussion) Gen. 2–3 wrestle with the relative merits of individual vs. collective accomplishment. It is thus no accident that the Bible's most lengthy and detailed narrative cycles (the Saul and David cycles of I/II Samuel) portray the conflicts of a primarily hierocratic king with a primarily charismatic son or protégé (Saul vs. Jonathan and David; David vs. Absalom). In both cycles, the hierocratic king is shown wrestling with a former

phase of his own career. It is not wide of the mark to suggest that these two contrasting social postures are summed up by the anthroposophical dichotomy *'adam/'ish* that is explored in the Garden story.

54. On the *Leitwort* in general: cf. Buber and Rosenzweig (cited in "Preliminaries," n. 20); Buber, *Werke: Schriften zur Bibel* II (Munich, 1964), 1095–1186; Everett Fox, "'We Mean the Voice': The Buber-Rosenzweig Translation of the Bible," *Response*, 5:3 (1971–72), 29–42; idem, "Technical Aspects of the Translation of Genesis of Martin Buber and Franz Rosenzweig" (Ph.D. diss., Brandeis University, 1974); Edward L. Greenstein, "Theories of Modern Bible Translation," *Prooftexts* 3:1 (Jan. 1983), 9–39.

55. See "Preliminaries," n. 28.

56. The connection of "myth" and "symbol" with a mimetic mode of representation is noted by de Man, 207 passim.

II. Is There a Story of Abraham?

1. Cf. chap. 1, n. 20.

2. For a useful skeptical perspective on these matters, cf. sources cited in "Preliminaries," n. 52.

3. Kugel, "On the Bible and Literature," 222ff.

4. See esp. Gunkel, *Legends of Genesis*, 13–36.

5. Cf. Claus Westermann, *Genesis 12–50: Erträge der Forschung* (Darmstadt: Wissenschaftliche Buchgesellschaft, 1975), 34; idem, *Biblischer Kommentar I, 2: Genesis 12–36* (Neukirchen-Vluyn: Neukirchner Vlg., 1981—hereafter abbreviated as "BK-2"), 15.

6. On the notion of a biblical story cycle, cf. Gunkel, *Legends*, 45–46; Westermann, BK-2, 15.

7. Cf. sources cited in chap. 1, n. 25.

8. Kugel, "On the Bible and Literature," 224ff.

9. Contra Kugel, 225: " . . . in terms of Israelite 'literary competence,' there is no evidence [that symmetry] was particularly prized." On the contrary, there is at least *some* evidence that the phenomenon at least *exists* (whether "prized," I am uncertain), and the imperfection of an alleged symmetry is not, in itself, grounds for dismissing the concept, as Kugel seems to suggest on 224–25. Flawed symmetry is still a form of symmetry, and, provided one keeps full accounting of the flaws and correctly identifies the elements that do converge properly, one can still offer a useful physiognomy of the text. Kugel's example, chosen from the apostle of chiasm, Fokkelman, is indeed a bad application of the concept, as Kugel correctly shows, and, as my citation of Kugel in n. 3, above, indicates, I concur with the main thrust of the argument he advances in his article.

10. Namely, episodes unfolding continuously within a single time-frame. One should note, in this regard, that, in addition to an abundance of temporal indicators that seem to stem from an effort to supply temporal consistency to the cycle (12:4, 6; 13:3b, 4a; 15:1a; 17:1a, etc.), there are certain *intrinsically* chronological factors that accord with the arrangement of the episodes: e.g., the "wife-sister" episodes must occur before a child is born to Sarah; Abraham's despair concerning the lack of a successor (15:2–3) occurs after the departure of Lot; Abraham is called "Abram" prior to chapter 17, and "Abraham" thereafter; Ishmael, born in chapter 16, is present at the circumcision scene in chapter 17, but not Isaac, who is not born until chapter 21; and so forth. This may belabor

the obvious, but it should make clear that the text either presupposes a fairly consistent sense of a single "story" of Abraham, or creates such a presupposition in the reader.

11. Compare the useful remarks of Michael Fixler in his review of Northrop Frye's *The Great Code: the Bible and Literature* (New York: Harcourt Brace Jovanovich, 1982), "Myth and History," *Commentary* (August, 1982), 76–78.

12. Cf. Westermann, BK-2, 19ff.

13. E.g., William F. Albright, *From the Stone Age to Christianity* (Anchor ed.; see "Preliminaries," n. 8), esp. 201–72; John Bright, *A History of Israel* (Philadelphia: Westminster, 1959, and later eds.; 1st ed. cited here), 60–93; Roland de Vaux, *The Early History of Israel*, trans. David Smith (Philadelphia: Westminster, 1978), 153–287; and the work of Kathleen Kenyon, G. Ernest Wright; E. A. Speiser; H. H. Rowley; Frank M. Cross, Jr., Henri Cazelles, et al.

14. Thomas L. Thompson, *The Historicity of the Patriarchal Narratives: The Quest for the Historical Abraham* (Berlin and New York: de Gruyter, 1974); John Van Seters, *Abraham in History and Tradition* (New Haven and London: Yale University Press, 1975).

15. On the affinity of these investigators with Wellhausen, cf. Westermann, BK-2, 21.

16. Thompson, in particular, seems thoroughly immersed in the data, perspectives, and methods of the investigations he attacks, and at no point does he offer any literary analysis of the material whose status as literature he seeks to vindicate.

17. Cf. the strictures in this regard by John T. Luke, "Abraham and the Iron Age: Reflections on the New Patriarchal Studies," JSOT 4 (1977), 35–47, who justly takes Thompson to task for his contention that " . . . no part of Genesis can be assumed to be history unless its literary character can first be shown to be historiographical . . ." (Thompson, 3).

18. See Westermann, BK-2, 19ff.

19. Ronald E. Clements, *Abraham and David: Genesis XV and its Meaning for Israelite Tradition* (London: SCM, 1967).

20. Westermann, 139–48; cf. idem, *The Promises to the Fathers: Studies on the Patriarchal Narratives*, (1976; trans. D. E. Green, Philadelphia: Fortress, 1980), 56–74. Westermann bases his symmetrical structure essentially on Gunkel's distinction between J^b (for "Beersheba") and J^h (for "Hebron")—the latter an interpolated "Abraham/Lot" Saga (see n. 23, below). Cf. Gunkel, *Genesis*, 159ff.

21. Apart from doxological references to the three patriarchs together in the remainder of the Pentateuch and beyond, cf. uses of "Abraham" in parallel or close association with "Jacob" or "Israel" in Isa. 29:22, 41:8, 66:16, Mic. 7:20, and Ps. 105:6, and, in parallel with "Isaac" in Ps. 105:9. Abraham is mentioned alone in an arguably pre-exilic tradition only in Ps. 47:10 (where the reference to "people of the God of Abraham" occurs in a specifically cosmopolitan context, in which the Israelite ancestor with the greatest number of kinship ties to neighboring peoples seems to be required), and, in an early exilic source, in Ezek. 33:24 (datable, according to 33:21, to the year 586 B.C.E., and clearly showing Abraham to have been present in popular tradition prior to that time). Significantly, this latter reference is used in a context *critical* of those Israelites who invoke the name of Abraham to justify their hold on the promised land. The reference to Abraham in Neh. 9:7, like those in Chronicles, presupposes Gen. 12–25. On the paucity of prophetic references to Abraham, cf. Clements, 61ff.

22. See Noth, *History of Pentateuchal Traditions* (see "Preliminaries," n. 6), 102–

15. But cf. the remarks critical of Noth in Westermann, BK-2, 14.

23. The common source-critical picture of Gen. 12–25 is more or less as follows: J—12, 13; 16; 18–19; 22:20–24; 24; 25:1–6. E—20; 22:1-19. JE (or various combinations of J and E)—15, 21. P—17; 23; 25:7ff.; and glosses of an archival nature throughout. As noted above, n. 20, Gunkel finds in J a "Hebron" strand and a "Beersheba" strand, and splits chapter 24 between J and E. Cf. Skinner, *Genesis*, 240ff.; Noth, *History of Pentateuchal Traditions*, 263–64; Pfeiffer, *Introduction to the OT*, 142ff.; 182ff.; Speiser, *Genesis*, Intro. and comm. ad loc. The notion of E as a "parallel" source to J has been challenged chiefly by Paul Volz and Wilhelm Rudolf, *Der Elohist als Erzähler: Ein Irrweg in der Pentateuchkritik?* BZAW 63 (Giessen: A. Töpelmann, 1933). But cf. Alan W. Jenks, *The Elohist and North Israelite Traditions*, SBLMS 22 (Missoula: Scholars Press, 1977). For a challenge to source criticism on Gen. 12–25, cf. Jacob, *Das erste Buch der Tora* (see "Preliminaries," n. 1), 970–90. On the anomalous Gen. 14, see next note. For convenience, I occasionally refer to the Abraham cycle as "Gen. 12–25," by which I mean more specifically 11:27–25:18.

24. On Gen. 14, cf. Skinner, 255ff.; G. von Rad, *Genesis: A Commentary* (see chap. 1, n. 49), 170ff.; Speiser, 99ff.; and, for a view dissenting from the mainstream, compare the worthwhile discussion by M. C. Astour, "Political and Cosmic Symbolism in Genesis 14 and in its Babylonian Sources," in Alexander Altmann, ed., *Biblical Motifs* (Cambridge: Harvard University Press, 1966), 66–111.

25. The discussion that follows is not intended to serve as a detailed literary study of the respective motifs, rather only to survey in brief the relationship of like motifs, and to explain the function of motivic pairs within the cycle as a whole.

26. Cf. Jacob, 333; Nahum M. Sarna, EJ, s.v. "Abraham," 114–15.

27. The coinage is rabbinic, based on the details of Gen. 15:9–11.

28. On the concept of "promise" narrative, cf. Westermann, *The Promises to the Fathers* (see n. 20, above), 2–30. For a treatment of the narratives as "covenant" narratives, cf. D. R. Hillers, *Covenant: History of a Biblical Idea* (Baltimore and London: Johns Hopkins, 1969), 93–119. Cf. also Clements, 9–22, who, with a great number of investigators, sees chapters 15 and 17 as the J and P versions, respectively, of the same basic tradition.

29. So argues, e.g., N. Lohfink, *Die Landesverheissung als Eid* (Stuttgart: Katholisches Bibelwerk, 1967), 33. Cf. Westermann, *Promises*, 110ff.

30. Westermann, *Promises*, 11–12, 106–107, and, on Ugaritic parallels, 165–86.

31. See n. 65, below, and its accompanying discussion.

32. Albrecht Alt, "The God of the Fathers," in idem, *Essays on Old Testament History and Religion* (Garden City: Doubleday/Anchor, 1968), 3–100, esp. 83–84. But cf. G. von Rad, "The Promised Land and Yahweh's Land in the Hexateuch," in idem, *The Problem of the Hexateuch and Other Essays* (see "Preliminaries," n. 15), 79–102, esp. 79–80, who categorizes the promises as those of land, progeny, blessing, and a new relationship with God; to which Westermann assents, *Promises*, 99. Cf. ibid., 97–98, et passim. I consider Alt's simpler categorization more relevant to an understanding of the literary unfolding of Gen. 12–25.

33. In chapter 12, Abraham is blessed with fecundity and told he will become "a great nation" in the far distant future; in 15:4, he is promised a *specific heir*, but the identity of the heir is not indicated; in 17, he is promised an heir named *Isaac*, but the time of conception is not indicated; finally, in 18:10ff., he is given the specific *time* of conception.

34. The inhabitants of Sodom, of course, are not explicitly condemned as child sacrificers. The relevant issue here is not who commits child sacrifice or how God views such sacrifices (there are ample views of both in Lev. 20:1–6, Deut. 12:29–31, II Kings 3:27, 16:21, 23:10, Jer. 7:30–31, 19:3–5, Ezek. 16:20–21, Mic. 3:32, Ps. 106:37–38, et al.), but rather what narrative reverberations, if any, exist between the Sodom and Akedah stories. (Lot's action in Gen. 19:8 is of course not child sacrifice, but child jeopardizing, though, in any case, Gen. 22, like Jephthah's action in Judg. 11:30–40, is a somewhat atypical and ad hoc enactment of child-sacrificial ritual.) A more pertinent clue is suggested by the end of Abraham's dialogue with God in 18:17–33, where the issue of how many righteous could suspend Sodom's destruction is curiously left hanging. Abraham's familiar step downward to fewer righteous is missing (though for five less, the righteous are saved and the city destroyed, as chapter 19 suggests), and the reader is left wondering if there might be some circumstance, analogous to Sodom or otherwise, in which God might require the death of *one* righteous person.

35. Cf. n. 30, above, and n. 37, below.

36. Compare rabbinic exegesis on the material: Gen. Rabbah 41:5–7.

37. One should consider, as well, the extensive ancient parallels to the annunciation episode, as adduced by Gunkel and Skinner, ad loc. (on Ugaritic parallels, cf. n. 30, above), and the fact that whereas the implied etiology of the name "Isaac" in 17:7 occurs in the thick of a continuing dialogue (the traditionary discontinuity with 17:8 notwithstanding), its analogue in 18:11–15 stands as the completion of the angels' visit with Abraham.

38. Cf. Gen. Rabbah 50:4.

39. Compare the form-critical analysis by Koch, *The Growth of Biblical Tradition* (see "Preliminaries," n. 4), 111–32, with the study of an alleged background in Hurrian legal institutions by E. A. Speiser in Alexander Altmann, ed., *Biblical and Other Studies* (Cambridge: Harvard University Press, 1963), 15–28 (contra Speiser: Thompson, 234–47; D. Freedman, JANES 2 [1970], 77–85; Van Seters, 71–76; et al.); and the traditiohistorical approach of Westermann, BK-2, 185–96; also, Gunkel, *Genesis*, 168–72, 220ff., 263ff. Westermann's conception of the interplay of familial and economic factors in the underlying tradition strikes me as the most pertinent approach, but no commentators have, in my opinion, satisfactorily explained the motive for Abraham's ruse, which seems rooted in socioeconomic factors of the Egyptian-Canaanite environment (immigration laws prohibiting entry of married couples?)—a conclusive discussion of which is presently beyond my competence to provide. Cf. next note.

40. No judgments are intended here about the *actual* marriage and kinship rules of the Egyptians—I refer only to a kind of circumstantial exogamy, as perceived by the narrator or his antecedent tradition. That is to say, the Nile Delta and Canaanite *shefelah*, being the most urbanized and cosmopolitan environments of the region, would quite naturally be perceived as an erosive force to the tribal solidarity of more parochial visitors, and its marital practices as *ipso facto* "exogamous." Cf. Gen. 21:21, 24:3–9; 26:34–35; 27:46; 34:1ff.; 38:2ff; 41:45, Ex. 1:8ff. (Ex. Rabbah 1:12ff. underscores the severe restrictions on family life incurred by Israelites in Egypt), et al. See also O. J. Baab, IDB, s.v. "Marriage," 281, regarding the sliding definition of "exogamy" and "endogamy," and the conflicting tendencies in Israelite marital practice. The suggestive studies of Edmund A. Leach, *Genesis as Myth, and Other Essays* (London: Jonathan Cape, 1969), showing how biblical narrative attempts to mediate contradictions between endogamous and exogamous bonds, should, perhaps, be taken into con-

sideration in the present context, though again I stress that our judgments regarding *actual* marital customs should remain circumspect.

41. Noth, *History of Pentateuchal Traditions*, 102ff., takes the Isaac version to be the "original" core of the tradition, and the variants in the Abraham cycle to be secondary developments (contra Noth: Koch, 122–27; Westermann, 187–88)— a matter on which I render no judgment. It should suffice to point out the close association of Abraham and Isaac with respect to this motif, and the complete absence of the motif in the Jacob cycle, where the question of a lineage emerging, or not emerging, from a single ancestral mother is not a factor.

42. On the formal similarity of at least 13:5–18 ("Streiterzählung") to its counterparts ("Brunnenstreit-Erzählung") in Gen. 21 and 26, cf. Westermann, BK-2, 200 (based on B. Gemser, SVT 3 [1955], 120–37). Cf. idem, *Promises*, 65–68.

43. Cf. Westermann, BK-2, 212, who stresses the importance of the peaceful resolution of Abraham's territorial conflicts in contrast to the more bellicose analogues outside of Genesis.

44. Cf. Westermann on "family" stories, *Promises*, 59–65.

45. More specifically of Isaac and Ishmael. See Gen. Rabbah 55:4; cf. 55:7; Rashi to Gen. 22:2.

46. Gunkel, for example, *Genesis*, 241–42, sees such a Canaanite substratum to the legend, though he acknowledges a secondary etiological stratum dealing with the *cessation* of child sacrifice in the Canannite or Israelite milieu. One should note that 22:18b (" . . . for you listened to my voice . . .") can just as easily refer to 22:12, the command to *stop* sacrificing Isaac, as to 22:2, the command to sacrifice him.

47. Erich Auerbach, *Mimesis: The Representation of Reality in Western Literature* (see "Preliminaries," n. 21), 1–20.

48. Cf. Westermann, BK-2, 46–48, who places special importance on 11:30 ("And Sarai was barren; she had no offspring") as a point of departure for the narrative material of the cycle. Likewise, Nahum M. Sarna, "The Anticipatory Use of Information as a Literary Feature of the Genesis Narratives," in Richard Freedman, ed., *The Creation of Sacred Literature* (Berkeley and Los Angeles: University of Calif., 1982), 76–82.

49. For other examples of this technique, cf. Sarna (see preceding note).

50. On the exceptionally discursive style of Gen. 24, cf. Noth, *History of Pentateuchal Traditions*, 199; von Rad, *Genesis*, 248–49; et al.

51. On the coda function of Gen. 23 and 24 ("accounts of success"), cf. Westermann, *Promises*, 69–70.

52. See chap. 1.

53. I refer here only to the division according to *parshiyyot*, not to the motivic structure I shall eventually demonstrate, which is slightly at variance with this pattern. On the relevance of lectionary divisions to an understanding of compositional structure, cf. discussion by Fishbane referred to in chap. 1, n. 14 and n. 25.

54. Cf. Westermann, BK-2, 389f., 412–13, 424–25, 490–93.

55. See Gen. 21:8–9, which pointedly exposes Ishmael playing (or "mocking") at the weaning ceremony of Isaac, and leads to the resolution of Sarah that "the son of that slave woman will not inherit with Isaac" (v. 10).

56. God reassures Abraham that his succession will pass, not to a servant, but to one born of his own loins (15:4), and to one borne, not by a servant woman, but by his wife Sarah (17:16ff., 18:9–15, 21:12), while nevertheless the child born to his servant Hagar will become a neighboring people to Israel (17:20,

21:13; cf. 16:10ff., 21:17ff.). God also gradually clarifies his intentions toward the Canaanite peoples he will displace from the land (15:13–21, 18:17–33): they will be removed when their "iniquity is . . . complete" (15:16), but God will spare their cities for as few as ten righteous people in their midst (18:32).

57. See n. 9, above. The symmetrical structure that I shall set forth in the discussion that will follow resembles in certain respects that argued by Gary A. Rendsburg in his conference paper "The Redactional Structuring of Gen. 11:27–22:24," summarized in *AAR/SBL Abstracts* 1982, 191–92—although I had worked out my own analysis without having seen Rendsburg's work. His analysis exhibits some especially interesting correspondences of *Leitwörter* that support, in the main, certain of my own observations. As my discussion will make clear, I depart from Rendsburg in the textual scope taken into consideration—for I hold Gen. 23:1–25:18 to be part of the symmetrical structure of the cycle, and, unlike Rendsburg, attempt to account for the *asymmetries* of the cycle, asymmetries that do not simply result from the effort to include additional texts in the pattern, but are an essential part of the dynamic unfolding of the narrative and depend on the symmetrical component of the cycle for their meaning. Cf. also George W. Coats, *Genesis—with an Introduction to Narrative Literature* (Grand Rapids: Eerdmans, 1984), 97–104.

58. See n. 42, above.

59. Furthermore, Phichol's statement to Abraham (21:22) that "God is with you in all that you do" would make no sense prior to chapter 21, in the light of Abraham's statement (20:11): "Truly, I had said, there is no fear of God in this place"—and Abraham's fear of the inhabitants of Gerar in the earlier episode contrasts strongly with his boldness in 21:5: "And Abraham admonished Abimelech concerning the waterwells the servants of Abimelech had stolen"—a boldness that presupposes the events of chapter 20.

60. On the concept of narrative syntax, see Vladimir Propp, *The Morphology of the Folktale* (Austin and London: University of Texas, 1968); Roland Barthes, "Introduction to the Structural Analysis of Narratives," in idem, *Image, Music, Text* (see chap. 3, n. 22), 79–124, esp. 97–104; idem, "The Struggle with the Angel: Textual Analysis of Genesis 32:22–32," ibid., 125–41.

61. Later Jewish tradition unequivocally identifies Mt. Moriah with the Temple Mount (II Chr. 3:1; Gen. Rabbah 55:7; Rashi to Gen. 22:2), and while no clear historical or textual evidence confirms this identification, it is congenial to the cycle's key themes. Gunkel, *Genesis*, 238–40, sees Gen. 22 as an etiology of "Yeru'el," a cultic site between Jerusalem and 'En-Gedi, referred to in II Chr. 20:16 (cf. "Peni'el" in Gen. 32:31), and the multiple plays on the roots *r'y* and *yr'* throughout the episode support such a reading, but the locale is of less significance than the perception that the story may obliquely refer to a known place. For Jerusalem, cf. "'Ari'el," Isa. 29:1, 2, 7. Jerusalem may appear once earlier in the cycle (14:17), in connection with "Melchizedek, king of Salem" (on "Salem" as Jerusalem, cf. Ps. 76:3; Gen. Apoc. 22:13; Onkelos; Josephus, El-Amarna letters; also, Skinner, Von Rad, Westermann, et al. to Gen. 14:17; contrast Albright BASOR 163 [1961], 36–54, esp. 52). Through the events of Gen. 22, one could say, "Salem" is transformed into "*Yeru*-Salem" (cf. Gen. Rabbah 55:10)—a witticism that may survive the inconsistency of Abraham's building of an altar at an already long-established Canaanite site of worship. The etiological culmination—"And Abraham named that site Adonai-yir'eh, whence is said today, 'On the mountain of YHWH *yera'eh*'"—yields an untranslatable term that can be read with three meanings: (1) He (YHWH) appeared. (2) It (a ram) was pro-

vided. (3) One should appear (namely, on the Temple Mount at pilgrim festivals—see *yera'eh* in Exod. 23:17, 34:23, Deut. 16:16). The foregoing considerations are, of course, an argument from silence, and the reason why the text should dissemble on the identity of Jerusalem remains in the present context unclear, but such dissembling is quite in character for the narratives of Genesis— cf. von Rad, *Gen.*, to 14:17–20. On *yeru-* as "founded," see BDB, s.v. *yeru'el.*

62. For a discussion of this dichotomy in the traditions about kingship, cf. Frank M. Cross, Jr., "The Ideologies of Kingship in the Era of Empire: Conditional Covenant and Eternal Decree," in idem, *Canaanite Myth and Hebrew Epic* (Cambridge: Harvard University Press, 1973), 219–73. Concerning a similar dichotomy in the Hebrew Bible as a whole, see Walter Brueggemann, "Trajectories in Old Testament Literature and the Sociology of Ancient Israel," JBL 98:2 (1979), 161–85. Robert Polzin, in *Moses and the Deuteronomist* (see chap. 1, n. 20), esp. 1–72, introduces a useful distinction between "dogmatic authoritarianism" and "critical traditionalism," to account for the orchestration of the "conditional/unconditional" ideologies in the Deuteronomistic history, at least through Deut.–Judges, which is the scope covered by Polzin's book.

63. The close association of this type of oracle with Isaac and his mate Rebecca is further suggested by 24:60. Westermann, BK-2 to 22:17, associates the bellicose segment of the oracle with the life of the tribes. On the background of the expression *'alfei revavah* in 24:60, cf. Gottwald, *The Tribes of Yahweh* (see "Preliminaries," n. 19), 279–81. One should note the interplay in Gen. 12–25 of two meanings to the verb *yrš*: (a) *familial:* 15:3–4, 21:10; (b) *military-political:* 15:17, 22:17, 24:60. On the latter, cf. Lev. 20:24, 25:46, Num. 21:24, Deut. 1:21, 2:24, 31, 6:18, etc., Josh. 1:15, 21:41, 24:4, etc., Judg. 1:21, 2:6, 18:9, etc., Jer. 49:1–2; Ps. 25:13, and a vast number of comparable examples.

64. The promise of 12:2, "I shall magnify thy name," could suggest military exploits; more pertinently, 12:3: " . . . and those that treat you contemptuously I shall curse." But, like the promise of fertility (cf. n. 33, above), these words are still far too general to associate with any concrete historical context. More specific is the oracle placed into the mouth of Melchizedek in 14:20: " . . . and blessed is El-Elyon who has delivered your enemies into your hands." But this applies to Abraham, and to the specific events of chapter 14. In 16:12, a bellicose oracle of sorts is applied to Ishmael: " . . . and he will be a wild ass of a man, his hand against everyone, and everyone's hand against him" (cf. 25:18). Only in 22:17 and 24:60 do we find oracles that explicitly apply to Isaac, and in language suggestive of the institution of holy war. One should note that attitudes toward war changed in Israel dramatically with the onset of the Exile, when the institutional basis of holy war disintegrated. Deut. 28:25–28, Jer. 31:15, Lam. 4:10, et al., reflect this newer ambience, and there the motif of child slaughter (or abandonment of children to slaughter) is prominent. Cf. E. L. Toombs, IDB, s.v. "War, ideas of," 798–99.

65. N. Habel, "The Form and Significance of the Call Narratives," ZAW 77 (1965), 297–323; W. Zimmerli, *Ezekiel 1: A Commentary on the Book of the Prophet Ezekiel, Chapters 1–24* (1969; trans. R. E. Clements, Philadelphia: Fortress, 1979), 95ff.; Wilhelm Richter, *Die sogenannten vorprophetischen Berufungsberichte,* FRLANT 101 (Göttingen: Vandenhoeck & Ruprecht, 1970); Uriel Simon, "Samuel's Call to Prophecy: Form Criticism with Close Reading," *Prooftexts* 1:2 (May, 1981), 119–32. Chief texts adduced: Exod. 3f., Judg. 6:11ff., I Sam. 3:1ff. (Simon), I Sam. 9:1ff., Isa. 6:1ff. Jer. 1:4ff., Ezek. 1:1ff.; material from Gen. 12– 25 discussed only passim, but Habel cites the *human* commissioning episode of

24:1 as related to the genre. James S. Ackerman, in a private correspondence, has cautioned me that the genre cannot be applied with any accuracy to the narratives examined here, and I must stress that it is not, strictly speaking, an identification of *genre* that I am attempting here, but rather only signs of the *influence* of the genre on the unfolding of the episodes in question, which properly exhibit features of an "annunciation" type-scene. Cf. next note.

66. Introductory word and/or commissioning: 15:1; 17:1–2 (cf. 18:1–2a). Hesitation or objection: 15:2–3, 8; 17:3 (?), 17–18; 18:12. Reassurance: 15:4–5; 17:19–22; 18:13–14. Sign: 15:9–16; 17:4–14; 18:14b (cf. 21:1). The most stable elements appear to be hesitation and reassurance—indeed, these are the sole elements common to all attested examples in the preceding note, in some form. Simon's stress on the great suppleness and variability of the genre should be kept in mind. "The hesitation of Abraham" is a topos that is further attested in the cycle in 18:23–33 and 21:11. It seems to be an essential ingredient in the prophet's assigned role of "intercessor" (see 20:7), as 18:23–33 makes clear. It should be noted that Abraham's *unquestioning* obedience is shown only at the beginning (12:4) and near the end (22:3) of the cycle. "Abraham the doubter" is thus sandwiched between two episodes of "Abraham the faithful"—a pattern quite similar to one shown in the book of Job by H. L. Ginsberg, EJ, s.v. "Job."

67. See n. 23 and n. 28, above.

68. We have in the so-called P example, if anything, the classic Davidic-Solomonic "nationalism" customarily attributed to J or his era, and, in the "JE" example, the "conditional" covenant frequently associated with "Elohistic" (and "Deuteronomistic") tradition.

69. One should note that there is a certain traditionary redundancy between the Hagar episodes and the brief gloss on Abraham's relation to Ketura in Gen. 25:1–6. Both bodies of material deal with ancestral mothers of bedouin groups living to the southwest and southeast of Palestine; both concern themselves with the question of Isaac's succession (see 25:5); and both record the explusion of the less favored children, presumably on the basis of some nominal legal settlement (25:6: "But to Abraham's children by concubines, Abraham gave gifts, and sent them away from Isaac's presence, while he was still alive, eastward to the land of the East.") Especially interesting is the fact that this redundancy is maintained in the Joseph story, for it is both Ishmaelites (children of Hagar) and Midianites (children of Ketura) who are the intermediaries in the sale and transport of Joseph to Egypt (Gen. 37:25–36; 39:1). For a worthwhile study of the literary effect of the ambiguity in the Joseph story, cf. Edward Greenstein, "An Equivocal Reading of the Sale of Joseph," in K. R. R. Gros Louis with James S. Ackerman, eds., *Literary Interpretations of Biblical Narratives*, Vol. II (Nashville: Abingdon, 1982), 114–25. Significantly, rabbinic exegesis (see Gen. Rabbah to 25:1) identifies Hagar and Keturah as the *same* person—suggesting that, traditiohistorically, at least, the notion of a clouded succession was a relatively archaic and stable element of the traditions about Abraham.

70. The verbal connection is quite precise: " . . . and they shall oppress [*we'innu*] them 400 years" (15:13); " . . . and Sarai oppressed her [*watte'annehah sarai*] and she fled" (16:6); "And [Pharaoh] appointed over [Israel] taskmasters so as to oppress [them] [*lema'an'annoto*]." Note also the metathesizing of the consonants '*ny* to '*yn*, when Hagar's situation is reversed: "An angel of YHWH found her by the desert spring" ('*eyn hammidbar*, 16:7); "God opened here eyes" (*wayyifqaḥ . . . 'et 'eyneyhah*, 21:19). The key word '*ny* was also pointed out by Martin Buber, *Werke: Schriften zur Bibel* (see "Preliminaries," n. 20), 1144ff.

71. Cf. Mendenhall, *The Tenth Generation* (see "Preliminaries," n. 19), xiv–xvi; John Bright, "The Modern Study of Old Testament Literature," in Wright, *The Bible and the Ancient Near East* (see "Preliminaries," n. 8), 23, n. 18.

72. See n. 40, above.

73. Contra Clements, Hillers, et al., who identify the Abrahamic covenant with a chiefly pro-Davidic ideology and nationalistic program over against the confederate covenants of Sinai and Shechem, and the prophetic movements and Deuteronomic theology.

74. The difficult and somewhat arcane insights of Hugh C. White, "Word Reception as the Matrix of the Structure of the Genesis Narrative," in Polzin and Rothman, ed., *The Biblical Mosaic* (see "Preliminaries," n. 21), 61–83, may be relevant in this connection.

75. Lev. 19:33–34; Deut. 23:8.

76. See my Epilogue.

77. Ex. 20:5, 34:7; Num. 14:18; Deut. 5:9—texts I interpret to mean that punishment can come *as late as* the third or fourth generation, when these generations persist in displeasing God. Cf. the conflicting interpretations of this formula by Rashi, Ibn Ezra, and Nachmanides to Ex. 20:5. Nachmanides, notably, establishes the connection to Gen. 15:16.

78. Michael Walzer, *The Revolution of the Saints: A Study in the Origins of Radical Politics* (New York: Atheneum, 1970), 188. The *locus classicus* of the concept of "new man" is the late Roman republic. Cf. Lily Ross Taylor, *Party Politics in the Age of Caesar* (Berkeley and Los Angeles: University of California Press, 1949, 1961). One recalls here Max Weber's reference to David's early retinue as "Catiline characters," *Ancient Judaism* (see chap. 3, n. 46, below), 45. Weber, in general, offers useful insights on the role of rootless political actors in ancient Israel. For more recent treatments of the phenomenon in ancient Israel, cf. Abraham Malamat, "Organs of Statecraft in the Israelite Monarchy," BAR 3 (1970), 163–98; Baruch Halpern, "Sectionalism and the Schism," JBL 93:4 (1974), 519–32; E. W. Heaton, *Solomon's New Men: The Emergence of Ancient Israel* (New York: Pica Press, 1974). While these studies focus on the period of the early monarchy, one should bear in mind the long history of the *ʿapiru*, the non-citizen or landless wayfarer, whose type is well known to historians of the Bronze Age. Cf. Moshe Greenberg, *The Ḥab/piru*, AOS 39 (New Haven, 1955); Mendenhall, *The Tenth Generation* (see "Preliminaries," n. 19); Gottwald, *The Tribes of Yahweh* (see "Preliminaries," n. 19), et al.

79. *Geʾon haggeʾonim* 26—cited in A. Steinsaltz, *Perush hammiqraʾ besifrut hashsheʾelot wehatteshuvot* (Jerusalem: Keter, 1978), 9.

III. David without Diagrams

1. Wellhausen, *Prolegomena to the History of [ancient] Israel* (see "Preliminaries," n. 3). Wellhausen deals in somewhat greater detail with this narrative in *Die Komposition des Hexateuchs und der historischen Bücher* (I cite from the 2d ed., Berlin: Reimer, 1899; cf. 4th ed., Berlin: de Gruyter, 1963), 258–63.

2. Works cited here: Albrecht Alt, "The Formation of the Israelite State" (1930), in idem, *Essays on Old Testament History and Religion* (see chap. 2, n. 32), 225–309 (quotation: 268); Robert H. Pfeiffer, *Introduction to the Old Testament* (New York: Harper & Row, 1948), 357–59; Gerhardt von Rad, "The Beginning of Historical Writing in Ancient Israel" (1944), in idem, *The Problem of the*

Hexateuch and Other Essays (see "Preliminaries," n. 15), 166–204 (quot.: 193); Otto Eissfeldt, *The Old Testament: an Introduction* (see "Preliminaries," n. 72), 141; John Bright, *A History of Israel* (I cite from the 1st ed., Philadelphia: Westminster, 1946, 1952), 163; Ernst Sellin and Georg Fohrer, *Introduction to the Old Testament* (German 1st ed., Heidelberg: Quelle & Meyer, 1963; trans. David Green, Nashville: Abingdon, 1968), 163. Cf. R. N. Whybray, *The Succession Narrative: A Study of II Sam. 9–20, I Kings 1 and 2* (Naperville: Allenson, 1968), 10–53. In some of the above citations, I have followed the excerpting of Whybray.

3. Hannelis Schulte, *Die Entstehung des Geschichtsschreibung im alten Israel* (Berlin and New York: de Gruyter, 1972).

4. Schulte echoes another frequent assumption of historical scholarship, namely, that historical sources bespeak only narrowly partisan or parochial interests of a class or faction. Cf. her remarks, 173–74, on the priestly origin of the Davidic histories. Her opponents on the matter note the general absence of "cultic" detail—an argument Schulte refutes, not by challenging its presuppositions headlong, but by explaining away the silence on cult as the result of an "estrangement" from the cult and priesthood in the "younger generation" of Jonathan and Ahimaaz. She thus preserves the presuppositions of the hypothesis she attacks, implicitly conceding that a priestly source *should* speak mainly of cultic matters—as if priests wait with bated breath for any opportunity to expound on sacral hardware. One need only consider the public addresses of Pope John Paul II in our own time: Does he speak about technicalities of the Eucharist, the names of the priestly vestments, the dimensions of the Vatican palace? No, he speaks of war and peace; of civil violence, poverty, hunger, and materialism; of marital fidelity and infidelity, and of the rights of the unborn. His priestly identity supplies the form, but not the content of his message. One might compare Rost (cited in next note), 82, regarding another alleged stratum in II Samuel: "[. . . Its two authors] spent time close to the king, . . . [one] apparently a prophet . . . not likely a priest, however, who would certainly not have missed the opportunity to bring, somehow, his office into mention."

5. Both Leonhard Rost, *Die Überlieferung von der Thronnachfolge Dawids* (Stuttgart: W. Kohlhammer, 1926), and Schulte, among others, offer useful observations on peculiarities of diction and style, which they hold to bespeak origin in a particular period. Schulte's adducement of affinities between the Samuel authors, the Judges 19 author, and the Yahwist are particularly suggestive, but far more useful than the assignation to period or author is the inventory of rhetorical tropes she provides in the process. See, among other places, *Entstehung*, 153, n. 65; 156–57, nn. 73–74. One should keep in mind that the extant language known as "biblical Hebrew" represents only an estimated one-fifth of the Hebrew language actually spoken in ancient Israel—see W. F. Albright in *Peake's Commentary on the Bible* (Edinburgh, 1962), 62, and Edward Ullendorff, "Is Biblical Hebrew a Language?" in idem, *Is Biblical Hebrew a Language?—Studies in Semitic Languages and Civilization* (Wiesbaden: Harrassowitz, 1977), 4ff.—and therefore that judgments as to the antiquity of a particular form are largely arguments from silence, and suspect as such.

6. On historical writing in general in the ancient Near East, cf. Robert C. Denton, ed., *The Idea of History in the Ancient Near East* (New Haven and London: Yale University Press, 1967). See also nn. 9, 11, below.

7. Cf. Eissfeldt, *OT Intro.*, 140–41, however, who notes that there is no hard evidence for contemporaneity of source—and contrast, say, J. A. Bewer, *The Literature of the Old Testament*, 3d ed., rev. E. G. Kraeling (New York and London:

Columbia University Press, 1962), 30: "All this is told by a man who had been present in all these situations, with all the variety of graphic and intimate details that bears the stamp of veracity on its face."

8. Cf. David M. Gunn, *The Story of King David: Genre and Interpretation* (Sheffield: JSOT Supplement Series 6, 1978), 31: " . . . If there is no internal or external evidence requiring a Solomonic date for the narrative, neither, I would argue, is there any inherent improbability in almost any date between Solomon's time and the exile."

9. The view of the court history as a "novella" goes back at least to B. Luther, "Die Novelle von Juda und Tamar und andere israelitische Novellen," in Eduard Meyer, ed., *Die Israeliten und ihre Nachbarstämme* (Halle, 1906), 177–206. Eissfeldt, *OT Intro.,* loc. cit., notes the prevalence of private scenes; cf. Whybray, 11–19; Wilhelm Caspari, "Literarische Art und historischer Wert von 2 Sam. 15–20," *Theologische Studien und Kritiken* 82 (1909), 317–48; Hugo Gressmann, *Die älteste Geschichtsschreibung und Prophetie Israels,* SAT 11:1 (1910); Jared J. Jackson, "David's Throne: Patterns in the Succession Story," CJT II (1965), 183–95; John Gray, *I & II Kings,* 2d ed., OT Library (London: SCM, 1970), 17–22; and the sources cited in the ensuing notes.

10. Charles Conroy, *Absalom Absalom!—Narrative and Language in 2 Sam. 13–20* (Rome: Biblical Institute Press, 1978); J. P. Fokkelman, *Narrative Art and Poetry in the Books of Samuel* (see "Preliminaries," n. 76). Fokkelman, a pioneer in synchronic study, is often a gifted interpreter, and my strictures in the discussion that follows should not obscure my debt to him.

11. See n. 8, above.

12. Gunn, *Story of King David,* 38.

13. Ibid., 26. Gunn's remarks are directed, on the one hand, toward Rost classically, as well as Theodorus C. Vriezen, "De Compositie van de Samuel-Boeken," *Orientalia Neerlandica: A Volume of Oriental Studies* (Leiden: Sijthoff, 1948), 156–89; and Whybray, esp. 20–21, 40–45—all of whom found the document to support the Solomonic cause—and, on the other hand, toward Gustav Hölscher, *Geschichtsschreibung in Israel: Untersuchungen zum Yahwisten und Elohisten* (Lund: Gleerup, 1952), and, contemporaneously to Whybray's study, L. Delekat, "Tendenz und Theologie der David-Salomo-Erzählung," in F. Maas, ed., *Das ferne und nahe Wort,* BZAW 105 (Berlin: Töpelmann, 1967), who found it to attack or criticize the Solomonic cause. Cf. Gunn, 21–26, esp. 22. Some have argued that the conflict of *Tendenz* possibilities undermines our conception of it as propaganda—see Gunn, 23; O. Eissfeldt, *Geschichtsschreibung im Alten Testament* (Berlin, 1948), 25–26. Cf. Schulte, 175.

14. This dating is argued classically by Rost (see n. 5, above); likewise, von Rad and Whybray (see n. 2, above). Cf. Walter Brueggemann, "David and his Theologian," CBQ 30 (1968), 156–81; T. N. D. Mettinger, *King and Messiah: The Civil Legitimation of the Israelite Kings* (Lund: Gleerup, 1971), 24–31. Eissfeldt, *OT Intro.,* 140–41, favors a ninth-century date; similarly, Hölscher, who sees the Yahwist's hand extending as far as I Kings 12. N. E. Wagner, "Abraham and David?" in J. W. Wevers and D. B. Redford, eds., *Studies on the Ancient Palestinian World* (Toronto: University of Toronto Press, 1972), 117–40, further expresses caution on a tenth-century origin. Cf. other sources and hypotheses adduced by Gunn, 124, n. 19.

15. On the question of boundaries, cf. Gunn, 65–84.

16. See Rost, 105, Cf. n. 54, below.

17. See Roland Barthes, *S/Z: An Essay,* trans. Richard Miller (New York: Hill & Wang, 1974), esp. 3–16.

18. Cf., in general, James A. Pritchard, ed., *Ancient Near Eastern Texts Relating to the Old Testament*, 3d ed. (Princeton: Princeton University Press, 1969); Henri Frankfort, *Kingship and the Gods: A Study of Ancient Near Eastern Religion and the Integration of Society and Nature* (Chicago: University of Chicago Press, 1948); Sigmund Mowinckel, *He That Cometh* (New York: Abingdon, 1954); idem, *The Psalms in Israel's Worship*, trans. D. R. Ap Thomas (New York: Abingdon, 1967); J. Gray, "Social Aspects of Canaanite Religion," SVT 15 (Leiden: Brill, 1965), 170–92; Roland de Vaux, *Ancient Israel: Social and Religious Institutions* (New York: McGraw Hill, 1965), 115–32; Ivan Engnell, *Studies in Divine Kingship in the Ancient Near East* (Oxford: Blackwell, 1967); A. R. Johnson, *Sacral Kingship in Ancient Israel*, 2d ed. (Cardiff: University of Wales, 1967), 132ff.; Tomoo Ishida, *The Royal Dynasties in Ancient Israel: A Study on the Formation and Development of Royal-Dynastic Ideology*, BZAW 142 (Berlin and New York: de Gruyter, 1977); Baruch Halpern, *The Constitution of the Monarchy in Israel*, Harvard Semitic Monographs 25 (Chico: Scholars, 1981).

19. See esp. Alt, "The Formation of the Israelite State," 238–67; Bright, *A History of Israel*, 163–208; Martin Noth, *The History of Israel* (1958; 2d ed., Harper & Row, 1960), 164–224; Ishida, *Royal Dynasties*, 26–54; Baruch Halpern, "The Uneasy Compromise: Israel Between League and Monarchy," in Halpern and Levenson, eds., *Traditions in Transformation* (see "Preliminaries," n. 52), 59–96.

20. One wishes, in a way, for a treatment that combines the perspectives of Perry and Sternberg, "Hammelekh bemabbaṭ 'ironi" (see "Preliminaries," n. 75) with that of Moshe Garsiel, *Malkhut Dawid: Meḥqarim behisṭoriyah we'iyyunim be-hisṭoriografiyah* (The Davidic kingdom: Studies in history and reflections in historiography; Tel Aviv: Society for Biblical Studies, 1975), 100ff., who perhaps correctly faults Perry and Sternberg for their inattention to institutional factors, but who sacrifices in the process their subtler grasp of the text's manner of ellipsis and indirection. Thus, what Perry and Sternberg have portrayed as an isolated moral failing on the king's part in his staying home from battle, Garsiel, with some justice, shows to represent a pivotal institutional change: the necessity of preserving the king's (dynastic) person as political figurehead, as summarized etiologically in II Sam. 21:15–17. Cf. further on in my discussion. Yet Garsiel, for his part, overlooks the general subordination of this "dynastic" etiology to the story's moral and psychological themes.

21. So MT^mss, LXX (ἐις τον καιρὸν της ἐξοδίας των βασιλέων), OL, Targ., Vulg., and I Chron. 20:1; cf. also Josephus *Ant.* 7:129, RSV; et al, But see Syriac. Fokkelman, preferring the MT as *lectio difficilior*, reads "envoys," with reference to the diplomats sent by David in II Sam. 10:2. Hans W. Hertzberg, *I & II Samuel* (1960; trans. J. S. Bowden, 4th printing, Philadelphia: Westminster, 1976), 303, 305, reading "kings," places the verse as the closing verse of the account of the Ammonite war in II Sam. 10. P. Kyle McCarter, *II Samuel: A New Translation with Introduction and Commentary*, Anchor Bible (Garden City: Doubleday/Anchor, 1984), 284–85, refers the "kings" to the Aramean coalition of 10:6, 11:1, thus marking the turning of one year since the original sally in defense of the Ammonites.

22. See Roland Barthes, "La lutte avec l'ange: Analyse textuelle de Génèse 32:23–33," in R. Barthes, F. Bovon, et al., *Analyse structurale et exégèse biblique* (Neuchâtel: Delachaux et Nièstle, 1971), 31. This essay appears in English in R. Barthes, *Image, Music, Text*, trans. Stephen Heath (New York: Hill & Wang, 1977), 125–41.

23. On the role of the king/judge in Near Eastern and Israelite institutions of holy war, cf. sources cited in n. 18, above, and G. von Rad, *Der heilige Krieg im*

Alten Israel, 5th ed. (Göttingen: Vandenhoeck & Ruprecht, 1969); R. Smend, *Yahweh War and Tribal Confederation* (Nashville: Abingdon, 1970); Patrick D. Miller, *The Divine Warrior in Ancient Israel,* HSM 5 (Cambridge: Harvard University, 1973); et al.

24. See I Sam. 8:20. Cf. 11:4–7. On the affiliation of royal investiture with procession into battle, cf. Halpern, *Constitution,* 132, who reads Isa. 51:9, 52:1–2, Ps. 93:1, and Job 40:10 as presuming a military context. Cf. Ishida, *Dynasties,* 47–48, who stresses the importance of the tribal leadership in securing a charismatic warrior-king in the era of Samuel and Saul. Cf. Alt, "Formation" (Anchor ed.), 258, on Saul's role in raising and leading troops. The narrative significance of David's remaining sedentary and in Jerusalem is stressed by Gunn, 70, concurring with G. P. Ridout, "Prose Compositional Techniques in the Succession Narrative" (Ph.D. diss., Graduate Theological Union, Berkeley, 1971); cf. T. Veijola, "Salomo—der erstgeborene Bathsebas," in J. A. Emerton, ed., *Studies in the Historical Books of the Old Testament,* SVT 30 (Leiden: Brill, 1979), 230–50. See also Perry and Sternberg, "Hammelekh bemabbaṭ 'ironi," 267ff.

25. Alt, 248, 264. Cf. I Sam. 22:1–2 (400 men, recruited from among the discontented of the land); 23:13, 27:2–28:3, 30:9 (600 men, now having the character of a mercenary army). Compare II Sam. 10:6.

26. On the background of David's relation to Nahash and Hanun, cf. Hertzberg, *I/II Sam.,* 203–204, McCarter, *II Sam.,* 273–74, and Fokkelman, 42, who associates David's homage to the house of Nahash the Ammonite with the latter's enmity toward Saul, as a consequence of the events told in I Sam. 11.

27. Concerning Saul's reliance on agents (*mal'akhim*), see n. 38 below.

28. It follows that the king need not be an ecstatic, since the display of his transported state is no longer the chief instrument for the raising and rallying of troops, as outlined classically for the "judge" pattern in Judg. 3:7–11, esp. v. 10 (but cf. 3:26, where the sounding of a ram's horm seems to substitute for this element). See also Judg. 6:34, 11:29, 13:25, 14:6, 16, 15:14, and cf. Robert G. Boling, *Judges: A New Translation with Introduction and Commentary,* The Anchor Bible (Garden City: Doubleday/Anchor, 1975), 81–83. P. Kyle McCarter, in *I Samuel: A New Translation with Introduction and Commentary,* The Anchor Bible (Garden City: Doubleday/Anchor, 1980), 187, views the prophetic pattern as a form-critical category influential in the shaping of Israelite tradition—similarly, B. C. Birch, JBL 90 (1970), 55–68, esp. 61–66; and Richter, *Die sogenannte vorprophetischen Berufungsberichte* (see chapter two, n. 65), 13–29—without, apparently, seeing in it an institutional basis appropriate to the period of judges, a matter made more explicit by Halpern, *Constitution,* 114. Cf. Halpern's allusion to the rarity of reference to prophetic inspiration in connection with Israel's kings (found only in II Sam. 23:2, and perhaps in I Kings 3:5ff.). While David, at his public debut in I Sam. 17:38ff., can be said to be "inspired" in a colloquial sense of the term, the episode is notable for the conspicuous absence of prophetic ecstasy, and for an emphasis on common sense and cunning.

29. I borrow this last expression from Num. 15:39. The unguarded or compromised posture of a king, prince, military leader, or hero is a frequent motif: cf. Judg. 3:15–25, 4:17–21, 5:24–27, 9:52–55, 16:15–21, II Sam. 2:23; 3:27, 32–34; 4:5–8, etc.

30. OL[115]: *per porticum;* Targ.[mss]: *'l 'ygr;* Vulg.: *ex adverso super solarium suum.*

31. Cf. permutations of this and similar expressions in Gen. 12:11, 14; 24:16, 26:7, 29:17, 39:6; 41:2, 4, 18; Deut. 21:11; I Sam. 16:12, 17:42, 25:3; II Sam. 13:1, 14:27; I Kings 1:3, 4; Esth. 1:11, 2:3, 7, etc.

32. Cf. I Sam. 14:33; 17:31; 18:20, 24; 19:19, 21; 23:7, 13; 24:2, 27:4 (all instances of reporting to Saul); I Sam. 15:12 (to Samuel); and I Sam. 18:26; 23:1, 25; 25:12; II Sam. 2:4, 3:23, 6:12, 10:5, 17:21, etc. (to David); II Sam. 19:2 (to Joab); I Kings 1:51 (to Solomon).

33. Cf. Abraham Levanon, *Yo'av: 'Iyyun besefer Shemu'el* (Jerusalem: Moses and Jacob Levanon Memorial Association, n.d.—henceforth, *Joab*), 35.

34. On the name "Araunah," cf. H. B. Rosen, VT 5 (1955), 318–20; Hertzberg, *I/II Sam.*, 414n.; McCarter, *II Sam.*, 507, n. 20, 512, comment on II Sam. 24:18.

35. On the problematic use of the term "Hittite" in the Bible, cf. R. de Vaux, *The Early History of Israel* (see chapter 2, n. 13), 134–36.

36. Cf. Levanon, *Joab*, 37, and II Sam. 23:39; 24:18–25; II Chron. 11:10, 41; 21:18–25.

37. Especially, Uriah's retort to David in 11:11, which bespeaks more the foot soldier than the professional officer (cf. my discussion further on), and his ready obedience in verse 14 in conveying an order he apparently is not authorized to unseal.

38. Compare Saul's use of *mal'akhim* (which, given David's reputation, would likely have been secret operations) in I Sam. 19:11, 14, 15, 16, 20, 21 (bis), and David's use (which, given David's precarious position at that time would have likely been secret) in I Sam. 25:14. Cf. also Judg. 11:17, where a context of secrecy is presumed, even though the line itself is spoken by *mal'akhim* in what appears to be a forthright delegation (cf. vv. 11, 14) to the Ammonite king Nahash. There seem to be several contexts of the word: as a secret delegation to a more powerful person, where the sender is outlawed or out of favor (e.g., Num. 2:26, Judg. 11:17, et al.); as a lawful but perhaps confidential communication where the sender proposes an alliance or beneficial assistance (e.g., II Sam. 2:5, 5:11); as an aggressive action, where the legal or moral grounds of the sender's demand is questionable (e.g., Num. 22:5, Saul's actions cited above, and David's in II Sam. 3:14 and 11:4). There is, in general, an undertone of covenant rhetoric (recital of favors past) in what often seems to be a request for return of good (*tov; tovah*) for good, kindness (*ḥesed*) for kindness, amid a general absence of *de jure* alliance.

39. Cf. Perry and Sternberg 270ff., among others.

40. On the complicated question of Uriah's awareness of the circumstances, cf. esp. Perry and Sternberg, 271–76.

41. See II Sam. 12:20–23; also, I Sam. 21:6, and McCarter, *I Samuel* (see n. 28, above), 365. Cf. Walter Brueggemann, "On Trust and Freedom: A Study of Faith in the Succession Narrative," *Interpretation* 26:1 (Jan. 1972), 7–8.

42. See Robert C. Culley, *Studies in the Structure of Hebrew Narrative* (Philadelphia: Fortress/Missoula: Scholars, 1976), 49–53; cf. McCarter, *I Sam.*, 385–87, 409–10; Hertzberg, *I/II Sam.* 195–98; 207–11.

43. See his remarks in v. 19, but compare his words to Abishai in v. 10.

44. Cf. I Sam. 9:16, 10:6; II Sam. 1:14, 16; McCarter, *I Samuel*, 384; also, Mowinckel, *He That Cometh*, 65, and others cited in n. 18, above.

45. But cf. Halpern, *Constitution*, who affirms a basic continuity between the eras of judges and kings, regarding the broad symbolic patterns of investiture borrowed from the surrounding milieus.

46. Information on this matter is sparse, and what exists applies mainly to David's *kingly* career, Cf., among others, Max Weber, *Gesammelte Aufsätze zur Religionssoziologie III: Das antike Judentum* (Tübingen, 1921); trans. H. H. Gerth

and D. Martindale, *Ancient Judaism* (New York: Free Press, 1952), 13–23, 45; Alt, "Formation," 258, 264, 271ff., passim; Bright, *History of Israel*, 184–86; idem, "The Organization and Administration of the Israelite Empire," in F. M. Cross, Jr., W. Lemke, and P. D. Miller, Jr., *Magnalia Dei: The Mighty Acts of God—Essays on the Bible and Archaeology in Memory of G. Ernest Wright* (Garden City: Doubleday, 1976), 193–208, esp. 197–201; Noth, *History of Israel*, 171ff., passim; Edward Neufield, "Royal-Urban Society in Ancient Israel," HUCA 31 (1960), 31–53, esp. 38–39; Abraham Malamat, "Organs of Statecraft in the Israelite Monarchy" (see chap. 2, n. 78), esp. 175–78; Levanon, *Joab;* and E. W. Heaton, *Solomon's New Men* (see chap. 2, n. 78); also, John H. Hayes and J. Maxwell Miller, *Israelite and Judean History* (Philadelphia: Westminster, 1977), 356–59. David's *staff* and David's *court* are hard to separate.

47. Cf. I Sam. 2:1–10; Pss. 18, 22, 23, 31, 35, et al.

48. See the statement attributed to Rav Ashi in Berakhot 3b.

49. Cf. n. 18, above; Ivan Engnell, "'Knowledge' and 'Life' in the Creation Story" (see chap. 1, n. 50); Fishbane, *Text and Texture*, (see chap. 1, n. 14) 111–20; J. S. Ackerman, "Satire and Symbolism in the Song of Jonah," in Halpern and Levenson, *Traditions in Transformation*, 213–46.

50. After II Sam. 14:17, 20. See Ernst H. Kantorowicz, *The King's Two Bodies: A Study in Medieval Political Theology* (Princeton: Princeton University Press, 1975), 8, n. 4.

51. Normally, as in Gen. 18:24, Prov. 30:18, Deut. 17:8, Job 42:3, Ps. 131:1, Jer. 32:17, the *nif'al* of the root *pl'* ("wonder"), takes a preposition *min* for the meaning "to be beyond the powers of." In the noun *pele'* ("wonder") and in the *nif'al* noun form *nifla'ot* ("wondrous things"), the word invariably designates wondrous acts of YHWH, performed either "in the midst of/in the presence of" a people (Ex. 34:10, Josh. 3:5, Mic. 7:15, Ps. 72:18, Neh. 9:1; cf. Ex. 15:11, Ps. 78:32, 196:7) or against a king (Ex. 3:20) or on a world stage (Ps. 9:2, 26:7, 40:6, 72:18, 75:5, 96:3, 98:1, 105:2, 106:7, 22, et al.). Cf. *pele'*: Ex. 15:11, Isa. 9:5, 25:1, Ps. 77:5, et al. and the numerous *hif'il* uses of the root. In some instances, it designates a more subjective *reaction* in wonderment of one person or a specific group, particularly when used with *be'eyney* (" . . . in the eyes of . . ."): II Sam. 1:26, Pss. 118:23, 119:18 (contextually), and Zech. 8:6 (where the verb is extended to God). In short: *lehippale' min* generally means "to be beyond the powers of" someone (to do or to contemplate), *lehippale' be'eyney*, "to be wondrous or wonderful to" someone.

52. Fokkelman, *Narrative Art*, 411–17, is close to the mark in showing a fairly precise connection between David's careless remark to Nathan in II Sam. 12:6 (that the "rich man" of Nathan's parable "should repay fourfold" the evil he had done) and the four principal disasters that befall David's (male) children: the death of the child conceived through his adulterous union with Bathsheba; the death of Amnon by the hand of Absalom; the death of Absalom; the death of Adonijah (after David's death) by command of Solomon. Rabbinic and medieval Jewish commentators (see Rashi to 12:6; Radaq, end of comm. on 12:1) advanced a similar notion, that David would witness the "eclipse" (*liqquy*) of four children: Bathsheba's firstborn to David; Tamar, Amnon, and Absalom.

53. Weber, *Ancient Judaism* (see n. 46, above), 45. Concerning the atmosphere of the court among the children of David and Solomon, cf. Malamat, "Organs of Statecraft," 175–78; Baruch Halpern, "Sectionalism and the Schism," JBL 93:4 (1974), 519–32.

54. Rost, 105, establishes succession as the theme of the court history by locating its thematic underpinning in the reference to Michal's childlessness in II

Sam. 6:23—thus, in the failure of the houses of David and Saul to unite dynastically. See also von Rad, "Beginning of Historical Writing," 177. K. Rupprecht, *Der Tempel von Jerusalem: Gründung Salomos oder jebusiter Erbe?* BZAW 144 (Berlin: de Gruyter, 1977) and F. Crüsemann, "Zwei alttestamentliche Witze. I Sam. 21:11–15 und II Sam. 6:16, 20–23," ZAW 92 (1980), 215–27, have similarly stressed the pivotal position of the David-Michal scene in the redactional montage uniting the Saul and David cycles. Contra Rost, cf. Schulte, *Entstehung,* 145–47. A. Weiser, "Die Legitimation des Königs Dawid. Zur Eigenart und Entstehung der sogenannte 'Geschichte der Dawids Aufsteig,'" VT 16 (1966), 325–54, ties the David-Michal scene to "the history of David's rise." Cf. McCarter, *II Sam.,* 187–89.

55. On the question of "wisdom" themes and influences in the court history, cf. Rost, 89–90; Whybray, 56–95; and the criticisms by James L. Crenshaw, "Method in Determining Wisdom Influence Upon 'Historical' Literature," JBL 88 (1969), 129–42; and by Gunn, 26–29.

56. The story's interlocking actantial structure as shown by Samuel Bar-Efrat, *Ha'izzuv ha'ommanuti shel hassippur bemiqra'* (Jerusalem: Sifriat Poalim, 1979), 231 (cf. his study of the story as a whole, 199–235) is relevant in this connection. No more than two characters appear in each scene, one of the two appearing in the scene preceding, the other in the one following—thereby highlighting the chain of agency that leads to the fateful actions. Cf. idem, "Some Observations on the Structure of Biblical Narrative" (cited in chap. 1, n. 19); Fokkelman, *Narrative Art,* 101–102.

57. Cf. Metzudat David to 13:11; Ralbag to 13:12; McCarter ad loc., *II Sam.,* 322–23, who, while noting that the term *nevalah* (sacrilege) " . . . is used especially of sexual misconduct," mentions only rape, promiscuity, adultery, and homosexual assault (see respectively, Judg. 20:6, 10; Deut. 22:21; Jer. 29:23; Judg. 19:23; and W. M. W. Roth, "NBL," VT 10 [1960], 294–409, cited by McCarter). Medieval Jewish commentators generally concur in acknowledging, for a variety of reasons, that the union between Amnon and Tamar, under orderly circumstances, would have been permissible—see Radaq to 13:1, Rashi to 13:13).

58. See also 4QSam[a] and McCarter *II Sam.,* 319, n. ad loc. The thematic importance of an absence of rebuke is not generalized in the Masoretic text until I Kings 1:6: "And [Adonijah's] father did not rebuke him during his lifetime by saying: 'Why have you done such-and-such'. . . ." See further in my discussion.

59. On the Calebite influence in Judean history, cf., among others, Clements, *Abraham and David,* 35–46; Jon D. Levenson, "I Samuel 25 as Literature and History," CBQ 40 (1978), 11–28; idem, with Baruch Halpern, "The Political Import of David's Marriages," JBL 99:4 (1980), 507–28. On the Judean background of David's early reign over the south, cf. in general, H.-J. Zobel, "Beiträge zur Geschichte Gross-Judas in Früh- und vordavidischer Zeit," SVT 28 (1974), 253–77.

60. Cf. Judg. 6:34; 11:29 (which, however, follows upon previous negotiation efforts); 14:19; 15:4; 19:29; I Sam. 11:7; cf. also II Sam. 13:22, 28; 14:30; 15:10. Absalom's actions, accompanied by a certain measure of deceit in the first, second, and fourth text cited, do not fit the classic pattern of an open challenge, or rallying of troops, in protest to a specific injustice, as his more direct action in 14:30 seems to suggest. Compare further on in my discussion of the terms "good and evil," and n. 76, below.

61. Cf. esp. I Sam. 17:45–47.

62. Cf. R. P. Gordon, *1 & 2 Samuel* (Sheffield: JSOT Press, 1984), 64.

63. See n. 59 above.

64. See Levanon, *Joab*, 40–47.

65. That this exemption coincides so fully with David's obvious aim to clear himself from suspicion of complicity in the deaths of Ishboshet and Abner (cf. vv. 36–37) has tended to obscure the underlying institutional premise of David's action. "It is the chief goal of this part of the story of David's rise to demonstrate the new king's innocence of the assassinations . . . that opened the way to his kingship in the north" (McCarter, *II Sam.*, 120; cf. idem, "The Apology of David," JBL 99 [1980], 489–504, esp. 501–502). McCarter's evaluation, which mirrors widespread critical opinion and has analogues in rabbinic and medieval Jewish exegesis (see Sanhedrin 20b; Radaq and Metzudat David to II Sam. 3:31), presupposes a narrowly propagandistic function to the narrative and a readership concerned only with David's motives (ultimately unimpeachable, in McCarter's judgment) vis-à-vis the Benjaminites, the house of Saul, and the northern league. This *realpolitisch* dimension, while undeniably present and of considerable dramatic interest, is not the principal ingredient of the political knowledge communicated here. The psychological subtlety of the scene flows from the contradiction between the policy David must affirm and his complex and continuing relationship with the close associates he must censure. David's pronouncements on blood feud, moreover, will return to haunt him, especially in II Sam. 14. The ambiguity of David's position is well conveyed by rabbinic interpretation—cf. Radaq to II Sam. 3:29: "Our rabbis have said [Sanhedrin 37b]: All of these curses were upheld against the seed of David, for he did not curse justly, for it was in his intention to order him [Abner? Joab?] killed, and so he did."

66. Contra Fokkelman, 22–40, who, given his customary delight in complicated motive and multiple meaning, uncharacteristically chooses sides in the matter.

67. Schulte, *Entstehung*, 143.

68. See n. 33, above.

69. This is further suggested by the fact that there is no clear referent for the particle -*hu* ("him") in David's final word—Joab, presumably, but not necessarily, in a text that chooses well its times of ambiguity. Who, indeed, is to be encouraged?

70. *Mauvaise foi.* See Jean-Paul Sartre, *Being and Nothingness,* trans. Hazel E. Barnes (New York: Washington Square Press, 1966), 56–86. In her Key to Special Terminology, 770, Barnes defines bad faith as "a lie to oneself within the unity of a single consciousness." By means of it one attempts to escape what Sartre calls "responsible freedom." Bad faith rests "on a vacillation between transcendence and facticity which refuses to recognize either one for what it really is or to synthesize them." Literary criticism usefully based on recognition of bad faith among the characters is the work of Harry Berger, Jr. (see "Preliminaries," n. 17 and 28), whose nuanced interpretations of various kingly heroes have partly influenced my own. See, among other works, Berger, "The Early Scenes of *Macbeth:* Preface to a New Interpretation," ELH 47 (1980), 1–31; idem, with H. M. Leicester, "Social Structure as Doom: the Limits of Heroism in Beowulf," in Robert Burlin and E. B. Irving, Jr., eds., *Old English Studies in Honour of John C. Pope* (Toronto: University of Toronto Press, 1974), 37–81. Also, idem, *"King Lear:* The Lear Family Romance," CR 23 (1979), 348–76, which bears useful comparison with the work of Cavell cited below.

71. Sartre offers the amusing paradigm of a classic seduction scene between a man and a woman, where a man places his hand over a woman's as they are

talking: "To leave the hand there is to consent in herself to flirt, to engage herself. To withdraw it is to break the troubled and unstable harmony which gives the hour its charm. The aim is to postpone the moment of decision as long as possible. We know what happens next; the young woman leaves her hand there, but she *does not notice* that she is leaving it. She does not notice because it happens by chance that she is at that moment all intellect. She draws her companion up to the most lofty regions of sentimental speculation; she speaks of Life, of her Life, she shows herself in her essential aspect—a personality, a consciousness. And during this time the divorce of the body from the soul is accomplished . . . ," *Being and Nothingness,* 67.

72. Stanley Cavell, "The Avoidance of Love: A Reading of *King Lear,*" in idem, *Must We Mean What We Say?—A Book of Essays* (New York: Scribners, 1969), 267–353.

73. David, to be sure, nowhere demands of his children the kind of counterfeit love requested by Lear in his famous "bequest" scene (I, i)—David's attitude toward the tribes in II Sam. 19:12–13 is more reminiscent of this. Nevertheless, the following remarks by Cavell are illuminating for the situation of King David: "Lear knows it is a bribe he offers, and—part of him, anyway—wants exactly what a bribe can buy: (1) false love; and (2) a public expression of love. That is: he wants something he does not have to return *in kind,* something which a division of his property fully pays for. And he wants to *look* like a loved man—for the sake of the subjects, as it were. He is perfectly happy with his little plan, until Cordelia speaks. Happy not because he is blind, but because he is getting what he wants, his plan is working. Cordelia is alarming precisely because he *knows* she is offering the real thing, offering something a more opulent third of his kingdom cannot, must not, repay. . . ." (289–90). Significantly, there is no character comparable to Cordelia among David's children—not even Absalom, perhaps David's most disenchanted child, is capable of challenging a counterfeit love; he only knows how to manipulate it to his advantage. The mutually dry-eyed "reconciliation" depicted at the end of chapter 14 illustrates Absalom's unreadiness for reconciliation as much as David's, and helps to suggest how much David's children are damaged and incapacitated from the start. Coldness and reserve toward kin are in some sense the sole constants of David's character from his earliest appearance to his deathbed moments, and this accords perfectly with the depreciation of kinship that forms the basis of his institutional revolution in Israel.

74. Preferential treatment of the eldest son in inheritance is reflected in the events of Gen. 27:1–4, and is present in legislation as late as Deut. 21:15–17, despite the narrative examples showing a switch in preference to a younger son (cf. Gen. 17:19–21, 48:13–20; I Kings 1:32–37; II Chron. 21:3). See, in general, O. J. Baab, IDB (1962), s.v. "Inheritance"; V. H. Kooy, ibid., s.v. "Firstborn," 270–72; R. de Vaux, *Ancient Israel: Social and Religious Institutions* (New York, Toronto: McGraw Hill, 1965), 41–55; J. Henninger, "Zum Erstgeborenrecht bei den Semiten," in E. Gräf, ed., *Festschrift W. Caskel* (Leiden: Brill, 1968), 162–83; idem, DBS 8 (1968), s.v. "Premiers-nés," cols. 467–82; H. Cazelles, ibid., 482–91. For the patriarchal period, cf. de Vaux, *The Early History of Israel* (see chap. 2, n. 13), 233–56.

75. "Benjaminite," that is, by territorial boundary. Ethnically speaking, Jerusalem was the city of the Jebusite, well into the era of David's rise. See Josh. 15:8; Judg. 1:21, 19:10–13; II Sam. 5–6. Some understand the reference to Jerusalem in I Sam. 17:54 to be anachronistic, anticipating David's later occupation of the

city (see NJPS, n. ad loc.), but the verse in its context is an interesting *traditum* that deserves to be taken at face value.

76. See above, n. 60, and its accompanying discussion. This difference in public styles is fundamental to an understanding of the institutional conflict underlying the civil war. It makes clear the meaning of Absalom's classic gesture of provocation, by counsel of Ahitophel, in 16:21–22, by which Absalom advances his rebellion. Still, Absalom, as noted earlier in my discussion, is decidedly *not* a confederate-style hero. His actions are robbed of political substance by the rubric of 15:1 ("Some time after, Absalom provided himself with a chariot, horses, and fifty runners"), which clearly delineates the court-bred nature of his public postures (cf. Deut. 15:16, I Sam. 8:10–18), and by the echoes of Reuben's ill-starred venture with Jacob's concubine Bilhah in Gen. 35:22, which sets Absalom's action against David in the light of more archaic oppositions of father and son.

77. On the theological and thematic importance of the three verses in the court history (11:27b, 12:24, and 17:14) that signify divine intention, cf. von Rad, "Beginning of Historical Writing," 198–201; McCarter, *II Sam.*, 298, 347. Also, Fokkelman, 220; Gunn, 108–109, 138, n. 9.

78. See my discussion of "The Imperium."

79. Rashi, reasoning from the latter half of the verse, explains: "Between good food and bad food." Cf. Fokkelman, 307. On the sexual connotation of the expression, cf. McCarter, *II Sam.*, 422. Also, see Deut. 1:39 and Isa. 7:15–16.

80. See my discussion on p. 110.

81. See n. 55, above.

82. Cf. Jonathan Z. Smith, "Wisdom and Apocalyptic," in idem, *Map is Not Territory: Studies in the History of Religions* (Leiden: Brill, 1978), 67–87, esp. 70.

83. Cf. Harry Berger, Jr., *The Allegorical Temper* (cited in "Preliminaries," n. 28), 211–40, esp. 237ff.

84. It should be clear from this and other examples offered in my discussion of the court history that the material of II Sam. 21–24 is no late interpolation, but an integral part of the story's intra-exegetical structure. The carefully wrought internal structure of this traditionary garland—a symmetry, in fact (famine; warrior exploits; psalm//oracle; warrior exploits and list; plague)—has been recognized as early as Budde's *Die Bücher Samuel* (Tübingen/Leipzig: Mohr, 1902), 304. But interest in the thematic relation of the garland to the court history as a whole is a relatively modern phenomenon among critical researchers. Cf., among others, R. A. Carlson, *David the Chosen King: A Traditio-Historical Approach to the Second Book of Samuel* (Stockholm: Almqvist & Wiksell, 1964), 194–359; Hertzberg (see n. 21, above), 415; Childs (see chap. 1, n. 3), 273–75; T. Veijola *Die ewige Dynastie. David und die Entstehung seiner Dynastie nach der deuteronomischen Darstellung* (Helsinki: Suomalainen Tiedeakatemia, 1975), 106–26; G. T. Sheppard, *Wisdom as a Hermeneutical Construct. A Study in the Sapientializing of the Old Testament*, BZAW 151 (Berlin and New York: de Gruyter, 1980), 144–58; Gordon, *1 & 2 Sam.* (see n. 62, above), 95–97; McCarter, *II Sam.*, 443ff.

85. Cf. sources cited in n. 18, above, and W. M. W. Roth, "You Are the Man! Structural Interaction in 2 Samuel 10–12," *Semeia* 8 (1977), 1–13. See also McCarter, *II Sam.*, 299, 204ff. On the so-called juridical parable, cf. Uriel Simon, "The Poor Man's Ewe Lamb: An Example of a Juridical Parable," *Biblica* 48 (1967), 207–42; J. D. Crossan, *The Dark Interval: Towards a Theology of Story* (Niles, Ill.: Argus, 1975); Gunn, *Story of King David* (see n. 8, above), 40–42; George W. Coats, "Parable, Fable, and Anecdote: Storytelling in the Succession

Narrative," *Interpretation* 35 (1981), 368–82. For an illuminating ethnographical-ly oriented study of the social assumptions and expectations underlying the role of a king and dynast, see James W. Flanagan, "Models for the Origin of Iron Age Monarchy: A Modern Case Study," *SBL Seminar Papers 1982*, 134–56, which draws suggestive comparisons of biblical kingship with that of Abdul Aziz ibn Saud, founder of the present ruling dynasty of Saudi Arabia.

86. Georg Lukács, *History and Class Consciousness: Studies in Marxist Dialectics*, trans. Rodney Livingstone (Cambridge, Mass.: MIT Press, 1968), xxiv.

87. See chap. 1, n. 50.

INDEX

250

Joel Rosenberg is Associate Professor of Hebrew Literature and Judaic Studies at Tufts University.